SIXTY UPANIṢADS OF THE VEDA

PAUL DEUSSEN

Sixty Upaniṣads of the Veda

Translated from German
by
V.M. BEDEKAR
G.B. PALSULE

VOLUME II

MOTILAL BANARSIDASS PUBLISHERS
PRIVATE LIMITED • DELHI

First Indian Edition: Delhi, 1980
Reprint: Delhi, 1987, 1990, 1995, 1997, 2004

First German Edition: Leipzig, 1897

ISBN: 81-208-0432-5 (Vol. II) (Cloth)
ISBN: 81-208-1469-x (Vol. II) (Paper)
ISBN: 81-208-0430-9 (Set) (Cloth)
ISBN: 81-208-1467-3 (Set) (Paper)

Also available at:

MOTILAL BANARSIDASS
41 U.A. Bungalow Road, Jawahar Nagar, Delhi 110 007
8 Mahalaxmi Chamber, 22 Bhulabhai Desai Road, Mumbai 400 026
120 Royapettah High Road, Mylapore, Chennai 600 004
236, 9th Main III Block, Jayanagar, Bangalore 560 011
Sanas Plaza, 1302 Baji Rao Road, Pune 411 002
8 Camac Street, Kolkata 700 017
Ashok Rajpath, Patna 800 004
Chowk, Varanasi 221 001

Printed in India
BY JAINENDRA PRAKASH JAIN AT SHRI JAINENDRA PRESS,
A-45 NARAINA, PHASE-I, NEW DELHI 110 028
AND PUBLISHED BY NARENDRA PRAKASH JAIN FOR
MOTILAL BANARSIDASS PUBLISHERS PRIVATE LIMITED,
BUNGALOW ROAD, DELHI 110 007

PART TWO

ALPHABETICAL LIST OF THE UPANIṢADS

[Pages in Antique occur in PART I]

THE ĪŚA UPANIṢAD
OF THE ŚUKLA YAJURVEDA

Introduction

This valuable small Upaniṣad, which according to its place in the Veda, is named Vājasaneyisaṁhitā-Upaniṣad or more usually, according to the words of the commencement, it is named as Īśa or Īśāvāsya-Upaniṣad; mostly in the Indian collection (of the Upaniṣads), the series of the Upaniṣads customarily begins with this Upaniṣad. Historically considered, in spite of its position in one Saṁhitā, it is wrong (to place it as the first) as it belongs to a pretty late stage of development; but in fact, it is not unsuitable (to place it in the beginning), so far as it affords an excellent glimpse into the basic doctrines of the Vedānta philosophy. According to its period, it is related with the latest parts of the Bṛhadāraṇyaka, according to all appearances, it is connected in verses 9-11 with the Kena 3b in its verse 3, it is reminiscent of Chānd. 8 8.5, it appears in many points more developed than the Kāṭhaka-Upaniṣad, with which it in its verse 8 concurs in respect of an important idea (cf. Kāṭh. 5-13); but on the other hand, it may appear to be older than the Śvetāśvatara-Upaniṣad, to which it supplies a precious supplementation from the ethical side, without participating in its heretical tendencies. The grounds in support of this will be given further on.—The basic thought consists in a description of one who knows the Ātman (verses) 1-2, 6-7, 11, 14) in contrast to those who persist in or maintain the standpoint of individual knowledge (verses 3, 9-10 12-13). This constrast or juxtaposition is repeatedly broken by a description of the nature of the Ātman, which is full of contradictions and is concluded (verses 15-18) with a glimpse into eschatology.

1-2 Ethical conduct of one who knows the Ātman.

3 The delusion caused by nescience.

4-5 Description of the Ātman.

6-7 The blessed state of one who knows the Ātman.

8 Once again the Ātman.

9-11 Condemnation of *Avidyā* and *Vidyā*.

12-13 Combating of becoming (of originating and decaying)

15-18 (=Bṛh. 5-15) A view of the beyond.

ĪŚA UPANIṢAD

[Verses 1-2. The ethical conduct of one who knows the Ātman.—After the assumption of plurality had been already rejected in Bṛh. 4.4.12 (Kāṭh, 4.10.11) in the severest terms, our Upaniṣad, basing itself on it, asks, in its commencing words, for sinking the whole plurality of the world in the depths of divine unity (literally, to clothe oneself all around or to cover oneself with God.) In renouncing the pluralistic world, there lies the true enjoyment (as it was already developed in the Bṛh. 5.12, in the words *vi-ram*), not in aspiring after another's goods. He who abides by this (*evam tvayi*), should continually carry on his work and wish for himself the full duration of life; no work clings to him. This thought is a great step far beyond the views prevailing in the Bṛh. 3.5.4,4,22. There a practical carrying out of world renunciation is demanded. Our passage concedes the enjoyment of life, when only there is the intention or a way of thinking of renouncing. It is the same step which was carried out by Jesus further than John the Baptist (Ev. Matth. 11.18-19) and in another respect, by the Stoics further than the Cynics.]

1. Sink this universe in God
   and everything that lives on the earth!
   He, who renounces, truly enjoys;
   Do not hanker after other's goods.

2. A man should wish to live a hundred years,
   carrying on his work!
   Therefore it stands (endures) if you do so, not otherwise;
   the taint of work does not cling to you.

[Verse 3. The delusion of the man who does not know. He who sees the self (*ātman*) in the body—of him, on that account, as it is expressed in the harshest terms, his soul (as the true Ātman) is murdered, (i.e. denied); he belongs to the demoniacal world, because he is a demoniacal man, as we should supplement from the Chānd. 8.8.6 (from which perhaps the thought stems).]

3. Indeed, demoniacal is this world,
   enveloped by blinding darkness!
   There in go all after death,
   those who have murdered their souls,
   (*ātmahano janāḥ*)

[The nature of Ātman, full of contradictions; it is the *coincidia oppositorium* (coinciding opposites), as has been already taught in the Atharvaveda 10.8.11 (see *Gesch. d. Phil.* I. 320), and as is stated in many more passages more closely in the Kāṭhaka-Upaniṣad, with which perhaps, our passage is connected; The Ātmạn is unmoved and yet it is the quickest of all, it is far and yet it is the nearest of all (of Kāṭh. 2.21), it is inside and at the same time outside of all (cf. Kāṭh. 5.9-11), it is one and at the same time all-encompassing, even like the primaeval waters which *Mātariśvan* i.e. "Prajāpati as the wind" lays in it; this last idea, indeed, traces itself back to the Taitt. Saṁh. 5.6.4.2 and 7.1.5.1) (cf. the translation of this passage in *Gesch. d. Phil.* I. 195).]

4. That one,—without movement and still quick as thought—
   advancing forward, not overtaken by gods
   standing still, it out-distances all runners,
   in it, the wind-god already puts or places the waters.

5. It is resting and yet restless,
   it is far and still so near!
   it is inside all
   and still outside all it is.

[Verses 6-7 : Joy of the one who knows the Ātman. He who knows himself as all beings and all beings as himself,—he never becomes afraid of and hides himself from the beings; the illusion of individual existence and that with sorrows bound up with it have ceased for him. Though the expression *vijugupsate* may also be traced back to the idea in the Bṛh. 4.4.15, Kaṭh. 4, 5-12 but in none of these passages it has been as sharply and finely expressed as in ours.]

6. He who recognizes all beings here
   in his own self
   and himself in all that lives,—
   —he never feels alarmed before any one.

7. In whom, all the beings have become
   the own self of him who knows,
   there, (in him), which illusion or delusion
   which sorrow would befall him,
   who sees realizes the unity!

[Verse 8 : Once again the nature of the Ātman or Brahman (therefore masc. and neuter used pellmell) is described mostly in negative definitions reminiscent of Bṛh. 3.8.8. The final line (in which the metre through the interpolated *yathātathyatao*' is broken up with complete irregularity) formulates a thought further which meets us less developed in words in Kaṭh. 5.13 (Śvet. 6.13) : *eko bahūnām yo vidadhāti kāmān.*]

8. It stretched itself around, bodiless and sinewless
pure, sole, unvulnerable, free from evil—
Viewing in advance, only the self through itself (*svayambhū*)
all-encompassing,
he has sketched (or planned) everything according to the
kind of direction or policy for a perennial period.

[Verses 9-11 : Condemnation of *Avidyā* and *Vidyā*. This verse (and along with it indeed the inserted verse in Bṛh. 4.4.10) are connected probably with Kena 3b and find, in every case, from the context there, their right elucidation. *Avidyā* is the empirical knowledge of plurality, Vidyā, the attempt to attain to God, whom one juxtaposes it as an object to be known (and to be adored). After the sharp severe remarks with which this attempt, in Taitt. 2.7, Kena 11, had been repudiated, it is indeed psychologically to be understood (anticipated), if our passage explains this supposed knowledge as evil, as the nescience (avidyā).]

9. Into blinding darkness they enter
who pay homage to the nescience;
into the still more blinding darkness enter those,
who are satisfied with the knowledge.

10. Different it is to which knowledge[1] leads,
and different it is to which ignorance or nescience leads !
Thus the teaching has been transmitted to us—
the doctrine by the ancient masters.

11. He who knows the knowledge and ignorance
—both (as inadequate)
—he transcends, through both[2] the death
and attains immortality.

---

1. The expression *anyad vidyayā* is boldly elliptical : "different (from what) (is attained) through knowledge. The elucidation lies in Kena 3b : *anyad eva tad viditāt*.

2. Particularly through the fact that he sees through knowledge and ignorance as being inadequate. No weight can be placed on (—or importance can be attached to—) the juxtaposition that he through the one transcends death and through the other attains immortality because 'to transcend death' and 'to attain immortality' is one and the same. The particular remark holds good for verse 14.

[Combating or refutation of becoming (of originating and persisting) : Already the old commentators wished to recognize here a polemic against the directions antagonistic to the Vedānta : Śaṅkara as also Dvivedagaṅga think of the Sāṁkhyas, Mahīdhara thinks of the Buddhists, Uvaṭa thinks of the materialists. All these explanations are to be rejected, as is evident from what follows. Both the basic definitions of Brahman (just like the '*one*' of Parmenides and the 'thing-in-itself' of Kant) are such that the one is spaceless and timeless and that it is unchangeable (changeless) (devoid of causality). Out of this, two things follow : (1) that there is no plurality and (2) that there is no becoming. The first statement is already often met with by us. The disputation about becoming is first undertaken by our passage in order to be carried further in a glorious manner by Gauḍapāda in the Kārikā on Māṇḍūkya-Upaniṣad (3.25 in it refers to our passage). Corresponding to it is *Saṁbhūti* in our passage; *Saṁbhūti* or *Sambhava* is the origination, *asambhūti*, *asambhava* is non-becoming, perishing, as already it becomes evident from the fact that afterwards it is again taken up by *vināśa*. Origination and destruction are two sides of becoming, which our author combats. The Mādhyandinas have this verse 12 already in Bṛh. 4.4.10.]

12. In blinding darkness he enters,—
he who believes that becoming is nothing;
into still more blinding darkness the other one enters,
—he who believes that becoming is something.

13. Different it is from becoming
different it is also from non-becoming;
thus the ancient masters
have transmitted the (teaching) doctrine to us.

14. He who knows becoming and non-becoming
both, as not existent,
he transcends through both the death
and attains immortality.

[Verses 15-18 : Epilogue concerning the beyond. This request (of a dying man, according to the acceptable opinion of Śaṅkara) to the sun in order that it should shove away its rays, that along with, the Puruṣa (man) in the sun should be visible and that union with him should take place, has already been described in its occurrence, in the Bṛh. 5-15.]

15. With a bowl wholly of gold
the mouth of truth is covered;
O Pūṣan, open this for me,
make it known to the one who is true to the truth.

16. O Pūṣan, the sole seer, O Yama,
O sun-god, O Prajāpati's son!
disperse your rays, amalgamate your splendour;
—indeed I see it,
your lovable form; and
that one there, the man there,
I am he himself!

17. Now, O breath, become the wind,
become the indestructible one and
this body should end in ashes!
Om!
O spirit, remember! remember the work!
O spirit, remember! remember the work.
O Agni, lead us on an even way
You, O God, who know the paths,
lead us to success!
Keep far away from us the crooked path of sin!
And we will proffer you the highest adoration.

E

THE UPANIṢADS OF THE ATHARVAVEDA

a. Pure Vedânta-Upaniṣads

MUṆḌAKA UPANIṢAD

PRAŚNA UPANIṢAD

MĀṆḌŪKYA UPANIṢAD

GARBHA UPANIṢAD

PRĀṆĀGNIHOTRA UPANIṢAD

PIṆḌA UPANIṢAD

ĀTMA UPANIṢAD

SARVA-UPANIṢAT-SĀRA

GARUḌA UPANIṢAD

THE UPANIṢADS OF THE ATHARVAVEDA

1. Introduction

While the Upaniṣads of the first three Vedas, excluding some exceptions, are the dogmatic text-books of actual Vedic schools, being connected with the *Brāhmaṇas* and serving as supplements to them and have been, therefore, named according to their names, the conditions are essentially different in the case of the numerous Upaniṣads reckoned as belonging to the Atharvaveda. According to the statement of Colebrooke (*Miscellaneous* I. 93) the first fifteen of the fiftytwo Upaniṣads enumerated by him are supposed to be ascribed as being the best mss., of the *Śākhā* of the Śaunakīyas, the remaining ones to the Paippalādis and others. Nārāyaṇa also occasionally mentions in his commentary on the Atharva-veda-upaniṣads that, one Upaniṣad '*ekādaśī Śaunakīye*' (the edition of the *Biblioδtheca Indica*, p. 260, 5), '*aṣṭādaśī Śaunakagrantha-vistare*' (p. 78, 10), '*aṣṭāviṁśī grantha-saṁghe śākhā Śaunaka-vartitā*' (p. 299,5), '*aṣṭamī Paippalāda-abhidhā*' (p. 60, 6), 'the *thirty-seventh Taittirīyake*' (p. 394, 13), 'the fortysixth *Ātharva-Paippale*' (ed. Pun. p. 183, 5); but the contradiction of this statement with that of Colebrooke indicates that we shall have to recognize in them hardly anything more than the later summaries of the Upaniṣadic-groups under the famous names of the ancient past; especially the Atharva-veda-upaniṣads (with a few and suspect exceptions like the Māṇḍūkya and Jābāla) are no more named, like the earlier ones after the Vedic Śākhās but with the names which are taken from the contents or from other circumstance. According to all appearances, the Atharva-veda-upaniṣads, so far as they are not wholly individual products, represent the expression of views of many neo-Vedāntic, mystic, sectarian ascetic communities and proclaim their contrast against the old Vedic Śākhās through the fact that they employ the Upaniṣadic form transmitted by them in order to present on their behalf an Upaniṣad, as it were, as its symbolic book; and when all these Upaniṣads were joined to the Atharvaveda the reason for it lay mostly not in an inner connection with the same but only in the fact that this fourth Veda, originally half apocryphal, was not preserved or protected like the three other Vedas through a competent surveillance by their Śākhas in the face of alien intruders. Thus most of these newly originated Upaniṣads have become, in general, the Upaniṣads of the Atharvaveda, so that later, after their original carriers had, in many cases, been forgotten, a beginning was made to assemble them and this collection was attached to the existing nucleus of the real or genuine and relatively older Upaniṣads of the Atharvaveda, beginning with Muṇḍaka and Praśna. While the great number of the Upaniṣads went on increasing up to the time when they were assembled into a collection (—Weber enumerated in 1876, all in all 235 names—) and while the apocryphal products under this name were smuggled into it (—even an Islamic Upaniṣad called the Allopaniṣad is available—) the attempt of those who assembled them could never have reached completion but was always directed to a selection of these Upaniṣads which were deemed as worthy, on account of their contents or their wide dissemination, of being included in the Veda—especially the Atharvaveda which was the only one still remaining open for this purpose. These collections are, therefore, an important criterion, for determining, not their worth, still, a more or less general estimate of the different Upaniṣads; and an Upaniṣad will deserve all the more attention (above all historical), if it appears generally in the collection and less in the miscellaneous multitude when it has been accepted only in one or the other of the same. We will give, in short, a survey of the four collections closely known to us—it may be the survey of all the Upaniṣads or it may be the survey of Upaniṣads of the Atharvaveda only.

2. The Collection in the Muktikā Upaniṣad

In this Upaniṣad, as the name signifies, dealing with the inquiry into the deliverance (*mukti*), Rāma appearing as the incarnation of Viṣṇu, recommends, to Hanumān, who puts questions to him, the Upaniṣads as the means of deliverance (verses 26-28 : edition Jīvānanda Vidyāsāgar, Calcutta 1872) :]

26. The Māṇḍūkya alone is sufficient
for the deliverance of the aspirant.—
If even then, the knowledge lacks,
then read the ten Upaniṣads.

27. Then, as soon as he has knowledge,
he will enter into my abode.—
He who, even afterwards, needs to be steadfast in knowledge,
O son of Añjanā !

28. he attains the goal
if he reads the thirtytwo Upaniṣads.—
If you just wish deliverance, while death is near,
read, then, the hundred and eight Upaniṣads.

These hundred and eight Upaniṣads are then enumerated by Rāma to Hanumān, in the following order :

1 *Īśā*, 2 *Kena*, 3 *Kāṭhaka*, 4 *Praśna*, 5 *Muṇḍaka*, 6 *Māṇḍūkya*, 7 *Taittirīya*, 8 *Aitareya*, 9 *Chāndogya*, 10 *Bṛhadāraṇyaka*, 11 *Brahma*, 12 *Kaivalya*, 13 *Jābāla*, 14 *Śvetāśvatara*, 15 *Haṁsa* 16 *Āruṇika*, 17 *Garbha*, 18 *Nārāyaṇa*, 19 *Paramahaṁsa*, 20 *Amṛtabindu*, 21 *Amṛtanāda*, 22 *Atharvaśiras*,

23 *Atharvaśikhā*, 24 *Maitrāyanī*,[1] 25 *Kauṣītaki*, 26 *Bṛhajjābāla*, 27 *Nṛsiṁhatāpanīya*, 28 *Kālāgnirudra*, 29 *Maitreya*,[2] 30 *Subālā*, 31 *Kṣurikā*, 32 *Mantrikā*[3], 33 *Sarvasāra*[4], 34 *Nirālamba*, 35 *Śukarahasya*, 36 *Vajrasūci*, 37 *Tejobindu*, 38 *Nādabindu*, 39 *Dhyānabindu*, 40 *Brahmavidyā*, 41 *Yogatattva*, 42 *Ātmabodha*, 43 *Nāradaparivrājaka*, 44 *Triśikhibrāhmaṇa*, 45 *Sītā*, 46 *Yogacūḍāmaṇi*, 47 *Nirvāṇa*, 48 *Maṇḍala-brāhmaṇa*, 49 *Dakṣiṇāmūrti*, 50 *Śarabha*, 51 *Skanda*, 52 *Tripādvibhūtimahānarāyaṇa*, 53 *Advayatāraka*, 54 *Rāmarahasya*[5], 55 *Rāmatāpanīya*, 56 *Vāsudeva*, 57 *Mudgala*, 58 *Śāṇḍilya*, 59 *Paiṅgala*, 60 *Bhikṣuka*[6], 61 *Mahā*, 62 *Śārīraka*, 63 *Yogaśikhā*, 64 *Turiyātītāvadhūta*[7], 65 *Saṁnyāsa*[8], 66 *Paramahaṁsa-parivrājaka*, 67 *Akṣamālikā*, 68 *Avyakta*, 69 *Ekākṣara*, 70 *Annapūrṇā*, 71 *Sūrya*, 72 *Akṣi*, 73 *Adhyātma*, 74 *Kuṇḍikā*[9], 75 *Sāvitrī*, 76 *Ātma*, 77 *Pāśupatabrahma*, 78 *Parabrahma*[10] 79 *Avadhūta*, 80 *Tripuratāpinī*, 81 *Devī*, 82 *Tripurā*, 83 *Kaṭha-(rudra)*[10], 84 *Bhāvanā*, 85 *Rudrahṛdaya*, 86 *Yogakuṇḍalī*, 87 *Bhasmajābāla*, 88 *Rudrākṣa-jābāla*, 89 *Gaṇapati*, 90 *Darśana*, 91 *Tārasāra*, 92 *Mahāvākya*, 93 *Pañcabrahma*, 94 *Prāṇāgnihotra*, 95 *Gopālatāpinī*, 96 *Kṛṣṇa*, 97 *Yājñavalkya*[11], 98 *Varāha*, 99 *Śāṭyāyana*, 100 *Hayagrīva*, 101 *Dattātreya*, 102 *Garuḍa*, 103 *Kalisaṁtaraṇa*, 104 *Jābāli*, 105 *Saubhāgyalakṣmī*, 106 *Sarasvatī-rahasya*, 107 *Bahvṛca*, 108 *Muktikā*.

That the *Muktikā* recommends the *Māṇḍūkya* as the first among the 108 Upaniṣads is understandable from its dogmatic (doctrinal) point of view, if we take into consideration along with it the fact that the Kārikā of Gauḍapāda is included in the collection; both offer an excellent survey or summary of the Vedānta-doctrine. The further recommendation of the first ten Upaniṣads, which follows, is fully understandable. They are the Upaniṣads of the three old Vedas besides the most important Upaniṣads of the Atharvaveda (Muṇḍaka, Praśna, *Māṇḍūkya*); however, the only exclusion of *Śvetāśvatara*, *Maitrāyaṇī*, and particularly of *Kauṣītaki* is striking. These ten first Upaniṣads enumerated by the *Muktikā* have been printed in India in all editions, in the serial order given by it. On the other hand, it is unintelligible when the passage in the *Muktikā* in its enumeration deliberately

1. It is the same as Maitr. 1-6,8. Instead of 4.4-6, there is the verse 6.34 (see *supra* Maitrāyaṇa-Upaniṣad 6.34). The Adhyāya 5 is counted at the end as the Adhyāya 4.

2. The beginning is just like that of Maitrāyaṇa-Up.—the further peculiarity.

3. It is another recension of the *Cūlikā*.

4. It is essentially *Sarvopaniṣatsāra*.

5. The first Adhyāya is *Hanumadukta-Rāmopaniṣad*.

6. It is, in its chief points, identical with *Āśrama*, Chap. 4.

7. It is an imitation of 19. *Paramahaṁsa*.

8. It is *Kaṇṭhaśruti* 1-2 with supplement.

9. It is *Saṁnyāsa* 2-5 in another recension.

10. It is *Kaṇṭhaśruti* 3-5, further expanded.

11. It is once again *Jābāla*-Up. 5-6 in metrical form.

gives a privileged position to the thirty-two Upaniṣads (after the first ten Upaniṣads). Among these, there are found works of doubtful origin, whereas many Upaniṣads recognized as the Atharva-Upaniṣads follow only later in the enumeration. Apart from the precedence given to the ten chief Upaniṣads, no principle is anywhere discernible in the serial order.

These 108 Upaniṣads are available in printed form since 1883, in Telugu characters in a volume of 124+902 pages which is without any commentary and which is printed without separating units of words and which is unfortunately incorrect in many places so that one cannot succeed in getting through its passages and before undertaking a thorough working over it, the new prospective printed edition of the 108 Upaniṣads undertaken in Bombay is awaited.[1] Many, otherwise known, Upaniṣads, appear in this collection entirely or partially, under other names (vide supra, the footnotes on the list of the Upaniṣads enumerated in the *Muktikā*), many of them in a completely changed order; several small Upaniṣads occurring in the remaining collection are expanded in the Telugu recension through supplements or additions which are tenfold or twentyfold in their extent, as we will note them on the appropriate occasion. Thus there appears before us in this case a peculiar Upaniṣad-tradition according to the South Indian tradition, which, anyway, merits a very careful and closer investigation. Indeed, as regards its credibility, it creates no favourable opinion, as of the 108 Upaniṣads, 10 are ascribed to the Ṛgveda, 19 to the Śukla (white) Yajurveda, 32 to the Kṛṣṇa (black) Yajurveda, 16 to the Sāmaveda and 31 to the Atharvaveda. This ascription appears to have been done arbitrarily without any semblance of justifiability. That this collection is only a selection out of still larger available material, can be concluded from the verse 44 of the Muktikā : *Sarvopaniṣadām madhye sāram aṣṭottaram śatam.* But even among these 108 Upaniṣads, there are many which have not been included in any of the collections appearing soon thereafter and which therefore, have not found general recognition.

3. The Collection of the Oupanekhat

In the year 1656 the Sultan Muhammed Dara Schakoh got together in Delhi learned Indian pundits from Banaras and got translated into Persian by them a collection of fifty Upaniṣads under the title *Oupanekhat* (in Persian); and this was translated by Anquetil Duperron into Latin

1. This edition was finally available to me (March 1896), while the printing of the present work was under way. Śvetāśvatara is placed before Brahma, Kaivalya and Jābāla and the passage in the book has confused Brahmabindu with Brahma, both being contrary to the serial order in the Muktikā. The Māṇḍūkya unfortunately appears there without Gauḍapāda's *Kārikā* and Mahānārāyaṇa is smuggled under Nārāyaṇa. Certain orthographical peculiarities appear to signify (wholly or partly) dependence on the Telugu printed edition.

(2 volumes, Argentorati 1801-1802), so literally that the Persian sentence-construction was retained in it; following this Persian-Latin translation and also drawing upon the Indian original, A. Weber offered for the first time, in the *Indische Studien* Vol. I, II and IX, this Upaniṣadic material in a remodelled worked-out form. In the preface of the Persian translation, it is said (by Anquetil I. 4) "...and the prophets of that time when they had made that book (the Upaniṣads) separate (had separated from the four Vedaṣ), wrote commentaries, expositions and complete explanations on it and they are reading it always, knowing it to be the best book on religion."[1] These words presuppose that the collection of the Upaniṣads must be older than the commentaries on the same; this assumption holds true in the case of Nārāyaṇa, who, as we shall see, had already before him a collection of the Atharva-Upaniṣads; but it does not hold true in the case of Śaṁkara who, in his introductory remarks (at the beginning of his commentaries) is accustomed to refer to the foregoing ritualistic parts, so that most of the Upaniṣads had been preserved in their contextual connection with the corresponding Brāhmaṇas. In any case, however, the cited words of the Persian translator prove that they (the translators) have not themselves introduced the arrangement of the collection of fifty Upaniṣads but that it was already ready (an accomplished thing) before them, it being even considered as originating in a period going far back. This collection contains the fifty Upaniṣads in the following order :

1 *Tschehandouk* (Chāndogya); 2 *Brehdarang* (Bṛhadāraṇyaka); 3 *Mitri* (Māitrāyaṇīya); 4 *Mandata* (Muṇḍaka); 5 *Eischavasich* (Īśa); 6 *Sarb* (Sarvopaniṣad); 7 *Narain* (Nārāyaṇa); 8 Tadiw (Tadeva=Vāj. Saṃh. 32. 1-2 translated in *Gesch. d. Phil.* I 291); 9 *Athrbsar* (Atharvaśiras); 10 *Hensnad* (Haṁsanāda); 11 *Sarbsar* (Sarvasāra=Ait. Ār. 2. including the Aitareya-Up.) 12 *Kok'henk* (Kauṣītaki); 13 *Sataster* (Śvetāśvatara); 14 *Porsch* (Praśna); 15 *Dehian band.* (Dhyānabindu); 16 *Maha oupanekhat* (Mahā.); 17 *Ātma pra boudeh* (Ātmaprabodha); 18 *Kioul* (Kaivalya); 19 *Schat roundri* (Śatarudrīyam=Vāj. Saṃh. abridged as Nīla-rudra-Up.); 20 *Djog Sank'ha* (Yogaśikhā); 21 *Djogtat* (Yogatattva); 22 *Shiw Sanklap* (Śiva saṁkalpa=Vāj. Saṃh. 34. 1-6 translated in *Gesch. d. Phil.* I, 335); 23 *Abrat Sak'ha* (Atharvaśikhā); 24 *Atma* (Ātma); 25 *Brahm badia* (*Brahmavidyā*); 26 *Anbrat bandeh* (Amṛtabindu, more correctly Brahmabindu); 27 *Tidj bandeh* (Tejobindu); 28 *Karbheh* (Garbha); 29 *Djabal* (Jābāla); 30 *Maha narain* (Mahānārāyaṇa); 31 Mandouk (Māṇḍūkya) 32 *Pank*[2]; 33 *Tschchourka* (Kṣurikā); 34 *Pram hens* (Paramahaṁsa); 35 *Arank* (Āruṇika); 36 *Kin* (Kena); 37 *Kiouni* (Kāṭhaka); 38 *Anandbli*

1. This is a translation of the Latin Original quoted by Deussen. —Translator

2. not *Sākalya*, as Weber had conjectured, but *Paiṅgala*, under which ti t it is found as No. 59 in the Muktikā collection.

(Ānandavallī=Taitt.2); 39 *Bharkbli* (Bhṛguvallī=Taitt. 3); 40 *Bark'he Soukt* (Puruṣasūktam=Ṛgveda 10.90 besides Uttaranārāyaṇam, Vāj. Saṃh. 31. 17-22; translated in *Gesch. d. Phil.* I. 156 ff; 290 ff.); 41 *Djounka* (Cūlikā); 42 *Mrat lankoul* (mṛtyu-lāṅgala); 43 *Anbratnad* (Amṛtanāda, better known as Amṛtabindu); 44 *Baschkl* (Vāṣkala ?)[1]; 45 *Tschhakli* (Chāgaleya ?)[1]; 46 *Tark* (Tāraka=Tārasāra 2, Telugu printed edition p. 745 and Rāmottaratāpanīya 2); 47 *Ark'hi* (Ārṣeya ?)[1]; 48 *Pranou* (Praṇava ?); 49 *Schavank* (Śaunaka ?)[1]; 50 *Nersing'heb atma* (Nṛsimha).)

In this collection, four constituent parts can be distinguished as follows :

1. Twelve numbers are made up by the eleven Upaniṣads of the three old Vedas, which have been totally included with the exception of Taitt. 1, while Taitt. 2 and 3 are reckoned as two Upaniṣads.

2. Mixed with these, there are twentysix Upaniṣads which have been also recognized by other chief collections. No principle is discernible in their order and arrangement. Among the most important works which are found missing in them, can be mentioned the *Kārikā* of Gauḍapāda, the first part of the Nṛsiṁhatāpanīya and (except a small work like 46. Tark) the Rāmatāpanīya Upaniṣad.

3. This collection includes four pieces or passages from the Vājasaneyi saṁhitā 16, 31, 32, 34 (Nos. 19, 40, 8, 22) of which the Śatarudrīyam (Vāj. Saṁh. 16) appears among other collections of the Atharva-Upaniṣads, in an abridged form as Nīlarudra-Upaniṣad, while the three remaining have not been included, as far as our knowledge goes, in any collection, presumably because they were presupposed as being well-known passages in the Vāj. Saṁh. They belong to the previous period in the history of the Upaniṣads and have been accordingly included in the form of their translations and elucidations in the *Gesch. d. Phil.* I (150 ff, 288 ff, 291 ff, 385).

4. Finally, the *Oupanekhat* contains eight works which are not included in the older Vedas and which accordingly have not been included in the chief collections. It may be that they were not known or if they were known, they may have been looked down upon as apocryphal. Among them is *Ātmaprabodha*, a short supplement to the *Nārāyaṇa Upaniṣad; Mṛtyulāṅgala, Paiṅgala, Ark'hi, Pranau* and *Schavank* appear to be very late and secondary products. *Baschkl* and *Tschhakli*, which appear to belong to the Ṛgveda and Yajurveda, produce an impression that they are

---

1. The Bāṣkala (=mantra) Upaniṣad, Chāgaleya Upaniṣad, the Ārṣeya Upaniṣad, and the Śaunaka Upaniṣad have since been reconstructed and edited from the single manuscripts of these Upaniṣads found in the Adyar Library, Madras. Vide these in the printed edition (pp. 358-376) of 'the Eighteen Principal Upaniṣads vol. I' edited by V.P. Limaye and R.D. Vadekar (Vaidika Samsodhana Maṇḍala, Poona) 1958.

—Translator

ancient. One cannot make a definite judgment about them as long as they are not available; from the circumstance that they have not been mentioned anywhere, in any way, they appear to be suspect.[1]

About the age of the Oupanekhat-collection, it is difficult to form a judgment, as long as the history of the Upaniṣad-tradition is wanting. From the circumstance that this collection, in contrast to the collections to be described in the sequel, not only included all old Upaniṣads but also other important texts in the Saṁhitā,—as there may have been the danger that they could have otherwise fallen into oblivion—, we may conclude that the collection may have been compiled in a relatively late period.

4. The Collection of Colebrooke

With this name we will describe the collection of 52 Upaniṣads which Colebrooke (*Misc. ess.* 1-93-98) first made known and which, according to the way in which Colebrooke and Weber speak about it, must have found a very general dissemination and recognition, so that they can be regarded as canonical in the case of the Atharva-Upaniṣads more than any other works. This collection contains "the fiftytwo Upaniṣads" (Colebrooke), in the following 'solemn order' (Weber) with which the *Cod. Bodl.* by Aufrecht 394b also exactly agrees (the deviations are, indeed, due only to oversight) :

1 *Muṇḍaka*, 2 *Praśna*, 3 *Brahmavidyā*, 4 *Kṣurikā*, 5 *Cūlikā*, 6 *Atharvaśiras*, 7 *Atharvaśikhā*, 8 *Garbha*, 9 *Mahā*, 10 *Brahma*, 11 *Prāṇāgnihotra*, 12-15 *Māṇḍūkya*, (with Gauḍapāda's *Kārikā*), 16 *Nīlarudra*, 17 *Nādabindu*, 18 *Brahmabindu*, 19 *Amṛtabindu*, 20 *Dhyānabindu*, 21 *Tejobindu*, 22 *Yogaśikhā*, 23 *Yogatattva*, 24 *Saṁnyāsa*, 25 *Āruṇīya*, 26 *Kaṇṭhaśruti*, 27 *Piṇḍa*, 28 *Ātma*, 29-34 *Nṛsimhatāpanīya;* 35-36 *Kāṭhaka*, 37 *Kena*, 38 *Nārāyaṇa*, 39-40 *Bṛhannārayaṇa*, 41 *Sarvopaniṣatsāra*, 42 *Haṁsa*, 43 *Paramahaṁsa*, 44 *Ānandavallī*, 45 *Bhṛguvallī*, 46 *Gāruḍa*, 47 *Kālāgnirudra*, 48-49 *Rāmatāpanīya*, 50 *Kaivalya*, 51 *Jābāla*, 52 *Āśrama* (cf. also Berl. HS. 2.88).

Most striking and therefore requiring elucidation is the circumstance that in this collection beginning with the *Muṇḍaka* and the *Praśna* and therefore, to all appearances, in a collection compiled originally of the Atharva-Upaniṣads, in a later order of the series and also in the middle of the series, among less significant, small works, four great and important Upaniṣads of the older Vedas have been included, namely : 35-36 *Kāṭhaka*, 37 *Kena* 39-40 *Bṛhannārāyaṇa* and 44-45 *Taittirīya*-Up. 2-3.—If this collection is supposed to be a general one (like the *Oupanekhat*), why are the remaining

1. Colebrooke (*Misc. ess.* I. 93 note) says "...in two copies, which I also obtained at Banares, the arrangement differs and several Upaniṣads are inserted, the genuineness of which is questionable; while others are admitted, which belong exclusively to the Yajurveda". These words of Colebrooke perhaps refer to the Sanskrit original.

Upaniṣads of the older Veda not found in it—above all the *Chāndogya* and the *Bṛhadāraṇyaka* ? If the collection was supposed to include only the Atharva-Upaniṣads, as the beginning with the *Muṇḍaka* unmistakably signifies, why then are the *Kena, Kāṭhaka,* and the *Taittirīya* texts inserted, by the way and as it appears, as it were in a supplement ?

This problem admits of different solutions. According to us, the most probable hypothesis is that this collection originated in a period and in a region in which the study of the three old Vedas—and that also of the Śākhās of the *Aitareyins, Tāṇḍins,* and *Vājasaneyins,*—besides their Upaniṣads (Ait. Chānd. Bṛh Īśa) thrived in its prime, whereas the parallel Śākhās were no longer studied and cultivated. Now, in order to at least snatch these Upaniṣads out of oblivion, an effort was made to incorporate them in an already existing collection which extended from *Muṇḍaka* to *Nṛsiṁhatāpanīya,* together with a supplement of ten later Atharva-Upaniṣads. The *Kauṣītaki,* the *Śvetāśvatara,* the *Maitrāyaṇīya* were passed over; it may have been due to their having been forgotten or otherwise to the misgivings that they raised, so that the striking later arrangement or collection therefore liked to include these three connectedly in the Muktikā-collection.

5. The Collection of Nārāyaṇa

If the Upaniṣad-collection of Colebrooke, through the special kind of its compilation, allows us to have a glimpse—though indeed only uncertain—into its history of origin, there is another collection which, if one will succeed in the task, will be certainly found serviceable for perhaps throwing some light on the further following history of the Upaniṣad-tradition. It is the collection to which the well-known Upaniṣad-commentator Nārāyaṇa continuously refers in the beginning of his commentaries (*Dīpikās*) on the several individual Upaniṣads and which was originally, evidently the same as Colebrooke's, though towards the end there is discernible a noticeable deviation from it. Regarding the personal details of Nārāyaṇa, we only know that he calls himself the son of Ratnākara (ed. *Bibl. Ind.* p. 393, 14) and that he lived later not only than Śaṁkarācārya (about 800 A.C.) but also later than Śaṁkarānanda, as he makes a mention of these (ed. Pun. p. 100, 3,—the *Bibl. Ind.* has indeed a different reading in the corresponding passage, p. 196, 10). In his (unpublished) commentaries on the *Muṇḍaka*, the *Māṇḍūkya*, the *Kaṭha*, the *Praśna*, the *Kena* and the *Taittirīya*, *Nārāyaṇa* (according to Jacob, Eleven Atharva Upaniṣads p. 2) is very dependent on Śaṁkarācārya, which he acknowledges at the conclusion of every commentary, by calling himself *Śaṁkara-ukti-upajīvin*. In contrast to this, at the conclusion of his *Dīpikās* on the remaining *Atharva-upaniṣads*, he almost continually calls himself *Śruti-mātra-upajīvin* by which, it appears, he wished to emphasise the independent character of his work. We will attempt to reconstruct the list of Nārāyaṇa out of his occasional utterances, so far as it is possible to do it with the material available to us. The numbers signify, when not otherwise stated, the pages and the lines of the edition in the *Bibliotheca Indica*.

1. *Muṇḍaka* — Nārāyaṇa is accustomed to count the Upaniṣads from it.
2. *Praśna* — on account of the back-reference to the same p. 197-7.
3. *Brahmavidyā* — on this ground and on account of the probable back-reference to the same p. 203.9.
4. *Kṣurikā* —on the same ground as well as on account of the possible back-reference to the same p. 203.9.
5. *Cūlikā* — because on page 219.5 it is designated as *pañcamī.*
6. *Atharavaśiras* — See page 229.4 : '*Śira ūrdhvam śikhā ucitā*'.
7. *Atharvaśikhā* — p. 229.5 *saptamī muṇḍāt.*
8. *Garbha* — p. 60.6. *aṣṭamī muṇḍāt.*
9. *Mahā* — ed. Jacob p. 91.6 *navamī.*
10. *Brahma*, p. 239, 5, *daśamī.*
11. *Prāṇāgnihotra* : p. 260.5 : *ekādaśī śaunakīye.*

12-15. *Māṇḍūkya* with *Gauḍapāda's Kārikā.* Although the commentary of *Nārāyaṇa* on this is not available, nevertheless he (like Colebrooke) must have regarded this as Nos. 12-15, as it appears certain from the words on p. 272.6 : '*asparśayogam uktvā*' which words can only refer to *Gauḍapāda* 4.2.

16. Nīlarudra, p. 272.4. *Ṣoḍaśī.*
17. *Nādabindu ?* — We could follow only this position from the analogy with Colebrooke.
18. Brahmabindu, p. 78.10 : *aṣṭādaśī Śaunaka-granthavistare.*
19. Amṛtabindu ? from the analogy.
20. Dhyānabindu, p. 102.2. *viṁśī.*
21. Tejobindu, p. 114.9 *ekaviṁśam.*
22. Yogaśikhā, p. 118.6. *dvāviṁśatitamā* (according to the reading in the Poona edition).
23. Yogatattva, p. 122.6 *trayoviṁśī.*
24. Saṁnyāsa, on account of the probable back-reference in Yogatattva verse 11 on page 128.4 and still more probable back-reference in Saṁnyāsa 4, on page 185.1.
25. Āruṇeya, p. 184.9 : *pañcaviṁśī.*
26. Kaṇṭhaśruti, on account of the probable back-reference to the same. on page 295.6.
27. Piṇḍa, p. 295.4 : *saptaviṁśati-pūraṇī.*
28. Ātma, p. 299.5 : *aṣṭāviṁśī.*

29-30. Nṛsiṁha; the commentary of Nārāyaṇa is available to us, but from the words *nārasiṁhe nirṇītam* on p. 305.3, it follows that this work must have been previously there and in another passage, there is no place for the six Upaniṣads of which it consists. Probably, *Nārāyaṇa* enumerated them according to the main parts only as two, as we may conclude from his analogous method in the *Varadatāpinī* (see below, 51-52).

31. Kāṭhaka ? } We could conjecture this position from the analogy
32. Kena ? } with that in Colebrooke's collection.

33. Nārāyaṇa ed. Jacob p. 49.15 : *trayastriṁśattamī.*
34. Mahānārāyaṇa (=Bṛhannārāyaṇa see among the Upaniṣads of the Black Yajurveda) ed. Jacob. p. 13. *Catustriṁśe.*

In the numbers from 1-34, the agreement with Colebrooke 1-40 is so preponderating that in the few cases in which it is not demonstrable, we can assume it as very probable. Among the following numbers 35-45 (Colebrooke 41-42) the specified Upaniṣads are the same in both (the collections) (in the case of two, it is not demonstrable), but their serial order is different.

35-36. *Rāmatāpanīya,* p. 304.6 : *pañcatriṁśattame;* p. 359.9 *Ṣaṭtriṁśam.* (In Colebrooke 48-49).

37. Sarvopaniṣatsāra, p. 394.13 : *saptatriṁśe caturdale* (Colebrooke 41).

38. *Haṁsa,* p. 405.9 : *aṣṭatriṁśattamīm* (Colebrooke 42).

39-42. Here, there appears a great confusion in numbers. No. 39 cannot be ascertained and Col. Jacob also, whom I asked about it, knows no answer.—Paramahaṁsa is designated on p. 417.6 as *catvāriṁśattamī* but in the following lines, according to all appearances, it is connected with the Haṁsa.—Jābāla, according to p. 437.9, should be *ekacatvāriṁśattamī* and refers itself back in the next line, to the Paramahaṁsa.—Kaivalya is similarly designated on p. 465.5 as *ekacatvāriṁśattamī* and is connected, in the immediately following words, with Jābāla.—Also Taittirīya has been commented upon by Nārāyaṇa and as (see Jacob, *Eleven Ath. Up.* p. 2) *Śikṣā—Brahmavallī-Bhṛguvallī,* has been consequently reckoned as one. Its position or place in Nārāyaṇa is not known. But as it follows after Kaivalya as No. 42 in the government collection at Poona (according to Jacob's friendly communication), this is also conjecturally its place in Nārāyaṇa. After this, in the given data, many mistakes are found, and Nārāyaṇa's serial order is probably : 38. Haṁsa (Colebrooke 42); 39. Paramahaṁsa (Colebrooke 43); 40. Jābāla (Colebrooke 51); 41. Kaivalya (Colebrooke 50); 42. Taittirīya (Colebrooke 44-45).—

43. Indefinite; possibly Āśrama, because this place alone remains for it; in Jacob's edition, no commentary is included at the end, as in Colebrooke in which the position 52 is given to it.

44. Garuḍa, p. 480.8 : Catuścatvāriṁśattamī. (Colebrooke 46).

45. *Kālāgnirudra*; ed. Jacob p. 17.9 : *pañcacatvāriṁśattamī* (Colebrooke 47).

While Nos. 1-34 evidently agree with Colebrooke's 1-40 in the names and in the serial order, and Nos. 35-45 agree with Colebrooke's 41-52 in the names but in serial order, there follow in Nārāyaṇa's further enumeration a series of texts which concern Kṛṣṇa and Gaṇeśa, which, however, find no place in Colebrooke's collection.

46-47. Gopālatāpanīya ed. Poona p. 183.5 : *Ṣaḍbhiś catvāriṁśatām ca pūraṇī* Ātharvapaippale; p. 205.15 : *Saptacatvāriṁśattamī Gopālottaratāpinī.*

48. Kṛṣṇa ed. Jacob. p. 3.7 : *aṣṭacatvāriṁśattami.*

49. Vāsudeva, ed. Jacob p. 25.11 : *Kṣudragranthagaṇe ca ekonapañcāśattamī matā.*

50. Gopīcandana, as ed. Jacob. p. 37.14 : *Vāsudeva-Upaniṣac cheṣabhūtā Gopīcandana-Upaniṣad ārabhyate.*

51-52. Varadapūrvatāpinī, ed. Jacob p. 111.6 : *ekapañcāśattamī* and consequently *Varadottaratāpinī*, on which no commentary is available.

Whether Nārāyaṇa's list concluded with the number 52, we cannot ascertain; we have not met with a higher number, although from his remark on No. 49, it follows that a larger collection of Upaniṣads was known to him; also among others, there is available a commentary by him on the *Śvetāśvatara* (according to Jacob, *Eleven Ath. Up.* p. 2). He has, perhaps, not included in his enumeration isolated small Upaniṣads, as e.g. he has treated the Rāma-Upaniṣad as a supplement to Rāmatāpanīya, Ātmabodha as a supplement to Nārāyaṇa, and Ṣaṭcakra as a supplement to Nṛsiṁha.

If it is presupposed that the list of Nārāyaṇa, as that of Colebrooke, included no more than the demonstrable 52 number, if it is also further presupposed that the sequential order ascertained by us will be ratified in the few doubtful places, the result would be that the 52 Upaniṣads in Colebrooke's list are summed up by Nārāyaṇa in 45 numbers (the last eleven with a few inconsiderable deviations in the series), after which there follow seven Upaniṣads from No. 46 to 52, not found in Colebrooke, concerned with Kṛṣṇa and Gaṇeśa.

These facts, if only fully ascertained, would get most simply clarified through the assumption that Colebrooke's list of 52 Upaniṣads had already attained a certain canonical authority, so that only the late eleven Upaniṣads —these only in a serial order which exhibited some fluctuations—attained recognition as the best of the recent ones or got incorporated into this canon as the recently originated Upaniṣads, in response to the desire (of the compilers) which asserted itself. With this aim in view, the Upaniṣads divided into more numbers in Colebrooke's list were again amalgamated into their natural unity and it was made possible, without overstepping the number 52 which had already received sanction, to incorporate into the acknowledged canon the seven Upaniṣads which had attained popularity through the growing worshipful regard for Kṛṣṇa and Gaṇeśa, or as one may say, they were smuggled into the canon. In any case, the fact deserves, in the interest of the history of the Upaniṣad-tradition, a closer investigation, than the one we can attempt at present.

6. Selection and Arrangement

To combine all the Upaniṣads in one edition or translation is, for the time being, impossible, as it is not even known how many Upaniṣads there are. Every attempt to work on them must therefore, confine itself to a selection. Any such attempt should, however, not depend on subjective judgement but on objective grounds according to which the more or less general recognition is chosen as the criterion for inclusion in the collection. From this point of view, we believe that we are right in restricting ourselves to 'the solemn series' of 52 Upaniṣads, as Colebrooke offers them in his list with which the collection of Nārāyaṇa (with the exception of a number of doubtful products in his collection —) as also that of the *Oupanekhat* essentially agrees.

On the other hand, what concerns the arrangement or order (of the Upaniṣads in these collections), all the collections described by us exhibit such a lack of any principle that they make an impression of having been mixed up confusedly by mere accident, so that the newest Poona edition has even gone to the extent of arranging the order of the Upaniṣads according to the alphabet. Such a procedure might, perhaps, be approved, if the contents of the Upaniṣads themselves had not most obviously called for an ordering of the Upaniṣads in different categories. These categories have been rightly recognized by Weber in their essentials, when he has distinguished three classes among the Atharva-Upaniṣads (*Literaturgeschichte*, 2 Auflage, p. 173) *:* "One (Class of Upaniṣads) continues in their direct investigation of the nature of the Ātman—the Universal Intelligence; another class is occupied with the method of going deep into the meditation (Yoga) on the Ātman; the third class, substitutes in the place of the Ātman any one of the four forms under which both the chief gods, Śiva and Viṣṇu, had come to be worshipped in course of time."

In this division, we miss to find, among the three mentioned kinds of different classes, one which seeks to attain, not in the mystical contemplation of Yoga, but in a more practical way, the goal set down by the Vedānta-doctrine as it posits the life of Saṁnyāsin — a religious recluse or mendicant—as the state to be most aspired for.

By the way, these are the three or four directions which, as Weber has already rightly emphasised, do not follow chronologically one after another but are regarded, in general, as running parallel with one another. There lies among them a development of the Vedānta-standpoint in different directions which, however, differ so little from one another, that in many, indeed, with a few exceptions, in all Upaniṣads, every one of these directions is found at least in a suggestive manner; above all, all of them stand on the common ground of the Vedānta doctrine Very generally the attempt exhibits itself, further to attain the primal cause or ground, which is not comprehensible in the intellectual way, but through a mystical communion, transcending intellect for which the syllable Om is offered as a vehicle or means by the Kāṭhaka; further there are a few Upaniṣads which do not join in the ideas already so forcefully emphasised by Yājñavalkya that the true conduct of the wise vis-à-vis against the world, is renunciation (*saṁnyāsa*); but concerned with the predilection for the sectarian way, they essentially spring out of the desire to win over for the Vedānta-doctrine a larger circle of the populace, sections from which paid homage in some form partly to Śiva and partly to Viṣṇu, because the chief god adored by them has been explained as a symbolical apparent form of the

Ātman—an attempt the first beginnings of which are already met with in the Upaniṣads of the three old Vedas.

With this premiss, therefore, that they deal with only an unfolding or if one wishes to say—with an expansion of one and general Vedānta-doctrine, we shall indeed proceed with this aim, when we arrange the Upaniṣads in the following five categories, each according to the point of view predominantly represented by it; in every one of these categories, there is a relatively old and again a very late product, because, as has already been remarked, these directions, in general, run, not chronologically one after another, but parallel along with one another; thus the circumstance is not excluded that according to the changing taste of the times, now the one, now the other attempt appeared forth more than the other in the foreground and found its expression in the corresponding Upaniṣads.

Accordingly, among the Upaniṣads of the Atharvaveda, we distinguish as follows :

1. Such, as essentially remain true to the old Vedānta-doctrine without considerably accentuating their further development into Yoga, Saṁnyāsa and Vaiṣṇavite or Śaivite symbolism, as it is in the old Upaniṣads;
2. others, which, presupposing the Vedānta-standpoint deal, overwhelmingly or exclusively, with the comprehension of the Ātman through the Yoga by means of the morae (the component parts) of the Om syllable;
3. again such others in which as a rule, though partially, the life of the Saṁnyāsin (anchorite) is recommended and described as a practically consistent conclusion of the Upaniṣad-teaching;
4. moreover, such others which interpret Śiva (*Īśāna, Maheśvara, Mahādeva* etc.) worshipped by the people, as a personification of the Ātman;
5. again, such as, equally reformulate Viṣṇu (*Nārāyaṇa, Nṛsiṁha* etc.) in the sense of the Vedānta-doctrine, as they consider his different *avatāras* as human incarnations of the Ātman.

Accordingly, the generally recognized Upaniṣads of the Atharvaveda have been grouped, according to the tendency predominant in them, below approximately, as follows :

1. *Purely Vedāntic Upaniṣads*

Muṇḍaka, Praśna, Māṇḍūkya (with the *Kārikā*), *Garbha, Prāṇāgnihotra, Piṇḍa, Ātma, Sarvopaniṣatsāra, Garuḍa.*

2. *Yoga-Upaniṣads*

Brahmavidyā, Kṣurikā, Cūlikā, Nādabindu, Brahmabindu, Amṛtabindu, Dhyānabindu, Tejobindu, Yogaśikhā, Yogatattva; *Haṁsa.*

3. *Saṁnyāsa-Upaniṣads*

Brahma, Saṁnyāsa, Āruṇeya, Kaṇṭhaśruti; Paramahaṁsa, Jābāla, Āśrama.

4. *Śiva-Upaniṣads*

Atharvaśiras, Atharvaśikhā, Nīlarudra; Kālāgnirudra; Kaivalya.

5. *Viṣṇu-Upaniṣads*

Mahā, Nārāyaṇa, Ātmabodha; Nṛsiṁhapūrvatāpanīya, Nṛsiṁhottaratāpanīya; Rāmapūrvatāpanīya, Rāmottaratāpanīya.

THE MUṆḌAKA UPANIṢAD OF THE ATHARVAVEDA

[The *Muṇḍaka-Upaniṣad* (occasionally also named briefly *Muṇḍa* —see Muktikop. verse 29; Nārāyaṇa on Atharvaśikhā 1 p. 229.5, on Garbha p. 60.6) does not belong to a definite Vedic school but is as the name signifies, "the Upaniṣad of those who have shaved their heads clean" (*Muṇḍa*), i.e. of a community of ascetics who, like the later Buddhist monks, shaved off the hair of their heads as an observance of vow. Correspondingly, it is emphasised at the conclusion of the Upaniṣad that it should be communicated to nobody who has not according to the scriptures, fulfilled the 'vow of (regarding) the head' (*Śirovratam*). That by this 'vow regarding the head' one should understand the carrying of fire (something like a basin containing coals or embers) on the head as Śaṅkara elucidates with the remark that "this vow occurs in the Atharvaveda", appears to us very doubtful; because there what has not yet been known to us will have to be demonstrated (I hope that one would not bring in its support Atharvav. 10.2.26; cf. about this passage *Gesch. d. Phil*, I, 269), and then still the question remains whether Śaṅkara gives his explanation on the ground of tradition or (as it so often appears) out of mere conjecture and whether we should not prefer, to his strange interpretation of the passage, the simple interpretation of *śirovrata* which lies in the word *muṇḍaka.*[1]

The *Muṇḍaka* is one of the most popular favourite Upaniṣads; in no collection of the Upaniṣads it fails to appear; among the ten Upaniṣads which the Muktikā and similar collections place ahead as the most important, it takes the fifth place after Īśa, Kena, Kaṭha, Praśna; Nārāyaṇa enumerates the Atharva-Upaniṣads, with it as the first one. Already Bādarāyaṇa devotes to it three of the 28 adhikaraṇas in which he deals with the Brahman-doctrine (*System des Vedānta* p. 130) and Śaṅkara cites it alone 129 times in his commentary on the Brahmasūtra (loc. cit. p. 32).

Our Upaniṣad deserves this favoured position not so much by its originality of its contents — because most of the ideas are demonstrably borrowed from older texts—but, on the contrary, on account of the purity

---

1. *Bhāskarānanda Svāmin* (an old Saṁnyāsin — a recluse, who has become my friend, with whom I often carried on philosophical discussions, when he, fully naked, sat on a stone-slab of the garden in Benares where he resides) appears to be of my opinion when he remarks, in his commentary which has already appeared on the eight Upaniṣads, at the beginning of his commentary on the Muṇḍaka : *asya ca śirovratibhir adhyetavyatvāt Muṇḍaka-iti-ākhyā*; from this indeed it is not correct to say that he reproduces the opinion of Śaṅkara on this passage.

with which it delivers the old Vedānta-doctrine and on account of the beauty of the verses in which it gives expression to it. It pre-supposes first and above all the Chāndogya, and very probably also the Bṛhadāraṇyaka and the Taittirīya, as well as the Kāṭhaka with which it has many passages in common; these passages occur in these Upaniṣads in the proper context, whereas they stand very abrupt in the Muṇḍaka. According to the language and other trends it may be placed next to the Bṛhannārāyaṇa and the Śvetāśvatara. With the later Upaniṣads, it has, in common, the poetic fervour, the deficiency of an ordered sequence of thoughts and the irregularity in metre; it is, however, less rich in original ideas and for that reason, is again free from theistic and heretical tendencies than they (the later Upaniṣads). Muṇḍaka has many important passages in common with the Śvetāśvatara on the one hand and with the Bṛhadāraṇyaka on the other; a comparison of the same (see footnotes in the sequel) makes it probable that the Śvetāśvatara has been used by the Muṇḍaka and the Muṇḍaka again by the Bṛhannārāyaṇa. Considered as a whole, however, all the three certainly belong to the same period.

A well-ordered arrangement of the Muṇḍaka-Upaniṣad, without straining at interpretation, cannot indeed be given and one can, only in general, say that of the three sections of which the Muṇḍaka consists, (of which every section again is divided again into two subsections), the first deals with the preparatory stages for the knowledge of Brahman, the second the doctrine of Brahman, and the third the way to the Brahman. But repeatedly comes the theme of the third section in the second, that of the second again in the third and both these again crop up in the first.]

FIRST MUṆḌAKAM

FIRST HALF

[First, the genealogy of this science of knowledge is given. It has reached through the following teachers :

Brahman
Atharvan[1]
Aṅgir[1]
Satyavāha Bhāradvāja
Aṅgiras

up to Śaunaka who is called *mahāśāla* (of great wealth) like the interrogator in Chānd. 5.11.1, and who puts to Aṅgiras a question which undoubtedly rests on Chānd. 6.1.2, and besides perhaps, on Bṛh. 2.4.5 (concluding part) and 7-9 : "What is that with the knowledge of which this whole world becomes known?"—Aṅgiras begins his reply with saying that he distinguishes

1. Aṅgir, which occurs only here, is indeed etymologically derived from Aṅgiras and Atharvāya must be nothing else than old mistake for Atharvaṇe.

the lower and the higher knowledge (*vidyā*)—this distinction first occurs here— ; by this, however, is not meant the *saguṇa* and *nirguṇa* vidyā, as in the later Vedānta; on the contrary, the lower knowledge includes the ritualistic knowledge as it is laid down in the four Vedas and in the six Vedāṅgas (auxiliary branches of Vedic knowledge) which are found enumerated here for the first time; the higher knowledge is the knowledge of the Brahman, or as it is called of the *Akṣaram* (the Imperishable). This name, as also the characterization of the same through negative attribute, indeed, rests on Bṛh. 3.8.8, while the following similes describing, here and in the continuation of the text 2.1.1, the arising forth of the world out of Brahman through (its) expansion, may have been taken from the Bṛh. 2.1.20. Towards the end, follows in the verse 8, a step-by-step or gradual series of the principles, regarding which verse 9 asserts that all of them (as they are again summarised without any order) have risen forth out of the all-knowing Ātman. Their sequence, with Śaṅkara's, is indeed not elucidating as to remain consistent (in verse 8, it is *prāṇa* while in verse 9 it is brahman=Hiraṇyagarbha).

Yaḥ sarvajñaḥ sarvavid (=*Brahmam*)
annam (=*avyākṛtam*)
prāṇaḥ (=*Hiraṇyagarbha*)
manas
Satyam (the elements), *lokāḥ*, *Karmāṇi*

If we compare this series with that placed together in Kāṭhaka (see above at the end of the introductory notes to the Kāṭhaka) it appears that in essentials it is the same only with the difference that, through the blending of *mahān ātmā* and *buddhi* with *prāṇa*, it has come a step nearer to the Sāṁkhya doctrine. Still, as the elucidations in Śaṅkara's commentary are uncertain, we would not like to use this observation to draw any further conclusion. Cf. also the footnotes on 2.1.2-3.]

1. Brahmā arose as the first of gods,
as the creator of this universe and its protector.
He taught his eldest son Atharva(n)
the knowledge of Brahman, the basic foundations of all knowledge.

2. What Brahmā formerly imparted to Atharvan
that Brahman-knowledge, Atharvan imported to Aṅgir,
This latter (Aṅgir) to Satyavāha Bhāradvāja,
and he (Bhāradvāja) imparted to Aṅgiras the highest and the deepest knowledge.[1]

---

1. The Sanskrit original is '*parāvarā*' (*para*+*avara* (vidyā). Deussen translates 'avarā'=deepest. According to Śaṅkara *parāvarā* means the 'highest and the most inferior' knowledge ' *avarā* (vidyā) is, according

3. It once happened that Śaunaka, a man of great wealth[1], approached Aṅgiras in the proper way and inquired of him: "O venerable one, what is that by the knowledge of which this whole world becomes known ?"

4. And he said to him: "One should know two sciences (or kinds of knowledge), that is what those who know Brahman say, namely: the higher and the lower.

5. The lower is the Ṛgveda, Yajurveda, Sāmaveda, Atharvaveda, the science of (properly) pronouncing the letters (of the Vedic Text) (Śikṣā), the lore of cult, grammar, vocabulary[2], prosody, astronomy.

But the higher knowledge is that through which that imperishable one (*akṣaram*) is known;

6. that which is invisible, ungraspable, devoid of pedigree
(agotra),
which is colourless, devoid of eyes and ears,
devoid of hands and feet,
which is eternal, all-penetrating, omnipresent,
which is hardly knowable,[3]
that is unchangeable,
which is viewed by the wise as the womb (source) of
beings.

7. Just as a spider spins out and holds (the threads of the
web)
just as the plants sprout forth out of the earth,
just as hair grow on the head and body of a man who lives,
similarly everything that is here arises out of the imperishable one.

---

to him, *avidyā* (ignorance), i.e. the knowledge of the phenomenal world which, as compared with *parā* (the highest knowledge of Brahman), is most inferior. —Translator

1. The Sanskrit original is *mahāśāla* which according to Śaṅkara means *mahāgṛhastha* i.e. a possessor of a large house, a great householder. —Translator

2. The Sanskrit original is *nirukti* which means 'etymological interpretation'. —Translator

3. The Sanskrit word in the original is 'Susūkṣma' which literally means "very subtle" (such as cannot be perceived by the senses)—Translator

8. Through *tapas* (penance) the Brahman expands itself,
out of it is produced food
out of food (arise) the breath, the mind, truth,
the world and, in works[1], eternity (Amṛtam).

9. The universal knower (*sarvajña*), the omniscient one (knowing all particular things=*Sarvavid*)
whose Tapas (penance) is (consists of) knowledge,
Out of it arise all these:
Brahman, name, form and food also.

Second Half

[This sub-section breaks the context (2.1.1 is connected with 1.1.7) and introduces the doctrine of the Upaniṣads differently than the previous subsection. There in the previous section, there was a purely intellectual motive, actuated by which, Śaunaka puts to Aṅgiras the question regarding that, with the knowledge of which, everything becomes known;—here it is the feeling of disgust towards the metempsychosis (transmigration of the soul) which does not cease (even) through the holiness (—produced by—) works; it is this disgust that drives the pupil with fuel in hand to approach the (proper) master. The isolated parts of this subsection are not quite consistent; first, the sacrificial cult is enthusiastically praised and recommended (1-6), and is then suddenly condemned in the severest words (7-10); Verse 8, on account of the mention of *Śreyas* in the preceding verse, appears to have been taken over from the context of Kaṭha 2.5; in verse 9, the same idea is still further spun out, Verses 10-11 describing *Pitṛyāṇa* and *Devayāna*, rest on Chānd. 5.10.1-3 (*tapaḥ-śraddhe*), whereas the passage (Muṇḍaka) 3.1.6 (Satyena) is reminiscent of the parallel passage in Bṛh. 6.2.15. — The whole subsection produces the impression that it must have been afterwards interpolated in the original composition.]

1. This is the truth:
The works, which the wise saw in the sacred songs,
are, in a manifold way, disseminated in the triad (of the Vedas)
You, who desire realization,[2] practise them continually;
path leads you to the world of the requital of works.

---

1. The Sanskrit original is *karmasu ca amṛtam* which according to Śaṅkara means "The actions performed during life according to one's class and station, produce their fruits which are unceasing (amṛta), like the actions which produce them. —Translator

2. i.e. requital; *satyam* is the same as *ṛtam* (Kaṭh. 3.1)

2. When the flame of fire leaps up licking (its blazing tongues)
when the sacrificial fire flames forth in splendour,
then, between the offerings of ghee
one should offer the gushing oblations
—it should be offered with faith.

3. He who does not follow up his fire-sacrifice
with new- and full moon sacrifices,
with four months sacrifice and offering[1] of the first products harvested in autumn,
and the hospitable treatment of guests
he, who does not sacrifice, nor makes offerings to the all-gods
he who sacrifices wrongly (not according to rules),
—he destroys his sacrifice up to all the seven worlds.[2]

4. The dark one, the fiercely grinding one,
the one as quick as thought,
the one highly red, the one flying into sparks,
the one which is smoke-coloured,
the one all glittering sublime one,
—these are the seven swinging or lolling flaming tongues of the sacrificial fire.

5. It (the fire) activates itself, sparkling with sparks,
and receives the gushing sacrificial oblations at the right time;
they (the oblations), like the sun's rays, lead him (the sacrificer) upwards,
there where reigns the one lord of the gods.

6. "Come! Come!" say the offerings rich with splendour
and they lead the sacrificer on the sun's rays upwards;

---

1. The Sanskrit original is *anāgrayaṇam, āgrayaṇam* is explained by Śaṅkara as *'śaradādi-kartavyam'* i.e. to be done in the beginning of autumn when the harvest season begins. The *āgrayaṇa* ritual prescribed the offering of grain or corn, the first product of the harvest. —Translator

2. The seven worlds are : *bhūr, bhuvaḥ, svar, mahas, janas, tapas, satyam.* These are, according to our knowledge, enumerated for the first time in Taitt. Āraṇy. 10.27-28.

speaking to him with sweet words and flattering him:
"There beckons to you the holy Brahman-world
of the pious."

7. Tottering and unsteady are these sacrificial rites[1]
the eighteen ones in which, the inferior ritual finds expression[2]
the fools, who greet it (the ritual) as the better one (*śreyaḥ*) (Kāṭh. 2. 1),
—they again sink into old age and death.

8. Meandering[3] in the depth of ignorance,
imagining themselves as the wise and the learned,
the fools knock about aimlessly hither and thither
like the blind men, whom, one who himself is blind, leads.

9. Meandering in manifold ways in ignorance,
the fools imagine themselves as having attained the goal of their desires,
before setting about to do useful work, they (on account of passion)[4] do not deliberate,
consequently falling into misery, when the reward is consumed.[5]

10. Regarding the sacrifice and other works as the highest,
the infatuated ones know not anything better.

---

1. The Sanskrit original for 'sacrificial rites' is '*plavāḥ yajñarūpāḥ* 'which means' the boats or the rafts in the form of sacrifice. Śaṅkara explains '*plava*' as 'perishable'. —Translator

2. According to Śaṅkara, the sixteen priests, the performer of the sacrifice and his wife are the *eighteen* ones. The expression *yeṣu karma uktam* appears, however, to point to Vedic scriptural works. Can they be thought of as the twelve divisions of the Veda i.e. the Saṁhitā, Brāhmaṇam, Sūtrām of each of the four Vedas besides the previously mentioned above (Muṇḍ. 1.1.5) six Vedāṅgas ?

3. Excepting the words jaṅghanyamānāḥ, the verse is=Kāṭh 2.5.

4. In the Sanskrit original there is here the word *rāgāt* (i.e. through passionate attachment) —Translator

5. The Sanskrit original here is *kṣīṇalokāḥ* which means "(whose stay in) the heavenly worlds attained through works whose fruits have been consumed has come to an end." —Translator

Having enjoyed themselves in the heaven obtained by works,
they sink back again into this world still deeper down.

11. Those, however, who practise in the forest the life of austerities and faith,[1]
calm, full of knowledge, living only on alms,
—they pass unpolluted (virajāḥ) through the portal of the sun,
to that place where there is the eternal spirit, the changeless Ātman.

12. The wise, critically pondering over the worlds brought about by their words,
—they turn away (from disgust)[2]; the uneffected (Brahmam) is not effected through works.[3]
In order to attain knowledge, he should seek and visit, with fuelsticks in hands,
The master who is proficient in scriptures and who is steady in Brahman.

13. He, who has approached in the proper way,
who is calm in heart and restful,
—to him the wise one then imparts the science (knowledge) of Brahman,
just as it is, the knowledge of the imperishable,
of the intelligent spirit, of the truth.

---

1. Just as the Pitṛyāṇa is previously described, here the Devayāna is also described, certainly not after the manner of Bṛh. 6.2.15; but according to Chānd. 5.10.1, which passage (*ye ca ime araṇye śraddhā tapa iti upāsate*) has not been quite rightly understood already here (as also in the parallel passage in Bṛh, 6.2.15). Whether our author sees also in the Devayāna only the fruit of lower knowledge and not of the highest knowledge cannot be ascertained according to his presentation. cf. Muṇḍ. 3.1 (our introductory remarks).

2. The Sanskrit original is 'nirvedam āyān' which means 'coming to the state of disgust'. —Translator

3. The uneffected world of Brahman. cf. *akṛto brahmalokaḥ* (Chānd. 8.13). The Sanskrit original is *nāsti akṛtah kṛtena* : It according to Śaṅkara means : "There is nothing that is not fruit of action; the fruit of action is perishable. The wise man realizes this and has no use for the actions done (Kim Kṛtena).—Translator

SECOND MUṆḌAKAM

FIRST HALF

[This subsection depicts the Brahman and its unfoldment into the phenomena of the world in a simile of great poetic beauty. The metre is very freely handled and dissolves itself in the several passages so much into rhythmical prose that we are compelled to give up the reproduction or counting of the number of syllables. The contents, at every step, remind us of the earlier Upaniṣad passages, without however, making it possible to pinpoint the borrowing with certainty. At the most, there is employed the description of the *Akṣaram* which Yājñavalkya depicts (Bṛh. 3.8) in his dialogue with Gārgī. Echoes of the Puruṣa-hymn in the Ṛgveda (10.90) are found and, as the footnotes thereon will show, echoes of many other passages are found. Only the concluding verse comes round to the thought that he, who knows this Brahman in his heart, would therethrough, untie or dissolve 'the knots of nescience'. (See the Footnote on Kāṭhaka-Up. 3.15.)]

1. This is the truth:
Just as out of the blazing fire
the sparks, alike in essence, arise a thousandfold
so also, O dear one, out of the imperishable
the manifold beings arise forth
and they again enter or merge in the same. (Taitt. 3.1)
2. Heavenly is the spirit (Puruṣa), the formless one (Bṛh. 2.3, 5);
It is outside and inside, (Īśa 5), the unborn one,
devoid of breath (*a-prāṇa*), devoid of desire (Bṛh. 3.8.8), the pure one,
Still higher beyond than the highest Imperishable.[1]
3. Out of it originates the breath, the mind and all the senses,
out of it arise ether, wind and fire
and the waters and the earth which bears everything.[2]

---

1. *Puruṣa* and *Akṣara* (the Ur-subject and the Ur-object) which were previously treated as a unity are here, however, distinguished from one another just as above (1.1.8-9) the *sarvajña* and *Brahman*.

2. The genealogy is similar to the above one in 1.1.8-9.

Puruṣa-Akṣaram
Prāṇa
manas
sense organs and elements. [Contd.

4. Its head is fire, its eyes the moon and the sun
the directions are its ears
Its voice is the revealed Vedas
The wind is its breath, its heart is the world
out of its feet (arises) the earth (Ṛgveda 10.90.14),
it is the inner self in all beings (Kāṭh. 5.9-12)

5. Out[1] of it originates the fire, the fuel of which is the sun (Chānd. 5.4.1)
out of Soma arises rain (Chānd. 5.5.2), plants out of earth,
The male sprinkles the fluid in the female mate (Chānd. 5.8.2)
many descendants are born from the spirit (puruṣa).

6. Out of it arise the hymns (Ṛc), songs (chants, Sāma), the sacrificial maxims (Yajus) (Ṛgveda 10.90.9)
out of it the consecration, the sacrifice, customs (*kratavaḥ*) and the sacrificial gifts
out of it arise the duration of the year and the sacrificer (Bṛh. 3.8.9) and the worlds
where light of Soma and the light of the sun are radiant.[2]

7. Out of it many gods have originated as also the blessed ones[3] (*sādhyāḥ*)
out of it originate men, cattle and birds (Ṛgveda 10.90.8)
"Inbreath and outbreath, rice and barley" (Atharvaveda), (11.4.13) faith,
self-mortification (austerities), truth, the practice of Brahman (Brahmacarya) and prescribed rules, (these have also originated out of it).

Cf. above the similar genealogy in our introductory remarks on Muṇḍaka I first half, and in the concluding part of our introductory remarks on the Kāṭhaka. Cf. also the sequence of the Sāṁkhya principles.

1. This is a short résumé of the doctrine of the five fires according to the Chānd. 5.3-10.

2. According to Śaṅkara : '*Somo yatra pavate punāti lokān yeṣu sūryas tapati*' i.e. where the Soma purifies the worlds and the sun shines' — Translator). That indicates the worlds of the Pitṛyāṇa and the Devayāna (Chānd. 5.10).

3. 'Gods and the blessed ones (sādhyāḥ)' rest on an inexact (vague reminiscence of the Ṛgveda 10.90.7.

8. Seven[1] organs (prāṇāḥ) have originated out of it,
with seven fuelsticks, seven flames, and sacrificial offerings
and also these seven worlds
in which they move about out of their cavities,
where seven respectively lay hidden.

9. Out[2] of it arise the seas and all the mountains,
out of it, the rivers flow in all forms
out of it have arisen the plants and nutrition-juice,
through which it continues to stay in the beings as their inner self.

10. Indeed, *Puruṣa* (the Spirit) is this universe (Ṛgveda 10.90.2),
he is the work[3], *tapas* (austerities), Brahman, the immortal one;—
he, who knows this (*puruṣa*) concealed in the cavity of the heart)
bursts asunder, O dear one, the knot of ignorance.

1-2. The activity of the seven senses (eyes, ears, nostrils, mouth) appear as sacrifice; the impressions or impacts (of the external world) on the senses are the fuel, the reaction of the senses against that impact is the flame; the sacrificial gifts are the perceptions of the senses, seeing, hearing, smelling, the sum of individual perceptions forms the world of concerned organs. All sense-organs are regulated by the *Manas* (mind) which has its seat in the heart. — We have already met with verses 8-9, with some veriants, in the Mahānār. 10.2-3. As the ideas in both the verses are entirely different, their occurrence in both the passages cannot be accidental; here a borrowing must have taken place. What is original between the two can be doubted. The whole subsection of the Mahānār. 10, as has been demonstrated by us, while dealing with that part, consists of borrowings. On the other hand, like so many passages in Muṇḍaka 2.1, the ninth verse in the same traces itself back to the speech of Yājñavalkya in Bṛh. 3.8. 8-9 and is a poetical reproduction of the same; it is not, however, a quotation borrowed from elsewhere. The verses 8-9 do not therefore, stem out of a common source—common for the Muṇḍaka and Mahānār., but they originally belong to the Muṇḍaka. The probable important result of this fact is that the Muṇḍaka-Upaniṣad must have been already used during the composition of the Taitt. Ār. 10.

3. The metrically surplus word *Karma* is missing in the quotation of the passage by Śaṅkara in his commentary on the Brahmasūtra (excepting two mss.). (See *Die Sūtras des Vedānta* p. 705, 11).

SECOND HALF

[This subsection continues further to glorify the highest supreme Being, when it refers, for a while, to the same dwelling in the heart and describes the way to reach it by means of meditation on the syllable *Om* and thus forms a preliminary to the views of the following part. The poet here displays an ecstasy of enthusiasm or inspiration in which the hearer or the reader is hardly able to follow him. The language is concise, abrupt, only suggestive, and hardly intelligible in some passages. Still here the apparent literary decadence is undeniable : most of the ideas can be demonstrated, with more or less certainty, to have been borrowed from the earlier Upaniṣadic literature. Particularly characteristic is the simile of the bow, the arrow and the target (verses 3-4) and the splendid verse 8, although it turns out to be only a happy summary of earlier thoughts.]

1. That which is evident (visible) and yet concealed
   dwells in the cavity (of the heart)—a great place,
   in which is fixed (as spokes) that which lives and breathes
   and shuts the eyes (Ṛgveda. 10.121.3),
   know ye what is higher than it, as what is and is not
   (Śvet. 4.18),
   transcending knowledge, the highest of creation,

2. that which is blazing forth like a flame
   that which is the subtlest of the subtle;
   on it rest the worlds and those who reside in those worlds,
   the imperishable one, the Brahman
   it is the breath, speech and mind;
   it is the truth, the immortal one
   that, indeed, O dear one, you should hit as the target.

3. Seize as the bow the great weapon of the Upaniṣads,
   fix the arrow, sharpened through meditation
   stretch it (the bow) through the mind directed on the existence of Brahman,
   and hit, O dear one, the imperishable as the target.

4. *Om* as the bow, the soul as the arrow,
   Brahman as the target —thus it is characterized;
   fixing the aim on it, without slackness (Kāṭh. 6.11),
   one penetrates into it, as the arrow penetrates the target.

5. In it are interwoven the heavens, the earth, and the aerial
   space (Bṛh. 3.8.7)

as also the mind with all the senses
know it as the Ātman, leave off other speech (Bṛh. 4.4.20)
it is the bridge leading to immortality (Śvet. 6.19)

6. In it are fixed the arteries of the heart (Bṛh. 2.1.19)
like the spokes in the navel (of a chariot wheel),
it stays in the inmost part and is born many times,
Om! thus speak about it and meditate the Ātman,
Hail to you! go to the bank beyond darkness
(Chānd. 7.26.2)

7. The all-knower, aware of all (Muṇḍaka 1.1.9),
the world displays its greatness to you (Chānd. 3.12.6)
in the heavenly city of Brahman (Chand. 8.1.9)
in the space of the heart it stays as the Ātman!
mind is its stuff, it directs the body of the living
(Chānd. 3.14.2),
rooted in food, it remains concealed in the heart
(Kāṭh. 6.17),
there the wise find him and discover
it in the form of bliss (Taitt. 2.5), the immortal and resplendent one!

8. He who sees the highest and the deepest,
for him, the knots of the heart are burst asunder
(Chānd. 7.26.2)
all the doubts are dissolved (Chānd. 3.14.4)
and his works come to an end (Bṛh. 4.4.22)

9. Behind a golden, excellent veil (Bṛh 5.15)
sits enthroned the stainless and partless Brahman;
it is full of splendour, it is the light of lights (Bṛh. 4.4.16)
and he who knows the Ātman knows it.

10. There[1] the son does not shine, nor the moon, nor the stars' splendour
nor do those lightnings flash there
let alone (not to speak of) the earthly fire,
it alone shines, everything else shines after it,
the whole world shines by its splendour.

1. Here also, as in Śvet. 6.14, we must conclude that the verse is borrowed from the Kāṭh. 5.15, as there alone it appears in its natural context.

11. Brahman[1] is the immortal one in the east,
Brahman in the west, Brahman in the south and the north;
Brahman extends itself below and above,
Brahman is this magnificent great universe.

THIRD MUṆḌAKAM

[*The first and the second halves* : This last muṇḍakam describes in its both parts, with manifold borrowings from the Chāndogya, Bṛhadāraṇyaka and other Upaniṣads, the doctrine of deliverance; in this description there are stated different viewpoints which this theme offers for consideration (e.g. contrast between the released and non-released, the way to deliverance, description of the supremacy of Brahman and of the blessed state of the delivered souls); these different viewpoints are not stated in an orderly manner but are thrown together pellmell. Worse than this defect in arrangement and orderliness which is not compensated or outweighed through the beauty of the verses in any way, is the unprincipledness which predominates in the eschatological ideas of our Upaniṣad. The basic view is that man attains Brahman through knowledge, why he becomes Brahman, as it is expressed more beautifully than elsewhere, in the celebrated passage 3.2.9 : *sa yo ha vai tat paramam brahma eva bhavati*, which has been rightly placed in the forefront as a motto by Anquetil Duperron in his translation of the *Oupanekhat*; he translated it concisely and appropriate to the purpose: 'quisquis Deum intelligit, Deus fit' ('Whoever knows God, becomes god); but repeatedly this presentation of the intellectual theory of deliverance is interrupted or broken by the ideas occurring in the Taittirīya 2 with the effect that the deliverance has become a trans-intellectual (mystic) communion (3.1.8 *jñānaprasādena*; 3.2.7-*karmāṇi vijñānamayaś ca ātmā*).— So also the doctrine of the five fires which gives the highest place to the Devayāna and the theory of Yājñavalkya according to which deliverance consists in a direct entry into or communion with Brahman (see regarding the contradiction in these views, our introductory remarks above at the beginning of Bṛh. 6.1) have been recited by our Upaniṣad side by side and confused with one another barring the consideration that the contradiction was removed through the later *kramamukti*-theory (Śvet 1.11; *Syst. des Vedānta* p. 430, 472) or that it distinctly came into awareness. Also here again is exhibited the basic character of our Upaniṣad : considerable beauty in isolated passages but deficiency in systematic clarity, on account of the dependence on older, contradictory ideas.]

1. The whole verse is modelled on Chānd. 7.25.1

First Half

1. "Two[1] pretty-winged, closely bound friends—
they hug one and the same tree;
one of them eats the sweet berry,
the other, not eating, only looks on."

2. On[2] such tree, the spirit (Puruṣa), sunken down,
caught up in delusion, grieves in his powerlessness;
when he, however, honours[3] and sees the omnipotence of the other and his majesty,
then his sorrow escapes away from him.

3. When[4] the seer sees him, shining like a golden ornament
—the creator, the lord, the spirit (puruṣa), the cradle (source) of Brahman,
then the wise man of knowledge shakes off the good and the evil (Chānd. 8.13)
– the stainless one enters into the highest unity.

4. He shines in all beings as their life
the wise one, the knower,—no one talks him down (*ativādī*)[5]
he plays with the Ātman, occupied[6] with it, rejoices in himself
thus, he is the excellent among the knowers of Brahman.

1-2. For verses 1 and 2, cf. the parallel passages in Śvet. 4.6-7. It is difficult to determine on which side the priority lies. The context is not decisive. The predilection for old Vedic citations emerging from the verses as well as the theistic inclinations are traits from which, otherwise, our Upaniṣad is free, (*īśa* however, occurs only in the following interpretative verse), whereas on the other hand, both these are directly characteristic of the Śvetaśvatara-Upaniṣad throughout.

3. The Sanskrit original is juṣṭam (īśam), which according to Śaṅkara means : 'the lord adored by the Yogins'—Translator

4. Quoted with changes in the concluding part, (indeed out of our Upaniṣad) in Maitr. 6.18.

5. 'ativādī' according to Śaṅkara means 'one who surpasses all in talking or debate. As the wise man of knowledge sees Ātman everywhere, there is none else left with whom he can talk or whom he can think of surpassing in debate. —Translator

6. The words *ātmakrīḍā*, *ātmarati-kriyāvān* (this is the better reading than *ātmaratiḥ kriyāvān*) have their source undoubtedly in Chānd. 7.35.2, in which *kriyāvān* sums up somewhat strikingly *ātmamithuna*, *ātmānandaḥ*. *Ativādin* occurring afterwards must be understood in the sense of Chānd. 7.15.4.

5. Through[1] truth, tapas (austerities), is the Ātman comprehended,
as also through perfect knowledge, constant practice of scriptural studies as a young student (brahmacaryeṇa) (Chānd. 2.23.1)
in the body, it (the ātman), consisting of light shines with lustre,
the ascetics whose sins or guilt is extinguished see (comprehend it).

6. He[2] gains truth, not untruth;
through the truth, the Devayāna[3] opens itself;
the wise, whose desires are fully accomplished, traversing on it (the Devayāna)
they attain to that place where there is the highest stronghold of truth.

7. It is great, heavenly, of inconceivable form,
finer (more subtle) than the fine (subtle),
it shines with splendour;
far away in distance, it is, however, here near enough;
concealed here in the hearts of those, who contemplate.

8. The eye, does not reach up to it, nor the speech,
no other sense-divinities, nor work nor (self-mortification) austerities;
When the knowledge is unruffled (serene),
when the heart is pure (Chānd.7.26.2),
then one sees it, meditating on it—the undivided one.

9. Secret it is, it can be known only through the heart,
in it the fivefold *prāṇa* has entered,
The mind (cittam) of all beings is interwoven with the *prāṇas*.
When it (the mind) is pure, then the Ātman unfolds itself

1. Cf. Bṛh. 4.4.22 Mādhy : *brahmacaryeṇa tapasā*.
2. He i.e, the ativādin (Chānd. 7.16) who has been mentioned above (verse 4).
3. This is in accordance with Bṛh. 6.2.15, not with Chānd. 5.10.1.

10. Whatever[1] world, which one pure in heart, imagines,
and all wishes which one may entertain,
one attains that world and also these desires;
that is why, he who desires happiness,
should adore the knower of the Ātman!

SECOND HALF

1. Because he knows that highest abode of Brahman (Chānd. 8.1.1)
enclosed in which the lights of the world shine (Chānd. 8.1.3)—
Indeed, he having been free from desires, adores the Puruṣa (spirit)
and transcends this world of birth (and death).

2. He who, still, entertains desires and indulges in them,
he is, on account of his desires, born in various places (Bṛh. 4.4.6)
but he, whose desires are stilled (Bṛh. 4.4.6)
whose self is already disciplined and prepared for getting knowledge (Chānd. 8.13)
—for him all desires disappear here below.

3. Not[2] through teaching is this Ātman attained
nor through reason and much erudition in scriptures.
Only by him whom it chooses, is it comprehended;
the Ātman reveals to him its nature.

4. This Ātman cannot be attained by one, who is powerless,
nor by one who is indolent (Kāṭh. 6.11);
nor by one who practises penance which is not genuine[3]

1. The whole verse, together with the reflections which it contains, depends on Chānd. 8.2. The verse 3.2.2 breathes a different spirit.

2. Verses 3-4 interrupt the context. Verse 3=Kāṭh. 2.2; verse 4 seeks to develop the thought further; still its importance lacks justification. Herein lies, indeed, a certain characteristic of the borrowing.

3. According to Śaṅkara, *tapas* here=*jñānam*, and *liṅgam*=*saṁnyāsaḥ*. In this way, everything can be interpreted out of anything. Probably, *aliṅgaṁ* tapas is the penance which swerves from the right character, particularly the characteristic of knowledge. Paulus (1.Kor. 13.3) demands another characteristic of genuine penances.

However, he who as a man of knowledge, strives through
these means,
—into the abode of Brahman his Ātman enters.

5. The wise, however, satisfied with their knowledge of the
self, having found it
with their self disciplined and prepared (kṛtātmānaḥ)
(Chānd. 8.13) dispassionate and serene,
– they, with their self well disciplined, enter from here
into the omnipresent allness (*sarvam*).

6. Those who have definitely grasped the doctrine of the
Vedānta,
—the recluses, completely devoted to renunciation and of
pure character[1]
—all these get into the world of Brahman on the end of
their life
becoming perfectly immortal and released.

7. The fifteen parts dissolve into wherefrom they had arisen,
and all gods (senses) each into its respective deity,[2]
but work and the Ātman of the nature of knowledge
(*vijñāna*)
—all get into communion in the highest eternal.

8. Just as the rivers flow and disappear
in the sea, giving up their name and form,
so also, the wise man, released from name and form,
enters into the divine highest spirit (puruṣa).

9. Truly, he who knows that highest Brahman becomes the Brahman. Nobody is born in his family, who has not known the Brahman. He goes beyond sorrow (Chānd. 7. 1.3), goes beyond the evil, and freed from the knots of the heart (Chānd. 7.26.2), he becomes immortal:

1. The expression *Śuddhasattva* (cf. 3.1.8.9.10; Chānd. 7.26.2) harks back, as so many expressions in the Muṇḍaka to Chānd. 7 and therefore, indicates that verse originally here, has been however, borrowed by the Mahānār. 10.22 from here.

2. The eye goes back to the sun etc. About the fifteen parts see our introductory remarks at the beginning of Praśna 6.

10. Regarding this, there is the following verse:
Those, during excellent work, proficient in scriptures
and truly devoted to Brahman,
sacrificing themselves, in all faith, into one sole Ṛṣi[1]
to such these, the knowledge of Brahman should be
imparted
if they have already properly fulfilled the vow[2] concerning
the head (*śirovratam*).

11. This is the truth, The wise
Aṅgiras has proclaimed it formerly.
Nobody, who has not fulfilled the vow,
should read or recite it.

Salutations to the highest wise men
Salutations to the highest wise men!

---

1. As 'the one Ṛṣi' according to Praśna 2.11 is the Prāṇa, so what is intended here is the Prāṇāgnihotram (see above our Introductory remarks at the beginning of Chānd, 5.11).

2. About the Śirovrata, see our introduction at the beginning of the Muṇḍaka above.

THE PRAŚNA UPANIṢAD OF THE ATHARVAVEDA

The Praśnopaniṣad connected with the Atharvaveda, and as it appears, connected with the Pippalāda-recension of the same, deals in six questions (*praśna*), which are put by six explorers of Brahman to the wise Pippalāda, with six main points of the Vedānta-doctrine :

1. Origin of matter and of the life of Prajāpati.
2. Superiority of Prāṇa over the rest of the life forces.
3. The Prāṇa and its ramification in man.
4. About dream-sleep and deep sleep.
5. Meditation over the syllable Om.
6. The sixteen parts of man.

The frame of the narration appears to be an imitation of Śatap. Br. 10.6.1ff, of Chānd. 5.11.1ff with the only difference that there in those passages, as it appears, much more fitting, the six Brāhmaṇas inquire of Aśvapati about one and the same common theme; while in the Praśna Upaniṣad everybody asks something different; consequently the joint quest of Pippalāda is not properly motivated, especially in the case of the last interrogator who states for his question quite a peculiar motive.

First Praśna

[The question, from where the beings originate, serves only as an occasion to divide nature, as the product of Prajāpati, into two parts : *rayi* (matter) and *prāṇa* (life). Under the first part the dark side of the world is grouped (viz. the moon, the winter, the dark half of the month, the night), while under the latter part the bright side of the world is grouped (viz. the sun, the summer, the bright half of the month, and the day). From *rayi* originates the *Pitṛyāṇa*, from *prāṇa* the *Devayāna*, in the description of which the author is akin to Chānd. 5.3-10 (not to Bṛh. 6.2). In conclusion, it is signified that procreation (*prajāpativratam*) belongs to the dark side whereas chastity (*Brahma-caryam*) corresponds to the bright side, leading to the deliverance of the Devayāna.]

1. Sukeśan Bhāradvāja, Śaivya Satyakāma, Sauryāyaṇin Gārgya, Kausalya Āśvalāyana, Bhārgava Vaidarbhi, and Kavandhin Kātyāyana—all these who regarded the Brahman as the highest and were deeply devoted to the Brahman, explored into the highest Brahman and saying (among themselves): "He, indeed, will explain all this", approached the exalted Pippalāda, with the fuelsticks in their hands.

2. The wise man said to them:

"You must live with me a year still from henceforth (cf. Chānd. 8.9.3; 8.10.4; 8.11.3) practising penance, the life of studenthood (chastity), and with faith (cf. Bṛh. 4.4.22), and afterwards you may put questions, if you like; provided we will know (the answers to them), we will explain to you."

3. Thereupon (after the expiration of the year) Kavandhin Kātyāyana approached him (Pippalāda) and asked:

"Exalted one, out of what, indeed, do these things originate?"

4. And he (Pippalāda) replied to him: "Prajāpati desired progeny; he practised tapas; after he had practised tapas, he created a pair namely *Rayi* (matter, in its real meaning wealth—) and *Prāṇa* (life); then he (Prajāpati) said: "Both these will create for me manifold progeny."

5. Indeed, the sun is Prāṇa and the moon Rayi; indeed Rayi is all this, what has form or what is formless; therefore, the form itself is Rayi.

6. Now when the sun rises and enters the easterly direction, it then encloses in its rays the eastern vital breaths (materialized in nature); and when it enters the southern, western, northern, the upper, the nether and the central directions, it then encloses, in its rays all the vital breaths, because it makes everything radiant.

7. This (solar) fire, disseminated in all (*vaiśvānara*) and omniformed (*vaiśvarūpa*) rises forth, as the *Prāṇa*. Regarding it is the following verse:

8. [I praise] The omniformed, golden, knower of beings (*jātavedas*) which there as the highest stronghold (parāyaṇa), shines as the one only light.
With a thousand rays, changing themselves hundredfold,
the sun, there, rises as the vital breath of beings.

9. Indeed, Prajāpati is the year; in the year there are two movements of the sun, the one towards the south, and the other towards the north. Now those, who practise worship with the words: "Sacrifice and pious works are what we have done", (cf. Chānd. 5.10.3), attain only to the moon as their abode.

These again return back. Those wise men who desire progeny go the southern way. And (*pitṛyāṇa*) is Rayi.

10. But by the Northern way, after they have aspired after the Ātman through penance, the practice of studenthood (*brahma-carya*=chastity), faith and knowledge conquer, or attain to the abode of the sun. This is the focal point of the *Prāṇas*. This is the immortal one, the fearless one, this is the highest stronghold or refuge. They never return from it. This is the exclusive description (of the way of the fathers and the way of the gods *vis-à-vis* one another). Regarding it, there is the following verse (Ṛgveda 1.164.12):

11. The father, fivefooted and of twelve-fold form,[1]
—he is physically, it is said, in the yonder side of heavens;
Still he, shining far and wide, is inserted
in the lower parts, with six spokes, seven wheels.[2]

12. Indeed, Prajápati is the month.
Its dark half is Rayi, its bright half Prāṇa. Therefore, these wise men (who adore the Prāṇa) offer the sacrifice in the bright half, others in the other (half).

13. Indeed, Prajāpati is day and night. What is his day, is Prāṇa, what is his night, is the Rayi. Indeed, they, who unite themselves in sexual pleasure during the day spill the Prāṇa (the life-force), and this is the practice of Brahmacarya (chastity) (applicable in the case of the Gṛhastha—a householder—) that one unites himself in sexual pleasure only in the night.

14. Indeed, prajāpati is food. From it is produced the semen out of which these beings originate.

15. Now those, who practise this observance of Prajāpati (Prajāpativratam), practise procreation (*mithunam utpādayante*), just as it is said of Prajāpati, above, that he procreates a pair—*mithunam utpādayate*).

1. According to Śaṅkara, the five feet are the five seasons of the year (Hemanta and Śiśira, the two wintry seasons being counted as one), and the twelve forms are the twelve months. —Translator

2. This verse which, indeed, originally refers to the parallelism between the starry heavens and the sacrificial fire (cf. *Gesch. d. Phil.* I. 111) is here very arbitrarily interpreted as referring to the Devayāna and Pitṛyāṇa.

16. Theirs is the world of Brahman—they, who practise penance,
and in whom true chastity is firmly rooted;
they attain the world of Brahman,
—those, who are taintless
devoid of crookedness, falsehood and deceitfulness.

Second Praśna

[Regarding the question concerning the number of vital organs in man and their order of preference or precedence, the narration of the quarrel among the vital organs about their rank or precedence' is carried out in an independent way (cf. Chānd. 1.2, 5.1; Bṛh. 1.3, 6.1; Kauṣ. 2.14). With it is connected the hymn to Prāṇa, which contains many echoes of the corresponding hymn in the Atharvaveda 11.4 (translated in *Gesch. d. Phil.* I. 302 ff).]

1. Then Bhārgava Vaidarbhi inquired of him (Pippalāda): "O Exalted one! How many gods maintain the created beings and which among them illuminates this body and who among them is most superior (to all others)?"

2. And he (Pippalāda) said to him: "The ether (*ākāśa*), indeed, is this god and the wind, and the fire, the waters and the earth, the speech, the *manas* (mind), eyes and ears. These, because they illuminate (the body) boast among themselves: "It is we who support this tubular mechanism (bāṇa=body) and maintain it."

3. Then the Prāṇa who was the most superior among them said to them: "It is not so ! You are all caught up in illusion. It is I alone who, dividing myself fivefold, support this tubular mechanism and maintain it !"

4. But they would not believe it. Then he made it appear as if he, out of (injured) pride, wished to escape upwards (depart from the body). And as he began to escape, all the others also wished to escape and as he remained abiding still (in the body), then the others also remained abiding. And just as when the king of bees leaves, the bees also leave following after it and just as the bees remain abiding as long as the king of the bees remains abiding, so also the speech, the *manas* (mind), the eyes, and the ears. Then they become satisfied and extol the Prāṇa.

5. It burns as the fire and shines as the sun
it is Parjanya, Maghavān (Indra) and Vāyu,
it is the earth, Rayi the god,
it is that which is, that which is not and that which is eternal.

6. Like the spokes in the navel of a wheel,
everything is fixed fast in Prāṇa,
the Ṛcs, the Yajus, and the Sāmans,
the sacrifice and the warrior and Brāhmaṇa class.

7. As prajāpati, you stay in the mother's womb,
are born anew
To you, O Prāṇa, the beings bring offerings (Atharvaveda 11.4.19)
when you stay with the (life-forces) vital organs.

8. You first bring to the gods the sacrificial offerings,
You first offer the refreshing drink (svadhā)
to the manes,
You are the work of the poet-sages
you are the truth of the Atharvāṅgirasas.

9. O Prāṇa, you are Indra in your vigour
you are Rudra, the protector,
you move in the aerial space as the sun,
you are the overlord of luminous[1] celestial bodies (*jyotis*).

10. O Prāṇa, when you rain over them,
your beings, filled with joy, continue to live here
saying, "Food will be produced for us
to fulfil our desire."

11. You are yourself consecrated,[2] O Prāṇa,
you are the wisest sage, the consumer, the lord of all,
we are the offerers of what you consume,
you are father to us, O Mātariśva(n) !

---

1. The overlord of the celestial luminous bodies is Brahman. See Kāṭh. 5.15.

2. The Sanskrit original is '*vrātya*'. According to Śaṅkara, vrātya means 'pure by nature (*svābhavata eva śuddhaḥ*)'. He explains it by saying that the primaeval Prāṇa being the first-born, had none to consecrate it (saṁskartur abhāvāt) and that it was primaevally pure. —Translator

12. The form in which you stay in speech,
    in the ears and in the eyes,
    That your form which is extended to Manas (mind)—
    Make that form auspicious for us,
    do not depart from us !

13. This universe is under the power of Prāṇa,
    whatever in the third heaven is;
    Protect us, as the mother protects her children,
    bestow on us prosperity and wisdom!"

THIRD PRAŚNA

[According to the verse occurring appended at the end of this subsection (3.12), one must know five things in order to attain immortality : (1) the origin of Prāṇa (2) its extension (*āyati*, already understood by the Upaniṣad as 'āyāti=entrance into the body) (3) its continuance in the body (4) its cosmic and (5) its psychical quintuplication. These five questions besides a sixth which concerns the departure of Prāṇa form the six themes of the section which as such already presuppose the knowledge of the contents and which therefore, do not appear very suitable for Āśvalāyana Kausalya in whose mouth the questions are placed.

(1) *The origin of the Prāṇa*:— It is here no more the highest principle itself in concrete form but as the highest principle which arises out of the Ātman (as Praśna 6.4, Muṇḍ. 2.1.3) and is related to it like the silhoutte, the image (chāyā) of the object.

(2) *The reason for its entrance into the body* :— The answer lies in the words *manokṛtena* which has been interpreted by Śaṅkara in the sense of the Vedānta: "On account of the actions done through his will"; grammatically, it would be more right to understand it as *mano'kṛtena* "without the aid of the will".

(3) *Continuance in the body* :—As five ramifications of the Prāṇa are enumerated *Apāna, Prāṇa, Samāna, Vyāna, Udāna;* among these, however, are understood, not as is generally done and as also it occurs in the fourth Praśna, not the vital breaths (the Prāṇas in the strict sense which stand beside the Manas and the Indriyas), but the vital powers (the Prāṇas in the wider sense, Manas and the Indriyas being included in them) as is mostly understood in the Brāhmaṇa-period (*Gesch. d. Phil.* I. 296). The customary nine Prāṇas of the Brāhmaṇa period, (corresponding to the nine openings in the body) are, in our passage, so distributed that the Apāna concerns the organs of evacuation and procreation, and Prāṇa (which has been thus identified with the Prāṇa in the wider sense) concerns the seven openings in the head (eyes, ears, mouth, nostrils). Besides, there are the Samāna as the nutritional power (which assimilates food : *annaṁ samaṁ nayati*) and

Vyāna as the power or force operating in the arteries (the power which regulates blood circulation). The number of main arteries had been fixed as 101 by the verse in Chānd. 8.6.6=Kāṭh. 6.16; in the Bṛh. 2.1.19, it was said that there are 72000 arteries. Through the combination of these passages and through the multiplication of the first by 100 our passage reaches up to 101 main arteries, every one of these with 100 ramifications of arteries, each among these again with 72000 auxiliary ramifications of arteries (pratiśākhā nāḍī); all these together amount to :

main arteries	101
ramifications of arteries (101 × 100)	10100
auxiliary ramifications of arteries 101 × 100 × 72000	727200000
Total	727210201

i.e. 72 crores, 72 lakhs, and 10201, as the commentary (according to the reading in the Ānandāśrama edition) rightly reckons.— The Udāna leads the soul through the 101st artery in the head running upwards beyond (later since the period of Maitr. 6.21, called suṣumnā) and leading (contrary to the verse mentioned in Chānd. 8.6.6=Kāṭh, 6.16) not only beyond the good but also beyond the evil.

4-5. The psychical quintuplication corresponds to the cosmic in the following manner : the Prāṇa found in the head corresponds to the sun, the *Apāna* moving downward to the earth, the *Samāna* opening in the middle or the centre corresponds to the space between them (*antarā yad ākāśaḥ*) and the Vyāna corresponds to the wind.

6. Finally the Udāna which carries the soul, corresponds to the Tejas in which (resting on Chānd. 6.8.6; 15.1), after it has received the Manas and the Indriyas in itself, it enters at the time of death.]

1. Then Kausalya Āśvalāyana inquired of him: "Exalted one ! From what does the Prāṇa originate ? How does it enter the body? How does it, dividing itself, continue in the same? Through which part does it depart? How does it behave in the external world and how does it behave in the self (the body)?"

2. And he (Pippalāda) said to him: "You go fer beyond the limit with questions (you ask questions exceeding the proper limit); I think, you are the best among those who love Brahman; therefore I will answer your questions. –

3. Out of the Ātman originates the Prāṇa; as the shadow cast by a man (arises out of him), so also it (the Prāṇa) extends out of the same (Ātman). Without the interference of the will, it comes into this body.—

4. And just as a king charges his officers to administer these or those villages, so also that Prāṇa appoints the remaining Prāṇas, each one of them separately (to do their task).

5. In respect of evacuation and reproduction, it orders the Apāna. It, the Prāṇa, has its own seat or abode in the eyes, the ears together with the mouth and the nose. In the middle (or the centre) there is the *Samāna* [so-called] because it is the *samāna* which contributes to the equal (*samam*) distribution of (or assimilates) the food which has been offered into the body (Chānd. 5.19 ff); out of it originate those 'seven sacrificial flames' (Muṇḍ. 2.1.8).

6. In the heart, however, dwells the Ātman; in that place itself, there are those hundred and one arteries (Chānd. 8.6.6); to every one of these arteries, belong respectively a hundred (ramifications); and to every one of these auxiliary ramifications, there are seventytwo thousand sub-ramifications, (Bṛh. 2.1.19); in them the Vyāna functions.

7. But through the one artery running upward, the Udāna leads a man to a holy world for his pious actions, to an evil world for his evil actions, to the world of men for both kinds of actions.

8. As the sun, that Prāṇa now ascends upward in the external world, as it is that (Sun) which renders assistance to the Prāṇa in the eyes; and the divinity which dwells in the earth, renders assistance through the fact that it supports the *Apāna* in man, that the space between them (the sun and the earth) is what is *samāna*; the wind is the Vyāna.

9. The fervour (*tejas*) (i.e. the vital force), is, however, the Udāna. Therefore, when the fervour (of the vital force) abates, then the man departs, to be born once again, together with the Indriyas (Chānd. 6.8.6) which have merged into the *manas* (mind),

10. and with the thought, with which one is preoccupied (in the hour of death), into the Prāṇa; and the Prāṇa bound up

with the fervour of the vital force through the Udāna leads it together with the Ātman over into that world imagined by him (in the hour of death) (cf. Chānd. 3.14.1, Bhagavadgītā 8.6).

11. He who having this knowledge, knows the Prāṇa—the line of his descendants or posterity does not become extinct and he becomes immortal. Regarding this, there is the following verse:

12. He who knows the origin, the dissemination, the abode,
and the fivefold distribution in the world,
and has himself the knowledge of Prāṇa,
—he attains immortality, he attains immortality.

Fourth Praśna

[This important subsection deals with four questions of which the first two concern dream-sleep and the latter two concern deep sleep. As the four questions are so framed that they already characteristically presuppose the knowledge of their answers—because they fall asunder from one another during the progress of the discourse—, the discourse (of Pippalāda) as an answer may have been the original nucleus and the questions may have been contrived only afterwards. The first germ of the whole, however, is, perhaps the one in a verse inserted at the end, which extols the imperishable (akṣara) unity, in which all subjective organs as well as the objective beings or things corresponding to them have been grounded.

The contents analysed according to the four questions are as follows :

(1) What is that which goes to sleep (in the dream-sleep) in man and that which wakes up ? — Answer : Just as the rays enter into (or merge into) the setting sun, so also, the ten Indriyas (senses) (hearing, sight, smell, taste, touch; — speech, seizing (with the hands), procreation, evacuation walking[1]) enter into the Manas (the mind) which remains awake in dream-sleep. Besides the Manas (mind),[2] there remain awake in the body—the city of Brahman, the Prāṇas as the live (ever awake) fires or—with the change of simile which is more familiar to the Indian mind,—as the sacrificial fires in which Apāna, Vyāna and Prāṇa have been equated with Gārhapatya, *Anvāhāryapacana* and *Āhavanīya*. Samāna is so called because it leads the outbreath and inbreath (—in 3.5 however, it leads the food into unity with the body—) into unity (*samam nayati*); *udāna* leads the Manas

1. This is (next to the Bṛh. 2.4.11), indeed, the oldest passage in which the ten *Indriyas* (senses and organs) have been systematically enumerated.

2. Manas and Indriyas are placed here, as in the *Vedānta*-doctrine vis-à-vis the five Prāṇas, whereas the prāṇas had been included under the Indriyas in the foregoing Praśna.

etc. into Brahman, not only as otherwise said during death, but also in deep sleep.

2. Which god (i.e. which organ) sees the dream-phenomena?— Answer : The *Manas* (mind), because it builds (these dreams) out of the things perceived earlier and those not perceived.

3. Who experiences the joy (in deep sleep)?—Answer : It originates through the fact that Manas, overpowered by the Tejas (which is equated with Udāna, see above 3.9), sees no dream-phenomena any more. It is not mentioned as to who experiences the joy but it can be gathered from what follows.

4. Which is that unity into which all the organs (*Indriyas*, manas, Prāṇas) are grounded ?— Answer : The highest Ātman (4.7) or the spirit consisting of knowledge (*vijñānātman*), and resting on the highest, imperishable Ātman (4.9). On it rest (a) the five elements (pṛthivī etc.) and the five fine subtle elements (pṛthivīmātrāḥ etc.) on which the five elements are founded); (b) The ten Indriyas (which have been once again, enumerated) and the objects of sense corresponding to them; (c) *Manas, Buddhi, Ahaṁkāra, Cittam, Tejas, Prāṇa*, and the functions belonging to them. Manas, Buddhi, Ahaṁkāra (the technical terms first occurring here and in the Śvet. 5 8, not the Chānd. 7.25.1) are reminiscent of the Sāṁkhya-system Cittam which is among these, is peculiar; to the *Tejas* (above it is equated; with *Udāna*) is attributed the function of illuminating (cf. Bṛh. 4.4.1-2); according to which the organs as *tejomātrāḥ* enter into the heart at the time of death and then the apex of the heart *pradyotate; tena pradyotanena eṣa ātma niṣkrāmati*); the function of Prāṇa is, as above described in Praśna 2, is *vidhāraṇam*.

The promise, held out in the concluding part 4.10—, is carried out in the wording of the verse which is quoted in 4.11.]

1. Then Sauryāṇin Gārgya asked him: "Exalted Sir! Who are they, that sleep in this man, and who remain awake in him ? Which is that god that sees the dreams ? Whose pleasure is that [of the deep sleep] ? In whom are they all established ?"

2. And he said to them:

"Just as, O Gārgya, the light-particles of the sun, when it sets, all become one in that disk of lustre and proceed again and again out of it when the sun rises, similarly all this also becomes one in the Manas as the highest Godhead; therefore it is that then man does not hear, does not see, does not smell, does not taste, does not touch, does not speak, does not take, does not procreate, does not pass stools, does not go here and there, but, as they say, sleeps.

3. It is the Prāṇa fires which are then awake in this city; the Apāna is the Gārhapatya fire, the Vyāna the Anvāhāryapacana fire; and the Āhavanīya fire, because it is carried forward from the Gārhapatya fire, is called Prāṇa from that carrying forward (*praṇayanam*).

4. Further, Samāna is so called because it carries equally (*samaṁ nayati*) the two sacrificial offerings of the out-breath and the in-breath. But the Manas is the sacrificer, and the fruit of the sacrifice is the Udāna; it leads the sacrificer into the Brahman day by day.

5. Then that God [the Manas] enjoys greatness in that it once more sees what was seen here and there, once more hears the things heard here and there, again and again experiences what was experienced in the place and in the region; seen and unseen, heard and unheard, experienced and unexperienced, he sees all, as all he sees it (Bṛh. 4.3.20).

6. But when it is overpowered by lustre, then that god sees no dreams and then that pleasure reigns in this body.

7. But, O dear, just as the birds betake themselves to the tree which is their residence (cf. Chānd. 6,8,2), similarly all these take their resort in the highest Ātman.

8. The earth and the earth-stuff, the water and the water-stuff, the lustre and the lustre-stuff, the wind and the wind-stuff, the ether and the ether-stuff; the eye and what is to be seen, the ear and what is to be heard, the nose and what is to be smelt, the tongue and what is to be tasted, the skin and what is to be touched; the speech and what is to be spoken, the hands and what is to be taken, the organ of procreation and what is to be procreated, the organ of excretion and what is to be excreted, the feet and the place to be gone; the Manas and what is to be conceived, the Buddhi and what is to be decided, the Ahaṁkāra (I-maker) and what can be conceived as I, the thought power and what can be thought over, the lustre and what can be illumined, the Prāṇa and what is to be supported.

9. Then this seer toucher, hearer, smeller, taster, conceiver, decider, doer, the spirit forming the conscious Self [the individual soul], he is established in the highest imperishable Self.

10. And into that highest Imperishable he enters, who O dear, knowing this shadowless, bodyless, bloodless, bright, this Imperishable, becomes omniscient and becomes all. Thereupon is this stanza:

11. Where the conscious Self with all the gods,
The vital breaths and the elements abide,
Knowing, O dear, this Imperishable,
One becomes omniscient, one becomes all.

FIFTH PRAŚNA

[The meditation of the Brahman on account of its utter imperceptibility requires an outward symbol; as such serves, the later the time the more, the old sacrificial exclamation Om, and after its importance had been already elevated as the essence of all the Vedas, (i.e. as the Brahman) in Kāṭh. 2,15-17, our passage takes a further step on the way so much trodden by the later Upaniṣads, in that it analyses the sound Om in its three moras (*a+u+m*) and promises for a meditation on one of these an immediate return to a privileged human existence (a conception which is incompatible with the doctrine of Pitṛyāna and Devayāna as it is described in the Chānd. 5.3.ff., Bṛh. 6,2 and as it is also recognized above, Praśna. 1); two moras lead, when meditated upon, to the moon and back to an earthly existence, corresponding to the Pitṛyāṇa, three moras into the Brahman, i.e. on the Devayāna, from which there is no return.]

1. Then Śaivya, Satyakāma asked him: "O exalted sir, he who among men meditates upon the sound Om upto his departure, which world does he win thereby ?" And he said to him:

2. "Verily O Satyakāma, the sound Om is the higher and the lower Brahman.[1] Therefore the knower when he takes his support on it reaches the one or the other.

3. If he meditates on one element of it, then, enlightened by the same, he atttains [after the death] quickly to the life. The Ṛg hymns lead him to the human world; there he acquires asceticism, Brahman-conduct and faith (cf. above 1,2) and enjoys greatness.

---

1. Here not to be understood in the later sense of this term *nirguṇam* and *saguṇam brahma* but to be understood as corresponding to the knowledge section and work section of the Veda, or to the higher and lower science in the Muṇḍ. 1,1,4-6.

4. When he reaches two elements in his meditation, then [after the death] he is carried above in the air to the world of Soma [to the moon] by the Yajus formulae. And after enjoying greatness in the world of Soma he again returns.

5. When on the other hand he meditates on the highest spirit through all the three elements of the sound Om, then after he has entered the light, the sun, he is freed from the sin as a snake from his slough (cf. Bṛh. 4,4,7); he is carried above to the Brahman-world by the Sāman songs; then he sees him who is higher than this complex of life, [i.e. than the individual soul[1]], the spirit living in the city [of the body]. On these there are these two verses:

6. Three elements, when one dies, employed,
Closely connected, and not unemployed,
So that for the outer, inner and middle practices
There is a full sufficiency, – then firm stands the spirit.

7. Through Ṛcs here, through Yajus' into the aerial region,
Through Sāmans there, what the wise proclaim,
The knower supported on Om reaches to him,
Who is that quiet, ageless, immortal, fearless Highest.

Sixth Praśna

[After one had accustomed oneself to regard Prajāpati as the "year having twentyfour parts [divided in twentyfour fortnights]" (*Gesch. d. Phil.* I, 208), it was natural to find him again in the fifteen-day fortnights also and to interpret the waning and waxing of the moon as that of Prajāpati himself, whose fifteen parts disappear gradually and originate again, while the sixteenth part, as containing his essence, remained constant (cf. particularly Bṛh. 1,5,14). Hence the more frequent description of Prajāpati as having sixteen parts (Vāj. Saṁh. 8,36) or even as having seventeen parts, since the life-principle was further distinguished from all parts.

Taking Prajāpati as the model, they further attributed sixteen parts to man also, of which fifteen decay but are replenished through food, while the sixteenth part vanishes with the life itself (cf. particularly the account in the Chānd. 6,7). By the way, how little one knew originally as to what these sixteen parts should be is clear from the fact that according to Śatap.

---

1. So according to Śaṅkara to Brahmasūtra 1,3,13 *System des Vedānta*, p. 214. The commentator of the Praśna Upaniṣad agrees fully with 'someone' mentioned in the commentary, loc. cit. Can he therefore be Śaṅkara ?

Br. 10,4,1,17) it is the sixteen syllables of the words *loman*, *tvac*, *asṛj*, *medas*, *māṁsam*, *snāvan*, *asthi*, *majjā* (hair, skin, blood, fat, flesh, sinew, bone, marrow) which are meant thereby.—The question of our section aims at these sixteen parts of man.

In the answer is shown, (a) how the sixteen parts proceed out of the Puruṣa (i.e. here out of the Spirit, the Ātman); (b) how they return in him.

(a) The Puruṣa creates 1) the *Prāṇa*, as the most important thing, on whose departure and stay depend his own departure and stay; out of it 2) *Śraddhā*, the faith, with which we are already acquainted in the Five-Fire Teaching as the most primitive germ of man (Chānd. 5,4,2. Bṛh. 6,2,9); 3-7) the five elements, whereby the nominative *vāyur*, *āpas* are to be explained as being due to the utilisation of a verse, with which we partly come across in Muṇḍ. 2,1,3 also; 8) *indriyam*, the ten sense organs looked upon as a unity; 9) *manas*, 10) *annam*, food, 11) *vīryam*, the strength depending on it; 12) *tapas*, 13) *mantrāḥ*, the hymns and the formulae, 14) *karman*, the deed based on them, 15) *lokāḥ*, the worlds whose acquisition is conditioned by the deed; 16) *nāman*, as the individual distinctness.

(b) The return of these organs into the Puruṣa results like that of the rivers into the ocean which is taught in similar words in prose as in a verse in the Muṇḍ. 3,2,8.

The whole section seems to have been composed out of the reminiscences of other passages.]

1. Then Sukeśan Bhāradvāja asked him:

"O exalted Sir, Hiraṇyanābha Kausalya, the prince, came to me and put me this question: 'Do you know that Puruṣa with sixteen parts ? To him, the prince, I said: 'I do not know him; for if I had known him, how would not have I told you about him? [According to Chānd. 5,3,5 and similar passage, where however the father speaks to the son.] He indeed dries up to the very root who tells untruth. Therefore, I cannot tell untruth'.—Then silently he mounted his car and went away. Now I ask you: Where is that Puruṣa ?"

2. Then he [Pippalāda] said to him: "Here in the body itself, O dear, is this Puruṣa in whom those sixteen parts originate.

3. This one [Puruṣa] thought to himself: With whose departure I myself shall be departed, and with whose staying I shall stay ?

4. Then he created the Prāṇa; from the Prāṇa the faith, the ether, the wind, the light, the water, the earth, the sense organs;

the Manas, the food; from food the strength, the Tapas, the Mantras, the work, the worlds and in the worlds the name also.

5. Just as these flowing rivers take their course to the ocean and on reaching the ocean they disappear in it, as their names and forms merge together and it is called only the ocean, similarly the same happens in the case of this all-seer, in that those sixteen parts take their course to the Puruṣa and when they reach the Puruṣa they disappear; their names and forms merge together, and it is called only the Puruṣa, who, however, continues to be without parts and immortal. On this there is this verse:

6. As spokes in the nave of a wheel,
The parts have their roots firm in him,
Him whom one must know, I know,
The Puruṣa, so that the death may not unnerve you too.

7. And to all of them he said: "This much I know about the highest Brahman, there is nothing beyond."

8. Then they worshipped him and said: "You are our father, you who lead us over from ignorance to the other bank."

Salutation to the great sages.
Salutation to the great sages.

THE MĀṆḌŪKYA UPANIṢAD OF THE ATHARVAVEDA

With the Kārikā of Gauḍapāda on it

INTRODUCTION

The Māṇḍūkya Upaniṣad, in prose, bears the name of a half-lost school of the Ṛgveda, but it is assigned to the Atharvaveda and is, as is shown not only by the numerous citations but the systematic compactness of its manner of representation, considerably later than the prose Upaniṣads of the three older Vedas. Its brevity and precision is in marked contrast with the verbosity of the older Upaniṣads. Many points of contact with the Maitrāyaṇa-Upaniṣad offer themselves and will require a close investigation to decide which side the priority lies. On the other hand, as opposed to the most of the Upaniṣads of the Atharvaveda, the Māṇḍūkya Upaniṣad makes a more archaic impression, particularly in so far as it distinguishes only three, and not three and a half moras in the word Om.

The fundamental doctrine of the Māṇḍūkya-Up. is that the whole world is pressed in the syllable Om. It adduces the following proof for this thesis : The world is Brahman, Brahman is the Ātman, the Ātman, however, is the sound Om, inasmuch as to its moras correspond the four quarters or feet, i.e. the four states of the Ātman. These four states are : 1) the waking, *Vaiśvānara* (so called because its impressions are common to all; perhaps, according to Śaṅkara, to be traced to the Chānd. 5.11-18), in which the Ātman perceives outward; 2) the dream state, *Taijasa* (the luminous, because in it the Ātman is its own light, *svena bhāsā, svena jyotiṣā prasvapiti*, Bṛh. 4,3,9), in which the Ātman perceives inward; 3) the deep sleep, *Prājña* (because in it the Ātman, according to the Bṛh. 4,3,21, becomes one with the *Prājña Ātman*, i.e. Brahman, for the time being; 4) the "Fourth" *Caturtha* (*Turīya, Turya*), in which the extinction of the world-expanse is not effected unconsciously as in the third state, but with consciousness. To the first state corresponds the *a* of *Om* (*a+u+m*), to the second the *u*, to the third the *m*, to the fourth the moraless (*amātra*) part of the word as is shown by an etymological play.

Astonishingly, Śaṅkara has not made use of the Māṇḍūkya Upaniṣad in his commentary on the Brahmasūtras; on the other hand it has not only exercised great influence on several Upaniṣads of the Atharvaveda but also, more than any other Upaniṣad, it has been useful, as a basis, for clever constructions of the Vedāntasāra, although with a modified interpretation of its basic concepts.

Its greatest importance however lies therein, viz. that it gave rise to one of the most remarkable monuments of Indian Philosophy, viz. the *Kārikā* of Gauḍapāda, a work whose appreciation has already been proclaimed by the fact that its four parts (the first of which includes the Māṇḍūkya-Upaniṣad) are usually regarded as four Upaniṣads. We cannot believe that the author of this *kārikā*, who represents the pure Advaita stand point in the bluntest way was the same Gauḍapāda who in his commentary to the *Sāṁkhyakārikā* glorifies the teaching of Kapila as the means to the salvation. And if later authors like Vācaspatimiśra and Vijñānabhikṣu have commented on the most diverse systems, it is still a different thing, for the *Māṇḍūkyakārikā*, in its last three parts is a completely independent work, and its author proclaims, obviously from deepest conviction, a standpoint which must make it impossible for him to get on, even temporarily, with the interpretation of the doctrine of duality which he fights so resolutely. On the other hand, it is quite likely that our Gauḍapāda was the teacher of Govinda who himself was the teacher of Śaṅkara; both, Gauḍapāda and Śaṅkara, hold the same views in all the essentials, and many ideas and imagery, in which Śaṅkara indulges, are already seen to occur in Gauḍapāda (reconciliation of the scriptures, polemic against the causality, the objectless perception etc.; serpent and rope, universal space and jar-space, dream, Māyā, mirage etc.); indeed, it can be said, that Śaṅkara developed the doctrines of Gauḍapāda into a system in the same way as Plato did those of Parmenides.

Gauḍapāda and Parmenides — this comparison will automatically press itself on every reader of the Indian poem translated for the first time, because the fundamental thought of both the philosophers is the same, indeed even the exposition of this thought often shows remarkable points of contact. All the statements of Parmenides amount to these two : (1) There is no plurality and (2) there is no becoming; and, correspondingly the Indian poem moves about from beginning to end in the two concepts of (1) the *advaitam*, non-plurality and (2) the *ajāti*, non-becoming; and even if, as is usual in India, we miss a well-ordered disposition so that the same ideas recur again and again in a wearisome manner, even if we often find only imagery instead of explanation, mere assertions instead of proofs, still every specialist will get the impression that Gauḍapāda's poem, as that of Parmenides is based on deep and genuine metaphysical insight although it may be only intuitive.

Here, we will indicate only the train of thought in its main features of the four parts, because for the rest we refer to our translation which through the exigencies of the metre and of the brevity it required could not everywhere be so literal as it would be desired on the other hand; still we hope that we have nowhere missed any idea. We do not however averywhere find ourselves in agreement with the commentary handed down in the name of Śaṅkara which certainly sometime goes wrong; e.g. when at 4.83, out of the four theses : 1. *asti*, 2. *na asti*, 3. *asti*, *na asti*, 4. *na asti iti na asti* 'he is not not' he takes the fourth one as synonymous with *na asti*, *na asti*, *iti* (perhaps he read it so) and refers to the *atyantaśūnyavāda*, i.e. the Buddhist school of the Mādhyamikas;—and so in many other cases.

I. The first part of the poem is essentially a metrical paraphrase of the *Māṇḍūkya-Upaniṣad;* peculiar to it is only the critique of the world-creation theories, v. 6-9 : The world is not an unfoldment of the power (*vibhūti*) of God, not a dream-like illusion (*svapnamāyā*) produced by Him; it is originated neither through the desire (*icchā*) of God nor through the power of Time (*kāla*), it has not come into existence for the enjoyment (*bhoga*) or sport (*krīḍā*), because *āptakāmasya kā spṛhā ?* "What can he wish, one who has everything ?" — rather it is God's own essence (*svabhāva*) and is so little differentiated from Him, as the rays from the sun, which are all one and the same, viz. nothing but light.

In contrast with this first section the other three are entirely independent and have no immediate connection with the Upaniṣad beyond whose thought they go widely : they have therefore characteristic titles also as *Vaitathyam*, *Advaitam* and *Alātaśānti*.

II. *Vaitathyam* 'falseness' of the empirical reality and of the theories adhering to it.

1. Verses 1-18. The plurality in the waking state also depends on delusion as the one in dream; and as the dream is sublated by the awakening, so is the waking again sublated by the dream (verses (6-7); in both *kalpayati ātmanā ātmānam ātmadevaḥ svamāyayā*, verse 12. At the end follows, in verses 17-18, the celebrated illustration of the rope which appears as a snake in darkness; similarly the Ātman appears as the world in the darkness of ignorance.

2. Verses 19-29. Every attempt to conceive the Ātman among empirical forms fails; everybody conceives of him according to what he knows of the world, as is illustrated by a long series of examples.

3. Verses 30-38. Again follow illustrations and the affirmation that there is no plurality and no becoming. The portrayal of a Muni, who has known this, forms the conclusion.

III. *Advaitam*, "the non-duality".

1. Verses 1-16. As against the 'wretchedness' of the theologistic God-worship, which brings down God into time and becoming, the poet develops the doctrine of *Advaitam*, the identity of the *Ātman* and the Jīva, the highest and the individual soul, on the brilliantly executed analogy of the world-space and the jar-space. This, he believes, is the view of the scriptures also, and where they speak differently, of world-creation etc., it is done only because that suits human mental capacity.

2. Verses 17-30. Polemic against becoming and plurality. Those who accept becoming get themselves entangled in contradiction; no object surely, can deviate from itself, from its own nature, and become something different since *prakṛter anyathābhāvo no kathaṁcid bhaviṣyati* is a main point to which the author returns again and again and which occurs verbatim

here as 3.21 and later on as 4.7 and 4.29. (This tenet is incontrovertible also, only that that very nature, which is eternally identical with itself, when pulled apart into states inherent in plurality, that is the becoming). The argumentation in verses 27 and 28 is quite Parmenides-like, the only difference lies therein that Parmenides has more the cause in view, Gauḍapāda the effect in order to show from it that it can neither as the existent nor as the non-existent come into being. He argues that neither as the existent nor as the non-existent can something originate; the former (*sato janma*) is impossible because in that case what is already there will have come into existence : *jātam jāyate* (o'úte pot' e'xpe e'óntos e'phèsei pístios i'skhús yinesdai ti par' au'to), the latter (*asato-janma*) is impossible because what is non-existent ("the son of a barren woman") can never come into being (o'út' e'x mè e'óntos e'àsō phasdai ou'dè noeĩn. ou' yar phatón ou'dè noéton e'stin ópos ou'x ésti).

3. Verses 31-48. The view on the practical again forms the end. That there is no plurality is evident from the fact that it disappears as soon as the Manas "comes out of itself", becomes non-Manas (*manaso amanībhāve*). This is effected through the Yoga and, indeed (since the author is not agreed with any and every Yoga, 3.39, as the Apostle Paulus not with any and every asceticism 1. Kor. 13.3) the *asparśayoga*, the "un-touch-Yoga" which consists therein that the objects are no more perceived by the conscience, they exist no more for it. This Yoga is achieved by suppressing the mind (*manaso nigraha*), the organ of imagination and desire and it is no doubt to be distinguished from loss of consciousness in sleep. In it the soul becomes one with the Brahman and exists in an inexpressible highest bliss as the pure subject of perception, containing the object within himself.

IV. Alātaśānti, the extinction of the firebrand-circle.

1. Verses 1-46 : The poet impresses once more the main doctrines of the previous section, that a becoming of neither the existent nor the non-existent is thinkable and that no object can ever become different since it is according to its nature and then demonstrates the contradictions in the concept of causality; the relationship of cause and effect (*kāraṇam* and *kāryam*), basis[1] and result (*hetu* and *phalam*), perception and what is perceived are inconceivable; therefore, there is no becoming, not of Saṃsāra

1. In this *Alātaśānti* section Gauḍapāda has used two pairs of words in connection with causality : (1) *kāraṇa* and *kārya*, and (2) *hetu* and *phala*. The choice of this or that pair seems to be governed by the exigencies of the metre. Deussen, however, almost always translates (1) *kāraṇa* and *kārya* by Ursache and Wirkung respectively, and (2) *hetu* and *phala* by Grund and Erfolg respectively. He however does not say what difference he makes between Ursache and Grund, and between Wirkung and Erfolg. Besides, in three places at least (verses 53, 76 and 78) he has translated *hetu* by Ursache and in one place (76) *phala* by Wirkung. Since ours is a translation, not of the Sanskrit original, but of Deussen's German translation of it, we have used two different sets of expression for the sake of

also, because Saṃsāra has never been, and not of salvation, which has always been there (verses 30-31). Also there is no becoming in the imagining subject : the fancies in the waking state are similarly based on error as those in the dream, as amplified here once more, so that neither in the subject nor in the object there is any becoming.

2. Verses 47-52 : But whence the appearance of plurality and becoming ? This question is answered through an illustration which is very highly original and brilliant in its form and which has given the name of *alātaśānti* to the whole book. *Alāta* (from *lā* to grasp, "that which cannot be grasped") is a splinter of wood glowing at one end. By swinging this a fiery line or fiery circle (*alātacakram*, also *Maitr*. 6,24; cf. also *Mahābh*. 7,1825) is produced, without thereby something added to the homogeneous gleam, or something emerging from it. The whole world is comparable to such a circle of gleam; it exists only in the conscience (*vijñānam*) all objects are the swingings of one and homogeneous conscience.

3. Verses 53-77. The poet returns to the impossibility of becoming, the relationship of basis and result, the affinity of dream and waking in order to explain, by referring to the previous illustration that everything objective and subjective is only *cittaspandanam*, swingings of the conscience (Verse 72). He again refers to the contradictions of the dualist, whereas according to him in the Vedānta the duality serves only as an educational aid that ceases after the final instruction.

4. Verses 78-100. At the end follows a portrait of the fool, who clings to the plurality, and of the 'awakened' (*buddha*) who has realized himself as that which all have been from eternity (*ādibuddha* and *ādiśānta*, verses 92, 93), as the eternal Identity, as pure objectless Intelligence, free from all worldliness.

---

consistency, translating (1) Ursache and Wirkung by cause and effect respectively and (2) Grund and Erfolg by basis and result respectively.—GBP.

MĀṆḌŪKYA UPANIṢAD

PART I

1

1. Om! This syllable is the whole world. Its explanation is as follows:[1]

The past, the present and the future, all this is the sound Om. And besides, what still lies beyond the three times, that also is the sound Om.

2. All this, verily, is Brahman, but Brahman, is this Ātman (the soul) and this Ātman is fourfold.

3. The *Vaiśvānara* present in the wakeful state, perceiving outwards, seven-limbed,[2] having nineteen mouths[3], the enjoyer of the gross, is his first quarter.

4. The *Taijasa*, present in the state of dream, perceiving inwards, seven-limbed,[2] having nineteen mouths,[3] the enjoyer of the selected[4], is his second quarter.

5. The state, "where he, asleep, no more experiences any desire and sees no vision", (Bṛh. 4, 3, 19) is deep sleep. The *Prājña*, present in the state of deep sleep, "become one" (Bṛh. 4, 4, 2) "consisting wholly of knowledge, through and through" (Bṛh. 4, 5, 13), "consisting of bliss" (Taitt. 2, 5), the enjoyer of the bliss, having conscience for his mouth, is his third quarter.

6. "He is the lord of all" (Bṛh. 4, 4, 22) he is "the omniscient" (Muṇḍ. 1, 1, 9), he is "the inner guide" (Bṛh. 3, 7), he is the cradle of the universe (cf. Muṇḍ. 1, 1, 6), verily he is creation and the disappearance of creatures.

---

1. The same expression in Chānd. 1,1.1.
2. Chānd. 5, 18, 2 (Śaṅkara).
3. Ten Indriyas, five Prāṇas, Manas, Buddhi, Ahaṁkāra, Cittam (Śaṅkara).
4. Bṛh. 4,2,3.

1. All-pervading, outward-conscious Viśva,
Inward-conscious is Taijasa,
Pure consciousness is Prājña,
One is it, who goes for three.

2. Out of the right eye looks Viśva,
In the Manas within, is Taijasa,
In the heart-space stays Prājña,
Thus threefold in body is his state.

3. Enjoyer of gross is Viśva,
Of choice, Taijasa,
Bliss-enjoyer is Prājña,
Thus threefold is his enjoyment.

4. With gross is satisfied Viśva,
With chosen Taijasa,
With bliss is satisfied Prājña,
Threefold is his satisfaction.

5. Who is in these three states
Enjoyer? What the object enjoyed?
Who knows these two well,
He enjoys and is not stained (Īśā. 2)

6. A source is of all creatures
As beings, that is certain:
The Spirit (*Puruṣa*) as vital force (*prāṇa*)
created them,
Separated only as the rays of the sun.

7. Some hold the world-creation
For unfoldment-of-power (*vibhūti*),
Others again for dream hold
The creation, and for delusion (*māyā*).

8. Many make the world-creation
At God's wish alone originate.
Others believe, it was Time
That produced all the creatures.

9. For own enjoyment, for a plaything
The God created them, hold others;—
No ! it is God's self-essence!
What can he wish, he who everything has ?

2

7. That which is neither inward-perceiving nor outward-perceiving, nor both way perceiving, that which does not consist of knowledge through and through, neither conscious nor unconscious,—invisible, unhandlable, ungraspable, uncharacterizable, inconceivable, unnamable established in the certitude of his own self, that which extinguishes the expanse of the universe, calm, auspicious, without the second,—that is the fourth quarter, that is the Ātman which should be known.

10. Capable of eradication
Of all sorrows, the unchangeable,
As oneness permeating all
Is the God, who the Fourth is called.

11. Effect-and-cause-bound
Are Viśva and Taijasa,
Cause-bound is Prājña,
Both apply not to the Fourth.

12. Neither of truth nor of untruth,
Neither of himself nor of other
Is Prājña ever conscious,—
Eternally the Fourth looks at all.

13. In the unawareness of plurality
Are Prājña and the Fourth alike;
Yet Prājña lies in the germinal sleep,
The Fourth knows no sleep.

14. Dream and sleep are of the first two,
Of Prājña, the dreamless sleep,
Neither dreaming nor sleeping
One ascribes to the Fourth, who knows him.

15. The dreamer perceives erroneously,
The sleeper perceives not at all;
Both err; where it vanishes,
There the fourth state is attained.

16. In the beginningless universal delusion
Sleeps the soul; when it wakes up,
Then wakes in it the secondless,
Sleepless, dreamless Eternal.

17. If the expanse of the universe existed,
It has to go some day;
But all plurality is delusion;
Without plurality is the reality.

18. Refutable are the assumptions
Only, if someone sets them up;
Here they are just educational aid;
To him who knows, plurality exists not.

3

8. This Ātman now is, in regard to the sounds (*adhyakṣaram*, used in analogy of *adhidaivatam*, *adhyātmam*) the syllable Om, specially with reference to its moras; the moras are the three quarters [of the Ātman], and the quarters are the moras, viz. the sound *a*, the sound *u*, and the sound *m*.

9. The Vaiśvānara present in the wakeful state is the *a*-sound, the first mora, from the reaching (*āpti*) or from the first existence (*ādimattvam*).—He who knows this verily attains all desires and becomes the first.

10. The Taijasa, present in the state of dream is the *a*-sound, the second mora, from the high-holding (*utkarṣa*) or from the being-on-both-the-sides (*ubhayatvam*).–He who knows this, verily holds high the tradition of knowledge [in his family] and is equally respected by both the sides [friend and enemy] and in his family no one is born who does not know the Brahman.

11. The Prājña, present in the state of deep sleep, is the *m*-sound, the third mora, from constructing (*miti*; from the root *mi*, *minoti*), or also from annihilation (*apīti*; from *mi minâti*).—He who knows this verily erects (out of himself) this whole world and is also its annihilation.

19. Very muchsimilar is Viśva to the *a*-sound
Through similarity of first existence,
Through moras' agreement
In attainment also they are alike.

20. Taijasa resembles the *u*-sound
In the high-holding clearly,

Through moras' agreement
In reciprocality also they are alike.

21. Very much similar is Prājña to the *m*-sound
Through similarity of construction,
Through moras' agreement
In annihilation also they are alike.

22. Since he, in the three states
Clearly sees this similarity through,
So is due to the high sage
From all creatures honour, and praise.

23. The *a*-sound leads to the Viśva, the goal,
The *u*-sound leads to the Taijasa,
The *m*-sound leads to the Prājña, the goal—
No goal of the moraless is.

4

12. Moraless is the Fourth, unhandlable, that which extinguishes the expanse of the universe, auspicious, without the second. In this way the syllable Om is the Ātman (the self).

One who knows this has his [individual] self merged in the [highest] self (Vāj. Saṃh. 32.11), – one who knows this.

24. Quarter by quarter knowthe Om-sound,
Its moras the quarters are;
Who knows the Om-sound quarter by quarter,
Needs know nothing further.

25. Meditating, be absorbed in the Holy Call,
It is Brahman, the fearless,
Who in the Holy Call is ever absorbed,
For him no fear is any more.

26. The Holly Call is the lower,
It is the higher Brahman too,
"Without the earlier and later,
"Without the inner and the outer" (Bṛh. 2, 5.19).

27. It is the beginning of everything,
Its middle and its end too,
Who thus knows the Holy Call,
Is merged in it forthwith thereon.

28. Know the Holy Call as the God,
Who is enthroned in the heart of all;
The sage, who the Om-sound knows
As all-pervading grieves not.

29. Partless and with unending parts,
Is the blessed cessation of duality;
Who as such the Om-sound knows,
He alone is a *Muni*, none else.

PART II

named Vaitathyam "The Untruth".

1. All that we see in dream,
Is untrue, the wise tell us,
For all this is inward,
For it lies locked up within us.

2. And because too short would be the time
To visit far off regions,
And because when we awake,
We are no more in those regions.

3. "There are no cars or no chariots,"
Teach us the scriptures (Bṛh. 4, 3, 10) and the logic;
Thus is the dream's untruth
Proved and revealed too.

4. Because plurality here is only inward,
It's so in the state of wakefulness too;
Here, as there, is only imagination,
Locked up within us, here as there.[1]

5. The state of dream and of wakefulness
Is the same to the wise,
Because plurality is common to both,—
For this well-established reason.

6. What is not before and not after too,
Is not in the meantime also;
Although untrue it is, it is
Seen not as untrue yet.

---

1. Read : *saṁvṛtatve na bhidyate.*

7. The acts of wakefulness are useful,
But no more so when we dream;
Therefore, as they begin and end,
Can depend on delusion alone.

8. Also what in dream new, springs it
From the mind only, and if the gods to him
Appear, he sees them just so,
As he was over them instructed.

9. Dreaming, what he builds in the mind
Within, that is unreal,
Although his mind grasped it outside,
As the thing seen both are untrue.

10. Wakeful, what he builds in the mind
Within, that is unreal,
Although his mind grasped it outside,
Logically untrue are both.

11. If now both kinds of plurality
In dream and waking untrue are,
Who perceives the two pluralities,
Who imagines them in the consciousness ?

12. Through self-delusion the God Ātman
Imagines his self by himself,
Perceiving both the pluralities,
Is the settled conviction of the Vedānta.

13. Transforming, He imagines as different,
What exists only in the consciousness,
As being outside and necessary
The Ātman imagines it within himself.

14. Mind is the chronometre of the inner,
Plurality that of the external,
Their difference lies only herein,
As imagination both are alike

15. Indistinct is the world within,
Distinct the world that lies outside;
Different according to the organ of sense,
As imagination both are alike

16. The soul is imagined first,
Then the peculiarity of objects,
External and internal;
As one knows, so one remembers.

17. As a rope, not perceived distinctly
In dark, is erroneously imagined
As snake, as a streak of water,
So is the Self (*Ātman*) erroneously imagined.

18. As, when the rope is distinctly perceived,
And the erroneous imagination withdrawn,
Only the rope remains, without a second,
So, when distinctly perceived, the Ātman.

19. When he as Prāṇas, as all
The diverse objects appears to us,
Then it is all mere delusion (*māyā*),
With which the God deceives himself.

20. To the Prāṇa-knowers he is the Prāṇas (Vaiśeṣikas),
Elements to him, who knows them (Lokāyatikas),
To the Guṇa-knowers he is the Guṇas (Sāṁkhyas),
Tattvas to him, who knows them (Śaivas).

21. To the quarter-knowers he is the quarters (Māṇḍūkya-Up.),
To the materiality-knowers materiality (Vātsyāyana),
To the world-knowers the worlds (Paurāṇikas),
Gods to the God-knowers (followers of the Veda).

22. To the Veda-knowers he is the Vedas,
To the sacrifice-knowers the sacrifice,
To the enjoyer-knowers the enjoyer,
The object of enjoyment, to those who know him so.

23. To the subtle-knowers he is subtle,
Gross to those who know him so,
Concrete to the concrete-knowers,
Formless to those who know him so.

24. He is time to the time-knowers,
For space-knowers he is the space,
To the art-connoisseurs he is the arts,
The spheres to those who know him so.

25. For Manas-knowers he is the Manas,
For Buddhi-knowers he is the Buddhi,
He is the Citta[1] for the Citta-knowers,
Right and wrong to him who knows them.

26. Twentyfivefold for those (Sāṁkhyas),
To those as the twentysixth (Pātañjalas),
Thirtyonefold for others (Pāśupatas),
Infinite is he for many (cf. *Cūlikā* 14).

27. Worlds he is to the world-knower,
Life-stages to him who knows them,
Three genders to the linguisticians.
To the others the higher and the lower (scil. Brahman).

28. For creation-knower the world-creation,
For dissolution-knower the world-dissolution,
The world-sustenance for sustenance-knower,—
So he is all everywhere.

29. Whatever existence one thus attributes
To the Ātman, he holds that view,
He cherishes it and, becoming it,
He surrenders himself to him as demon.

30. He himself is all forms of existence,
From which he appears different,—
Who knows this, will imagine himself,
Unawed, what he really is.

31. As one looks at dream and delusion,
As at mirage in desert,
So he looks at this universe,
Who is versed in the Vedānta.

32. There is no dissolution and no becoming,
No bound one, nor an aspirant,
No seeker of emancipation,
No emancipated, in truth.

33. As unreal forms of existence
And as the one he is thought,

---

1. For this word of the original, Deussen has used the word 'Geist'—GBP.

Yet who muses on them, is always the one,
And so victorious is the oneness.

34. Not on the Ātman the plurality rests
And also never on its own self,
Not beside him and not through him
It can exist, that is certain.

35. Giving up fear, anger and inclination
The Muni who knows the Veda,
Sees that secondless and changeless,
In which the expanse of the world dissolves.

36. Who thus the essence of the world knows,
He shall hold on to the oneness faithfully,
Certain of all absence of duality,
He goes indifferent along the world.

37. From glorification free, and from songs of praise,
From even the worship of the Manes, indeed,
In everything, whatever exists, at home,
He lives so "just as it comes to him" (Bṛh. 3, 5).

38. Seeing the essence in himself,
Essence in the world outside,
Becoming it, reposing in it,
He holds on to the essence, firmly and faithfully.

PART III

named Advaitam "Absence of duality"

1. Worship the command requires
Of Brahman as born,
Ere it became, was nothing there,
Therefore wretched the worshippers are.

2. What is not wretched, hear now,
The unborn, same everywhere,
And why nothing originates whatsoever,
Although originating everywhere.

3. The Ātman is like the world-space,
The Jīva like the space in pot,
The pots are the bodies —
That is 'origination', the metaphor shows.

4. When the pots are broken,
What becomes of space in pot ?
It is merged in the world-space,—
So the Jīva in the Ātman too.

5. As, when in some pot-space
Dust is found, or smoke,
Not all the spaces share it, though,
So too the Jīvas joys and sorrows.

6. Forms, functions and names
Differ, forsooth, according to their places,
Yet the space, which they occupy,
Is the same by itself,—so the Jīvas too.

7. As the pot-space of the world-space
No product is, and no part also,
So is the Jīva of the Ātman
No product and no part of him also.

8. Just as the sky to the childern,
[Although colourless] appears as blue,
Similarly the Ātman to the unexperienced
Appears as soiled with stain.

9. In the matter of dying and being born,
Going away and coming back,
And permeating all the bodies,—
He is alike the space.

10. As dream, surely, all bodies
As delusion, the Ātman projects;
Neither as similar, nor as dissimilar
In degree they let be judged.

11. As soul (*Jīva*) in the five sheaths,
So teaches the Taittirīyakam (Taitt. Up. 2),
The highest Ātman lies concealed,
He, whom we liken to the space.

12. In the Honey-section (Bṛh. 2.5) is in pairs
The highest Brahman shown,
As in the earth and in the belly,—
He, whom we liken to the space.

13. If the scripture, through equation,
Declares Jīva and Ātman as one,
Condemning all the plurality,
So it is true in the fullest sense.

14. And even if before the creation
The scripture holds the two apart (Chānd. 6.3.2),
That applies figuratively, not primarily,
And only to that who is supposed to become.

15. And if at all the scripture creation teaches,
In pictures of the clay, the ore, and the sparks,
(Chānd. 6, 1, 3. Bṛh. 2.1.20).
That serves only as an educational aid (cf. 1.18),
For "there is no plurality whatsoever" (cf. Bṛh., 4, 4, 19).

16. There are three grades of students:
Weak, mediocre, excellent;
For their sake, out of compassion
Brahman becomes the object of worship.

17. The dualists take their stand,
With assurance, on their own doctrines,
Yet they are at variance among themselves,
With us there is no such contradiction whatever.

18. In truth there is non-duality,
Duality only in the world of division;
They teach duality both ways,
With us there is no such contradiction.

19. Only as delusion exists the division
Of that, which is one and eternal,
For if the division existed in reality,
What eternal is would mortal become.

20. Of existence that is unborn
Those teachers assume a becoming,—
The unborn, immortal,
How could it turn into mortal ?

21. The immortal cannot become mortal,
Nor the mortal immortal,
Nothing can ever be otherwise
Than what its nature is.

22. If an immortal being
Were to turn into a mortal one,
Only fictitious would be its immortality,
What would become of its eternality ?

23. Speaking in earnestness or ostensibly,
The scripture uniformly teaches the same
About creation; certain and well reasoned
Is what it says and not otherwise.

24. "There's no plurality here" says it (Bṛh. 4, 4, 19),
"Manifold through delusion Indra goes about"
(Bṛh. 2, 5, 19),
"As unborn becomes manifold" (Vāj. Saṁh. 31, 19)
Through delusion only he is born.

25. Through the denial of Saṁbhūti (Īśa 12)
Origination is warded off;
"Who could bring him forth ?"
These words (Bṛh. 3, 9, 28) show him as a causeless one.

26. The words: "he is not so, not so" (Bṛh. 4, 2, 4),
Denying all expressible,
Can, as the imperceptibility shows,
Refer to Him and none else.

27. The existent cannot come into being,
It would be so only through delusion;
Who makes it originate in reality,
He brings into being what already was.

28. Not in reality, nor as a delusion.
Can the non-existent ever originate;
A son of the barren women is born
Not in reality, nor in appearance.

29. As in dream the mind is active,
Appearing as many only through illusion,
So in waking the mind is active,
Appearing as many only through illusion.

30. The mind, though it's one, appears
As many in dream,—that is obvious;
The mind, though it's one, appears
As many when awake,—that too is obvious.

31. In mind alone everything comes to view,
This plurality, movable and immovable;
And when the mind comes out of itself,
Plurality is no more to be seen.

32. As soon as the mind ceases to imagine,
When Ātman, the being, dawns on it,
Then, as non-mind, it perceives no more,
For there remains nothing to be perceived.

33. As the eternal changeless knowledge
is not different from the known,
The Brahman is over cognized,
By the eternal the eternal is known.

34. This procedure consists therein,
That forcibly all the movements
Of the mind are suppressed,—
It is different in deep sleep.

35. The mind is dissolved in deep sleep;
Suppressed, it is not dissolved,
But becomes one with the Brahman,
The fearless, light-of-knowledge.

36. The eternal, sleepless, dreamless one,
Without name, without form,
"Shining at once" (Chānd. 8, 4, 1), all-knowing
No worship whatever applies to it.

37. All lamentation retreats from it,
In it no anxiety anymore,
Quite content, the ever light is,
Firm and fearless meditation.

38. No taking is there, no giving,
Where no anxiety remains whatsoever,
Then there is, reposing in itself,
Eternal knowledge alone, its own like.

39. That is called the Touchless Yoga,
Even for the Yogins difficult to see,
Because even the Yogins shy at it,
Afraid of the fearless one.

40. The suppression of the mind is necessary
For every Yogin to attain
The fearless, the sorrowless,
The awakening, eternal rest.

41. As of a drop, merged in ocean,[1]
That rested on blade of grass,
So the suppression of the mind
Follows with no difficulty whatsoever.

42. One has to suppress the mind methodically,
Distracted in desire and lust,
Then will it come to rest and disappear,
Its disappearance is like pleasure of love.

43. Knowing that everything is painful,
One turns away from desire and lust,
Knowing that everything is Brahman,
One no more sees what has come into existence.

44. Wake up the mind, if it falls into slumber,
Collect it, when it is distracted;
Know this well, that both are sinful;
Disturb it not, when it's Brahman-like.

45. No pleasure he enjoys any more,
Of no intense desire conscious,
His mind working undisturbedly,
He keenly strives after unity.

46. And when the mind is not vanished
in sleep, nor it distraction seeks,
Then it steps forth as the Brahman,
Still, and from appearance free.

47. Free, calm and quiet, painless,
Inexpressible highest pleasure,
Eternal, conscious of the eternal object,—
That is how the wise describe it.

48. No soul is ever born,
No originating of the wide world,
It is the highest holy truth,
That there is no such thing as becoming.

---

1. Perhaps *udadhau* is to be read. I cannot decide upon the interpretation of the commentator.

PART IV.

named Alātaśānti, "The extinction of the firebrand."[1]

1. One who like the clouds in the space
Knows the pluralities in the One,
The subject and at the same time the object
Is,—him I adore, the Puruṣa.

2. That one called the Touchless Yoga,
Friendly and beneficial to all,
Without contradictions, incontrovertible,
Shown to us (3.39),—adoration to him.

3. "What exists alone comes into being,' So many a thinker says;—
"No! It's what existed not", say others,
Each challenging the other's view.

4. "What exists cannot come into being,"—
"Nor that what existed not";—
Thus disputing, they testify
To the non-becoming, like non-dualists.

5. We are delighted when they thus show:
It's impossible, to come into being;—
That there is no contradiction among us
As in them all, now listen.

6. The becoming of what had not become
Those disputants accept,
Still, the unborn, the immortal,
How could it mortal become ?

7. The immortal cannot become mortal,
Nor the mortal immortal,
Nothing can ever be otherwise
Than what its nature is (=3.21).

---

1. That probably means : "The refutation of the (apparent) circle of spark (which appears when a fire brand is swung around)."

8. If an immortal being
Were to turn into a mortal one,
Only fictitious would be its immortality,
What would become of its eternality (=3, 22) ?

9. Permanent, inherent in itself,
Inborn and unmade,
Never giving up its own essence,
Such is, what they call, 'the Nature' (*Prakṛti*).

10. Unborn and undying,
Are individualities (*dharma*) by nature;
He, to whom they originate and die,
Is ignorant of the individuality.

11. He, to whom the cause becomes the effect,
He makes the cause be born,—
How can, what is eternal, be born ?
How, what is inherent, be divorced ?

12. If the cause itself becomes effect,
Then the effect is already there for ever,
And yet it becomes ! And its becoming
Makes the cause vanish into air.

13. No! Him no practical proof avails,
Who makes the Eternal come into existence;
And one who originates what already is,
He sinks into unending regressus.

14. If the result[1] were the source of the basis,[1]
And the basis the source of the result,
Then both will be beginningless,
Basis and result, how can it be ?

15. If the result were the source of the basis,
And the basis the source of the result,
Then the origination of both, forsooth,
Is like the son begetting the father.

16. Basis and result, if originated,
Do require an order of succession;

1. For Deussen's translation of *phala* by Erfolg (here result) and of *hetu* by Grund (here basis), see our note above, page 608.

For if they originate simultaneously,
Like two horns, there goes the bond.

17. That from the result should spring up
The basis itself, is unprovable,
And if the basis is unprovable,
How can it effect the fruit ?

18. If out of the result the basis followed,
And out of the basis the result,
Which one of the two is earlier,
And its following only relative?

19. Thus the impossibility (4,14), the absurdity (4,15)
And the confusion in the time sequence (4,16-18),
In which the opponents invariably fall,
Bear testimony to the non-becoming.

20. The case of seed and plant,
Is only seemingly decisive;[1]
And what only seemingly decisive is,
It counts not as a valid proof.

21. The absurdity of the time-sequence (4,15)
Only confirms the non-becoming;
For what becomes would surely refer
Back to something, an earlier one.

22. Not out of itself, nor out of else,
Can anything ever come into being;
Not as existent, nor as non-existent,
Nor as both, it can originate.

---

1. The relationship between the seed and the plant must either have a beginning or it must be without a beginning; both alternatives, however, are impossible. It has no beginning : for every plant always already presupposes the seed, every seed in its turn the plant. It cannot also be without a beginning : for every plant, every seed originates in time and therefore has a beginning. Or should all the members be temporary, and their relationship alone be beginningless ? That also is impossible; *na hi vīja-aṅkura-vyatirekeṇa vīja-aṅkura-saṁtatir nāma ekā abhyupagamyate;* for the relationship is only a bond between the members and so it already presupposes them and is nothing without them (according to Śaṅkara).

23. Basis and result, if beginningless,
Rule out the becoming from themselves,
For which there is no beginning,
For that there is no beginning.

24. Perception must have a source-object,
Otherwise its variation would be impossible,
Also independent of us should be
Pain and perception, – they think.

25. Perception must have a source-object,
So they cleverly argue with us, –
But that the source has no source,
So the meditation on reality tells us.

26. The mind does not touch the objects,
And also not the appearance of objects,
And when the objects are unreal,
So too their appearance, divorced from mind.

27. Also never, in the three courses of time,
Does an object touch the mind;
A causeless appearance is rarer still;
How could it become the cause ?

28. So there is no such thing as becoming,
Not in the subject, not in the object;
Who makes it take place in both,
He walks in skies only.

29. Since otherwise the eternal would come to be,
So the substance is unchanging;
Nothing can ever be otherwise
Than what its nature is (=3,21. 4,7).

30. If the Saṁsāra were beginningless,
It could not be ending;
If the liberation had beginning,
It could not be unending.

31. What is not before and not after too,
Is not in the meantime also;
Although untrue it is, it is
Seen not as untrue yet (=2,6).

32. The acts of wakefulness are useful,
But no more so when we dream;
Therefore, as they begin and end,
Can depend on delusion alone (=2,7).

33. What we in dream perceive,
Is false, for its only in the body;
How would objects let be seen
In this closed space ?

34. And the time, too, is not sufficient
To go there, so as to see them;
And we don't find ourselves there
On awakening, where we saw them.

35. And what with others one discusses in dream,
It exists not, when one awakes;
And what was grasped in dream,
Awakened, one holds it in hand no more.

36. And also what we dream of the body,
Is untrue and not what it is;
Untrue like this, is everything,
What the mind takes as true in waking.

37. What we, as if wakeful, see in dream,
That has its basis within us;
So too has its basis within us,
What in waking we take as true.

38. Origination is inconceivable;
Everything is eternal, so teaches the scripture;
At no time can emerge
The non-existent (becoming) from the existent.

39. Wakeful we see the non-existent;
The dream image is of the like stuff made:
The non-existent we see in dream;
When we wake up, there is nothing.

40. Non-existence does not bring forth non-existence,
Non-existence does not bring forth existence either;
And existence also does not bring forth existence;
Existence cannot bring forth non-existence.

41. Just as in waking one may by error grasp,
Something impossible, as if it really existed,
So in dream too, out of error,
One sees objects appearing themselves.

42. From perception and tradition
They hold on to realism;
Becoming is all that they know,
Recoiling in horror from what is.

43. Many a one,[1] recoiling from existence,
Even when not a pure perceptionist
Escapes not the defects of becoming;
Defects do remain, although insignificant.

44. From perception, from tradition
Even delusion is called elephant;
From perception, from tradition
An object also is called existent.

45. Becoming is appearance, movement appearance,
The objective is sheer appearance;
Non-becoming, motionless, unobjective,
Calm, dualityless, reality is.

46. Thus there is no becoming in the subject,
No becoming in the object either;
Who has known this once for all,
He does not fall back into the contrary.

47. As the swinging of the fire-brand gives the appearance
Of lines straight and curved,
So swinging of consciousness the appearance
Of perception and the perceiver.

48. Just as a fire-brand unswung
Does not appear, does not originate (as circle),
So consciousness unswung
Appears not and originates too not.

---

1. The followers of the (religious) tradition (*samācāra*), who passes the existent in the form of the becoming, the truth in the clothing of myth.—The restraint, with which they are censured here, is remarkable.

49. If the fire-brand swings, comes the appearance
Not from outside in any way,
Not from something other than the swing,
It is not an addition to the fire-brand.

50. Nor does it escape from the fire-brand,
For it has no real existence,
The same is the case with perception,
For this too is sheer appearance.

51. If the perception swings, comes the appearance
Not from outside in any way,
Not from something other than the swing,
It is not an addition to the consciousness.

52. Nor does it escape from the consciousness,
For it has no real existence,
Because of unreal causal nature
It is unthinkable as real.

53. One object, they say, can be the cause
Of existence of another object,
But for the spirit there is
No objectness and no otherness.

54. Neither from the mind springs the existence,
Nor from existence springs the mind;
Therefore, the wise accept no becoming
Either of the basis or of the result.

55. He who accepts basis and result,
To him they originate from each other;
One who is freed from this assumption,
For him the two originate no more.

56. He who accepts basis and result,
Far and wide is the Saṃsāra for him;
One who is freed from this assumption,
He is free from the Saṃsāra too.

57. The mentally benighted sees becoming everywhere,
Of the eternal he knows nothing;
Everything, in reality, is eternal,
There is no such thing as extinction.

58. The beings, which originate,
They originate not in reality;
Their origination is like delusion,
And delusion is not a reality.

59. Just as, where the seed is mere delusion,
The plant also is equally alike,
Not real, nor destructible,
So it is with all objects here.

60. Since all objects are unreal,
There is neither constancy nor disappearance;
Where all colours fade away,
No differentiation is there.

61. As in the apparent plurality of dream
The mind is entangled erroneously,
So in the apparent plurality of waking
The mind is entangled erroneously.

62. As in dream, the mind, non-plural
sees the apparent plurality,
So in waking, the mind, non-plural
Sees the apparent plurality.

63. Roaming about in dream
In the different regions of space,
What one believes to have seen:
Animals, birds, insects.

64. All that nowhere exists
But in the dreamer's mind,
So everything he then sees, is
Just the consciousness of the dreamer.

65. Roaming about in waking
In the different regions of space,
What one believes to have seen:
Animals, birds, insects.

66. All that nowhere exists
But in the mind of the awake,
So everything he then sees, is
Just the consciousness of the awake.

67. The object and its imagination
They presuppose each other;
Everything in itself is transitory,
Only in consciousness they are there.

68. As we merely dream of somebody,
That he is born, and he dies,
So are all these worldly beings,
They are, and are not too.

69. As we see in hallucination,
That somebody lives and then dies,
So are all these worldly beings,
They are, and are not too.

70. As the black magic makes us see,
That somebody lives and then dies,
So are all these worldly beings,
They are, and are not too.

71. No soul is ever born,
No originating of the wide world,
It is the highest holy truth,
That there is no such thing as becoming (=3,48).

72. What appears twofold as subject-object,
Is just swinging of consciousness (4,47);
The mind is eternally objectless,
"Nothing sticks him" says the script (Bṛh. 4,3,15).

73. As it is artificial, a mere make-belief (3,15),
So it is not there in reality;
What other schools accept,
Exists only for them, not in reality.

74. What they accept as eternal
Falsely, is not eternal in reality;
And becoming, it shows as erroneous
the conclusions of other school.

75. Accommodation of what exists not
Does not prove that there is duality;
If its absence is perceived,
Away goes accommodation, no more purposive.

76. When one does not accept causes
In all the realms of nature,
Then there is no imagination too;
With the cause goes the effect too.

77. Mind is causeless; the non-becoming,
Free from duality, is ever its own;
Duality is nothing but the appearance of mind
In that Eternal, which is all.

78. Knowing as real the causelessness,
Throwing away the causes of isolation,
One goes to the place that's free from fear,
Free from desire, and free from grief.

79. Accommodating itself to what is not,
The mind remains entangled in such;
Having known the non-existence of objects,
It returns to that unattached one (4,72).

80. He who grasps this and lets not go,
unshakable remains his position then;
Of wise the goal's that eternal one,
Free from duality, the identical being.

81. Free from slumber, free from dream,
The eternal one is luminous by itself
(Bṛh. 4, 3, 14. Kāṭh. 5.15);
"For ever luminous" (Chānd. 8,4,1) is this entity,
Such is its nature itself.

82. Easily He is ever hidden from us,
He unveils His essence with great difficulty,
So long as we continue to apprehend
This object and that, – He, the Holy.

83. "He is" ! "Is not" ! "Is and is not" !
"He is not !" thus deeming Him
Unstable, stable,[1] twofold, negative,
The fool hides His nature from himself.

1. One expects: "Stable (He is), unstable (is not)".

84. Because of these four points of view
[By fool] pursued, remains ever hidden
The Holy one, untouched by these,—
He who sees Him, has seen everything.

85. He who fully possesses the omni-vision,
The Brahman-abode, free from duality,
Devoid of beginning, middle and end,
For him nothing remains to strive after.

86. That is called real peace of mind,
That the real discipline of priests,
That's the taming of own nature,
He who knows this, attains peace.

87. Perceptible and objective
Is the dual worldliness (Waking);
Perceptible and unobjective,
Is the pure worldliness (Dream).

88. Imperceptible and unobjective,
That is called the super-worldliness;
It subject is at the same time object,
So the wise have always taught.

89. The subject and the three objects (4,87-88)
When known one after another,—
Therefrom follows the omni-vision
In all directions, of the high-minded.

90. One shall first ask: What should be
Avoided, known, attained and ripened ?
The perception passes for knowledge,
And so it is with the other three.

91. All beings are by nature
Boundless and resemble the space (3, 3ff),
And there's no plurality whatever
In them, in no sense ever.

92. All beings are by nature
Awakened from beginning (*ādibuddha*), that's certain;—
Who lets this suffice for himself,
He is ripe for deathlessness.

93. They all are by nature
Calm from the beginning, full of bliss;
All alike and indivisible,
Perennial, pure identity.

94. Yet this purity is no more,
When they fly into manifold bits;
Sunk into plurality, and divided,
They are therefore called wretched (3,1).

95. But in whom grows into conviction
The eternal identity,
He, in this world, knows the Great,
But the world understands it not.

96. Knowledge of the Eternal is eternal,
And it's concerned with nothing else;
Being unconcerned, it is called
Knowledge the unattached (4,72.79).

97. Yet when the untrained mind
Looks upon the smallest difference as real,
Then there is neither the unattachment
Nor the retreat of obscurity.

98. All souls are by nature
Free from obscurity, free from stain,
Awakened from beginning, liberated from beginning
They awake, so says the master.

99. As the sun shines by himself,
So also the knowledge, without the objects;
All objects are only knowledge, –
Inexpressible to the awakened himself.

100. Knowing to the best of our capacity, we salute
The obscure, wholly deep,
Perennial, pure Identity,
Which is the home of unity.

GARBHA UPANIṢAD[1]

The *Garbha Upaniṣad* (i.e. "Esoteric Doctrine over the Embryo") contains, subjoined to a prefixed verse, all sorts of views on the elements and the parts of human body, and describes particularly the development of the embryo in the mother's body. Accordingly, this text would have rather belonged to a manual on physiology and medicine than to a collection of the Upaniṣads and the designation : 'Pippalāda's Doctrine of Salvation" occurring at the end would have very little justification, — had it not been for the idea, contained in its middle part in the course of the description of the development of the embryo, an idea which is based on such passages as Ṛgveda 4,26,1. 4,27,1. 10,177,2 (*Geschichte der Philosophie* I, 253) and which is interesting on account of its analogies with the Western Philosophy, that the embryo in the mother's body is already in possession of the

1. On the order of sequence. Among the Upaniṣads of the Atharvaveda, which strive to continue the study of the Vedānta without encroaching materially on the territory of the Yoga, the Saṁnyāsa, Śiva- and Viṣṇu-cults, the most important and most universally accepted by the Vedānta theologists are the three presented so far : *Muṇḍaka*, *Praśna Māṇḍūkya*. A fourth, the Brahma Upaniṣad, which could be assigned to this circle according to Weber (*Literaturgesch.*, 2. ed. p. 178) will, in view of its most characteristic third part, find its place better at the beginning of Saṁnyāsa Upaniṣads as the transitional link from the purely Vedāntic to the Saṁnyāsa Upaniṣads. So only a gleaning of six Upaniṣads remains for us for this class which partly pursue more closely only individual points of the Vedānta doctrine (*Garbha*, *Prāṇāgnihotra*, *Piṇḍa*), partly undertake a recapitulation of the fundamental concepts of the Vedānta (*Ātma*, *Sarvopaniṣatsāra*), on which may follow a text (Gāruḍa) standing in isolation. In the arrangement of this whole group we adhere to the order of sequence in the list of Nārāyaṇa and Colebrooke because this same is possibly of importance for the age of origination of the individual texts.—Our translation here and in the following is based upon the text of the Calutta edition, supplemented by Jacob's *Eleven Ātharvaṇa Upaniṣads* (Bombay 1891). Besides variant readings of the manuscripts made use of by Weber (*Ind. Studien* I. II. IX), as also those of the Telugu print have been drawn upon. Those which appeared during the issue of printing and could be still used subsequently are : The "32 Upaniṣads in the Ānandāśrama Series (Pune 1895) as also the new reprint of 108 *Upaniṣads* (Bombay 1896). The reader comparing the original texts will nowhere be in doubt as to the reading adopted by us. A thorough discussion of the exceedingly numerous and deep-going mutual differences in the individual texts lies beyond the limits of our present task and so must be reserved for future occasions.

knowledge (of its previous births, of the difference between good and bad etc.), but all this is forgotten (*pāsa mádēsis a'námnēsis*) when it comes out of the mother's womb.—The standpoint of the author is, as the juxtaposed references to Sāṁkhya-Yoga, Maheśvara (Śiva), Nārāyaṇa (Viṣṇu) and Brahman seem to indicate, conciliatory in the highest degree, though we do not have before us here (cf. to Chānd. 8,14, above) formulae for the different creeds.

The text is considerably damaged and full of gaps, and the confusion in the commentary of Nārāyaṇa is only surpassed by the carelessness and ignorance of its editor in the *Bibliotheca Indica.*[1]

Om !

1. Consisting of five, connected with each of the five,
Supported on six, burdened with six qualities,
Having seven constituent elements, three impurities, twice procreated.
Partaking of fourfold food is the body,

Why is it "consisting of five" [and "connected with each of the five"] ?

Because it consists of earth, water, fire, wind and ether.

In this body "consisting of five" what is earth, what water, what fire, what wind, what ether ?

In this body "consisting of five" what is hard it is earth, what is liquid it is water, what is warm it is fire, what moves about it is wind, what is hollow it is ether.—Hereby [it is "connected with each of the five" inasmuch as] the earth serves it for support, the water for assimilation of food [*piṇḍīkaraṇam*, cf. Chānd. 6,8,3], the fire for illumination, the wind for the distribution [of substances], the ether for giving room. — In another way[2] [it is " connected with

---

1. To page 64, 13 *stoścubhiścu āvartate* he cites in the note from the Cod. the variant reading : *stoścunāścuḥ āvataṅsa, iti* and adds : *kintu ubhayapāṭho'pi durbodhaḥ* ! So he did not know that he had a Sūtra of Pāṇini (8,4,40 : *stoḥ ścunā ścuḥ*) before him which certainly stands at a wrong place in the commentary, because it can only refer to *rasāc choṇitam* of the text.—Also the Poona edition does not seem to have understood the citation because it quotes it after *allopo'nas* (*Pāṇ.* 6,4, 134) in order to explain the form *majjñaḥ*.

2. The Poona edition reads with Nārāyaṇa *pṛthustu* "but it (the body) is (indeed) space-filling."

each of the five" inasmuch as] the ears serve for the perception of the sound, the skin for the touch, the eyes for seeing, the tongue for tasting and the nose for smelling. —[Or, again, inasmuch as] the sexual organ serves for sexual enjoyment, the Apāna for evacuation, while the body perceives with the Buddhi, imagines with the Manas, speaks with the speech.

Why is it " supported on six"?

Because it finds (in the food, out of which it develops) sweet, sour, saline, bitter, pungent and astringent tastes.

Further there are *ṣaḍja*, *ṛṣabha*, *gāndhāra*, *madhyama*, *pañcama*, *dhaivata* and *niṣāda* (as the seven notes of the scale). Further [the above enumerated fivenesses] become, through their application, tens according as they are characterized by the words "acceptable" and "unacceptable."[1]

2. Why is the body "Having seven constituent elements" ?

Because in it 1) white, 2) red, 3) black, 4) smoke-coloured, 5) yellow, 6) brown, 7) pale [liquid is found], according as substances [read *dravyāṇi* with Nārāyaṇa] become objects of food for, say, Devadatta. [The common source however, of all the seven constituent elements] is, in so far as they have the quality of wateriness common with each other, the sixfold [above mentioned : sweet, sour, saline, bitter, pungent, and astringent] food-sap.

Out of the [1. white] food-sap originates the [2. red] blood, out of the blood [3. black, i.e. opaque] flesh, out of the flesh

1. This second reference to the fivenesses is difficult to explain; more difficult, how all of a sudden the seven notes of the scale drop in in advance. Nārāyaṇa thinks, with the reference to the *ṣaḍguṇayogayuktam* of the verse, on the application of the seven notes in the six Rāgas and in the six times six Rāgiṇīs belonging to them; Śaṁkarānanda explains the enumeration of the seven notes as a *Pūrvapakṣa* to the question about the "seven constituent elements" although this question is raised only later on. Besides, his reading and the word order are too different to allow us to go into them. Further, the Telugu edition offers entirely different readings, and yet other readings seem to have offered themselves to the *Oupnekhat*. — *Quot capita, tot sensus*. The corruption of the passage consequently seems to be quite desperate.

the [4. smoke-coloured] fat, out of the fat [*snāyavaḥ snāyubhyas* is to be struck off with Śaṁkarānanda and the Telugu edition] the [5. yellow] bones, out of bones the [6. brown] marrow, out of the marrow the [7. pale] semen.

From the union of the semen and the blood develops the embryo; "in the heart are the partings" as they say. Particularly in the heart is a fire, and by the fire is bile, and by the bile is wind, and where the wind is, there goes forth the heart [of the child] in consequence of a creative process.

3. From the pairing at the time of the season there originates after one night a nodule, after seven nights a bubble, within a fortnight lump, within a month it becomes hard, after two months originates the head, after three months originate the parts of foot, in the fourth month ankles, belly and hips, in the fifth the vertebral column, in the sixth the mouth, the nose, the eyes, the ears, in the seventh the embryo is equipped with the soul [*jīva*], in the eighth it is complete in all parts.

By the preponderance of the father's semen originates a male, by the preponderance of the mother's semen a female; in the case of the preponderance of the semen of both a hermaphrodite; in the case of stupefaction of the mind are born the blind, the lame, the hunch-backs and the dwarfs. If the semen pressed in by the winds on both sides goes as under, then the body also becomes twofold and a twin is born.

The [embryo] "consisting of five [elements]" is capable of living [in the eighth month, of course — the preceding sentences on the procreation are parenthetical remarks], and his fivefold Buddhi has, by reason of the intelligence, the perception of smell, taste etc. Since, however, according to the text "he then thinks over the imperishable syllable Om" he perceives this one syllable [as the Puruṣa], so further the eight productives [*Prakṛti*, *Mahat*, *Ahaṁkāra*, 5 *Tanmātrās*] and the sixteen products *Manas*, 10 Indriyas, 5 Bhutas [to sum up, therefore, all 25 principles of the Sāṁkhya doctrine] are also present in the body of this embodied soul. Then his *Prāṇa* also swells on account of what is eaten and drunk by the mother which reaches him by means of a vein. Finally in the ninth month he is complete in all parts and in perception; then he remembers (so long as he is still in the mother's body) his earlier births and has a knowledge of his good and bad deeds:

4. After I had thousands of times before
Lived in the mother's womb,
I enjoyed many kinds of food,
And drunk many a mother's breast.
Born was I, died again
And was continually born anew.

What I did for my fellow-creatures,
Work, good or bad,
For that I must suffer alone;
Those who enjoyed it, are gone.
Alas ! sunk in the ocean of grief,
I see no remedy.

If once I escape from mother's womb
I shall turn to Maheśvara,
Who destroys all the evil
And bestows the reward of liberation.

If once I escape from mother's womb.
I shall turn to Nārāyaṇa,
Who destroys all the evil
And bestows the reward of liberation.

If once I escape from mother's womb,
I shall study the Sāṁkhya Yoga
who destroys all the evil
And bestows the reward of liberation.

If once I escape from mother's womb.
I shall meditate on the Brahman.

But then, when reaching at the opening of the genital organs, oppressed by the squeezing, he is hardly born, then touched by the Vaiṣṇava wind, [i.e. the wind of the outer world as against the wind in the body,] he can no more remember his births and deaths and has no knowledge any more of good and bad deeds.

Why is he called "the body" (*śarīram*)?

Because in it lie (*śriyante*) close fires, namely the fire of knowledge, the fire of seeing and the gastric fire. Here it is the gastric fire which digests what is eaten, drunk, licked, sucked. The fire of seeing effects the seeing of forms. The fire of knowledge knows the good and bad deeds.

[Besides] there are three places of fire; in the mouth is the Āhavanīya fire, in the stomach the Gārhapatya fire, in the heart the Dakṣiṇa fire. The Ātman is the sacrifice, the Manas the Brahman [the priest of this name], greed, etc. are the victims, perseverance and contentment are the sacrificial consecration, the organs of sense are the sacrificial utensils, the organs of activity are the offerings; the head is sacrificial potsherd, the hair the Darbha grass, and the mouth the inner sacrificial ground.

The head has four skull-bones, and on [each of] their both sides are sixteen tooth-cells. [In the body] there are 107 weak parts, 180 joints, nine times hundred sinews, 700 veins, 500 muscles [Yājñav. 3,100; according to the commentator it should be *majjā* for *peśī*], 360 bones, and four and a half *Koṭi* (45 million) hair.

The heart weighs eight Pala (364 grams), the tongue twelve Pala (546 grams), the bile a Prastham (728 grams), the phlegm an Āḍhaka (2912 grams) the semen a Kuḍavam (182 grams), the fat two Prastha (1456 grams), excrement and urine are uncertain, depending on the quantity of food.

This is the science of liberation by Pippalāda, the science of liberation by Pippalāda.

PRĀṆĀGNIHOTRA UPANIṢAD

The thought underlying this *Upaniṣad, of Prāṇa-agnihotram* "the fire-offering made to the Prāṇa" (or the sacrifice offered in the Prāṇa-fire) has developed through the following stages.

1. After one had discovered the all-encompassing universal soul in the individual self, it was natural to see old-Vedic natural gods embodied in the individual body, the sun as the eyes, the wind as the breath, and so on for which the older Upaniṣads offer numerous examples.

2. It was a consequence of this view (cf. already Bṛh. 1, 5, 2) when the Agnihotram daily offered to the gods was replaced by an offering to the gastric fire in the body (to the fire *Vaiśvānara*, Bṛh. 5, 9) i.e. by feeding, which followed among certain ceremonies. This sacrifice made to the Prāṇa (life) is described in Chānd. 5, 19-24, in connection with the doctrine of *Ātman Vaiśvānara* Chānd. 5, 11, 18; since the vital breaths are satisfied, the sense organs and the corresponding gods and the accompanying quarters are equally satisfied. —In an adjacent passage, Chānd. 5, 2, 2 (Bṛh. 6, 1, 14) the rinsing of mouth laid down before and after eating is allegorically looked upon as a dressing of the Prāṇa.

3. A combination of both the ideas, the feeding and the dressing of the Prāṇa, beside some formulae to be employed in the ceremony is there in the Maitr. 6, 9. The invocation to the wise who have praised this sacrifice, which is found there at the beginning, can probably refer to Chānd. 5 only. In order to make the procedure still more similar to the usual fire-sacrifice, an analogy therein is found to the second offering also to be made silently, in that after the five offerings one eats the rest of the meal silently, *yatavāg aśnāti*.

4. The repetition of this last feature as also the recurrence (with variants) of the verses *prāṇo'gnir* and *viśvo'si* in the *Prāṇāgnihotra Upaniṣad* render it probable, that this [Prāṇāgnihotra-Up.] is based not only on Chānd. 5,19-24 but on Maitr. 6,9 also and that it represents a further embellishment of the ceremony prescribed there. There the two verses, to be sure, precede the ceremony while here they follow it and they are prescribed to be recited before a triad and a couple of verses which in this association are found neither in the Ṛgveda nor in the Atharvaveda and accordingly they seem to presuppose a collection other than both of these. The glorification of water which then follows doubtless refers to the rinsing of the mouth which precedes eating. Further follow the five offerings to the Prāṇas with special instructions upon the use of particular fingers, whereupon the silent offering appears, spread out to five offerings in the five fires of the body. The rinsing of the mouth after the meal and the explanation of the five fires in the body mentioned (in the head, mouth, heart, navel and abdomen) form the contents of the second part.

As the first and the second part are based on Chānd. 5 and Maitr. 6, 9, similarly the third and the fourth part of our Upaniṣad contain a further depiction of the idea occurring in Chānd. 3, 17 and Mahānār. 64, to interpret allegorically the manas the sacrifice. This little agrees with the first two parts; there the five Prāṇas receive the offerings, here they are sacrificial priests. Besides the beautiful and ingenious thought of the original has not gained in detail in the course of interpretation.—It is remarkable that Śaṅkara to Brahmas. 3, 3, 24 (my translation p. 582 ff.) where he discusses the Chānd. 3, 16-17 and the Taitt. Ār. 10.64 passages, does not mention our Upaniṣad, may be that he did not know it or did, not recognize it.

I

Now, therefore, let us explain the sacrifice offered in one's own body, (the sacrifice) which forms the essence of all the Upaniṣads, which is helpful for knowledge of the Saṁsāra, which is studied [in the Veda, Chānd. 5, 19-24], and which has food as its authority.

Liberation from Saṁsāra is possible in this present human body, even without the Agnihotram, and without Sāṁkhya and Yoga. In this belief one puts down food on the ground, each according to the prescription applicable to him, and consecrates it with the three stanzas: "The herbs which are in Soma's realm" and with the two verses: "Give us, O Lord of food" etc.

The herbs, which are in Soma's realm
Many, different in hundreds of ways,
Which Bṛhaspati created in past,
They should protect us from fear.[1]—

Those bringing fruit, and those fruitless,
Not blossoming and blossoming,
Which Bṛhaspati created in past,
They should protect us from fear.[2]

1. Atharvav. 6, 96, 1. The first hemistich is Ṛgv. 10, 97, 18 also. [The second hemistich is ṚV. 10, 97,15cd also—GBP.]

2. Ṛgv. 10, 97,15.

As re-invigorating I apply to you[1]
The herb Nagharīṣā;
May it bring you fresh life-force[2]
And scare away the demons.[3]

Give us, O Lord of food,
Wholesome and powerful food,
Lead the sacrificer forth and forth,
Give us strength, to the bipeds and quadrupeds.

What indigestible I eat so often,
Fore-tasted by Rudras, by Piśācas,
May the Lord make it all free from danger
And auspicious; svāhā to the Lord!

You abide within the beings
In the cavity of heart and everywhere,
You are the sacrifice, are Brahman, are Rudra, are Viṣṇu, are the exclamation Vaṣaṭ.
Water, light, essence, the immortal, Brahman, Bhūr, Bhuvaḥ, Svar, Om, Salutation![4]

By waters may the earth be purified.
Purified, may she make me pure!
By Brahmaṇaspati, Brahman
Purified, may she make me pure![5]

What sticks[6] me, what uneatable,
What misdeed I committed,
ay the water wash me pure of all,
And from the gifts of the wicked!

1. Read : *ā te badhnāmi.*
2. With the Telugu ed. : *yā ta'āyur upāharat.*
3. [Quarter a=AV. 8.2.6a—GBP.]
4. We have already come across this formula, whose first part is called the Śiras (of Gāyatrī), at Maitr. 6,35; cf. Amṛtabindu 10, Note.
5. I have translated Deussen literally. The Sanskrit original of the last two quarters in the editions available to me is : *Punantu Brahmaṇaspatir Brahmapūtā punātu mām* which I have not been able to understand.—GBP.
6. 'anklebt' (Deussen). The Sanskrit original, however, in the editions available to me is *ucchiṣṭam* 'remainder of food after somebody has eaten it; hence impure for others to eat'.

O water, you are Amṛtam, (ambrosia, nectar) you are bed of Amṛtam (Taitt. Ār. 10, 32). I offer Amṛtam in the Prāṇa! In us, O ward, you are fed [1]!

Svāhā to the Prāṇa, the most pre-eminent!—Svāhā to the Apāna!—Svāhā to the Vyāna!—Svāhā to the Samāna! Svāhā to the Udāna!

With these words he offers (read: *juhoti*) with the little finger and the thumb to the Prāṇa, with the nameless (ring) finger to the Apāna, with the middle finger to the Vyāna, with the fore-finger to the Samāna, with all fingers to the Udāna.

Then he silently makes an offering to the Ekarṣi (the sun), two to the Āhavanīya (in the mouth), one to the Dakṣiṇa fire (in the heart), one to the Gārhapatya (in the navel), one to the All-atonement fire (below the navel).

Then he says [to the water]: "You are the covering! For immortality I superimpose you!" and therewith he rinses out the mouth, takes once more of it and rinses out once more. Then he takes the water in the left hand (read: *savye pāṇau apo gṛhītvā*) lays hold of the heart therewith and murmers:

The breath-fire, by five winds
Encircled, who the highest Ātman is,
Who gives peace to all the creatures!
I shall not be born any more!

You are all, all-human, multiform,
You sustain the universe born out of you.

May all sacrificial offerings enter (read: *viśantu*) into you, there where you Brahman, immortal in all, are.

Great is, and refreshment, that spirit,
Which lives on the tip of the thumb;
Him I will moisten with water,
May he bring immortality in the place of finger-tips.[2]

1. *amā, śiṣya, anto'si.* The explanation of these mysterious words given by the scholiast seems to us extremely doubtful.

2. *so'sya ante amṛtāya yonau*; the superfluous syllable certainly shows that the passage is corrupt.

One should meditate on this Ātman and think: "I make him a fire-sacrifice". Because he is a son [foster-child, ward] of all.

Thus in order to put the sacrifice in circulation he makes the offering in his own body, thinking: thereby I put the sacrifice in circulation.[1]

Four fires [and the All-atonement fire as the fifth, were mentioned above at the end of the first part]; what are their names?

The sun as fire, in the form of the solar disc, surrounded by a thousand rays, is located as Ekarṣi in the head, because it is said about him (perhaps Maitr. 6, 8).

The optic fire (cf. Garbha 3.; or perhaps *daśanāgnir* the tooth-fire ?) is located as the quadrangular *Āhavanīya*-fire in the mouth.

The gastric fire, promoting digestion, manages the sacrificial food[2] and is located as the crescent-shaped Dakṣiṇa fire in the heart.

Then comes the intestinal fire. This so-called intestinal fire which cooks (read: *śrapayitvā*) what is eaten, drunk, licked, and masticated is located in the navel as the [round] Gārhapatya fire.

The All-atonement fire finally is below the same, [has the three main arteries Iḍā,, Piṅgalā, Suṣumnā] as three wives and brings about procreation by means of the moon-light, conducted through them (arteries).[3]

3

In this sacrifice offered in the body, adorned with sacrificial posts and sacrificial ropes, who is the sacrificer ?—Who his wife? —Who are the Ṛtvij ?—Who the Adhvaryu? —Who the Hotar? Who the Brāhmaṇācchaṁsin (assistant of the Brahman priest) ?

---

1. Read : *atha yajñaparivṛttaye āhutīr homayati.*

2. One has to read *havir avaskandati* with the Telugu ed. The reading of other texts is quite impossible.

3. "This fire is the same which effects procreation by means of the moon-light (from the lunar disk situated on the forehead flowing down as semen through the arteries). The roots of the procreation-limb are located in the midst of the fire-pot; through it the semen falling in the fire-pot, after it has risen up high through the Prāṇa, is led to the progeny. Therefore it is said that the body consists of Agni and Soma (fire and moon)". (Nārāyaṇa).

—Who the Pratiprasthātar (assistant of the Adhvaryu)?—Who the Prastotar (assistant of the Udgātar)?—Who the Maitrāvaruṇa (assistant of the Hotar)?—Who the Udgātar? — Who the partners in the feast?—Which the sacrificial utensils?—Which the sacrificial food?—Which the sacrificial bed?—Which the northern fire-hearth?—Which the Iḍā(Milk-offering)?—Which the Somavat?—Which the cart?—Which the sacrificial animal? Which the Dhārāpotar (stream-strainer)?—Which the grass-bunch?—Which the Sruva-laddle?—Which the pot of the clarified butter?—Which the two sprinklings of fat?—Which the two portions of the sacrificial clarified butter (for Agni and Soma)? —Which the preceding offering?—Which the subsequent offering?—Which the recitation of the hymns?—Which the Śaṁyor formula?—Which the Ahiṁsā (non-injury of the Yajamāna through a wrongly applied formula, Ait. Br. 1, 30, 11)?—Which the Patnī-saṁyājas (offerings made to the wives of the gods)?—Which the sacrificial post?—Which the sacrificial rope?—Which the Iṣṭis?—What the reward of the sacrifice? Which the concluding bath?

4

In this sacrifice offered in the body, adorned with sacrificial posts and sacrificial ropes the Ātman is the sacrificer;—the Buddhi his wife;—the Vedas the chief Ṛtvij;—the Prāṇa the Brāhmaṇācchaṁsin;—the Apāna the Pratiprasthātar;—the Samāna the Maiṭrāvaruṇa;—the Udāna the Udgātar;—the Ahaṁkāra the Adhvaryu; the mind the Hotar;—the body the sacrificial bed;—the nose the northern fire-hearth;—the head the Somavat;—the right hand the Sruva-ladle:—the left hand the pot of the clarified butter;—the ears the two sprinklings of fat;—the eyes the two portions of the sacrificial clarified butter;—the neck the Dhārā-strainer;—the subtle elements (*tanmātra*) the partners in the feast;—the gross elements the preceding offering;—the elements the subsequent offering; the tongue the Iḍā;—teeth and lips the recitation of the hymns;—the roof of the mouth the Śaṁyor-formula;—memory, compassion, patience and non-injury (ahiṁsā) are the four Patnī-Saṁyājas:[1]—the sound

1. According to this the *ahiṁsā* occurs, indeed, twice in the answer, while the question about the *Ahiṁsā* has remained undisposed of.

Om the sacrificial post;—the hope the sacrificial rope;—the Manas the cart;—the desire the sacrificial animal;—the hair the bunch of grass;—the organs of sense the sacrificial utensils; —the organs of activity the sacrificial food;—the non-injury (*ahiṁsā*) the Iṣṭis;—the renouncing the reward of the sacrifice; —the concluding bath results through death.

All the godheads, indeed, there are
Enclosed in this body here !
He who passes away in Benares[1]
Or he who reads this sacred text
To such a man after this life
The liberation will surely come,
—The liberation will surely come.

---

1. As I was wondering in Benares that so many old people often travelled to Benares with great sacrifice and hardships in order to lay down their lives there, Pandit Priyanatha explained to me that this was so because he who dies in Benares attains liberation.—"How can you, a learned man, cling to such a superstition !" I exclaimed; "you know as well as I that according to the Vedānta one who has attained knowledge is liberated no matter where he dies, and that without knowledge liberation is not possible even if one were to die in Benares !"— "It is true" he replied in tones of deep conviction, "but it is particularly a special grace of Śiva that all those who die in Benares come into possession of the knowledge at the moment of their death".

PIṆḌA UPANIṢAD

[The Gods and Ṛṣis asked the (personal) Brahmán two questions :

1. How can the dead ones receive the meal-balls (*piṇḍa*) because they are without any consciousness (*acetasaḥ*))?

2. When the body is dissolved into elements on death, where does the soul (*haṁsa*) live ?

The answer to the second question is given first (verse 3).

After the death the soul lives for three days (*tryaham* to be read everywhere with the Poona Edition) in water, three in fire, three in ether and one in wind, who then (thus we have probably to understand) at the end of the tenth day as *phukhopomp ós* brings it [the soul] to its destination as in Bṛh. 3, 3, 2.

As a reply to the first question Brahman describes how through the offerings of ten meal-balls the organs and functions of the body are gradually given back to the dead. According to the scholiast and according to a related passage from the Garuḍapurāṇam cited by him this offering of the ten Piṇḍas takes place on ten successive days, may be the same ten days spoken of in the answers to the second question, or ten days following them.

Presupposing the correctness of this statement, the whole ritual cannot naturally refer to the Śrāddha offering (in which on every new moon day water is poured in three earth cavities of the breadth of a hand and three meal-balls for the father, the grand-father and the great grand-father are placed), but it must be understood as belonging to the activity previous to it, through which the individual departed one first becomes capable of participating in future in the Piṇḍa-offerings made to the manes on every new moon day.]

1. The gods all and the wise
To Brahman asked this question:
"How can the dead receive
Without consciousness their balls of meal ?"

2. "And when into the five great elements
The body dissolving returns back,
And the soul (*haṁsa*) departs from it
At which place does it abide then ?"—
Brahmán spoke:

3. "In water it stays for three days.
Three days it stays in fire,

Then it goes through the ether three days
And for a day then in the wind.

4. Then with the first meal-ball
The atoms reassemble again;
And with the second meal-ball
Originate new flesh, skin and blood;

5. And with the third meal-ball
Consciousness (*mati*) originates in him anew;
And with the fourth meal-ball
Originate the bones and the marrow;

6. And with the fifth meal-ball
Hands and fingers, head and mouth;
And with the sixth meal-ball
Are formed the heart, neck, palate;

7. By the seventh meal-ball
Vitality for a long life;
And with the eighth meal-ball
He attains the power of speech;

8. And with the ninth meal-ball
All organs are tightened,
And with the tenth meal-ball
Come the powers anew in the stream;

9. Thus is formed through the offerings of balls
A new body from ball to ball."

ĀTMA UPANIṢAD

[The doctrine of the three Ātmans or Selves, the external Self (the body), the innerself (the individual soul), and the highest Self (the highest Brahman), which had found its expression in a beautiful poetic form in the Prajāpati myth, Chānd. 8, 7-12, is here handled in the most dry scholasticism through an enumeration of the parts of the body, properties and functions of the three Selves in the course of which there are considerable back-references to the older Upaniṣads.]

1

Then spoke Aṅgiras:

Man is threefold, namely external Self, inner Self and the highest Self.

That Self in which there are skin, bones, flesh, marrow, hair, fingers, thumbs, vertebral column, nails, ankles, belly, navel, genitals, hips, thighs, cheeks, brows, forehead, arms, sides, head arteries, eyes and ears, and that which is born and dies, that is called the external Self.

2

Now the inner Self:

The one, who

on the one hand through [the perceptions of] the earth, the water, the wind, the fire, the ether, as also through desire, hate, lust, pain, greed, delusion, misunderstanding etc., while he possesses the characteristic of memory,[1] on the other hand through speaking—with a high tone, low tone, short, long, extra long, faltering, shouting, blurting out,—through dancing, singing, playing, swooning, yawning etc., becomes a listener, smeller, taster, thinker, perceiver, and doer, and who as the conscious Self, as Person (*puruṣa*) knows to distinguish in the activities of hearing– whether it is a Purāṇam, Nyāya, Mīmāṁsā or Dharmaśāstra—, of smelling, drawing towards oneself,

it is this one who is called the inner Self.

1. I follow the reạding of the Poona ed., which is supported by a remark (dropped in the *Bibl. Ind.*) of the commentator.

3

Now the highest Self:

The one, who

to be worshipped according to the constituents [of the word *Om*] while one meditates over him (—*cintakam* adverbial) as one's self, by breath-control, withdrawing inwards from the objects of sense, meditation and Yoga-practices, as seed of the fig tree (Chānd. 6, 12, 1), as seed of the millet (Chānd. 3, 14, 3), is not comprehended or grasped through a hundred-thousandfold splitting of the hair's end (Śvet. 5, 9., Dhyānabindu 6) and the like who is not born and who does not die (Kāṭh. 2,18), does not wither up (Chānd. 6, 11, 2) and is not burnt (Chānd 6, 16, 2), does not shake (Praśna 5,6., Yogaśikhā 1), is not divided (Chānd 6.12.1) and is not split up (Bhag. G. 2, 23), who is the Guṇa-less observer (Śvet. 6,11), the pure, limbless Ātman, the subtle, partless, spotless (Śvet. 6, 19), free from self-illusion (Maitr. 6, 30) free from sound, touch, taste, form and smell, changeless (Brahmb. 8), desireless, all-penetrating (Śvet. 1-16), he, the inconceivable and indescribable, who purifies the impure and the unholy, whom no work sticks nor the effect of a work—that is the highest Self, the Puruṣa,—that is the highest Self, the Puruṣa!

1. In the editions available to me, thirtyone stanzas follow here, source of which are met with elsewhere such as the *Māṇḍūkyopaniṣat-Kārikā* and the *Vivekacūḍāmaṇi*.

SARVA-UPANIṢATSĀRA[1]

[Like the *'óroi, Definitions* in the corpus of the Platonic writings, some very late and secondary writings occupy a similar position in the collection of the Upaniṣads which, on the basis of the older Upaniṣads, particularly as it appears, enumerate and explain the main concepts of the Vedānta system for the purpose of teaching and learning. The *Nirālamba-Upaniṣad* treated by Weber (*Ind. Stud.* XVII, 136-160) is of such a kind, which discusses 29 basic concepts; the *Śārīraka-Upaniṣad* proceeds in a more classifying way; and the *Nirvāṇa-Upaniṣad*, difficult to judge, also seems to belong to this circle. —Our *Sarva-Upaniṣat-sāra*, or also called *Sarva-Upaniṣad* which occurs not only in Colebrooke's and Nārāyaṇa's collections, but also as Sarb (not to be confused with *Sarbsar*) in the *Oupanekhat* and as *Sarvasāra* in the *Muktikā* collection, has received greater recognition than the above three included only in the Muktikā collection. It explains on the basis of older Upaniṣadic passages yet with an independent attitude, following twentythree terms :

1-4 : *bandha* and *mokṣa*, *avidyā* and *vidyā*;

5-8 : The four states in the Māṇḍūkya;

9-13 : The five sheaths in the Taitt. 2;

14-16 : *kartar*, *jīva*, *kṣetrajña*;

17-19 : *sākṣin*, *kūṭastha*, *antaryāmin*;

20-22 : *pratyagātman*, *paramātman*, *ātman*;

23 : *māyā*.]

Om!

1. What is the bondage ?
2. What is liberation ?
3. What is ignorance ?
2. What is knowledge ?

5-8. What are the states waking, dreaming, deep sleep and Turyam ?

9-13. What is the sheath consisting of food,
Consisting of breath, consisting of Manas,
Consisting of perception, consisting of bliss ?

1. Named in some editions as *sarvasāropaniṣat*. — GBP

14-19. What is the doer, Jīva, Kṣetrajña,
On-looker, standing on high, inner guide ?

20-23. What is the inner Ātman, the highest
Ātman, the Ātman and the Māyā ?

1. The Ātman is God. When however one fancies the body, etc. which is not the Ātman to be the Ātman then this fancy is called bondage.

2. The annihilation of this fancy is the liberation (*mokṣa*).

3. What brings about this fancy is the ignorance (*avidyā*).

4. That through which the fancy is annihilated is the knowledge (*vidyā*).

5. When one perceives gross objects like sound, etc. by means of the fourteen organs beginning with Manas, which unfold outwards and which are supported by deities like Āditya, then this is called the waking (*jāgaraṇam*) of the Ātman.

6. When one, freed from the impressions of waking, perceives only by means of four organs [Manas, Buddhi, Cittam, Ahaṁkāra] without the sound, etc. being there, sound etc. based upon those impressions then that is called the dreaming (*svapnam*, here neuter!) of the Ātman.

7. When one in consequence of the reposing of all fourteen organs[1] and out of the cessation of particular objects [is without consciousness], then this is called the deep sleep (*suṣuptam*) of the Ātman.

8. When, on cessation of the three states mentioned, the spirit, standing as a spectator towards the existence, exists by itself as a non-differentiatedness freed from all existence then this spirituality is called the Turīyam (the Fourth).

9. The collection of the six sheaths (bones, marrow, fat, skin, flesh, blood) formed from food is called the sheath consisting of food (*annamaya*).

---

1. *Manas, Buddhi, Cittam, Ahaṁkāra,* five *Jñānendriyāṇi,* five *karmendriyāṇi* (*Nārāyaṇa*). *Cittam,* as a special organ also at Praśna, 4.8. Cūlikā V.14.

10. When in the sheath consisting of food there are also fourteen kinds of wind, *Prāṇa* etc. [*prāṇa, apāna, vyāna, udāna, samāna*; *nāga, kūrma, kṛkara, devadatta, dhanaṁjaya; vajrambhava, sthānamukhya, pradyota, prakṛta*], then this is called the sheath consisting of breath (*prāṇamaya*).

11. When the Ātman, bound up with these two sheaths, brings about sounds and other objects, as also the activities of imagination by means of the four organs of Manas etc. (Manas, Buddhi, Cittam, Ahaṁkara), then it is called the sheath consisting of manas (*Manomaya*).

12. When the Ātman, bound up with these three sheaths, appears as perceiving the differences and similarities based on those activities [of imagination etc.], then it is called the sheath consisting of perception (*vijñānamaya*).

13. When he remains in the knowledge that he himself is the cause of the four sheaths, as the fig seeds of the fig tree, then it is called the sheath consisting of bliss (*ānandamaya*).

14. When, supporting himself on the perception of joy and sorrow, he becomes a doer (*kartar*) within the body, then perception of the desired object becomes the perception of joy, the perception of an undesired object becomes perception of grief; but the causes of joy and sorrow are sound, touch, form, taste and smell.

15. When he brings about the separation with the present body and a union with a future body in consequence of good and bad deeds, then he is called, while he is involved with these bodies, the individual soul (*jīva*).

16. The Manas with the rest [Buddhi, Cittam, Ahaṁkāra], the Prāṇa with the rest [Apāna, Vyāna, Udāna, Samāna], the Sattvam with the rest [Rajas and Tamas], the desire with the rest[1] and the good with the rest [evil, perception, impression],

---

1. The scholiast understands the enumeration of the functions of Manas occurring at Bṛh. 1,5,3 : "desire, deciding, doubt, belief, disbelief, firmness, infirmity, shame, perception, fear"; —hardly correctly, because *icchā* is certainly no member of this series. More correctly one will have to think of *icchā, dveṣas, sukham, duḥkham* (Śaṁk. to Brahmasūtra p. 660,7) or of the five Kleśāḥ (*avidyā, asmitā, rāga, dveṣa, abhiniveśa*) of the Yoga (Yogasūtra 2,3).

—these are the five groups. The supporter of these five groups, who does not perish until the knowledge of the Ātman arises, and is perceived as eternal in the vicinity of the Ātman although it is only a determinant (*upādhi*) of the Ātman, that is called the Liṅga-body or the heart-knot; and the spirituality, which appears in it, is called the Body-knower (*kṣetrajña*).

17. The one who perceives the subject, the object and the activity of knowing in their appearance and disappearance, while he himself neither appears nor disappears but is light in himself, this is called the witness (*sākṣin*).

18. In so far as he is noticed without any distinction in the consciousness of all living beings from the Brahmān down to the ant, as being in the consciousness of all living beings, he is called the one standing on high (*kūṭastha*).

19. When the Ātman, as the cause of the natural disposition of distinctions endowed with the one standing-on-high etc., appears interwoven in all bodies, as a thread through a string of pearls, then he is called inner guide (*antaryāmin*).

20. When the Ātman, freed from all determinants, like pure gold, appears in its nature as consisting of knowledge and spirit then it is called inner Ātman (*pratyagātman*) denoted by the word "thou" [in *tat tvam asi*].

21. The Brahman is real, knowledge, unending, bliss. Real i.e. imperishable is that which does not perish simultaneously when the name, place, time, body and the cause perish. This imperishable one is further called knowledge, that is to say as the spirituality not subject to the origination and destruction, i.e. as knowledge. Further it is called unending that is to say, as the clay in the case of clay utensils, the gold in the case of gold products, the thread in the case of the texture, similarly the spiritual one precedes all objects coming from the unmanifest one and penetrates them all, and as such is called unending. Further, it is called bliss: the one consisting of joy and spirituality, the infinite ocean of bliss : the one by his nature consists of joy without any distinction, is called bliss. That one, which has these four and essential factors [being, knowledge, unending, bliss] as its characteristic, and which remains immutable in space, time and causality, that one, denoted by the word "that"

[in *tat tvam asi*] is called the highest Ātman (*paramātman*) or the highest Brahman.

22. The one who is different from the word[1] "thou" affected with determinants, different from the word[1] "that" affected with determinants, is pure and absolute like ether, and consists only of existence, is designated as the self (the essence, the soul, the Ātman) of the word "that".[2]

23. The one, which is without a beginning but still is not without an end (read: *antavatī*), which behaves similarly towards valid means of knowledge and towards what are not valid means of knowledge, what is not existent, yet not non-existent, nor existent and non-existent, which does not exist inasmuch as one imagines the cause (i.e. Brahman) for the created object arising out of what itself is not created, and which exists in so far as one does not imagine it (remaining on empirical plane), what defies all these characteristics is named delusion (*māyā*).[3]

---

1. Rather "different from the content of the word 'thou' and of the word 'tat' ". —GBP.

2. There seems to be some confusion here in the German original. The paragraph, which I have translated literally, is not quite clear to me. —Besides the editions available to me speak of param Brahma, and not of the Ātman. —GBP.

3. The editions available to me add a number of verses here. —GBP

GĀRUḌA UPANIṢAD

[This snake-charm, named after Garuḍa, the bird of Viṣṇu and the sworn enemy of snakes, owes its inclusion in the Upaniṣads probably to the seriousness which the danger from being bitten by snakes still possesses in India down to the present day. It is not so much for the European who is equipped with strong footwares and who can avoid to go out in dark. It is however all the more for the natives who must wander with naked feet at night or must perform their work in fields or forests in which case the possibility of treading over a snake inadvertently and consequently to be bitten by him is not small. The danger is increased through the commandment of Ahiṁsā which does not allow an orthodox Hindu to kill a snake but only to take him, at his own peril, and to carry it there where in his opinion it can do no harm. Also in the masonry of old houses snakes not seldom nest, without being exterminated by the inmates of the house, because on account of a widespread superstition people see souls of the ancestors in them and there is also the rumour that they never do any harm to the house-mates.

The present snake charm, raised to the dignity of an Upaniṣad has a double purpose, to guard one against a snake-bite as also to obviate evil effects of a snake-bite when it has taken place.

Our translation follows the recension given in Jacob's edition (*Eleven Ātharvaṇa Upaniṣads* pp. 83-88). Weber has edited our Upaniṣad in an enlarged form (*Ind. Stud.* XVII, 161ff).]

1

Om !

I will preach the Brahman-science. Brahmán taught it to Nārada, Nārada to Bṛhatsena, Bṛhatsena to Indra, Indra to Bhāradvāja, Bhāradvāja to his pupils who desired to preserve their life.

2

[He taught them the science] which achieves this, which achieves good, removes poison, destroys poison, overcomes poison, annihilates poison:

"*Struck is the poison, annihilated is the poison, destroyed is the poison; it is struck by Indra's thunder-bolt, svāhā! May it originate from snakes, from vipers, from scorpions, from cankers, from salamanders, from amphibious animals or from rats.*

May you be Anantaka's messenger, or be Anantaka himself,[1]
May you be Vāsuki's messenger, or be Vāsuki himself,
May you be Takṣaka's messenger, or be Takṣaka himself,
May you be Karkoṭaka's messenger, or be Karkoṭaka himself,
May you be Śaṁkhapulika's messenger, or be Śaṁkhapulika himself,
May you be Padmaka's messenger, or be Padmaka himself,
May you be Mahāpadmaka's messenger, or be Mahāpadmaka himself,
May you be Elāpatraka's messenger, or Elāpatraka himself,
May you be Mahailāpatraka's messenger, or be Mahailāpatraka himself,
May you be Kālika's messenger, or be Kālika himself,
May you be Kulika's messenger, or be Kulika himself,
May you be Kambalāśvatara's messenger, or be Kambalāśvatara himself !"

3

For twelve years snakes do not bite him who hears this great science on the new-moon night. The snakes do not bite him as long as he lives who, having recited this great science on the new-moon night, wears it [as an amulet].

He who teaches it to eight Brāhmaṇas, he releases (from the effects of snake-bite) by merely touching with grass, with a piece of wood, with ashes. One who teaches it to a hundred Brāhmaṇas he releases by a mere glance. One who teaches it to a thousand Brāhmaṇas, he releases by the mere thought, — by the mere thought.

Thus spake the exalted Brahmán, —the exalted Brahmán.

Thus is the Gāruḍa-Upaniṣad.

1. At the end of the formula of exorcism follows this enumeration of twelve chief snakes.

b. Yoga Upaniṣads

BRAHMAVIDYĀ UPANIṢAD

KṢURIKĀ UPANIṢAD

CŪLIKĀ UPANIṢAD

NĀDABINDU UPANIṢAD

BRAHMABINDU UPANIṢAD

AMṚTABINDU UPANIṢAD

DHYĀNABINDU UPANIṢAD

TEJOBINDU UPANIṢAD

YOGAŚIKHĀ UPANIṢAD

YOGATATTVA UPANIṢAD

HAṀSA UPANIṢAD

BRAHMAVIDYĀ UPANIṢAD[1]

[*Brahmavidyā Upaniṣad*, "the esoteric teaching of the science of Brahman", with this much promising name denotes this small Upaniṣad consisting of only 14 ślokas in our recension (in the Telugu ed. it has about eight times the expanse of this). But once in the older Upaniṣads the complete imperceptibility of the Brahman had been already taught (*neti* ! *neti* ! — *yato vāco nivartante,—avijñātam vijānatām*, etc.), a proper science of Brahman could no more be formulated. For it would then be as a science of the symbol under which the imperceptible Brahman was looked at and worshipped. Already since Kāṭh. 2,15 the old sacrificial syllable *Om*, consisting of three moras (*mātrā-s*) $a+u+m$ serves as this symbol, to which was added as a $3\frac{1}{2}$th mora the buzzing reverberation (*nāda*) of *m*, which, along with this latter, was denoted by a point (*bindu*) of Anusvāra placed above the syllable. This syllable Om as a symbol of the Brahman had an advantage of keeping away from the Brahman all predicates of the external world on account of its (Om's) being completely without any meaning. But it had also the disadvantage in that it could not put any limits to unbridled fancy. As in the case of so many other Upaniṣads of the Atharvaveda, a probe into it also appears here.

The Introduction (verses 1-3) proclaims the intention to impart the Brahman-lore, in which the origination and the course of all things are recognized through and in Brahmán, Viṣṇu and Śiva (verse 1). Particularly it is the esoteric doctrines of Viṣṇu and his human incarnations which are glorified as the Dhruva fire in the Brahman-lore. *Dhruva* (constant) is, like *Akṣaram* (imperishable, syllable) a characterization of the highest essence (*dhruvaṁ Viṣṇusaṁjñitam*, Maitr. 6.38) and thereby that of the sound Om also (cf. Rāmatap. Up. ed. Weber p. 335, 14 and Mahābh. 1, 24,30[2] *dhruva-akṣaram*). The Om sound particularly is, as verse 3 declares, the Brahman, whose knowledge is to be taught here, and this

---

1. On the order of sequence. As the second class of the Atharva-Upaniṣads, we let follow, maintaining again the order of sequence in Nārāyaṇa and Colebrooke, the eleven Yoga-Upaniṣads admitted by them. The first of these groups (3-5) is formed by *Brahmavidyā*, *Kṣurikā*, *Cūlikā*, the second (17-23) by *Nādabindu*, *Brahmabindu*, *Amṛtabindu*, *Dhyānabindu*, *Tejobindu*, *Yogaśikhā*, *Yogatattva*, the third by the *Haṁsa-Upaniṣad* standing by itself. The contents of the last-named one show that it is much later than the others, which also corresponds to its position; in the case of the remaining, their sequence in the collections mentioned may hardly correspond accurately to the time of their origination.

2. =1.57.85 (The Critical Ed. by the BORI). —GBP.

consists of 1) *śarīram,* the body, 2) *sthānam,* the location, 3) *kāla,* the time i.e. here the terminus, 4) *laya,* the vanishing of the Om sound from perception. Herewith the four parts of the Upaniṣad (verses 4-7. 8-10. 11-12. 13-14) are shown in advance.

I. *Śarīram,* the body of the sound Om, verses 4-7. As such are mentioned :

	Three Vedas :	three fires :	three worlds :	three gods
Body of the *a*-sound :	Ṛgveda	Gārhapatya	earth	Brahman(n)
,, ,, *u*-sound :	Yajurveda	Dakṣiṇa	mid-region	Viṣṇu
,, ,, *m*-sound :	Sāmaveda	Āhavanīya	heaven	Śiva.

In addition to this comes the 3½th mora which is merely mentioned (verse 4). The arrangement is as in Praśna 5.

II. *sthānam,* location of the sound Om, verses 8-10. Within the 'brain-conch' (*śaṅkha*) shines the *a*-sound as the sun; in it (shines) the *u*-sound as the moon; further, (we have probably so to understand) the *m*-sound shines in it as the fire while the 3½th mora rises from it as a pointed flame (*śikhā*). (cf. Maitr. 6,38).

III. *kāla,* the time, i.e. probably the terminus of the sound Om, verses 11-12.

The meaning of these verses, which are very problematic in text and interpretation, seems to be this : resembling the sun, and comparable also to a pointed flame in splendour is also the artery *suṣumnā* : when the end (*kāla*) approaches, the sound Om breaks through the sun in the brain described above (verse 8) as also through the 72000 remaining arteries and reaches (on to that Suṣumnā), penetrating in the head (*bhittvā mūrdhani*) through the Brahmarandhram to the point where it becomes the all-creator and all-penetrating.

IV. *laya,* the vanishing of the sound Om, verses 13-14.

Just as a metal utensil or a gong, when struck, gives out a sound which fades away slowly, similarly one should let the sound Om also die away slowly; the peace (*śānti*) in which it fades away, is the highest Brahman; for the sound Om (*dhruva*) is Brahman and helps towards immortality.]

INTRODUCTION

1. I proclaim the Brahman-lore,
   Which is omniscience, which the highest;
   It shows as origination and end
   Brahman, Viṣṇu Maheśvara.

2. Viṣṇu, working with his miraculous power,
   Becomes, at intervals, a human being through compassion,
   His secret, as the Om-fire,
   Lies in the Brahman-lore.

3. The syllable Om is the Brahman,
Thus, verily, teach the Brahman-knowers;
Body, location, time and dying away
Of this syllable, I will proclaim.

I. The body (*śarīram*) of the sound Om.

4. There are three gods and three worlds,
Three Vedas and three fires,
Three moras and the half mora
In that trisyllabic, blissful one.

5. The Ṛgveda, Gārhapatya,
The earth and Bráhman as god,
That is the body of the *a*-sound
As expounded by the Brahman-knowers.

6. The Yajurveda and the mid-region,
And the fire Dakṣiṇa,
And the holy god Viṣṇu
Thus is the *u*-sound proclaimed to us.

7. The Sāmaveda and heaven,
The Āhavanīya fire also,
And Īśvara, the highest god
Thus is the *m*-sound proclaimed to us.

II. The location (*sthānam*) of the sound Om

8. In the midst of the brain-conch
Like the sunshine glitters the *a*;
Within it is situated
The *u*-sound of moonlike splendour.

9. The *m*-sound too, like the fire,
Smokeless, resembling a lightning flash —
Thus shine the three moras
Like the moon, the sun, and the fire.

10. Thereupon a pointed flame
Like a torch light exists;
Know it as the half mora
Which one writes above the syllable.

III. The terminus (*Kāla*) of the sound Om.

11. Yet one, like a pointed flame
Subtle, like lotus-fibre, shines
The sunlike cerebral artery
[Passing through it] penetrates [the Om].

12. Through the sun and seventytwo thousand
Arteries, breaks through the head,
And remains as bringer of blessings to all,
Pervading the whole universe.

IV. The vanishing, the fading away (*laya*) of the sound Om.

13. And just as the sound of a metal utensil
Or of a gong dies in silence,
So he, who seeks the All,
Lets the Om-sound fade away in silence.

14. For that wherein the sound fades away,
Is the Brahman, the higher;
Yea, the whole sound is Brahman
And conduces to immortality.

KṢURIKĀ UPANIṢAD

[This passage is named "The esoteric doctrine of the *kṣurikā* (sc. *dhāraṇā*), of concentration which cuts like a razor (*kṣura*)". Along with the features of the Yogic practice well known from other Upaniṣads (the place and the way of sitting verse 2; the withdrawing of the Manas from sense objects and locking it up in the heart, verse 3; three kinds of breath-regulation, *pūraka, kumbhaka, recaka,* verses 4-5), it contains an original thought, the details of which are often difficult to indicate on account of the uncertainty of readings, grammatical incorrectness of diction and the defectiveness of the commentary.

The Yogin has to detach himself not only from all external objects, but also from his own corporeality. This detachment appears as a successive cutting away of the individual parts of the body which is accomplished by means of the Manas as a razor (*kṣura*, verse 11, —hardly consistent with the locking up of the mind in the heart, verse 3) through a process in which attention is concentrated (*dhāraṇā*) on the individual parts of the body and thereby one secludes himself from them successively (*nirodha;* in verses 6-7 *dve* should be supplemented by *dhāraṇe* and *trayas,* as the scholiast states, by *nirodhāḥ*). Thus one detaches oneself successively from one's toes, ankles, knees, anus and penis and reaches to the navel; from here along the *suṣumnā* (already Chānd. 8,6,6, although not mentioned with this name, but as the 101st main artery) to the heart and further in the neck where the Suṣumnā serves as the support (*taittilam,* pillow) of all other arteries and is specially surrounded and protected by two of these, viz. *Iḍā* and *Piṅgalā.* One again cuts away all other arteries with the mind-razor and goes along the suṣumnā upwards and out, while one leaves behind in it all good and bad states (*bhāva*), one as it were stuffs the Suṣumnā-pillow with them (verse 20; cf. Sāṁkhyakārikā verse 40; *bhāvair adhivāsitam liṅgam*). Since in this way one cuts off all parts of the body by meditative concentration on them, one breaks all the chains of the Saṁsāra and is no more required to be born again (verses 21-24). —Particularly striking is the application of *dhāraṇā,* which otherwise means fettering of the mind, here however the concentration of attention on the individual parts of the body for the purpose of detachment from them. Similarly striking is the contradiction related with it and which is already mentioned, viz. that the Manas is locked up in the heart (verse 3), and at the same time it is supposed to be a razor (*kṣura*) with which one cuts off the individual parts of the body, from which the whole Upaniṣad has received its name.]

1. The cutting concentration I will proclaim
For accomplishing the Yoga,
He who attains it as a Yogin,
Is no more born again.

2. As the main contents of the Veda,
As precept, Svayaṁbhū expressed this;
Choosing a silent place,
And a proper kind of posture,

3. Like a tortoise one draws in the limbs,
Locks up the Manas in the heart;
Employing the twelve moras[1]
Under Om-saying gradually

4. The whole body one fills with breath,
And shuts all its doors,
Leaning by degrees to the heart,
Breast, hips, face and neck.

5. Thus lets the Yogin flow in
The breath, which goes through the nose;
After the breath has stayed in the body,
He releases it slowly again.

6. Through fixed moras making steady
The breath, first in the big toes,
Then in the two ankles, two calves,
Three to the right, three to the left,[2] deepening,

7. Then in the knees and thies,
Anus and penis, two times three,[2]
Finally one enters the location of the breath,
The region of the navel.

---

1. Cf. Nādabindu, verses 8-11.
2. "Accomplishing three restraints (*nirodhāḥ*) every time". (Schol.)

8. There is the Suṣumnā artery,
Many arteries surround it.
Pale red, yellow and black,
And from deep red to dark red.

9. But one should slip into the subtle
And delicate white artery,
There upwards climbs the vital breath,
As a spider along a filament.

10. So he comes to the great seat of the Puruṣa,
Which looks like a lotus red,
Which as "the little lotus flower"
The Vedānta texts delineate to us.

11. Penetrating through it, along that artery
He ascends to the neck.
And seizes the sharp razor of Manas,
Shining bright with knowledge,

12. Sharpens it and cuts off completely
The forms and names,
And through Manas, the sharp,
Gives himself permanently to the Yoga.

13. Glorious like Indra's thunderbolt,
One praises the joints and legs as firm,
Until through power of meditation, through Yoga,
Through concentration he cuts them off.

14. Shifting himself into the thies,
He cuts off the breath and the joints,
Through Yoga, repeated four times,
Without hesitation cutting them off.

15. Then gathers together within the neck
The Yogin his host of arteries,
Of which a hundred and one
Are regarded as the best of them.

16. Where on the left guards Iḍā
And on the right the Piṅgalā,
Between them is the chief spot;
He who knows it, knows the Veda.

17. Dustless, entering into Brahman,
The Suṣumnā is related to it,
It's the pillow on which rest
The seventytwo thousand [arteries].

18. The concentration-Yoga splits everything,
The Suṣumnā it splits not.
With the lightning-sharp razor of Yogic power
Which shines like the fire.

19. He should split the hundred arteries,
The wise one here on earth itself.
And just as with Jasmine flowers
A pillow is perfumed.

20. So the Yogin stuffs the artery
With states good and bad.
Thus prepared he moves off,
From future birth liberated.

21. Then, well conscious in the mind,
He chooses a quiet place,
Freed from worldly inclination and expectation,
A real knower of Yoga, by and by.

22. Just as a bird, cutting the cord,
Soars fearless into the sky,
So the soul, cutting the cord,
Rises above the Saṁsāra.

23. Just as a flame, having burnt,
At extinction comes to nought,
So the Yogin, having burnt
His actions all, comes to nought.

24. Who as a Yogin with the razor,
Pointed with breath-control, sharp with moras,
Sharpened on the stone of renunciation,
Cuts the cord in two, remains free.

25. He attains immortality,
Who frees himself from desires,
Who, giving up all wishes,
Cuts the cord in two, remains free.

CŪLIKĀ UPANIṢAD[1]

[*Cūlikā* (from *cūlā*, *cūḍā* "the tip" in a variety of meanings) is, according to the introductory verse of the commentary, "pointed top of a pillar". The pillar (we may perhaps explain it so) would be probably the Sāṁkhya philosophy and its tip the theism of the Yoga in which our author makes the Sāṁkhya philosophy end. At first he stands on the ground of the Sāṁkhya doctrine, certainly not the same as we know it from the Sāṁkhya-kārikā and the Sūtras, but of an older form as appears, e.g. in the Maitr. 5 (cf. our introduction there), which does not yet bluntly contrast the Puruṣa with the Prakṛti, but makes him develop out of the Sattva. Similarly our author declares the Puruṣa as "staying in the Sattvam" (verse 2) and portrays him (if our interpretation of verses 3-4 is agreed upon) as the one who with the Prakṛti creates the world, but then as an infant sucks at her breast, and that he can be observed only in this condition (*aśakyaḥ so 'nyathā draṣṭum*). Among the numerous soul-infants, who thus drink the sense-objects, is a soul who, as God (the Īśvara of the theistic Yoga system), enjoys her at will, and who is seen as eating the sweet berry by the Snātakas and the Adhvaryus at the sacrifice (according to Ṛgv. 1,164,20,22), but in reality is entirely devoid of activity (*udāsīna;* verse 8). Besides the sacrifice of the Adhvaryus, all the Śāstras of the Bahvṛcas and all the seven Stomas of the Chandogas also are meant for him (verse 9), but particularly the Saṁhitā and the Brāhmaṇa of the Atharvaveda extols him as Brahman in the esoteric teaching of the Mantras "with a series of designations" (*pada-krama-samanvitam*, verse 10). This series is then presented in verses 11-13; the Brahman appears as :

brahmacārin Atharvav. 11,5 (*Gesch. d. Phil*, I, 277-282);

vrātya, a wandering ascetic, Atharvav. 15;

skambha, a pillar, Atharvav. 10,7.8 (*Gesch. d. Phil.* I, 310-324);

palita, the "grey with age", Atharvav. 9,9.10 (Ṛgv. 1, 164; *Gesch. d. Phil.* I, 105-119);

anaḍvān, bull, Atharvav. 4,11 (*Gesch. d. Phil.* I, 231-233);

rohita, the red one who has arisen (the sun-god), Atharvav. 13,1.2.3 (*Gesch. d. Phil.* I, 212-230);

ucchiṣṭa, the remaining, Atharvav. 11.7 (*Gesch. d. Phil.* I, 305-310);

kāla, the time, Atharvav. 19,53.54 (*Gesch. d. Phil.* I, 210-212);

prāṇa, the vital breath, Atharvav. 11.4 (*Gesch. d. Phil.* I, 301-305);

bhagavān ātmā, the exalted Ātman, Atharvav. 10,8,44 (*Gesch. d. Phil* I, 324);

---

1. Named Māntrika-Upaniṣad (32) in the collection of 108 Upaniṣads.

puruṣa Atharvav. 19,6 (Ṛgv. 10,90; *Gesch. d. Phil.* I, 150-158);
Śarva, Bhava, Rudra, Atharvav. 11,2;
Īśvara along with *Puruṣa* Atharvav. 19,6,4;
Prajāpati Atharvav. 4,2 and often repeated (Cf. however *Gesch. d. Phl.* I, 189-190).
Virāj Atharvav. 8,9,10;
Pṛśni (to be so read for *Pārṣṇi*) Atharvav. 2,1 (*Gesch. d. Phil* I, 253).
salilam, primordial water, Atharvav. 8,9,1.

The Atharvans know him as the Head (perhaps with reference to Atharvav. 10,2,26-27.10,8,9), while some as the 26th (the Īśvara of the Yoga along with the 25 principles of the Sāṁkhya) or as the 27th (probably by differentiating the Cittam from Buddhi, Ahaṁkāra, Manas) or as the revered one who brings to Vyaktam the 24 principles hidden in the Avyaktam (verses 14-15). But he is also one, two, three - five etc. as the verse 15 (with a reference evidently to Chānd. 7,26,2) assures, he is the source and the place of dissolution of beings. One who proclaims him (exoteric) as life-principle obtains inexhaustible food for himself and for his ancestors, one who perceives him (esoteric), whether or not he is a Brāhmaṇa, he enters into him for perennial rest.

The Upaniṣad may have found its place at a time when the theistic Yoga developed out of the Sāṁkhya doctrine which had not still been finalised systematically, and would, if this view proves to be correct, be of a special value as a proof of this transition.]

1. The bird, radiating, eight-footed[1]
Three-stranded,[2] eternal jewel,
Having flames of fire, wandering twofold,[3]—
Everyone sees him and sees him not,[3]—

2. When at the time of creatures' delusion
The darkness around God is torn,
Then He is seen in the cavern of Guṇas,
In Sattvam, by the Guṇaless one.

3. For He is not to be seen otherwise,
As when like an infant He sucks[4]

1. Illuminating the eight regions of the heaven.
2. *trisūtram*, perhaps because fettered with the three Guṇas.
3. Everyone sees Him as the sun-bird, and does not see Him as the Ātman.
4. Read *dhayamānaḥ*.

Māyā, the mother of all that becomes,
Eternal, firm, of eightfold form.[1]

4. Lying,[2] he sucks at her breast;
And again she becomes excited and broad
And brings forth for the Puruṣa,
By whom she was covered before.

5. With the cow's voice lows[3]
The procreatress, who cultivates the beings,
The black, white and red,[4]
Milking all desires for the master alone.

6. Countless indeed are the infants,
Who drink the world of senses,
But only one as God drinks her,
Freely following His own will.

7. Through his thought and deed
He enjoys first, the holy God,
The all-bestowing milch-cow,
Who is worshipped by all sacrificers.

8. In her they see the great Self
As bird, that eats the fruit,[5]
Although it eternally sits idle,
Sacrificing householders and priestly class

9. After Him, speaking, repeat
the Ṛg-singers, in tradition versed,
Him in Rathantaram, Bṛhat,
In all seven[6] applies the song.

---

1. Māyā (Prakṛti) is eightfold, perhaps in the sense of the eight forms of Śiva which occur in the Nāndī of the Śākuntalam.

2. Literally : "She (the Prakṛti) is lain upon, sucked, by him" (read *dhīyate*).

3. Cf. Ṛgv. 1,164,28 (Atharvav. 9.10.6).

4. Following Śvet. 4,5; the three Guṇas are meant.

5. Ṛgv. 1,164,20 (*Gesch. d. Phil.* I. 113).

6. The seven forms of Stoma may have been meant; Rathantaram and Bṛhat are of course Sāmans. (For the names of the seven Stomas, see *Ind. Stud.* IX, 276).

10. As Brahman in the esoteric lores
Of Mantras, in a series of words
Him proclaim the Atharvans,
The topmost sons of Bhṛgu.

11. As Brahman-student,[1] as wanderer,[2]
As supporter[3] and as grey-with-age,[4]
As bull,[5] remainder[6] and Rohita[7]
Him proclaims the Bhṛgu-work.

12. As time,[8] as Prāṇa,[9] as Ātman,[10]
The exalted one, as Puruṣa,[11]
As Śarva, Bhava and Rudra[12]
As God and Puruṣa[13] together.

13. As Pṛśni[14] and as primordial water,[15]
As Virāj[16] and prajāpati[17]
In the prescriptions[18] coupled with aphorisms
Of the Atharvans, the Lord is praised.

14. Many as the twentysixth,[19]
Also as the twentyseventh,

---

1. *Brahmacārin*, Atharvav. 11,5.
2. *Vrātya* Atharvav. 15.
3. *Skambha* 10,7,8.
4. *Palita* 9,9,10.
5. *Anaḍvān* 4,11.
6. *Ucchiṣṭa* 11,7.
7. *Rohita* 13, 1.2.3.
8. *Kāla* 19,53.54.
9. *Prāṇa* 11,4.
10. 10,8,44; *bhagavān* sums up the epithets appearing there.
11. *Puruṣa* 19,6.
12. *Śarva* (read thus), *Bhava Rudra* 11,2.
13. *Īśvara* and at the same time *Puruṣa* 19,6,4: The Poona edition reads *Syāvāśvaḥ* (Atharvav. 11,2,18) *sa-asuras tathā*; anyway *Puruṣa* occurring twice is striking.
14. *Pṛśni* 2,1; *pārṣṇi* is meaningless, because we cannot probably expect the author to have thought of something like *kena pārṣṇī* etc. 10,2,1.
15. *salilam* 8,9,1.
16. *Virāj* 8,9 and 10.
17. *Prajāpati* 2,1 and often, mostly to give a new meaning to it.
18. Perhaps refers to the Brāhmaṇas (*vidhi*) of the Atharvaveda.
19. C f. Gauḍapāda, Māṇḍūkya-Kārikā 2,26.

The Atharvans know him as the head
The Sāṁkhyas as the Guṇaless Person.

15. Who makes the Avyaktam visible
As Vyaktam, in twentyfour ways;
As one without and with duality,
As threefold, fivefold, Him they know.[1]

16. Through the eye of knowledge
The Brāhmaṇas see the One alone
Extending throughout, from Brahman
Down to the world of plants.

17. In whom is woven this universe,[2]
All that moves and does not move,
In Brahman also merges everything
As bubbles in the ocean.

18. In whom enter all the objects
Of world, in whom become invisible,
In whom they merge and emerge again
To view like so many bubbles.

19. That in body as soul he dwells,
The wise show with reason,
And that as God, again and again,
He changes His dwelling thousandwise.

20. Who, as a Brāhmaṇa true to law,
Teaches this at the time of the Śrāddha meal (Kāṭh. 3. 17),
He obtains for himself and forefathers
Food and drink inexhaustible.

21. Yea, who, Brāhmaṇa or not
Knows the Brahman and its commandment,
He disappears, entering
Into the one who rests in the Brahman,
—Into the one who rests in the Brahman.[3]

---

1. A reference to Chānd. 7,26,2.
2. Bṛh. 3,6.
3. Literally : "they are merged in the Brahman (*tatraiva*), in that [as in the case of rivers, Chānd. 6,10. Muṇḍ. 3,2,8] their mouths disappear (*līnāsyāḥ*) for a union with the one who [already] exists in the Brahman-ocean (*brahmaśāyine*, Dative of purpose)."

NĀDABINDU UPANIṢAD

[*Nāda* the tone, especially the buzzing nasal sound, in which the word Om fades away; —*bindu* the point, especially that of the Anusvāra, which denotes the third mora of the sound Om as also its reverberation as 3½th mora; —therefore *nādabindu-upaniṣad* "the secret meaning of the nasal-point".

The philosophical rigour, with which the older Upaniṣads had excluded all identifications of the empirical reality from the Brahman (*neti, neti*), brought with it that in order to satisfy the necessity of worship one had to catch hold of symbols and, as remarked above, in the interest of philosophical truth there was nothing at all wrong if, as a symbol, such a meaningless thing as the word Om with its three or later three and a half moras ($a+u+m+$reverberation) came to be chosen. According to our Upaniṣad the true Yoga, and with it the way to salvation consists in the meditation of this Om along with the renouncing of all sense perception, through the Indriyas and the Manas (verse 18) and the annihilation of attachment to the world of sense (verse 19).

In the first part (verses 1-6a) the Ātman appears, with an appeal to the Atharvav. 13,3,14 (*Gesch. d. Phil.* I, 228), as the bird (*haṁsa*) which "spreads its wings broad like thousand days" and carries the Yogin on high. The 3½ moras of the word Om and the three Guṇas of the Sāṁkhya doctrine are designated the parts of the body of this bird, *dharma* and *adharma* (it observes the right and the wrong of men) its eyes, and its body extends upwards through all the seven worlds : *bhūr*, *bhuvaḥ*, *svar*, *mahar* (cf. Taitt. 1,5), *jana(r)loka*, *tapoloka*, *satyaloka* (cf. with Muṇḍ 1,2,3 above).

Further (verses 6b-7) it is taught, that of the 3½ moras of the word Om, *a* is dedicated to Agni, *u* to Vāyu, *m* to the sun, and the reverberation to Varuṇa.

Each of these four moras, the text thus goes on (verses 8-11), has a threefold aspect (is *kalātrayānanā*), from which originate the following twelve objects of meditation :

ghoṣinī,	—	*vidyunmālī*,	—	*pataṅgī*,
vāyuveginī	—	*nāmadheyā*,	—	*aindrī*,
vaiṣṇavī,	—	*śāṁkarī*,	—	*mahatī*,
dhruvā,	—	*maunī*,	—	*brāhmī*.

According as one meditates on one of these twelve forms at the time of death, —thus the development in verses 12-17 is in evident imitation of Praśna 5, —one attains, as his reward :

king in India, —Yakṣa, —to become a Vidyādhara, to become a Gandharva,— Somaloka, —communion with Indra, communion with

Viṣṇu, — Rudra (Paśupati), Maharloka, dhruvam, — Tapoloka, —Brahman;

from where only then he reaches the Brahman which is *sadoditam* (=*sakṛdvibhātam*, Chānd. 8,4,2), from where the luminaries rise (Kāṭh. 5,15, the germ already in Ṛv. 10.121,6).]

The Ātman as bird

1. Its right wing is the *a* sound,
The *u* is its left wing,
The *m*-sound is its tail-feathers,
The half mora is its head.

2. Rajas and Tamas its feet,
The Sattva is called its body,
Righteousness is its right,
Its left eye is the wrong.

3. At his feet is Bhūrloka,
At his knees Bhuvarloka,
Svarloka at the hip region,
At the navel is the Mahar-world.

4. At the heart is Jana(r)loka,
At his neck the Tapas-world,
Between his forehead and the brows
Is located the Satyaloka.

5. "He spreads to a thousand days' width"
In this hymn (Atharvav. 13,3,14) he is meant,
It is the bird on which ascends
The knower of the Yoga.

6. He is not slave to work,
Him do not bind many a thousand sins.

The three and half moras of the word Om

The first mora is sacred to Agni,
To the Vāyu the one that follows;

7. The mora, which comes as the third,
Has the lustre of the solar orb.
The three and halfth, the highest
The wise name it after Varuṇa.

The twelve partial moras of the word Om

8. Each of three moras has its own
Aspect in three parts;
That's how the Om sound is interpreted,
Listen to it with attention and thoughtfulness.

9. The first mora is rich in sound,
The second is wreathed with lightning,
As third follows the flight-enjoyer,
The fourth is swift as wind.

10. The fifth is the namable,
The sixth is called sacred-to-Indra,
The seventh after the God Viṣṇu,
after Śaṁkara (Śiva) the eighth is called.

11. The ninth is called great,
The tenth is regarded as the firm,
The eleventh is the silent,
The twelfth is called the Brāhmic.

Reward for the meditation at the time of death

12. Meditating on the first mora,
If one gives up life,
Then in the Bhārata Varṣa
He is born as a sovereign king.

13. Who in the second departs,
Becomes a high-souled Yakṣa,
The third makes a Vidyādhara,
A Gandharva the fourth one.

14. And who, while giving up the life,
Meditates on the fifth mora,
He lives among gods, he roams
In the Somaloka magnificently.

15. The meditator of the sixth with Indra,
Of the seventh, with Viṣṇu,
With Rudra, with Paśupati lives he,
Who meditates on the eighth.

16. The ninth leads to the World-of-greatness[1]
The tenth to the firm place,
The eleventh to the Tapoloka,
To the eternal Brahman the twelfth.

17. And then to the pure, partless,
Omnipresent, holy,
To the eternal light of Brahman,
From which the luminaries originate.

The Yoga and its reward

18. When, free from senses and Guṇas.
The Manas is dissolved in itself,
Not comparing, not imagining—
That is called the correct art of Yoga.

19. Serving him and attached to him,
He is gradually liberated from the body
prospering in the Yogic practice,
Free from all worldly attachment.

20. Then all bonds are loosened,
And pure, unstained and free,
Becoming Brahman, he goes there through
Into the highest bliss,
Into the highest bliss.

1. i.e. Maharloka (GBP)

BRAHMABINDU UPANIṢAD

[The name of this Upaniṣad *Brahmabindu Upaniṣad* (*Amṛtabindu Upaniṣad* in Śaṁkarānanda, Anquetil, in the Telugu edition and in a few manuscripts) must no doubt mean "the esoteric instruction on the point which signifies the (higher) Brahman," i.e. on the Anusvāra of the word Om, which, in so far as it denotes the reverberation also, refers to the higher wordless Brahman, while the word Om as such represents only the "Word-Brahman" symbolically (verses 15-17). Accordingly, the verse 7 teaches that through the sound (Om) one can only 'begin' the Yoga, but the highest one must remain wordless. For the rest nothing further is said of Om and its reverberation. The Upaniṣad rather treats of the dissolution of the Manas (verses 1-10), the relationship of the Brahman with the world of appearances (verses 11-17), the worthlessness of the external perception, bookish learning etc. (verses 18-22) in a way which makes it (Upaniṣad) appear like a link between the older Upaniṣads and Śaṁkara, whose favourite illustration of the space in the jar and the universal space already appears here (verses 13-14), as also the verse 12 which is indeed cited by Śaṁkara under Brahmasūtra p. 810,1, possibly from our Upaniṣad. Also it has five verses (1.2.4.5.17) in common with the Maitrāyaṇa Up. (6,34 and 6.22), which appear there as citations, and as more torn off than in our Upaniṣad, in whose context they are woven quite naturally. It is therefore quite probable that Brahmabindu Up. is cited in the Maitr. Up.—Of sectarian inclinations there is no trace, with the exception of Vāsudevaḥ at the end, which can, however, by reason of its metrical impossibility, be surely recognized as an interpolation by one or the other worshipper of Viṣṇu-Kṛṣṇa and which has dislodged the original end (something like *iti smṛtam*).]

Verses 1-10

The withdrawal of Manas from the sense objects and liberation as its result

Om!

1. The Manas, they say, is twofold,
Either impure or pure,
Impure, when it imagines desires,
Pure, when it is free from desires.

2. The Manas therefore is the cause
Of bondage and liberation to us:
Of bondage, when attached to object,
Of liberation, when free from it.

3. Since by the objectless Manas
Liberation is conditioned,
So one who aspires after it,
Should free his mind from object.

4. Free from attachment to sense world,
Who locks up his Manas in the heart,
And thus reaches Manas-lessness,
He goes into the highest one.

5. Restrain your Manas so long,
Until it is annihilated in the heart,
This is knowledge, this liberation,
The rest is all learned trash.

6. Not thinkable and not unthinkable,
Thinkable and unthinkable together,
Free from every partisanship
Is Brahman, which he then reaches.

7. Beginning the Yoga with Om,
Meditate wordlessly on the highest one,
Since through wordless meditation
Is being attained, not mere non-being.

8. That is Brahman, the partless,
Changeless and without deception;
"I am that Brahman", so knowing
One surely reaches the Brahman.

9. The changeless, endless,
Causeless, incomparable,
Without limits and without beginning,
One knows as the highest bliss.

10. There's no death, no becoming,
None bound, none aspirant,[1]
No liberated existence, no desire for it,
That is the highest reality.

---

1. *Na baddho na ca sādhakaḥ* with the Telugu ed. and Śaṁkarānanda.

Verses 11-17

The Ātman and the world of appearances

11. Know the Ātman as one,
Then, waking, dream and deep sleep,
Throwing off these three states,
You will never be born again.

12. A single being-self there is,
It dwells in each and every being,
Uniform and yet multiform
It appears like the moon in pond.

13. As the space, which a jar encloses,
When the jar is broken to pieces,
The jar alone breaks, not the space,
Life is like the jar.

14. All forms are like the jar;
Unceasingly they break to pieces;
When departed, they are unaware,
Still he is aware eternally.

15. One who is enveloped in word-delusion,
Remains caught up in the heart-lotus,
But when the darkness grows clear,
He sees the unity all alone.

16. Brahman is the syllable of the Om-sound;
When it fades off, what remains,
The wise meditate on that eternal one,
The seekers of the peace of soul.

17. Two sciences are necessary,
The Word-Brahman and the uppermost;
One who is versed in the Word-Brahman,
Attains to the highest Brahman too.

18. The wise, searching through books
For real insight into knowledge,
Throws off the mass of bookish stuff,
As one the chaff, who strives after corn.

19. The cows, to be sure, are many-coloured,
But uniform is the colour of milk;
The Self-knowledge is like the milk,
Its characteristic like cows.

20. Like butter, hidden in milk,
True knowledge dwells in all that lives;
Ever, with mind as the churning rod
Everyone should churn it out in himself (Āryā).

21. Using the whirling rope of knowledge,
One should obtain, like fire by friction,
That partless, stainless silence;
"I am that Brahman", as it's said.

22. That which is the abode to all beings,
To which all beings are abode;
Which holds in it all affectionately,
That I am, the Vāsudeva,
—That I am, the Vāsudeva.

AMṚTABINDU UPANIṢAD

[*Amṛta-bindu Upaniṣad or Amṛta-nāda Upaniṣad* as it is already called by Sāyaṇa (who cites its 10th verse under Taitt. Ār. 10, 27, page 849) and elsewhere (also in Śaṁkarānanda's commentary) means : "The esoteric doctrine of the (Anusvāra) point (*bindu*) or of the reverberation (*nāda*) of the word Om, which signifies the Immortal (Brahman)" or also "which grants immortality". In view of the positiveness with which every sound element is excluded in verses 4 and 24 the former name is more appropriate, as also better attested. The interchange of the names can be explained in this way that the name Brahmabindu was dropped by scribal oversight and was replaced by Amṛtabindu, so that it was necessary to choose a new name for our Upaniṣad also.

The contents consist of an introduction, four parts, and a concluding verse

The Introduction (verses 1-4) not only condemns all bookish learning but it also considers the sounding elements of Om as pure means to the end. Only the soundless *m* (*asvara makāra*), which is also signified by the Anusvāra-point (*bindu*) is to be meditated.

I. Verses 5-16. Of the eight members of the Yoga system our Upaniṣad, like Maitr. 6, 18, mentions only five to which, as there, *tarka*, is added as the sixth.

1. *pratyāhāra*, withdrawing of the Manas and the Indriyas from the sense objects (explained in verse 5, which would better stand after the verse 6).

2. *dhyānam*, meditation, whose explanation is missing.

3. *prāṇāyāma*, breath-controlling, consisting of (a) *recaka*, emptying, (b) *pūraka*, filling, (c) *kumbhaka*, retaining of the breath in the chest.

4. *dhāraṇā*, locking up into the Ātman of the Manas drawn away from the sense objects.

5. *tarka*, reflecting, missing in the Yogasūtras, and explained differently from Maitr. 6, 18.

6. Communion in the Ātman, the Self, "which one meditates, although one already possesses it" (*yaṁ labdhvā api eva manyeta*).

II. Verses 17-27. Rules for the conduct of a Yogin : ways of sitting, of meditating over Om etc.; verse 27 would better stand at the beginning, before verse 17.

III. Verses 28-31. Reward of the Yoga. The five moras, which are imagined here, correspond to the five properties : smell, taste, sight, touch sound; the earth has all the five, the water four, the fire three, the air two, the ether one. By concentrating on the half mora one liberates oneself from all these.

IV. Verses 32-37. The Prāṇa and its five ramifications, to which here not only a particular seat but also (similarly as in Chand. 8,6,1 to the arteries of the heart) five different colours have been assigned.

V. Verse 38. Final promise. The term *maṇḍalam* here and in verses 17.26 is not clear; in verse 17 the same is to be muttered, in verses 26 and 38 a transition point of the outgoing soul, in 38 before its exit from the body and in 26 after it; also, as it appears, the word *maṇḍalam* has three different meanings at the three places which is not without doubt in so small a work.]

Verses 1-4.

Superiority of Brahman over the book learning and over the audible part of the word Om

1. The wise who read the text books,
   And studied them again and again,
   When partaking of the Brahman's knowledge,
   Throw them off, as if they burnt.

2. He mounts the car of Om,
   His charioteer is Viṣṇu,
   He seeks the abode of the Brahman-world,
   To win the Rudra for himself.

3. But the car is useful,
   Only so long as one is on the highroad;
   Who has come to the end of the highroad,
   Leaves the car, and goes on foot.

4. So one leaves the word-symbol also,
   And only with the silent *m*
   From Om one comes to the soundless,
   Silent, invisible place.

Verses 5-16

The six limbs of the Yoga

5. The five objects of sense
   And the Manas, the mobile,
   Are only the reins of the Ātman,
   To know this is withdrawal.

6. Withdrawal and meditation,
Breath-control and chaining,
Reflecting and communion,
Are the six limbs of the Yoga.

7. As by melting, the slag
Of the raw ore is completely burnt,
So by restraining the breath
The faults of senses are completely burnt.

8. By breath-control is burnt the fault,
By chaining, the sin.
Having thus annihilated the sin
One should think of the shining one.

9. [While thinking of] the shining one
One breathes out and in again,
There are three controls of breath,
Emptying, filling and retaining.

10. The Gāyatrī with its head
Along with Vyāhṛtis and Praṇava
Say thrice in one breath,
That is called the breath-control.[1]

11. When one, expelling the breath out,
Makes contentsless, empty space,
Restraining himself to this emptiness,—
It is, what they call, the emptying.

13. [2]Pursing one's lips like a lotus-stalk,
One is accustomed to drink water;[3]

---

1. =Viṣṇusmṛti 55, 9. Further this verse is cited by Sāyaṇa under Taitt. Ār. 10, 27 (which section contains the entire formula prescribed here), p. 849, and, indeed, as occurring *Amṛtanādopanisadi.* The "head of the Gāyatrī" is the formula which crowns it (follows it) : *Om āpo jyotī raso'mṛtam brahma* (auch Maitr. 6, 35. Prāṇāgnihotra-Up. 1 above), upon which should follow the Vyāhṛtis (*bhūr, bhuvaḥ, svar*) and the Praṇava (*Om*).

2. See note 1 on p. 694 —GBP.

3. According to the Telugu ed. and Śaṁkarānanda : *vaktreṇa utpalanālena toyam ākarṣayen naraḥ.*

One should similarly draw in wind also,
It is, what is called, the filling.[1]

12. When one breathes neither out nor in,[2]
And doesn't move his limbs also,
And when the air is thus held fast,
That is called the retaining.

14. Look at the forms like the blind,
Hear the sound like deaf,
Regard the body as a log of wood,
Then you are called the pacified.

15. Who sinks into the Self the Manas
As the organ of imagination
And thus remains chained to himself,—
That is renowned as the chaining.

16. Thinking, which does not run counter
To the accepted doctrine, is called reflecting.
What one already has, and still ponders over[3]
That is the object of communion.

---

1. Nārāyaṇa's codex, as also that of Weber, have (on the other hand), *kumbhaka* (retention) in verse 13 and *pūraka* (filling) in verse 12. Weber's suggestion to transpose the two is supported by the Telugu ed. and Śaṁkarānanda's text, which also explain the cause of confusion, in that in both of them verse 13 rightly comes first, then verse 12. Some copyist transposed them through oversight, and a later copyist established the sequence *recaka, pūraka*, kumbhaka required by verse 9 in such a way that he simply interchanged the two terms in verse 13 and verse 12, which gave rise to the naive remark of Nārāyaṇa that here a special kind of Kumbhaka has to be understood.

2. The *Bibl. Ind.* reads : *na ca ucchvaset, na anucchvaset*, which would be an example of a privative *a* prefixed to a finite verb (*nañas tiñā samāsaḥ*); Weber reads : *na ucchvasen na anūcchvāsayet;* but *anu+ud+śvas* does not occur and it can scarcely mean "breath in". The Telugu ed. has probably the correct reading : *na ucchvased na ca niśvāsāir* (scil. *śvaset*); or one can read with Śaṁkarānanda and the Bombay edition : *na ucchvasen, na ca niśvaset*.

3. According to Weber's MS : *yaṁ labdhvā api eva manyeta*. Nārāyaṇa reads: *yaṁ labdhvā api avamanyeta* and draws attention to Bhag. G. 6,22; the Telugu ed. (with Śaṁkarānanda) : *samaṁ manyeta yal labdhvā*, cf. the well-known : *maṁa samadṛśo yāntu divasāḥ Ind. Spr.* 2nd ed. No. 844.

Verses 17-27

Rules for the Yoga

17. Upon a level ground,
which is lovely and free from defects,
He should take care of his Manas
And mutter a Maṇḍalam;[1]

18. Twining properly as Yogic posture
The lotus-posture, the cruciform-posture,
Or even the luck-posture[2] as well,
He remains facing the north.[3]

19. He closes one nostril with a finger,
And takes the air in with the other,
Blocks in himself the energy-fire[4]
And meditates on the sacred sound.

20. Om ! This syllable is Brahman,
With Om alone he should breathe out,
With this divine sound frequently
He washes away the stains of the soul.

21. Then he should meditate and utter
The formula in the sequence mentioned (verse 10),
Repeatedly, more than repeatedly,
No excess here is too much.[5]

22. Casting down his eyes within himself
Sideways, above and downward,
He sits motionless, firm of manner,
Then he really practises the Yoga.

---

1. According to Nārāyaṇa a formula referring to the solar orb, such as : *yad etan maṇḍalaṁ tapati*. Śaṁkarānanda otherwise.

2. *padmāsanam, svastikam, bhadrāsanam* are three modes of postures with crossed legs.

3. Cf. Maitr. 6, 30.

4. i.e. probably the energy (*tejas*), of which Maitr. 6, 35, 37 speaks. [The Skt. original simply reads *agnim*. —GBP]

5. With Weber's Ms : *na atimūrdham atikramaḥ* (Nār., Śaṁk., Weber otherwise).

23. Rhythm [in breathing], resignation,[1]
Chaining[2] and union,[3]
The Yoga too, of twelve moras,[4]
Is regarded as fixed according to tempo.

24. Voiceless, neither a consonant nor a vowel,
Not guttural, palatal, labial, nasal,
Without the burring sound, with both lips unmoved.—
The sacred syllable, which sounds silently.[5]

25. With this sound he sees the way,
The way, along which his Prāṇa goes,
Therefore should one always practise it,
So that he goes along the right way.

26. Through heart-gate, wind-gate,
The gate, which leads upward,
And the opening of the gate of liberation,
Which they know as the open orb.[6]

27. Against fear, against anger, against sloth,
Against too much waking, too much sleeping,
Against too much eating, not eating,
A Yogin shall always be on his guard.

Verses 28-29
Reward of the Yoga

28. If in this way, at all times,
He practises the Yoga according to rules,
Then without doubt in him will arise,
The knowledge in three months.

---

1. *yoga* according to Nārāyaṇa=*samādhi*.
2. *dhāraṇā* chaining of the Manas, cf. verse 15.
3. Of the individual soul and the highest soul according to Anquetil, of Prāṇa and Apāna according to Nārāyaṇa. Śaṁkarānanda differently.
4. For the twelve moras, see Nādabindu, verses 8-11.
5. The word-play between *akṣara* and *kṣarate* (Cf. Talav. Up. Br. 1,24,1), almost untranslatable, here allows to be replaced by another one.
6. Nārāyaṇa thinks of the solar orb (Śaṁkarānanda differently).

29. After four months he sees the gods,
After five he's as strong as they,
After six, without doubt,
He attains to absoluteness at will.

30. Through five moras he becomes akin to earth,
Through four to water;
Akin to fire through three moras,
Through two moras alike the wind.

31. Through one mora space-akin;
Yet he meditates on the half,
Then he is finished with the mind,
He thinks through him and in him alone.

Verses 32-37

The Prāṇa and its ramifications

32.[1] Thirty fingers broad space there is,
Where Prāṇa resides with the Prāṇas,
The breath, so called, as it serves
As play-ground to the breath outside.

33. Hundred and thirteen multiplied by thousand,
Plus hundred and eighty times[2]
Results the incoming and outgoing breath[3]
In the interval of a day and night.[4]

34. The Prāṇa, to begin with, dwells in the heart,
The Apāna has the bowel as its place,

---

1. According to the (corrected) Telugu text :
triṁśad vārddhāṅguliḥ prāṇo yatra prāṇaiḥ pratiṣṭhitaḥ,
eṣa prāṇa iti khyāto vāhyaprāṇasya gocaraḥ.

2. Weber's conjecture *aśītiś ca śatam* is supported by the Telugu ed. and Śaṁkarānanda.

3. *viniśvāso* Telugu ed.

4. The number 113180 divided by five (since all the five Prāṇas participate therein) gives 22636 respirations in 24 hours or 15. 7 in a minute which is correct for the grown-up on the average. Elsewhere the number of daily respirations is given around 21600 (Sarvadarśanasaṁgraha p. 175, 4) or even 21000 (under Maitr. p. 79, 4). The Haṁsa Upaniṣad fixes it at 21606.

Samāna there, where the navel is,
Udāna, where there is the neck.

35. The Vyāna, finally, continually
Runs, ruling, through all the limbs.
Now the colours of the five Prāṇas,
As they follow in order.

36. The Prāṇa resembles in lustre
A red-hued precious stone,
The Apāna shines reddish
Like a cochineal insect.[1]

37. The Samāna shines in belly
Like a milk-coloured mountain-crystal.
The Udāna is pale yellowish,
The Vyāna of the hue of a flame.

Verse 38

Summary

38. In whom, breaking through this ring,
The vital breath ascends to the head,
No matter where he dies,
He is never born any more,
—He is never born any more.

1. *indragopasamaprabhaḥ* of the Sanskrit original translated as 'Wie ein Marienkäferchen' by Deussen. —GBP.

DHYĀNABINDU UPANIṢAD

[The *Dhyānabindu Upaniṣad*, i.e. "the esoteric doctrine of the point (*bindu* of the Anusvāra in Om), to which the meditation (*dhyāna*) relates" contains an introduction and four parts.

The Introduction (verses 1-3) promises, in two stanzas taken over out of context from Yogatattva 1-2 and in the third of its own, eradication of all sins as a reward of the Yoga.

I. (Verses 4-6). The complete silence of meditation is in accordance with the infinite subtlety of its object, which is explained by the illustration of the split hair-end taken from the Śvet. 5, 9.

II. (Verses 7-10). Through a series of original and pertinent illustrations it is shown how the Ātman penetrates through all of its appearances, omnipresent in the whole as also in every individual part. The shade (*chāyā*) in verse 10 does not offer any useful illustration and its emendation into *śākhā* suggests itself, even though it is not unobjectionable and is justified only by the word *sakala* which appears beside it to interpret *niṣkala* 'the partless' as part i.e. as non-whole.

III. (Verses 11-17). After bringing the meditation of Viṣṇu, Brahmán and Śiva into relationship with the three breath practices *pūraka*, *kumbhaka* and *recaka* in verses 11-13, there follow verses 14-17, a difficult section, which I cannot make up my mind, with Nārāyaṇa and Anquetil, to again connect with the Triad for there is no basis for thus hacking the verses of the text. I rather believe that in contrast to Viṣṇu, Brahmán and Śiva the Ātman himself is described here, how as imminent he penetrates the world and still remains transcendent (on the other side of the sun and the moon). As individual soul (lotus flower) he is plucked after death and carried to the moon and the sun along the Pitṛyāna and the Devayāna according to the seed.

IV. (Verses 18-23). The meditation of Om is described towards the end in abundant, but partly borrowed, metaphors; verse 19 stems from Muṇḍ. 2, 2, 4, verse 20 from Śvet. 1,14, verse 21 from Amṛtabindu 13. In verse 22 there is in original comparison of the heart with a well from which (as even today in India) water is drawn up by means of a rope along an inclined plane, usually by a pair of bulls until, poured out, it comes to rest above. So also the Manas at the spot between the eyebrows and the nose as the dwelling place of the highest Ātman, cf. Jābāla 2.]

Verses 1-3
Value of the Yoga

1.[1] I will proclaim the truth of the Yoga
For the well-being of the Yogin,
Who listens to it and recites,
He is freed from all sins.

2. Viṣṇu is called a great Yogin
Great in magic power and penance,
As a lamp on the way of truth
He shines, the highest Puruṣa.

3. Even if the sins are like mountains
Stretching miles after miles,
Yogic meditation pierces thro' them,
Nothing else ever penetrates them.

Verses 4-6
The silence of the meditation corresponds to the subtlety of the Brahman

4. Higher than the first syllables
Is the point, higher than resonance,
The syllable vanishes with the sound,[2]
Silent is the highest place.

5. The sound which remains unbeaten,
There is something higher than this sound,
The Yogin who meditates on this
As highest, doubts break off from him.

6. A thousandth of a hundredth part
Of hair's tip, a part of this part,
And of this a half part further,—
So subtle is the pure being.

---

1. Verses 1-2=Yogatattva 1-2, where they suit better, and from which context they are secondarily taken over here, since they are missing in the two Poona MSS and the Telugu ed.

2. *sa śabdaś ca akṣare kṣiṇo*, Telugu ed.

Verses 7-10

Brahman and its appearances

7. As fragrance is in flower,
As butter is in milk,
As oil is in oil-seeds,
As gold is in ore.

8. As the thread is in pearls,
So firm in Ātman are all beings,
Therefore the knower of Brahman, with mind
Firm on Brahman, stands unconfused.

9. As the oil pervades the oil seeds,
As the fragrance the flower,
So in the body of man
He is in it and outside too.

10. Know the tree as the whole,
The branch[1] is only a non-whole,
In the whole as also in the non-whole
Everywhere the Ātman dwells.

Verses 11-17

Viṣṇu, Brahmán Śiva and the Ātman pervading them all

For *pūraka, kumbhaka, recaka*, see above, Amṛtabindu Up. 11-13.

11. Comparable to a flax flower
Having his place at the navel,
The heroic Viṣṇu of four arms,
On him one meditates with Pūraka.

12. With Kumbhaka on him,
Whose lotus-seat is in the heart,
On the god Brahman, the ur-father
Red white, having four faces.[2]

---

1. I read *śākhā*.
2. Out of the descriptions like Ṛgveda 10, 81, 3 : "eye on all sides and face on all sides" etc. (comparable to Xenophanic o'ulos 'orᾶ etc.), grew by materialisation god Brahmán with four faces. —In a similar way in the biblical field, what were still concepts in the *Romans* 1, 3-4, have taken a concrete shape in the imagination of *Math.* 1,18. *Luk.* 1,35, in order to be intelligible to the common people.

13. With the *recaka* he meditates
Over the three-eyed enthroned on forehead,
Resembling a pure rock-crystal,
Destroying sins, free from patches.

14. Of eight petals,[1] blooming downward,
The stalk on high, calix down,[2]
Resembling a banana flower,
He is the essence of gods.[3]

15. The flower with a hundred petals,
Which surround the seed-pod all around,
Meditate on him beyond fires,
Beyond the moon and the sun.[4]

16. Plucking off the lotus flower,
In order to carry it away
To the lunar fire,[5] to the sun,[6]
The Ātman surely the seed directs.

17. Of three places[7] and three paths,[8]
He is the threefold Brahman and holy sound.
Having three and a half moras,—
Who knows him, has the knowledge.

Verses 18-23

The meditation on the Om-sound and on the reverberation

18. Long-drawn like a drop of oil,
Long-humming like the sound of a bell,
Silently reverberates the tip of Om,
Who knows it, has the knowledge.

---

1. Perhaps the eight regions of the heaven.
2. Probably immitation of Kāṭh. 6,1 *ūrdhvamūlo avākśākha eṣo 'śvatthaḥ sanātanaḥ*.
3. Editions available to me read *sarvavedamayam* for *sarvadevamayam*. —GBP.
4. Beyond the goals of Pitṛyāna and Devayāna.
5. Along the Pitṛyāna.
6. Along the Devayāna.
7. Nevel, heart and forehead.
8. Perhaps, Pitṛyāna, Devayāna and Tṛtiyam Sthānam; or as Śvet. 1, 4.

19. Om is the bow, the soul the arrow,
The Brahman the target of the arrow,
That one should hit unflinchingly,
Identifying oneself with it like an arrow.

20. Making one's body the friction-wood,
With the Om-sound as the upper stick,
Through meditation's friction one sees the God,
Like the fire hidden in the wood.

21. Pursing one's lips like a lotus stalk
One is accustomed to drink water,
One should similarly draw in wind also,
When as a Yogin one practises the Yoga.

22. Using the half mora as a rope,
Draw out of the well of heart-lotus
The Manas upward along the path of artery,
Between the brows, where it melts away.

23. For the forehead between the brows,
Where there is the root of the nose,
Is the perennial dwelling place,
The great resting place of all.

TEJOBINDU UPANIṢAD

[This Upaniṣad bears the name *Tejo-bindu* "the point (of the Anusvāra in Om), which denotes the power (Brahman)" probably on account of the first word (similarly as in Kena and Īśa), for otherwise there is no further discussion, either of Om or of its moras etc., in the fourteen verses which alone constitute our recension.

They rather deal with, in a clearly ordered manner, the most important of the main features of the Vedānta doctrine one after another :

Verses 1-2. Difficulty of meditation (*dhyānam*).

,, 3-4. The requirements of one qualified for it.

,, 5-8. The place of the Brahman as its object.

,, 9-11. The enigmatic nature of the Brahman.

,, 12-14. Portrayal of one liberated alive.

Although the train of thoughts here is on the whole clear, the individual passages are often equally difficult and have already demanded from the Indian commentator the most jaw-breaking exegetical acrobatics. But when he e.g. in verse 9 puts up with *brahmāṇam* instead of the required *brahma* with the remark that here is only a confusion of gender and case (*liṅga-vibhakti-vyatyayaḥ*), or when in verses 12 ff. he supplies *śritā na vidur* (subject, copula, negation and predicate) to the accusatives *lobham* etc., which are completely hanging in air, to make them intelligible, — then we shall not follow him here as in much else but we will find ourselves facing the alternative as to whether the language feeling was already so completely blunted[1] in the original author of these verses, or whether we are dealing with an enormously corrupt text-transmission. The latter alternative would seem to be supported by the numerous but not better readings of the Telugu ed. in which our 14 stanzas form only the beginning of the Tejobindūpaniṣad, which is followed by discussions in verses and prose which exceed more than thirty times the extent of our recension.]

Verses 1-2
The meditation (*dhyānam*)

1. At the power-point aims the highest meditation,
Supremely enthroned in the heart,
Subtle, blissful, powerful,
First gross, then fine, then superfine,

---

1. Even for the title the majority of the manuscripts used for the Poona edition offer *Tejabindu* which is impossible.

2. Difficult to accomplish, difficult to reach,
Difficult to look at, difficult to establish,
Difficult to execute is this meditation
Even for the wise and the lonely.

Verses 3-4

Who is qualified for the meditation

3. One who conquers greed and anger,
Worldly attachment and senses' lust,
Who lays aside duality, I-consciousness,
Free from expectation, from wife and child.

4. Who makes the inaccessible accessible,
Strives only for teacher's respect and gain,
Who, stepping through the three gates,[1]
Becomes the Haṁsa dwelling in the three worlds.

Verses 5-8

The place of the Brahman

5. Mysterious is the place,
Brahman, groundless and unmanifest,
With parts subtle like ether;
That is Viṣṇu's highest step.

6. It has three eyes,[2] three Guṇas,[3]
It surrounds three invisible worlds,
Unmoving, unchanging,
Without props, without foundation.

7. Free from all determinations,
Beyond the range of word and thought,
To be grasped by Self-absorption alone;
No word names it, no mesh of words.

---

1. According to the commentary : renunciation, patience and respectfulness towards one's teachers.
2. Ostensibly the three Vedas.
3. Sattvam, Rajas, Tamas.

8. Rapture indeed, yet beyond pleasure,
Difficult to see, endless, beginningless,
Free from the mind's bossing,
Eternal, firm, impossible to shake.

Verses 9-11

The enigmatic and contradictory nature of the Brahman

9. This Brahman, which dwells in the Self.
This first cause, this highest aim
Of unthinking thinking, is the soul
And the highest haven of refuge.

10. Unempty, it appears as empty,
Above emptiness it stands majestically,
Nor thought it is, nor thinking,
Unthinkable and yet, indeed, thinkable.

11. It's all and yet it is nothing,
There's nothing higher than it,
Unthinkable unawakened it is,
It's not real and is not known.

Verses 12-14

Portrayal of one who is liberated alive

12. Essentially associating with the lonely,—
He who is God, sure knows the highest,—
Greed, delusion, fear, pride,
Anger, love, sin renouncing,

13. Cold and warm, hunger and thirst,
And intentions, which ever change,
Not proud of the Brāhmaṇa descent,
Not of the rubbish of liberation texts,

14. Knowing no fear, nor lust, nor pain,
Nor respect, nor disrespect any more,—
Because from all these is free
Brahman, the highest goal of all endeavour,
—Brahman, the highest goal of all endeavour.

YOGAŚIKHĀ UPANIṢAD

[The *Yogaśikhā* from which this Upaniṣad gets its name is either to be understood as "the peak, the highest result of the Yogic meditation" or as "the pointed flame" in the heart, in which the Yogin sees the highest being according to the verse 6.

After an introductory verse (No. 1), a brief and clear picture of the Yogic meditation is first given (verses 2-3). More mystical is the following part (verses 4-7) which takes for granted symbolically a sun situated in the body, be it in the head (as in the Brahmavidyā 8 ff) or, probably more rightly, in the heart (Nārāyaṇa); in its midst is a fire which projects into a pointed flame, in which exists, to be seen, the highest being; a concept which has developed probably out of old passages as e.g. Kāṭh 4, 12-13. Mahānār. 11, 9-12. Maitr. 6.38. It must be the departure of the Yogin's soul after his death, referred to when it is described further how the Yogin penetrates through the above-mentioned solar disk, in order to attain to the union with the Highest through the *suṣumnā* (actually already Chānd. 8, 6, 6= Kāṭh. 6, 16) and the coronal suture (Ait. 1, 3, 12). But it is odd, and raises doubt about the correctness of the text, when further here (verses 8-9) for those who would not or would not practise the Yoga, it is replaced by a much simpler means, viz. to recite thrice daily this small Upaniṣad, which leads to the same goal, just as the Āraṇyakas replaced the sacrificial cult by a mental view of it. This goal is, as the verse 10 says, the annihilation of sins and the dissolution of Saṁsāra which is [otherwise] not possible in thousands of re-births. An Interpretation of verses 8-9 quite differed from this one which already underlies Nārāyaṇa's commentary is testified to by the variant readings in the Telugu ed. (see below), in which the extent of the Yogaśikhā Upaniṣad is about 40 times that of our recension, consisting of six Adhyāyas, in the first of which the ten verses of our recension are incorporated with many partly quite good variants.]

Verse 1

Proclamation

1. I will proclaim the peak of Yoga,
Which is the highest of knowledge,
He who meditates this holy word,[1]
Never shall his limbs tremble.[2]

---

1. Either the syllable Om or this Upaniṣad is meant.

2. According to the reading of the Telugu ed. *gātrakampo na jāyate*. Cf. Kauṣ. 3, 1 end.

Verses 2-3

A brief account of the Yogic meditation

2. Choosing the posture of the lotus type,
Or whichever else may please him,
Fixing the gaze on the nose tip,
With hands and feet pressed close,

3. Controlling the Manas on all sides,
The wise shall meditate,
Continuously on the syllable Om,
Enshrining the highest God in heart.

Verses 4-7

Penetrating to the God and the flight to Him after the death

4. Upon one pillar,[1] three posts,[2]
With nine doors,[3] having five gods,[4]
Stands a temple, body it is,
In it one shall seek the highest.

5. Therein glows a sun,
With flamelike rays surrounded,
In its midst is a fire,
Which burns like the wick of a lamp;

6. As large is its pointed flame,
So large the highest God there.
Practising the Yoga repeatedly,
The Yogin penetrates through the sun,

7. Then zigzag he goes upwards
Through the shining door of Suṣumnā;
Breaking through the cerebral dome,
He finally sees the highest one.

---

1. The vertebral column.
2. The three arteries *iḍā*, *piṅgalā* and *suṣumnā* or the three Guṇas *sattvam*, *rajas* and *tamas* (schol).
3. The nine openings of the body.
4. The five senses.

Verses 8-9

A substitute for the Yoga[1]

8. Yet, who, inattentive and lazy,
Does not see his way to meditation,
He can penetrate to the highest place,
If he daily thrice recites.

9. The pure speech that I proclaimed
After participating in the Yoga,
After reaching, what is to be known,
The gracious, the highest God.

Verse 10

End

10. Who through thousands of births
Does not consume the debt of sins,
He finally beholds through Yoga
The dissolution of the Saṁsāra here.

---

1. According to the readings of the Telugu ed. the idea rather is: "He who goes through this meditatingly thrice a day reaches, from out of laziness and inattentiveness, to the pure bliss"

YOGATATTVA UPANIṢAD

[This Upaniṣad, which bears its name *Yogatattva* "The essence of the Yoga" either according to the initial word or according to the main contents, consists of only fifteen Ślokas in our recension while in the Telugu ed. it has a considerable augmented form. The two initial stanzas are the same there, but then follow about a hundred Ślokas, after which again stanza 2, and stanzas 3-13 and 15 as the end, partly with quite different variant readings. Whether these rest on an original tradition or only on a later arrangement, we do not undertake to decide for the time being. In our recension the text is so corrupt and the commentary so defective, that the translation can be looked upon only as an experiment in order to reproduce the contents in a somewhat intelligible form.

After the initial verses (1-2), which less suitably form the beginning of the Dhyānabindu also, follows in verses 3-5 a very drastic picture of the ceaseless rotation of re-births and in verses 6-8 an exposition, how the 3½ moras of the Om sound include everything in themselves, wherein the verse 8 is again the same as Dhyānabindu 7, but this time it stands there better suited; —accordingly it appears that Yogatattva and Dhyānabindu are dependent, not on each other, but both on a common source which however is probably to be sought only in individual stanzas, which were transmitted orally in the Yoga circles and which, considerably altered, were finally admitted in these Upaniṣads. This also applies to the following verses (9-11), which, according to the model of the Mahānār. 11, 8 and in repeated agreement with the Dhyānabindu 12-14, picture the heart, the seat of the Manas, as a lotus flower facing downward, which opens in meditation but becomes motionless with the quieting of the Manas, whereupon the soul reflects in itself the highest Being as the rock-crystal the ray of the sun (verse 11). Verse 12 probably refers to the *Pratyāhāra*, the withdrawing of the organs, while the breathing still continues, verse 13 to the Prāṇāyāma, the breath control, which has its acme in the *Kumbhaka* (Amṛtabindu 13. Dhyānabindu 12), verse 14 to the exit of the soul through the *Suṣumnā* and the *Brahmarandhra* (cf. *Yogaśikhā* 7), verse 15 finally deals with the selection of the proper place for meditation, and the indulgence on the part of the Yogin towards all living beings.]

Verses 1-2

Importance of the Yoga[1]

1. I will proclaim the truth of the Yoga
   For the well-being of the Yogin.

---

1. Verses 1-2 = Dhyānabindu 1-2.

Who listens to it and recites,
He is freed from all sins.

2. Viṣṇu is called a great Yogin,
Great in magic power and penance,
As a lamp on the way of truth,
He shines, the highest Puruṣa.

Verses 3-5

The rotation of the migration of the soul

3. The breast at which he once drank,
Later he squeezes lasciviously,[1]
On the womb, which once gave him birth,
He sates his carnal desire.

4. She, who was once his mother,
Now becomes his wife, and wife mother,
His father becomes his son,
He, who son was his father.

5. Thus in the rotation of Saṁsāra
Like a bucket on the water-wheel[2]
Running round, he's once more born
In the mother's womb.[3]

Verses 6-8

All-comprehensiveness of the sound Om

6. There are three worlds, three Vedas,
Three times of day, three gods,
Three sacrificial fires, three Guṇas,
The Tri-syllable comprehends all in it.

---

1. *Yaḥ stanaḥ pūrvapītas tam niṣpīḍya mudam aśnute* (Telugu ed.).

2. Even today one sees quite frequently this wheel for drawing water furnished with bucket around. When this is turned through a stream flowing under it, the buckets merged in it are filled with water and when they reach up, they empty their contents into a channel which carries the water to the fields.

3. *yonijanmāni śritvā* (Telugu ed).

7. And who at the end of the Tri-syllable
Meditates on the half syllable also,
He pervades through all this
And finally goes to the highest place.

8. As fragrance is in flower,
As butter is in milk,
As oil is in the sesame,
As gold is in the ore,[1]...

Verses 9-11

Reward of the meditation on Om

9. The lotus flower, that occupies
The space in the heart, calix down,
The stalk on high, dewing down,
Therein the Manas has its seat.

10. With the *a*-sound it become luminous,
With the *u*-sound it opens out,
With the *m*-sound it resounds,—
Motionless is the half sound.—

11. And just as in a crystal perchance
Is reflected the light of the sun,[2]
So shines in the soul, inspiring it,
The highest spirit by means of Yoga.

Verses 12-13

Pratyāhāra and Prāṇāyāma

(See Introduction to the Amṛtabindu Up.)

12. Like a tortoise he draws within
The hands and feet and head,[3]
While the breath still plays around
The gates. Then it's called "fill in! fill in!"

---

1. This Śloka can be fitted with the preceding one only artificially (by means of the all-pervasion of the sound Om) and is perhaps taken over from the context which is there for the Dhyānabindu 7ff.

2. *ātmā labhate sphaṭikasaṁkāśam, sūryamarīcivat*, "the soul takes on the glow of the mountain-crystal, as [when] a ray of the sun [touches it.]."

3. We read with the Telugu ed. ; *śiraś ca.*

13. When after closing the nine gates,
He seeks to breathe out and in
Like a torch in a jar
Without wind, that's called "detaining".

Verse 14

Exit through the Brahmarandhra

14. Till, breaking, as through a lotus petal,
The impetuous wind leads him,
Whom they know as the guileless,
Between the brows and the forehead.[1]

Verse 15

Relationship of the Yogin with the outer world

15. At an unprohibited, far off, place,
Calm and quiet, undisturbed,
The Yogin guarantees protection
To all beings, as to his own self.[2]

1. Cf. Dhyānabindu 23. Jābāla 2.
2. Literally: "Through the Yogic service the sanctity of beings who form the self (of the Yogin) is guaranteed."

HAṀSA UPANIṢAD

[This Upaniṣad, included in the *Oupanekhat* also as *Hensnad* (i.e. *Haṁsanāda*), belongs, as is already shown by its position in the collections of Colebrooke and Nārāyaṇa, but more so by its contents, to a later stage of development than the Yoga-Upaniṣads treated so far. The assertion about the words *haṁsa haṁsa* as being the Mantrarāja (King of the aphorisms, i.e. as an aphorism running through the whole of the Upaniṣad) and the way how the beginning, the middle and the end (*vījam, kīlaka, śakti*) are distinguished in it, and how the employment of the aphorism is taught as a diagram, make our Upaniṣad appear in closest relationship with the circle of thoughts of the Nṛsiṁhatāpanīya and the Rāmatāpanīya.

As the fundamental thought can be shown that the *Haṁsa* [the individual soul) becomes the *Paramahaṁsa* (the highest soul) through the meditation of the sound Om, and particularly of its reverberation.

The main contents are the following. The division into paragraphs is our own, because the one in the Calcutta edition and that in both the Poona editions (with the commentary of Nārāyaṇa and of Śaṁkarānanda) are conflicting and are not sufficient for the purpose.

1. Introduction. The verse at the beginning as also the one at the end are missing in Śaṁkarānanda's recension.

2. The individual soul is called as Haṁsa through the combination of sounds of out-breath (*han*) and in-breath (*sa*).

3. Just as the Kṣurikā Upaniṣad teaches a successive detachment of the self from the several parts of the body, similarly our Upaniṣad teaches an ascent through six mystical circles differentiated in the body on to the Brahmarandhra. This ascent is accomplished through meditation of the syllable Om and particularly of its reverberation.

4. The *haṁsa haṁsa* repeated 21606 times in day and night through the respiration of the (fivefold) Prāṇa appears as hymn (as the Mantrarāja) whose poet, metre and the deity are determined, and whom the *vījam* (germ, initial syllable), the *kīlaka* (stem, middle syllable), and the *śakti* (power, final syllable) are differentiated.

5. This king-of-aphorisms, which as such has (cf. Nṛsiṁhap. 2, 2. Rāmap. 61), six physical parts (heart, head, tuft of hair, armour, three eyes and weapon) is, under specific invocations (to be supplied from the commentary) of these parts, put down (the exact way of executing this is not given) as a diagram (evidently to be worn as an amulet) and besides, as it appears, it is also laid on the hands.

6. Symbolical interpretation of the individual Ātman conceived in the form of a bird as *Haṁsa* (goose).

7. Identity of the *Haṁsa* and the *Paramahaṁsa* (of the individual and the highest Ātman).

8. Portrayal of *Haṁsa* who has yet to become *Paramahaṁsa.*

9. Its becoming one with the *Paramahaṁsa.*

10. The ten ways in which the reverberation can be brought forth (cf. Chānd. 2, 22. Maitr. 6,22); The tenth of these is recommended for practice The verses which follow differ.

11. Dissolution of the Manas and unification with the highest Ātman.

The context makes it appear conceivable that those sections of this Upaniṣad which make it look far more modern than the other Yoga Upaniṣads (particularly 3-5) rest on later insertion.]

1. Gautama spake:

The awakening of the Brahman-lore,
Which is familiar with all duties,[1]
Which comprises the content of all texts,[1]
Through what, O sir, is it effected ?

Sanatsujāta spake:

Pondering over all the Vedas
And grasping firmly their content,
Śiva expounded to Pārvatī
The truth;—learn it from me.
Indescribable and shrouded, equally,
Is the mystery of the Yogins;
Which spreads out the path before the Haṁsa,
Bestows joy and the fruit of liberation.

Now we will impart precise information over the Haṁsa and the Paramahaṁsa for the Brahman-student who is passionless, restrained and devoted to the teacher.

2. With the sound *haṁ-sa haṁ-sa* (outbreathing and inbreathing) it (the breath) stays continually in all bodies, filling them completely, as the fire in the fuel or the oil in the sesame seeds. He who knows it, does not fall into the hands of Death.

1. Editions available to me read *sarvadharmajña sarvaśāstraviśārada* (both vocatives) which certainly give a better meaning.—GBP.

3. Closing the anal opening, one should send the wind upward from the abdomen-circle (*ādhāra*), going around the sexual-circle (*svādhiṣṭhānam*) thrice, keeping it on the right, ascend to the navel-circle (*maṇipūrakam*), should go beyond the heart-circle (*anāhatam*), should maintain the breath in the neck-circle (*viśuddhi*), should think over the circle-between-the-brows (*ājñā*), should meditate over the Brahman-opening, and all the while also the expression" I am that one [Om sound] which consists of the three moras", and further, from the abdomen-circle upto the Brahman-opening, should think over the reverberation, which is like a pure rock-crystal, for it is that which is called Brahman, the highest Ātman.

4. In the case of this aphorism [namely *haṁso haṁsa*] the Haṁsa is the poet, *Paṅkti*[1] the metre, the Paramahaṁsa the deity, the word *ham* the germ (the initial syllable), *sa* the power (the final syllable), *so'ham* the stem (the middle). There are 21,606 of the [haṁsa, i.e. outbreathings and inbreathings].[2]

5. With the words: "To the sun (*om sūryāya hṛdayāya namaḥ*), to the moon (*om somāya śirase svāhā*), to the spotless one (*om nirañjanāya śikhāyai vaṣaṭ*), to the lustreless one (*om nirābhāsāya kavacāya hum*), tanu-sūkṣma (*om tanusūkṣma netratrayāya vauṣaṭ*) and pracodayāt (*om pracodayāt astrāya phaṭ*)" and with addition [everytime]: "to Agni and Soma *vauṣaṭ*" the constituent aphorisms are laid [as diagram] on the heart etc. [heart, head, tuft of the hair, armour, three eyes and weapon] of the king of aphorisms and also laid on the hand.

6. When this is done, one should meditate on the essence of the Haṁsa in the eight-petal [lotus-flower which is] in the heart. [One thinks of him in the form of a bird, as Haṁsa a goose:] Agni and Soma are his wings, the Om-sound his head, the anusvāra-point his eye [or also] his mouth; Rudra and Rudrāṇī his hands and feet, Kāla and Agni his both sides (right and left), "sees" and "homeless" are his two remaining sides [above and below].

1. The Poona ed. reads: "the unmanifest Gāyatri".
2. On this number, see Amṛtabindu 33.

7. And this [*Haṁsa*, i.e. the individual soul] is that *Parama-haṁsa* [the highest soul], which shines like ten million suns and pervades this entire world.

8. His behaviour, however, [so far as he abides in the eight-petal lotus-flower of the heart] is eightfold: On the eastern petal his mind is directed to holy acts, on the south-eastern sleep and laxity overcome him, on the southern his mind is cruel, on the south-western he strives after sin, on the western after play, on the north-western he desires going etc., on the northern love-enjoyment, on the north-western acquisition of property. Renunciation rules in the middle, the state of waking in the filament, sleep in the seed-pod, deep sleep on the stalk, the Turyam at the spot where the lotus flower ends upward.

9. But when the Haṁsa is merged in the reverberation, then appears what is called above-the-Turīya, Unthinking, Conclusion-in-non-muttering. All this happens at the will of the Haṁsa. Therefore the Manas is allowed to run; however, he [the worshipper] enjoys the reverberation in ten million mutterings. All this happens at the will of the Haṁsa.

10. The reverberation can be brought about tenfold: the first sounds as *ciṇī*, the second as *ciñciṇī*, the third like the sound of a bell, the fourth like the blowing of a conch, the fifth like the string music, the sixth like clapping, the seventh like the note of a flute, the eighth like the beating of a drum, the ninth like that of a kettle-drum, the tenth like a thunder. One should avoid the ninth [and those preceding it] and practise the tenth alone.

In the case of the first his body
Imitates *ciñciṇī*, in second it crumples,
In the third he is very tired,
In the fourth his head shakes,

In the fifth his palate runs,
In the sixth he drinks Amṛtam,
In the seventh he has esoteric knowledge,
In the eighth skill in speech.

In the ninth power to disappear
And a clear-seeing eye divine,
In the tenth he becomes the Brahman,—
Brahman and Ātman become one.

11. In him the Manas vanishes, and in the Manas are burnt desire and doubt, good and bad. But he, ever blissful, with all penetrating power, omni-present, glows through his own light as pure, enlightened, eternal, spotless and calm.

Om! that is the Veda-explanation,—Veda-explanation.

c. Saṁnyāsa Upaniṣads

BRAHMA UPANIṢAD

SAṀNYĀSA UPANIṢAD

ĀRUṆEYA UPANIṢAD

KAṆṬHAŚRUTI UPANIṢAD

PARAMAHAṀSA UPANIṢAD

JĀBĀLA UPANIṢAD

ĀŚRAMA UPANIṢAD

BRAHMA UPANIṢAD[1]

[According to Nārāyaṇa the *Brahma-Upaniṣad* consists of four parts,[2] two in prose of a more archaic bearing and two in verse which show a more modern character in respect to the form and content.

1. In the first part Pippalāda "the Aṅgiras" (contrast with this the beginning of the Atharvaśikhā) answers four questions of Śaunaka in this way that he refers to the Prāṇa (the Ātman, the Brahman) as the life-principle of the organs and characterises its behaviour in deep sleep, dream and waking in the manner of the old Upaniṣads and with considerable accord with these (particularly with Bṛh. 4, 3-4). The style is extremely abrupt and reminds one of the manner of Sūtras which consist of referring, by a casual expression, to a context known to the reader. This whole section is missing in most of the manuscripts; Śaṁkarānanda's commentary ignores it and even Nārāyaṇa mentions, without approving of it on his part (p. 239,10), that according to many the Upaniṣad began with the second part. Probably they omitted the first part because the style there is so concise and the transmission so uncertain that it is possible only with a straining to extract a meaning from it, and that too remains problematic.

2. The second part mentions the four physical seats and (without assigning to these) the four states of the Ātman in order then to dwell upon a complete negation of this as also on its residence in the heart-space, which, with an appeal to the Veda (*vaidya=vaidika*), i.e. probably the Chānd. 8,1,3, is compared to the universal space (*suṣiram ākāśam*, neutr.)

---

1. On the order of succession. The *Brahma Upaniṣad*, in view of its third part, can be considered as a transition from the Vedānta and the Yoga-Upaniṣads to those texts, which see the highest goal, in the Saṁnyāsa. This is followed, according to the order in the lists of Colebrooke and Nārāyaṇa, by two groups of Saṁnyāsa Upaniṣads, (1) *Saṁnyāsa*, *Āruṇeyī*, *Kaṇṭha-śruti*, all three characterised by their fragmentary form and dilapidated transmission, and (2) *Paramahaṁsa*, *Jābāla*, *Āśrama*, whose presentation is more orderly, and whose late position in the canon cannot be an evidence of its posteriority. Only the last-named one will have to be placed, on account of its systematic character, at the end of the whole line of development.

2. The determination of these originates partly from us, since the divisions in the Calcutta and both Poona editions (with the commentary of Nārāyaṇa and that of Śaṁkarānanda) are partly confused and partly they are of no use whatever. In the Telugu ed. our Upaniṣad exists in two entirely different recensions, without the first part as *Brahma Upaniṣad*, and with it as *Parabrahma Upaniṣad*.

3. The most original and most intimately connected with the Saṁnyāsa Upaniṣads is the third, more modern part in verse, which recommends the Brahman-knower to do away with the *śikhā* (the hair-tuft which is not cut off for religious reasons) and the *Yajñopavītam* (the sacred sacrificial thread) and to carry knowledge alone as *śikhā* and *yajñopavītaṁ*.

4. A series of verses follow as a supplement, which, it seems, are meant to explain the prose portion. The first four are taken from the Śvet. 6,11.6,12. 1,14. 1.15. Then follow three verses for explanation of the metaphor of the spider, of the heart as a lotus flower, which the Brahman occupies, and of the four places of Brahman which are here paralleled with the four states for which purpose, however, *nābhi* has been replaced by *netram*. The two following Ślokas recommend the *saṁdhyā* as a symbol of oneness with God and oneness of all beings; here, there is a play, difficult to reproduce, on the words *saṁdhā* and *saṁdhyā*.—A reminiscence of Taitt. 2,4 and the verse Śvet. 1,16 conclude the whole which is built up of such a variety of constituent parts.]

1

Om!

Once it so happened that Śaunaka, a highly rich man, asked Pippalāda, the worthy Aṅgiras:

In the divine, lovely Brahman city [in the body] how are they (the gods of the vital organs) established?

And how do they break forth [outwards]?

And from whom originates this power of theirs?

And who is he, who has become this power of theirs?

He then explained to him the most splendid doctrine of Brahman and said:

It is the Prāṇa, is the Ātman; from the Ātman originates their power; he is the vital power of the gods [of the vital organs] he is the [place of] disappearance and appearance of gods.

He, who shines in the divine Brahman-city as the dustless indivisible, pure, imperishable Brahman (cf. Muṇḍ. 2, 2, 9), controls them, [and they follow him] as the bees the bee-king.[1]—And as the female fly-destroyer [the spider] spreads its net out of a thread and withdraws it within itself again to that thread (according to Muṇḍ. 1,1,7), similarly the Prāṇa also, when he

1. According to Praśna 2,4, with which passage *makṣikāvat* has to be read. The corruption is due to the following *yathā makṣikā*.

goes into [the arteries] withdrawing the spread-out within itself. For all the arteries [in which he goes] recognise the Prāṇa as the godhead in deep sleep, [which happens] as with the falcon and atmosphere (reference to Bṛh. 4,3,19). Just as the falcon, to wit, after soaring high in the sky, goes to his nest, similarly the one in the deep sleep also. For he says it [after waking up: "I have slept well". Comm.]

But just as anybody [in deep sleep; e.g.] Devadatta, as long as he is not struck with a stick or the like [read: *yaṣṭi-ādinā atāḍya-māna*, in view of the Kauṣ. 4, 19], does not stir about, similarly he is not soiled by sacrifices and pious works, by good and by bad. But just as a child, which has as yet no desires, lives in bliss, so also every Devadatta lives in bliss during [deep—] sleep. For he then cognises the highest light, and because he loves the light, therefore it makes him blissful.

Further he passes into dream with this one [highest Ātman], like a caterpillar,—that is to say, just like a caterpillar which propels itself from leaf-edge to leaf-edge, propelling its front part and dragging the hind part behind it (read *saṁdhayati aparam*), but does not leave the hind part in lurch. And he [the Ātman] is also the one who is called the waking one; and just as one [who wants to perform a sacrifice] keeps the eight potsherds together, similarly he bears it (the body with the organs); he as it were hangs on his bosom [cf. Bṛh. 4,3,21: *yathā priyayā striyā pariṣvakto*, and Cūlikā-Up. 3-6 above], he, who is the source of the Vedas and the gods.[1]

When men awake, their good and bad is an expression [manifestation] of this God who, as the origin of the world [if one does not read *saṁprasāda*, Chānd. 8,12,3], as inner guide (Bṛh 3,7), as bird, as crab,[2] as lotus flower, as Puruṣa, as Prāṇa,

---

1. According to Nārāyaṇa "It (the deep sleep, dream, waking) hangs on him (the Ātman) like a woman's breast; he is the source of the Vedas and the gods". The sense of the whole passage (extremely obscure in the origin) seems to be that the highest Ātman wholly and undividedly accompanies man through all the three states of deep sleep, dream and waking.

2. The comparison of the Ātman with a crab (*karkaṭaka*) makes no particular meaning and is isolated in the Upaniṣad literature.

as non-harm, as the higher and the lower Brahman, as Ātman makes the gods (of sense-organs) conscious.

He who knows this, grasps that the local soul (*kṣetrajña*) is the highest abode of Brahman, – he grasps that the local soul is the highest abode of Brahman (Cf. Muṇḍ. 3,2,1).

2

There are four dwellings of this Puruṣa; the navel, the heart, the neck and the head. In them the Brahman shines with its four quarters which are: the waking, the dream, the deep sleep, the Turīyam (Fourth); in the waking as Brahmán, in the dream as Viṣṇu, in the deep sleep as Rudra, in the Turīyam as the highest Imperishable.

This is Āditya, Viṣṇu and Īśvara, this is Puruṣa, this is Prāṇa, this Jīva, and this is the god-filled fire, which keeps guard (Praśna 4,3) in the Brahman-city of the body; in those (four dwellings) the highest Brahman shines.

Itself, however, it is without Manas, without ear, without hand and foot and wanting in light; in it there are not[1]

worlds and non-worlds,
gods and non-gods,
Vedas and non-Vedas,
sacrifices and non-sacrifices,
mother and non-mother,
father and non-father,
daughter-in-law and non-daughter-in-law,
cāṇḍāla and non-cāṇḍāla,
Paulkasa and non-Paulkasa,
ascetic and non-ascetic,
animals and non-animals,
penitent and non-penitent,

but it is only the one highest Brahman, which shines.

1. What folllows is a citation from Bṛh. 4,3,22 which, however, has acquired a completely different meaning on account of the prefixed *na* (not) : neither the objects nor their contradictory counterpart can be ascribed to the Brahman. (Śaṁkarānanda differs).

In the space in the heart is the Brahman, as consciousness, the space; and this very space is the hollow (universal) space because that is the space in the heart taught by the Veda (Chānd. 8,1,3), and in it stirs to and fro he in whom the whole world is sewn lengthwise and crosswise (Bṛh. 3,6). The creatures (or creation) must be viewed as His own Self, of the All-mighty. In him prevail no gods, no worlds, no wise, no forefathers, but only the awakened, the all-knowing.

In the heart are all gods,
In it the vital breaths also,
In the heart is life and light,
And the threefold thread[1] of the world.

In the heart, in the spirit, all this exists.

3

The sacrificial thread, the highest means of purification,
which in past originated along with Prajāpati,
The powerfully highest, pure, put it away!
May now strength and energy be your sacrificial thread.

Shearing off the tuft of hair too,
The wise one should cast off the external thread,
And wear the imperishable, highest
Brahaman as his sacrificial thread.

The thread is so called from untying,[2]
So the thread is called the highest place too,
He who has understood this thread,
He is wise, grounded in the Veda.

Everything is interwoven in him,
Like pearls strung on a thread,
Let the Yogin wear that as his thread,
He who sees the truth in the Yoga.

---

1. *Sattvam, Rajas* and *Tamas*.
2. Literally : "from making visible" (*sūcanāt sūtram*); the same etymology in Āruṇeya 3. (below).

The wise one casts off the external thread,
Who practises the Yoga as the highest,
He is the knower, wearing the thread,
Woven out of the Brahmanness.
He who wears such a thread,
Never lacks in purity, nor in purification.

Who, wearing the thread within,
Has the knowledge for his sacrificial thread,
He is the knower of the world-thread,
He is the wearer of the sacrificial thread.

To him the knowledge is the hair-tuft,
The permanent quarters and the thread.
The knowledge is to him the highest,
Incomparable means of purification.

Who like the pointed flame of fire,
Wears only a tuft of knowledge,
He really wears the hair-tuft,
The others only grow hair.

Yet one who, as a Brāhmaṇa,
Is engaged in Vedic activities,
Such an one may wear the external thread,
Which is a part of the accessories to works.

Who wears the knowledge as hair-tuft,
And the knowledge as the sacrificial thread,
He is the true Brāhmaṇa,
So teach us the Brahman-knowers.

Whom knowledge the highest sacred thread,
Whom knowledge the highest aim is,
That wise one has the sacrificial thread,
He is versed in sacrifice, is sacrifice himself.

4

The one God, hidden in all the beings,
All-pervading, inner soul of all,

The observer of works, filling all with perfume,
Witness, pure spirit and devoid of Guṇas,[1]—

The one wise, who multiplies
The eternal oneness into many, by nature inactive,
Him, the wise one who sees dwelling in the heart,
He has eternal peace, and none else.[2]
Making oneself the lower churn-stick,
And the Om-sound the upper wood,
One sees, after diligent thought-stirring,
The God, latent like the fire.[3]

Like oil in oil-seeds, butter in milk,
Water in streams, fire in the Churn-stick,
So one finds that Ātman in his own self,
He, the wise, who looks with truth and austerities.[4]

Like a spider which projects
And withdraws the thread within,
So the soul goes out in waking,
And goes in sleep again [5]

A space, resembling a lotus-calyx,
With its tip inclined downward,
Is the heart, and it is, know,
The basis that supports the universe.[6]

In waking he dwells in the eye,
In the neck during the dream,
In the heart during deep sleep,
As Turīyam he dwells in the head.[7]

---

1. =Śvet. 6.11.
2. =Śvet. 6.12 (free).
3. =Śvet. 1.14.
4. =Śvet. 1.15 (free).
5. Explanation of the metaphor of the spider, above para 1.
6. Explanation of part 2, end, =Mahānār. 11,6-7 (Atharva-recension).
7. Explanation of the beginning of part 2, with the substitution of the eye in the place of the navel mentioned there.

When through the knowledge dawns[1]
The individual self into the highest self,
That is the twilight-prayer,[1]
Worship, therefore, in the twilight!

The twilight-worship checks,[2]
Wards off the need of body, of speech,
Dams into a unity all beings
So the carriers-of-one-staff[3] practise it.

That from which words turn back,
Along with the Manas, without finding him,[4]
That is the bliss of the life's spirit;
The wise one knows him and becomes free.

The all-pervading Ātman,
Like butter concealed in milk,
In self-knowledge, self-discipline rooted,
Is the final goal of the Upaniṣad;[5]
Is the core of the All-One doctrine,
Is the final goal of the Upaniṣad,
—Is the final goal of the Upaniṣad.

---

1. A word-play between *saṁdhā* joining, *saṁdhin* (here probably : joining) and *saṁdhyā* twilight-prayer.
2. Read *nirodhakā*.
3. A particular class of Saṁnyāsins, here probably for the latter in general.
4. According to Taitt. 2,4.
5. =Śvet. 1,16.

SAṀNYĀSA UPANIṢAD

[In this Upaniṣad we have before us a very much damaged piece of old-Indian literature which, in prose with interspersed verses, portrays the transition from the position of the householder to that of the forest resident (*vānaprastha*) and the monk (*saṁnyāsin*), which two are not distinguished here.

1. The first chapter portrays the difference of the Saṁnyāsin from the sacrificial ritual. Retiring into the forest he performs once more a sacrifice to manes, as if sufficient for the whole future; then the Brahman-sacrifice (*brahmeṣṭi*) in which, to judge from the description, a real sacrifice to Brahman must be understood. Finally he throws into fire, under the recitation of the entire book Atharvav. 18, both the fire-sticks which he no more needs in the future, which his consecration (*saṁskāra*) is complete. From now on he pays homage to the sacrificial cult only symbolically in that, according to a notion familiar from Manu 6,25.38, he contains sacrificial fires in the body.

2. In the second chapter follows in verses a short description of the Brahmacārin and of the Gṛhastha and then a sketch of the Saṁnyāsin not differing from the Vānaprastha.

3. In the third chapter follows the consecration (*dīkṣā*) and the sketch of the Saṁnyāsin according to his outward appearance.

4. The same forms the subject of verses with which the fourth chapter begins. To them is added a section in prose which shows how elevation to Brahman is accomplished through meditation, connected with Taitt. 2,1, on the origination of all beings from the Brahman (here represented by Manas). The external behaviour of the meditator and the reward of his meditation are the subject of the verses which then follow.

5. The fifth chapter, linked with these, describes in prose the ascendence to the Brahman through the coronal suture after death.

These are the main contents of the Upaniṣad as existing in the very corrupt text of the Calcutta and Poona editions.[1] The commentary of Nārāyaṇa printed there is very defective, and its explanations are partly extremely forced and partly completely unacceptable.

Under these circumstances the translation here and there could be established only with some violence and it may serve as makeshift as long as a better text of the Upaniṣad is not available.]

---

1. The Telugu ed. could offer help only rarely, since the recension, in which our text appears there (p. 660-662) under the name Kuṇḍikā Upaniṣad, differs too much from ours. On the other hand the *Saṁnyāsa-Upaniṣad* of that collection is different and corresponds, in substance, to our *Kaṇṭhaśruti* 1-2.

1

When one who had deposited sacrificial fires dies, the consecration of the deceased takes place through Vedic formulae;—or also, when one in good health entertains a desire to reach over to the life's stages.

Then he brings together a collection of vegetables required for a sacrifice to departed forefathers, goes into the forest, and after depositing for the last time the sacred fires towards morning on the new-moon night, and after satisfying the forefathers by funeral offerings, he should then offer a Brahman-sacrifice (*brahmeṣṭi*), at which time he utters the words (the first line, the Muṇḍ. 1,1,9):

The all-knower and omniscient,
With knowledge as his penance,
Him for immortality may help
This divine sacrificial pouring !

and then further [in rhythmical prose] :

The Brahman, which rose to heaven as abode,
Filling this world and that everywhere,
May it, all creating, all blessings to us
Grant as well-disposed Godhead.

Then after making the offering with the verse:[1]

Brahman first, in former times was born,
[And later the seer discovered it shining,
While he its deepest, highest forms,
The womb of what exists and what not, unlocked.—]

and with the words: "To the Brahman, Atharvan, Prajāpati, Anumati and Agni Sviṣṭakṛt" and further, after offering both the fire-sticks to the fire with the formulae:

O sacrifice, go to sacrifice,
[Go to the dark spouse,
Go to your cradle! Svāhā!

1. Atharvav. 4,1,1; cf. our translation and discussions of the song, *Gesch. d. Phil.* I, 255.

and:

This is your sacrifice, O lord of sacrifice,
And your manly formula,
Enjoy it! Svāhā!]

he should make offerings of the butter with the four Mantras which begin with: "Hereby I will be friend—" etc. Atharvav. 18, 1-4).

Through these [Mantras] it [the consecration] takes place.

Then, with the words :
[In me,] O fire, [I receive] the fire,
[Together with strength, dignity and vigour,
In me I contain posterity and life ! Svāhā !]

he should receive in himself the two fires [in which he offers the fire-sticks] (cf. Manu 6,25,38) and maintain his vows without slackening.

2

About this are the verses :

1. Who, weary of Brahman-studentship,
Having fully learnt the Vedas,
Is discharged by teacher he had ev'r obeyed,
Such an one is called the Āśramin.

2. Choosing a wife of equally high birth,
He should deposit the sacred fires,
And bring to those deities,
The Brahman-sacrifice, day and night.

3. Until, dividing among the children
His property, abstaining from conjugal pleasures,
He gives himself to the forest-life,
Wandering in a pure region.

4. Living on water and on air,
And on such fruit as proper,[1]

1. In the explanation of the corrupt *vihitānottaraiḥ phalaih* Nārāyaṇa shows at his greatest. Read : *vihitan nottaraiḥ phalaiḥ*. [Here *vihitān*= *vihitāt* in saṁdhi. Other editions have a smoother reading : *vihitaiḥ kandamūlakaiḥ*.—GBP.]

Fire within body, he abides on earth
Without obligations, without tears.

5. But when he takes with him the fire,
How then is he called a renouncer ?—
How would the fire be similar,
By which he is called a renouncer ![1]

6. Therefore, a fire, which is unpolluted
By reward, does not vitiate renunciation,
It's such a fire that goes to the Forest,[2]
Accompanying the retiring recluse.

7. From the world into the forest
He goes, accompanied by his wife.—
Still he casts off there every desire,
How can fear then assail him ?

8. What can pain hold against him,
Since he runs away from lovely pleasures ?—
Dreading a fresh womb of mother,
A new pain through heat and cold.

9. I want to enter into my heart,
Where the dwelling is free from grief !—

3

After renouncing the sacrificial fire in this way, he does not return [to it] any more.

Then he should solemnize the consecration (*dīkṣā*), while muttering the formulae relative to the Self.[3]

---

1. The meaning of the obscure verse seems to be : Although he takes with him to the forest the sacrificial fires which he has received into the body, he is still a renouncer (*saṁyasta*, active), because these fires are essentially different from the real sacrificial fires which bring a reward.

2. Read *agnir vanam*.

3. Atharvav. 11,8; translated and explained in *Gesch.d.Phil.* I, 270-277.

[As self] Manyu a wife
[Out of the House of Saṁkalpa] chose,

Wearing a brownish red robe, with hair in armpit and on private parts removed, he should remain with an arm stretched up, free in the choice of his road. When, living in this way, he takes his food obtained by begging, he should carry a filter with him in order to [filter his drinking water and to] save germs [which may be there].

4

About this are the verses :

1. Pot, goblet and water-flask,
The three staves,[1] the pair of shoes,
A speckled mantel, giving protection
From cold and heat, a loins-cloth,

2. Bath-towel and cloth-strainer,
Threefold staff and upper shawl,
What lies beyond this,
All that an ascetic shall avoid.

3. Sleeping on the sandy banks of rivers,
Or in temples before the door,
Not straining the body too much,
Whether in pleasure or in pain,

4. With holy waters he should exert
After bathing, meditation[2] and purification,
Not rejoicing when praised,
Not cursing those who abuse him.

---

1. *triviṣṭapam* "the three-staff"; the Petersberg *Wörterbuch* would read *triviṣṭabdham* for it, but even the Kaṇṭhaśruti p. 292 and the Telugu ed. (Kuṇḍikā-Up. p. 661.8) read *triviṣṭapam.* On the other hand the repeated *tridaṇḍakam* may have been corrupted in the next verse because of a metrical error, and because Kaṇṭhaśruti and Kuṇḍikā concurrently read *eva ca.*

2. 'Nachsinnen'. Editions of the Up. available to me read *pānam* 'drinking'.—GBP.

5. Only begged food and dehiscent fruit,
Drinking and bathing material are allowed.
Adhering to this way of life,
He mortified his sensuality.

The cohesion of science (i.e. of the word of the Veda, of the Brahman) is in the Manas, through the Manas is originated the ether, out of the ether the wind, out of the wind the light, out of the light the waters, out of the waters the earth; [one who knows] in this way [the origination] of creatures out of the earth, goes into that unaging, immortal, indestructible imperishable, when in the devoted study of the same he restrains the outbreath and the inbreath.

About this are the verses:

1. Between Apāna and the testicles
He conceals the hands clasped together,
Pressing with his teeth the tongue
protruding, of the size of a barley-corn.

2. The eyes of the bean-size open,
The gaze on ear and eye-brow
Directing, nor smelling odour,
Hearing the sound, feeling with the skin.[1]

3. Then follows the state of blissfulness,
That Brahman, the highest goal;
For the sake of earlier births
The Ātman bestows it to the pious.

4. Establishing, with this means,
The heart in the restraint of penance,
The breath leaves the body upward,
Piercing through the head to the eternal one.

1. As the metre already shows, the passage is altogether corrupt. It would somewhat help if one reads : *aśravaṇo, na gandhāya nāsike, na tvaca spṛset,* but also in many other ways.

5

Then leaving behind the head, he overgrows it;[1] that is the road of those, who go to him; and those who have found the highest way [they ascend along it], they do not again return from the highest highplace,—from the highest high-place (*parama-vasthāt* for *paramāvasthānāt*).

1. *asya* is supposed to be equivalent to *kṣiptvā*, and *deha* to *dideha* (*upacaye*). An Indian scholiast is never at a loss.

ĀRUṆEYA[1] UPANIṢAD

[Āruṇi asks Prajāpati how he can get rid of works in such a way that nothing remains, and (so we must add) of the wandering of the soul which depends on them. Prajāpati refers him to the life as a Saṁnyāsin, who is here understood in the strict sense and is distinguished not only from a *Brahmacārin* and a *Gṛhastha*, but also from a *vānaprastha* and from a *kuṭīcara* (the 'hut-visitor',) cf. on this Āsrama-Up. 4 below). The rules which are laid down here for his life certainly let miss the systematic arrangement as also a perfect harmony, but they nonetheless give, particularly when one requisitions closely allied Upaniṣads for supplementing with, a vivid and in essentials a truly correct picture of that remarkable cultural phenomenon of asceticism, which would not have developed and preserved itself down to the present day, if the disposition to it had not been founded deep in human nature. But he who wishes to study Man wholly and perfectly cannot afford to neglect any side of him which has come into prominence in the course of history. Asceticism, it is true, has become quite foreign to our age and part of the globe, but it is not completely ruled out that Man will once more come back to it, since what gave birth to it lies in Man, lies in all of us.]

1

Āruṇi came to the world of Prajāpati. And approaching him he said: "How can I, O exalted sir, get rid of works, so that nothing remains of them ?"

Prajāpati said to him:

"[Renounce] your sons, brothers, relations and [friends]; one should renounce the hair-tuft and the sacrificial thread, the sacrifice along with the thread and also the Vedic studies, one should renounce the [seven higher] worlds: Bhūr, Bhuvaḥ, Svar, Mahas, Jana, Tapas, Satyam, and the [seven lower] worlds: Atala, Pātāla, Vitala, Sutala, Rasātala, Mahātala, Talātala, and the egg of Brahman (the universe);—one should take hold of a staff, an upper garment and a loins-cloth and should give up everything else,—should give up everything else.

1. Named *Āruṇika* in some editions and *Āruṇeyī* by Deussen himself above (*Brahma-Up.*, Introduction, note 1).—GBP.

2

Whether he be a householder, a Brahman-student or a forest-resident, he should deposit the sacrificial fires, which bring him worldly returns, in his gastric fire [in which he further offers the *Prāṇa-Agnihotram*] and the Gāyatrī in his speech-fire. He should, however, bury the sacrificial thread and the hair-tuft in the earth or sink them into the water.

If he is a hut-visitor (*kuṭīcara*) or a Brahman-student, he should renounce his family, renounce his vessel, renounce his filter renounce the staffs [which distinguish between a Brāhmaṇa, a Kṣatriya and a Vaiśya] and renounce the worlds; and he should also renounce the sacrificial fires which bring worldly returns! "so said [Prajāpati].

"From now on he should live without [the liturgical] Vedic formulae and renounce the ascendence [in the wandering of the soul conditioned by them].

On the other hand he should take a bath at the three junctures of the divisions of the day, practise the merging into the Ātman in meditation, recite the Āraṇyakam from all Vedas, recite the Upaniṣad,—recite the Upaniṣad".

3

" 'Verily, I am Brahman. The Brahman, as the manifesting (*sūcanāt*), is the [true] thread (*sūtram*, cf. Bṛh. 3,7,1), I myself am the thread, who knows as such!' The knower, who knows as such, should discard the threefold spun, [sacrificial] thread away.

'I have renounced, I have renounced, I have renounced!' he should say thus thrice and take up the bamboo staff [of the ascetic] and the loins-cloth.

He should take food only sparingly like medicine, he should take food only sparingly like medicine!

'All beings are safe from me, for everything has proceeded from me'; [he says thus and turning towards the staff]: 'You are my friend, guard me, you are energy and friend to me, you are Indra's thunderbolt'.

Chastity, non-violence, possessionlessness and truthfulness, you should observe this assiduously,—observe this assiduously!"

4

"Further as highest wanderers and pilgrims, it is your duty [to practise your homelessness] by sitting and lying on the ground, and as Brahman-students [who live on begging] [to carry] an earthen bowl, or a gourd-bowl or a wooden bowl.

He should give up desire, anger, lust, delusion, pride, deceipt, envy, egoism, self-conceit and untruth.

During the rainy season he should stay at one place, but in the remaining eight months, as an ascetic he should wander alone, or he should wander for two months,—wander for two months.

5

"Verily, he who grasps the meaning of the Veda may, after his initiation by the preceptor or even before that, renounce all this: his father and his son, the sacrificial fire and the sacrificial thread, his work and his wife and everything in this world.

Then as ascetics they enter the village only for begging food, with the belly as the bowl, or with the [palm of] the hand as the bowl. 'Indeed Om, indeed Om, Indeed Om!' He should bear this as an Upaniṣad [on the parts of the body]. Verily, he is a knower who knows this as an Upaniṣad.

Discarding the staff of Palāśa-wood, of Bilva-wood, of Aśvattha-wood [as the Brāhmaṇas, the Kṣatriyas and the Vaiśyas carry it], the hide, the girdle and the sacrificial thread, he becomes a conqueror, who knows thus".—

And the highest step of Viṣṇu
The patrons see for ever
Like an eye, stationed in heaven.
And wondering over this highest step
Of Viṣṇu, the priests, wide-awake,
Enkindle the sacrificial fire.[1]

Thus runs the instruction upon the Nirvāṇam, the instruction of the Veda,—the instruction of the Veda.

1. These verses (from Ṛgv. 1,22,20-21) form a favourite conclusion of many an Upaniṣad; cf. Skanda-Up. 15-16. Nṛsiṁhap. 5, 10. Vāsudeva 4. Muktikā, end.

KAṆṬHAŚRUTI UPANIṢAD

Kaṇṭhaśruti, the name of this Upaniṣad first cropped up in Colebrooke's catalogue *Misc. Ess.*, 2.ed., p. 86, note 3, and in Bergstedt's transcript, *Ind. Stud.* I, p. 302, but it was changed into *Kaṭhaśruti* by Weber, *Ind. Stud.* II, p. 396 and *Lit.* 2. *Aufl.*, p. 181 (with reference to a prosodial error in the initial and concluding verses of Nārāyaṇa's commentary). It was subsequently accepted in the Petersberg *Wörterbuch* (see under *Kaṭha*) as well as by Jacob, *Concordance* pref. p. 7; by both rather hastily : because with the exception of Telugu ed. (and, correspondingly the manuscript of the India Office, Eggeling p. 127) which, according to the enumeration of the Muktikā Up. verse 37 (Bombay) followed by it, calls the work *Kaṭha Upaniṣad* (*Kaṭharudra Upaniṣad* in the new Bombay ed.), as also possibly with that of Nārāyaṇa[1], all the manuscripts known to us (besides those mentioned above at the beginning : probably all the manuscripts of the Calcutta ed., since in any case no variant reading is noted,—two manuscripts of the India Office, Eggeling p. 110. 112,—the Oxford manuscript, Aufrecht p. 394b,—Stein's Catalogue of Kashmirian Manuscripts, which contains three copies of the Upaniṣad, p. 25—the Poona Collection in a catalogue prepared for me most kindly) offer, with a remarkable unanimity, *Kaṇṭhaśruti*. That this was corrected here and there into *Kaṭhaśruti* is as conceivable, as it is inconceivable that the name of one of the best known Vedic schools should have been corrupted uniformly in different parts of India, into the rare and unintelligible *Kaṇṭhaśruti*. We shall have therefore to regard this latter as the original name and we must make an attempt to find out an explanation for it.—If one considers the contempt in which these ascetics held the writing (how in the concluding verses of our

1. How Nārāyaṇa read, remains doubtful. The prosodial error in the initial and the concluding verses means nothing in the case of a 'versifex' who concludes so many of his Ślokas with *Upaniṣad-dīpikā*. The corrupt initial verse must be read (as already seen by Jacob, *Concordance* p. 5) as :

Yajurvede tu carakā dvādaśa, eṣāṁ kaṭhās trayaḥ |
Saṁnyāsa-upaniṣat-tulyā catuḥkhaṇḍā ka(ṇ)ṭhaśrutiḥ ||

"In Yajurveda there are twelve Caraka schools, three among them being Kaṭhas (*Kaṭhāḥ, Prācyakaṭhāḥ, Kapiṣṭhala-Kaṭhāḥ, Ind. Stud.* III. 257); [on the other hand] the *Ka(ṇ)ṭhaśruti* consisting of four [of five according to the edition; possibly a text with a different division than the present one was there before Nārāyaṇa] Khaṇḍas is like the Saṁnyāsa-Upaniṣad." Whether at the end Nārāyaṇa read *Kaṇṭha* or *Kaṭha* cannot be ascertained in the absence of manuscripts, because the contrast with the Kaṭha schools of the Yajurveda which he wants to stress makes both appear as possible.

Upaniṣad also the Vedas are expressly prohibited to them), and if one reminds oneself, that for 'learnt by heart' the expression *kaṇṭhastha* 'residing in the throat' (cf. par coeur=by heart) is quite common in (at least in the present day, spoken) Sanskrit, then the hypothesis will perhaps not be found altogether rash, that *kaṇṭhaśruti* could denote a "Śruti meant to be learnt only by heart, not to be written down" (in contrast to the Veda already written down).

The motley confusion of the rules for ascetics, which constitute the contents of our Upaniṣad, matches this unordered way of transmission.

Ch. 1. The last sacrifice of the Saṁnyāsin (a *Vaiśvānara* sacrifice).

Ch. 2. Parting with the son. Food, dwelling and dress of the Saṁnyāsin.

Ch. 3. Myth for recommending of the *Maunam* (silence). Parting with the son, once more and in detail.

Ch. 4. The last sacrifice (a twelve-day milk sacrifice), differing in performance from Ch. 1. Saṁnyāsin's way of life.

Ch. 5. Consecration (*dīkṣā*) of the Saṁnyāsin. His equipment, his way of life. Everything excepting a tattered piece of cloth (for filtering a drink) is denied him, even those very objects which are permitted to him in the parallel passages of the Saṁnyāsa Upaniṣad (above).

One could make an attempt, on ground of the last-mentioned contradiction, to construct different tendencies of milder and stricter observances, had not every attempt been still inadvisable for the time being to draw definite conclusions on account of the fluctuating nature of the text from the very beginning, the incredible naïveté of the commentator and the disgraceful carelessness of the editor.

It would be similarly hazardous to undertake a division of our text into more than one Upaniṣad, such as the Telugu ed. offers (Ch. 1-2=Saṁnyāsa-Up. there, 3-5=Kaṭha-Up; to both of these is appended a comet's tail of further verses) on account of contradictions and repetitions found in it. Also the agreement, partly verbatim, and the disagreement standing side by side with it, between Kaṇṭhaśruti 5 and Saṁnyāsa 3-4 (above) remain for the time being still unclarified.

And only this much can be known for the present, that among the Saṁnyāsins all kinds of rules, prose formulae and verses circulated, that the products of this mendicant-poetry or mendicant-philosophy gradually fused into small wholes, naturally circulated orally (*kaṇṭhastha*), until finally these disorderly jumbled up passages, partly repeated, partly mutually contradictory, found their recorder and they were received into the Atharva-Upaniṣads as Kaṇṭhaśruti-, Saṁnyāsa-, Āruṇeya-Upaniṣad and so on.

KAṆṬHAŚRUTI UPANIṢAD

1

One who renounces the world in the right order of succession (of the four stages of life), he is a renouncer.

What is this renunciation (*Saṁnyāsa*), and how does one become a renouncer ?

He who has made himself well-protected by good deeds may, after requesting the mother, the father, the wife, sons, friends and relatives for their consent, and after choosing once more as in the past all his previous sacrificial priests, offer the *Vaiśvānara* sacrifice,[1] then give up all his possessions and cause the transportation of the parts of his, the sacrificer's body to all the sacrificial implements through the sacrificial priests, while he lets the Prāṇa, the Apāṇa, the Vyāna, the Udāna and the Samāna to be transported into the Āhavanīya, Gārhapatya, Anvāhāryapacana, Sabhya and Āvasathya fires all in all – lets all transported in all.[2]

2

After removing the hair on the head including the hair-tuft (*śikhā*) and discarding the sacrificial thread, he goes out, takes a look at his son and greets him with the words: "You are Brahmán, you are the sacrifice, you are the universe." If he has no son, then he thinks in this way on himself, and then he wanders, without looking back, towards east or towards north.

---

1. Cf. Chānd, 5, 11-24 above, but also Kaṇṭhaśruti 4 and Jābāla 4 below.

2. "This transportation of the parts of the body and the vital breaths of the ascetic takes place in order to disembody him; for he whose limbs are transported to the sacrificial utensils etc. continues to exist, purged of them" Nārāyaṇa. The transportation (*samāropa*) of the vital breaths into the sacrificial fires occurring here is no doubt to be distinguished from the receiving (*samāropa*) of the sacrificial fires into the vital breaths, to which texts like Śatap. Br. 13,6,2,20 (*ātman agni samārohya*), Manu 6,25 as also the Prāṇāgnihotram refer.

Then he should beg among all castes, for his subsistence, eat his meals out of his hand as a pot, should take it as though it were his medicine, should eat according as he receives, only to keep his body and soul together, and in such a way that he does not put on fat, and remains lean.—He can stay one night only in a village, five nights only in a town, whether in a village or in a town, he can spend only the four months of the rainy season.[1] For clothing he should wear a torn one or a similar one made of tree-bark, he cannot wear another one.—If he is weak, he should practise austerities only so far as no complaint arises.

One who renounces in the proper order of succession, and also one who deviates from it, what serves him as the sacrificial thread? and what as the hair-tuft ? and how is his washing and rinsing of the mouth done ?—And he[2] said to them: The meditation of the Ātman is his sacrificial thread, and the knowledge is his hair-tuft, while he performs the work [of washing] with water as found everywhere, with water itself as the utensil [i.e. without a utensil]; his abode is on the river-bank, say the Brahman-teachers.—But after the sunset, how can he perform the washing and the rinsing of the mouth [because at night nothing can be taken out from the pond]?—And he said to them:

As by day so it is at night too,
For him there is no day and no night;

therefore it is said by the Ṛṣi also: "Then it is over the day" (Chānd. 3,11,3). Who knows this, does not mix with such-like,—does not mix with such-like.

3

Once upon a time the gods jointly said to Prajāpati: "We do not know it, we do not know it !" — And he said to the holiest

1. Here the Telugu ed. (p. 609, 19) inserts the observation : *pakṣau vai māsā*; *iti dvau māsau vā* (instead of four) *vaset*,—which is evidently a commentarial gloss.

2. Perhaps Prajāpati, and one could think of placing initial lines of the third chapter at the beginning of the present paragraph, had not the whole Upaniṣad too much the character of a fragmentary patchwork.

ones: "Hear it from me, while I impart it". Thereupon [after he had imparted it] it so happened that the holiest ones did not speak any further, did not speak any further. That is all [to be said in recommendation of silence]. He who knows this, attains to participation in dignity, world and life in common with gods.

After removing the hair on the head including the hair-tuft (*śikhā*) and discarding the sacrificial thread, he goes out, takes a look at his son and says: "You are Brahmán, you are the sacrifice, you are the Vaṣaṭ-exclamation, you are the Om sound, you are the Svāhā wish, you are the Svadhā-greating [to the manes], you are the creator, you are the ordainer, you are the modeller, you are the foundation". Thereupon the son says: "I am Brahmán, I am the sacrifice, I am the Vaṣaṭ-exclamation, I am the Om sound, I am the Svāhā-wish, I am the Svadhā-greeting, I am the creator, I am the ordainer, I am the modeller, I am the foundation"; all this [he repeats]. When he then accompanies the father, he should not shed tears, for if he sheds tears he cuts off his progeny and his knowledge [they show that he does not feel as identical with the father]. Then while they turn around towards the right, they go along their way, without looking back here and there. That is the heaven—that is the heaven.

4

After a Brahman-student has studied the Veda or two Vedas or all the three Vedas, observed a Brahmacārin's code of conduct, taken a wife, begotten sons, established them in suitable stations of life, and performed sacrifice according to the capacity, then renunciation (*saṁnyāsa*) is due for him. After taking the leave of his teachers and relatives, he goes out into the forest and for twelve days [first] performs the Āgnihotram with milk, while he subsists on milk for twelve days. At the end of twelve days [he offers] to the Agni Vaiśvānara and offers to Prajāpati a Prajāpati-oblation (of rice, barley and pulse) and to Viṣṇu a cake in three potsherds. Then, consigning to fire, he offers his old wooden utensils to the fire, offers his earthen, utensils in the water, and gives the metallic ones to the teacher. "May you not, leaving me, go away from me. May I not, leaving you, go away from you!" so says he to the Gārhapatya fire, so to the Dakṣiṇa fire, so to the Āhavanīya fire while, according to some, he drinks a handful of ashes from region of the fire-sticks.

After removing the hair on the head, including the hair-tuft, and discarding the sacrificial thread he offers the same with the words: "to the earth svāhā" into the water. Then he may set out on the great journey, while he abstains from food, goes into water, goes into fire or chooses a hero's death; or he may also betake himself to a hermitage of the old.

What then he eats in the evening, that is his evening-sacrifice; what in the morning, his morning sacrifice; what on the new-moon day, his new-moon-sacrifice; what on the full-moon day, his full-moon-sacrifice; and when in spring he causes his hair on the head, beard, hair on the body and nail to be cut, that is his Agniṣṭoma,—that is his Agniṣṭoma.

5

After renouncing the sacrificial fire, he should not restore it back. He should mutter the formulae relating to the Self (Atharvav. 11,8, *Gesch. d. Phil.* I, 270 ff):

When Manyu for himself a bride
[From Saṁkalpa's house] chose,

and after saying: "May all beings prosper! "he may solemnize the consecration (*dīkṣā*). His garment should be brownish red, he should remove the hair in the armpit and on the private parts; he should live with a small tonsure, without the sacrificial thread, having his belly as the utensil; why so ? because his meditation aims at the soul. With his arm stretched up, he should wander about without a place of residence; living by begging, he should give no alms;[1] he should carry only a rag (*lava*) with him in order to [filter his drinking] water and to save the germs [that may be there].

---

1. *bhikṣāśī na dadyāt* (Saṁnyāsa 3: *bhikṣāśanaṁ dadhyāt*): perhaps in our passage *bhikṣāśī 'ṣad adyāt* "one living by begging should eat frugally" is to be read.

On this there are these verses also:

1. Pot, goblet and water-flask,
The three staves, the pair of shoes,
A speckled mantel, giving protection
From winter cold, the loins-cloth,

2. Bath-towel and cloth-strainer,
And further, an uppper garment,
The sacrificial thread and the Vedas,–
All that the ascetic ṣhall avoid.[1]

3. With holy waters he should exert
After bathing, meditation and purification,
Lying on the sandy bank of rivers
Or in temples he may sleep.

4. Not straining the body too much
Whether in pleasure or in pain,
Not rejoicing, when praised,
Not cursing those who abuse him.

5. That is the conduct, practising which
They accomplish the mortification of senses.

---

1. Verses 1-2 recur at Saṁnyāsa 4, verses 1-2, with a slight change which, however, exactly reverses the whole idea; the things enumerated there are the only ones which are allowed to a Saṁnyāsin, while according to the stricter custom of our Upaniṣad even they are forbidden to him. [Stanzas 3-4=Saṁnyāsa 3-4, with a variation in the sequence cf. lines.—GBP].

PARAMAHAṀSA UPANIṢAD

[*Haṁsa*, the wandering (wild) goose, whose roaming is already mentioned in the Ṛgveda (1,163,10.3,8,9) and more frequently in the Upaniṣads (Chānd. 4,1. Śvet, 1,6.3,18) is a symbol, on the one hand, of the migrating soul and on the other, of the homeless Parivrājaka on pilgrimage who is called *Paramahaṁsa* 'supreme wandering bird' in the stage of his highest perfection. Our Upaniṣad draws a lovely and vivid picture of him, portraying how he renounces the world and all inclination towards it, in order to find a full recompensation for it in the consciousness of unity with the Brahman, with the *Bhagavān*. By the *Bhagavān* it is not here Sanatkumāra who is to be understood, as Nārāyaṇa does with a reference to Chānd. 7, but as remarked by Śaṁkarānanda, only Hiraṇyagarbha, i.e. the Brahman consceived as person (Cf. the words at the beginning : "All his thoughts are always about me; so I am also always in him"). The picture of the perfected ascetic drawn by the Bhagavān agrees essentially with the one sketched in previous Upaniṣads but on the whole it makes an impression of belonging to a later period in which the inserted verse as also the warnings at the end give it to understand, that the position of the Saṁnyāsin and his immunity from law was already occasionally utilised as a cloak for licentious lust.]

1. Nārada, approaching the Bhagavān, asked him : "Which is the way of the Yogins, the Paramahaṁsas ? And what is their position ?"

The Bhagavān said to him :

This way of the Paramahaṁsas is difficult to find in the world and it is not much trodden. But when one treads it, he remains in constant purity, he is the Veda-man, so think the wise, is a great man. All his thoughts are always about me; so I am also always in him.

He renounces children, friends, wife, relatives, the hair-tuft and the sacrificial thread, Vedic study and all works, he renounces the whole world and takes up loin-cloth, staff and a covering and endeavours just to preserve his body and help others.—

But this one is not the highest; and if you ask, who the highest is,—it is he,

2. who, as a Paramahaṁsa carries no staff, no hair-tuft, no sacrificial thread, no covering any longer, who no longer

cares for cold and heat, for pleasure and pain, for respect and disrespect, who on the contrary, is free from the six waves [of Saṁsāra: hunger, thirst, grief, illusion, old age and death], in that he leaves behind censure, pride, jealousy, deceipt, haughtiness, desire, hatred, pleasure, pain, longing, anger, greed, illusion, joy, irritation, egoism and all things of that kind; and while he looks upon his own body only as a corpse, he turns away for ever from this depraved body which is the cause of doubt, perversity and error, directs his perception continually on it [Brahman], abides in that alone, knows of it, the quiet, immutable : "That timeless, consisting of bliss and knowledge I am myself, He is my highest abode, my hair-tuft, my sacrificial thread !" Then the dividing wall between the two is pulled down with the knowledge of the identity of the Ātman and the Paramātman, and that is the true union-time (also : twilight-prayer, *Saṁdhyā*).

3. Who, giving up all desires,
Abides in the secondless, supreme one,
Carrying the staff of knowledge alone,
He is truly called a one-staffed one (ascetic)

But he, who, without knowledge
carrying the high staff, eats from anybody,
He goes to terrible hell,
Which is called 'the great howler'.

He who understands this difference is a Paramahaṁsa.

4. The space is his garment, he knows no obeisance, no sacrifice to manes, no censure nor praise, no sacrificial call, but lives just as it comes to him,[1] as a mendicant. He does not attract, and he does not repulse; for him there are no Veda-formulae any more, no meditation, no obeisance, nothing fit to be seen and nothing unfit to be seen, nothing separate and nothing inseparate, no I, no you and no world. Without a lodging, he lives as a mendicant; he has nothing to do with gold and such things, for him there is nothing to be seen or looked at. But do you mean to say that he may not harm himself by merely looking ? He may harm himself thereby. Because

1. Cf. Bṛh. 3,5. Gauḍap. 2,37 (above).

he is an ascetic, therefore, if he looks at gold longingly, he becomes a Brāhmaṇa-killer; because he is an ascetic, therefore, if he touches gold longingly, he becomes a Paulkasa; because he is an ascetic, therefore, if he grasps gold longingly, he becomes a self-killer. Therefore an ascetic should not look at, touch or grasp gold longingly; he should turn away from all desires that may come to his mind. Firm-minded in grief, not seeking after joy, renouncing all desires, not attached anywhere, neither to the good nor to the bad, he is without hatred and without pleasure. The impulse of all senses comes to rest, he abides in the knowledge alone, well-established in the self. That is the true Yogin, is the knower; his consciousness is permeated with that whose only taste is perfect bliss. That Brahman I am, he knows it and has that goal achieved,—that Brahman I am, he knows it and has the goal achieved.

JĀBĀLA UPANIṢAD

[The Jābālas are enumerated as a branch school of the Yajurveda in the Caraṇavyūha (*Ind. Stud.* III, 262). In the commentary to the Brahmasūtras Śaṁkara cites as '*Jābālānām*' or '*Jābālānām śrutiḥ*' thirteen passages, out of which nine are found in our Upaniṣad (*System des Vedānta*, p. 33), and already even Bādarāyaṇa (Brahmasūtra 1,2,32) seems to refer to one of these. Further, the beginning of the sixth chapter of our Upaniṣad has been quoted by Sāyaṇa under Taitt. Ār. 2,11 p. 246 as a text of the *Jābāla-śākhā-adhyāyinaḥ*. From this it appears that a Śākhā of the Jābālas in reality existed, of which, however, our Upaniṣad formed only a part (as the citations of Śaṁkara, which are not any more traceable to it, already show), which, to judge from its whole attitude, certainly seems to stand on the same footing as the other Saṁnyāsa Upaniṣads and anyway not much removed in antiquity it can be compared with the related passages of the Bṛhadāraṇyaka Upaniṣad.

According to the pattern of the Bṛh. 3-4, here also it is Yājñavalkya who in the first five chapters answers the questions put to him by Bṛhaspati, Atri, The Brahman-students, Janaka and by Atri once more.

1. On Avimuktam as the sacrificial place of the gods and the Brahman-seat of all beings. *Avimuktam* 'that which is never left [by Śiva]' is a region in Banaras, in a wider sense Banaras itself. By the grace of Śiva liberation is granted to him who dies there (*Prāṇāgnihotra Up.* above, last foot-note). But the Parivrājaka carries this Avimuktam on himself as the point between the eyebrows and the nose (just as he has admitted the sacrificial fires and the sacrificial thread in his self). This allegorical explanation of Avimukteśvaram, it is true, comes later on only in the next section, but it is already presupposed here, because it is fully understandable only to the initiated.

2. Near Banaras two small streams flow into the Ganges : on the upper side of the city the Asī, mostly dry, on the lower side of it the Varaṇā, similarly very small; the city of Banaras is supposed to have got its name from these two. This place between the Varaṇā and Asī, on which the supreme Ātman rules is always carried by the Parivrājaka on himself as the spot where both the eyebrows meet together at the root of the nose, just like the two streams meeting together near Banaras. The name of the city is falsely analysed into Varaṇā and Nāsī, in order to achieve a word-play with *vārayati* and *nāśayati*.

3. Yājñavalkya recommends the *Śatarudriyam* (Vāj. Saṁh. XVI) as a means of immortality to the Brahman-students who had questioned him, because the hundred Rudras, who occur there, are conceived as many epithets of the Immortal (i.e. the Ātman).

4. Janaka asks Yājñavalkya (in connection with Bṛh. 4,4,22, it appears) about the departure of the Saṁnyāsin, at which it is described quite similarly as in other Saṁnyāsa Upaniṣads. Like the Vaiśvānara sacrifice in the Kaṇṭhaśruti 1, here a sacrifice to Agni as a representative of Prāṇa, and a sacrifice to the three Guṇas of the Sāṁkhya doctrine is prescribed for the person renouncing. The inhaling of the fire probably means that thereby it is symbolically received into the body of the Saṁnyāsin.

5. Upon the enquiry of Atri, feeding and dressing of the Prāṇa in the sense of the Chān. 5,19ff and 5,2 is recommended to the Parivrājaka as his only duty. At the end the words *eṣa panthāḥ* etc. are repeated from Bṛh. 4,4,9 and refer to the Saṁnyāsin.

6. The concluding section portrays, according to the enumeration of a number of great models, the procession, the way of life and the place of residence of the Saṁnyāsin; the whole section recurs similarly at the end of the Bhikṣuka Up. and partly at the end of the Āśrama Up. also.]

1

Om !

Bṛhaspati said to Yājñavalkya : "[Tell me that] which is next to Kurukṣetram itself as a sacrificial place of the gods and as Brahman-seat of all beings".— He said : "Verily, Avimuktam is the [true] Kurukṣetram, the sacrificial place of gods and the Brahman-seat of all beings.

Therefore, wherever he may be wandering, he [the Parivrājaka who does not restrain himself to any holy places any longer] should think : here, verily, is the [true] Kurukṣetram, the sacrificial place of gods, the Brahman-seat of all beings. For here, when the vital breaths depart out of a person, Rudra imparts the saving formula, by which one participates in immortality, participates in liberation. Therefore, one should revere Avimuktam, one should not leave Avimuktam [which is not left] !"—"It is so, O Yājñavalkya."

2

Then Atri asked Yājñavalkya : "This infinite, not manifest Ātman, how can I know him ?"—And Yājñavalkya said : "In Avimuktam he is to be revered ! that infinite, not manifest Ātman, he is to be found in the Avimuktam".—"But where is this Avimuktam-place to be searched for ?" — "It is to be searched for between the Varaṇā and the Nāsī."—"But what is the Varaṇā and what the Nāsī ?"—"Varaṇā is so-called because she wards off (*vārayati*) errors committed by the organs of the body; while Nāsī is so-called because she destroys (*nāśayati*) sins committed by the organs of the body".—"But where is the place of this Avimuktam ?"—"It is the meeting place of the eyebrows and the nose. For that is the connecting place of the world of heaven and the highest world [of Brahman]. Therefore, the knowers of Brahman revere this connecting place as the union-time (twilight). For in Avimuktam, so they know, one should revere him [the Ātman]. He who knows thus, proclaims his knowledge as *avimuktam* (unforgettable)".

3

Then the Brahman-students said to him : "By the muttering of which [prayer] one attains immortality, tell us that !"—Yājñavalkya said: By the "*Śatarudriyam*; for these are the names of Immortality, and through them one becomes immortal".—"It is so, O Yājñavalkya !"

4

Then Janaka, the king of Videha, approached Yājñavalkya and said : "Explain to me, O exalted sir, the renunciation (*Saṁnyāsa*)!" And Yājñavalkya said: "If one has finished the Brahman-studentship, one may become a householder; after one has been a householder, one may become a forest-resident; after one has been a forest-resident, one may wander about on pilgrimage [as *Parivrājaka, Bhikṣu*, Saṁnyāsin]. Or one may even directly go on pilgrimage after Brahman-studentship, or after householdership, or after the forest-residentship. And even otherwise, whether he may have observed a vow or not, whether he has taken the final ablution or not, whether he has caused the household fires to extinguish or whether he is [already] without fire,—from that day on, on which he renounces, he should wander as a pilgrim. Here some perform a sacrifice to Prajāpati;[1] one

1. In the place of sacrifice to Prajāpati (which, as it appears, means redeeming oneself from the obligation of propagation) comes a sacrifice to the Prāṇa (an ascetic requires no progeny, Bṛh. 4,4,22).—Here there seems to be a polemic against the precept given in the Kaṇṭhaśruti 4 (above).

should not do that, but offer a sacrifice to Agni alone, for Agni is the Prāṇa; so thereby one offers to the Prāṇa. Then he should offer the *Traidhātavīya* sacrifice; thereby the three Dhātus (elements), namely Sattvam, Rajas and Tamas are worshipped.

This is the place, which is rightfully yours,
Where, as soon as born, you shone brilliantly;
Knowing it, Agni, ascend it
And make our riches grow!

With this formula (Atharvav. 3.20,1) he should inhale the fire. The Prāṇa, verily, is the seat (place of origination, *yoni*) of the fire, and he says thereby "Go to the Prāṇa, *svāhā* !"

Or [the priest] may also bring the fire from a village and make him [the Saṁnyāsin] inhale the fire as described. If he cannot get fire, he should make an offering in water, for water is all godheads. And after performing the sacrifice with the words "Om, I offer to all godheads, svāhā" he should take out of it and eat the wholesome sacrificial food along with clarified butter. Thereby he will find that the liberating formula [Om] is all the three Vedas; for this is the Brahman, that one should worship. It is so, O exalted sir".

Thus spoke Yājñavalkya.[1]

5

Then Atri asked Yājñavalkya : "I ask you, Yājñavalkya, how can a Brāhmaṇa be without the sacrificial thread ?"—And Yājñavalkya said : "This very thing is his sacrificial thread, namely the Ātman; that he feeds himself, and that he rinses the mouth, that is the sacrificial precept of the Parivrājakas, whether for the rest he chooses a hero's death or abstains from taking food, or goes into water, or goes into fire or sets out on the great journey [otherwise].

Thus it comes to pass that the pilgrim, with colourless garments, with shaven head, without belongings, pure, free from deceipt, living on begging, becomes fit for Brahmanhood.

1. Here, as also at the end of sections 1 and 3, editions available to me read *Yājñavalkyaḥ*. Still Deussen's way of translation there suggests that he reads Yājñavalkya (i.e. a vocative) there. He should have done the same here also. The word *bhagavan* (which should properly refer to Yājñavalkya) and the absence of any word for 'spoke' in the Skt. original also indicate this.—GBP.

If he is too ill [to observe this mode of life], then he may practise the renunciation only mentally and by words.

This is the path found out by Brahman, the renouncer goes along it, the knower of the Brahman (Cf. Bṛh. 4,4,9).

This is the case with him, O exalted sir."
Thus spoke Yājñavalkya.[1]

6

Thus were the men called Paramahaṁsas, a Saṁvartaka, Āruṇi, Śvetaketu, Durvāsas, Ṛbhu, Nidāgha, Jaḍabharata, Dattātreya, Raivataka and others, without a visible sign and with their conduct concealed, behaving like insane, but not insane.

Three staves, water-vessel, drinking bowl, water-flasks, water-filter, hair-tuft and sacrificial thread, all this one should throw into water with the words "*bhūḥ svāhā*" and seek the Ātman.

Naked as he was born, above the pairs of opposites (joy and sorrow etc.), without belongings, wholely devoted to the way to truth, the Brahman, with a pure heart, going out, without any restrictions, aimlessly for begging alms at prescribed hour only to sustain his life, with the belly as his utensil, even-tempered whether he gets anything or not,—staying homeless, whether in a deserted house, in a temple, on a heap of grass, on an ant-hill, at the roots of a tree, in a potter's workshop, in a fire sanctuary, on a river bank, in a mountain cave, in a ravine, in a hollow tree, at a waterfall or on bare ground, not striving, free from the feeling of 'mine', given to pure contemplation, firmly rooted in the supreme Self, eradicating all evil deeds,—who becomes free from the body by means of renunciation, he is called a Paramahaṁsa,—he is called a Paramahaṁsa.

1. Editions available to me read here *Yājñavalkya* (i.e. a vocative). Also there is no word corresponding to 'spoke'—GBP.

ĀŚRAMA UPANIṢAD

[For the four Āśramas or the 'exercise-stages' in which the life of an Ārya was supposed to proceed, see above Introduction [at the beginning of this work] and the Chānd. Up. Introduction to 23rd *khaṇḍa*. The last stage of life is that of the *Saṁnyāsin*, *Bhikṣu*, *Parivrājaka* who, as the names signify "throws away everything", "lives on begging" and "wanders about on pilgrimage homelessly." The division of these Saṁnyāsins into four kinds as *Kuṭīcaras* (or *Kuṭīcakas*), Bahūdakas, Haṁsas and Paramahaṁsas is often met with. To conclude from the names, this division originally seems to refer to the different places of residence of the Parivrājaka (near huts, near water, sometimes in towns and sometimes in villages, wholely uncertain) and only later to have attained to a hierarchy of gradually increasing perfection. Thus a verse of the Mahābhārata (13,6478)[1] runs :

Caturvidhā bhikṣavas te, kuṭīcaka-Bahūdakau,
Haṁsaḥ Paramahaṁsaś ca; yo yaḥ paścāt, sa uttamaḥ.

With this may be compared particularly passages from older authorities collected by Mādhava in Aufrecht, *Oxf. Cat.* p. 269a.

These four stages of the Saṁnyāsa are shortly characterised in an Upaniṣad text which has found a place in the Muktikā Collection (No. 60, Telugu ed. p. 552) under the name of Bhikṣuka-Upaniṣad. This text forms (in a somewhat different recension) only the fourth chapter of the present Upaniṣad, to which three others are prefixed, which also examine the remaining three Āśramas in a similar way and distinguish four classes in each of them. What is not clearly perceptible is whether all these varieties are to be thought of as different, coexisting tendencies or whether as ascending stages, following one another, in the first three Āśramas also. Probably here we are dealing with, as in the case of the Āśramas themselves, varieties which originally existed side by side and were later combined in the system into an ascending graded sequence. In any case this systematisation is only secondary and artificial; also the names do not quite agree in many cases with the description given. Particularly unintelligible is how the Prājāpatya, according to its first definition, can be assigned to the class of Brahmacārins. The names given here and their explanations are therefore to be accepted rather cautiously and may serve as a source for the knowledge of the Āśrama life, only so far as they are corroborated from other side.

Our Upaniṣad, which is the last one in Colebrooke's list, is missing in the *Oupanekhat*, and about Nārāyaṇa also it cannot yet be shown with

1. =BORI Crit. Ed. 13.129.29 (with variants).

certainty (above, Introduction to the Upaniṣads of the Atharvaveda, section 5), that he has presented and commented upon it in his list, also how uptil now no commentary at all on it has come to light.]

1

Now it is to be further said that there are four Āśramas with sixteen subclasses.

The Brahmacārins are fourfold, viz. *Gāyatra*, *Brāhmaṇa*, *Prājāpatya* and *Bṛhan*.

Gāyatra is he who, after the initiation, not eating salty food throughout for three [days and] nights, remains occupied with the Gāyatra-formula.

Brāhmaṇa is he, who adheres to the Vedic study for fortyeight years throughout, twelve years for each Veda, or only so long, until he masters the Veda.

Prājāpatya is he who, content with his wife, approaches her at the time of the Ṛtu and always keeps himself away from other women.

Or also : *Brāhmaṇa* is he who lives in the house of the teacher for twentyfour years, *Prājāpatya* who lives there for fortyeight years.

Bṛhan is he, who as *Naiṣṭhika* (constant in chastity) does not leave the teacher until his death.

2

Also the Gṛhasthas (householders) are fourfold viz. *Vārttākavṛttis*, *Śālīnavṛttis*, *Yāyāvaras* and *Ghorasaṁnyāsikas*.

Vārttākavṛttis (living on farm-produce) are they who, engaged in agriculture, cattle-breeding and trade without ill repute and performing sacrificial acts lasting for a hundred years, strive after the Ātman.

Śālīnavṛttis (living a settled life) are they who, sacrificing without making one sacrifice, studying without teaching, giving without taking and performing sacrificial acts lasting for a hundred years, strive after the Ātman.

Yāyāvaras (wander lusty) are they who sacrificing and making one sacrifice, studying and teaching, giving and taking and performing sacrificial acts lasting for a hundred years, strive after the Ātman.

Ghorsaṁnyāsikas (practising a fierce renunciation) are they who doing their work with selected and filtered water only, managing their maintenance with ears of corn picked up daily and performing sacrificial acts lasting for a hundred years, strive after the Ātman.

The Vānaprasthas also are fourfold viz. *Vaikhānasas, Udumbaras, Vālakhilyas* and *Phenapas.*

Vaikhānasas (followers of Vikhānasa) are they, who, tending the sacred fires with creepers and trees which grow on uncultivated land, and with ritual performed outside a village and thus observing the practice of the five great sacrifices, strive after the Ātman.

Udumbaras (*Audumbaras ?* fig-gatherers) are they who, when they get up in the morning, gather corns of fig-trees, jujube, rice and millet from the region on which his glance falls and tending the sacred fires with them and thus observing the practice of the five great sacrifices, strive after the Ātman.

Vālakhilyas (bald-headed) are they who, wearing hairlocks with a cloth rag, clad in hide or tree-bark, offering flowers and fruit on the full-moon day of the month of Kārttika [the festival day of Śiva], procuring their subsistence in the remaining eight months [until the beginning of the rainy season], tending the sacred fires and thus observing the practice of the five great sacrifices, strive after the Ātman.

Phenapas (foam-drinkers) are they who, while they, like insane, subsist on fallen leaves and fruit, dwelling wherever they be tending the sacred fires and thus observing the practice of the five great sacrifices, strive after the Ātman.

4

The *Parivrājakas* also are fourfold, viz: *Kuṭīcaras*, *Bahūdakas*, *Haṁsas* and *Paramahaṁsas.*

The *Kuṭīcaras* (hut-visitors) are they who, carrying on begging in the houses of their children, strive after the Ātman.

The *Bahūdakas* (the water-friends) are they who, equipped with the three-staff, water-pot, water-flask, side-locks, water-filter, drinking bowl, shoes, seat, hair-tuft, sacrificial thread, loins-cloth, and reddish brown garments, carrying on begging in well brought-up families of Brāhmaṇas, aspire after the Ātman.

The *Haṁsas* (wandering birds) are they who, carrying a single staff, without hair-locks, wearing a sacrificial thread, with the waterflask and water-pot in the hand, staying for one night only in a village and five nights in a town and in holy bathing places, still threat undertaking throughout one or two nights difficult vows like the fasting according to the lunar course, aspire after the Ātman.

The *Paramahaṁsas* (highest wandering birds) are they who, without staff, bald-headed, clad in rags and loins-cloth, without any particular mark and without any particular mode of life, moving about like an insane one although not insane, discarding three-staff, water-pot, water-flask, side-locks, water-filter, drinking bowl, shoes, seat, hair-tuft and sacrificial thread, dwelling in a deserted house or in a temple, no longer know right, wrong, untruth, put up with everything, remain patient with everybody, regard earth-clods, stones and gold equally and, begging alms among all the four castes where they happen to be, liberate their soul,—liberate their soul.

d. Śiva Upaniṣads

ATHARVAŚIRA UPANIṢAD

ATHARVAŚIKHĀ UPANIṢAD

NĪLARUDRA UPANIṢAD

KĀLĀGNIRUDRA UPANIṢAD

KAIVALYA UPANIṢAD

ATHARVAŚIRAS
(Atharvaśira Upaniṣad)[1]

This Upaniṣad, which calls itself (p. 10,9, Calcutta ed.) *Atharvaśiras* (which probably means : "The main point of the Atharvaveda",—cf. *Vedānta* "The final goal of the Veda") and quotes, at 9,3, the verse Atharvav. 10,2,27 (probably misunderstood) for an explanation of this name, extols as the principle of all things and as the highest goal, *paramaparam* (not *param-aparam*[2]), *parāyaṇam*, Rudra (Īśāna, Bhagavān Maheśvara,—the name Śiva does not occur). Rudra is the past, the present and the future, he is all-embracing and is the innermost of all objects, he is the visible and the invisible. He who knows him, thereby knows everything (1,12); he is to be proclaimed through silence alone (7,13). His symbol is the sound Om, and especially the three-and-halfth (imaginary) mora of it (4,10). Rudra dwells in the heart (4,10) and pervades the entire creation (8,10ff), which consists of nine heavens, nine atmospheric regions and nine earths (9,5). When he coils himself together as a snake, he absorbs the world and releases it again through his breath (9,10ff). He is the unity of the life-organs and the corresponding deities (6,1 ff). The man is his creation (*paśu*) and is bound by the cord (*pāśa*) of earthly existence. The liberation from birth, sorrows, death (5,10) follows when one surrenders anger and lust (tṛṣṇā), the earth as the root of the causal chain (*hetujālasya mūlam*) and all possessions to Rudra (7,3.8,3).—The Upaniṣad seems to belong to a sect of the Pāśupatas, as whose vow (*vratam pāśupatam*) the symbolical smearing with ashes is mentioned (8,8). The further systematisation of the Pāśupatas, however, does not appear in this Upaniṣad. The text of this Upaniṣad is considerably corrupt, so that help had to be taken from conjectures.

---

1. On the sequence. Now follow five Upaniṣads which look upon the god Śiva as a symbolical personification of the Ātman, viz : *Atharvaśiras*, *Atharvaśikhā*, *Nīlarudra*, *Kālāgnirudra* and *Kaivalya*. We adhere to this sequence which follows from the lists of Colebrooke and Nārāyaṇa, although it does not certainly quite correspond to the time of origination, since the *Nīlarudra Upaniṣad*, in so far as it offers only an abstract of the Vāj. Saṁh. 16 and similar passages, is by far the oldest piece. Also to judge from its contents, the *Kaivalya Upaniṣad*, in spite of its late position in the above lists, could have originated in a comparatively old age, an age close to that of the *Śvetāśvatara*, *Muṇḍaka* and *Mahānārāyaṇa Upaniṣads.*

2. But the foregoing pairs of expressions like *hutam ahutam* favour this interpretation rejected by Deussen.—GBP.

1

Om! Once the gods went to heaven. And they asked Rudra: "Who are you?"—And he said: "I am that one [which] existed at first, I exist, and I shall exist. None else is there apart from me. I am that [which] entered the inner from the inner. I am eternal and non-eternal, visible and invisible, Brahman and non-Brahman. I am eastern and western, southern and northern, I am below and above (Chānd. 7,25,1), I am the quarters and the sub-quarters. I am masculine and neuter and feminine (Atharvav. 10,8,27). I am the Sāvitrī and the Gāyatrī, I am the Triṣṭubh, the Jagatī and the Anuṣṭubh. I am the appearance and the reality. I am the fire Gārhapatya and Dakṣiṇa and Āhavanīya. I am the cow and the she-buffalo. I am Ṛc, Yajus and Sāman and I am the Atharvāṅgiras'. I am the eldest, the noblest and the best (Bṛh. 6,1,1). I am the water and the fire, I am hidden in the fire-sticks. I am the imperishable and the perishable. I am the lotus flower and I am the Soma-filter. I am the powerful, I am within and without, I am 'the light [born] in the East' (Atharvav. 4,1,1). I am all, I am the unending.[1] He who knows me, becomes all at the same time. He knows the gods and all the Vedas and the Vedāṅgas. And I am also that, I who with my power satisfy the Brahman by the Brāhmaṇas, the cow with the cows, the Brāhmaṇas with the Brāhmaṇahood, the sacrificial food with the sacrificial food, the life with the life, the truth with the truth, the law with the law".—Then the gods asked Rudra, the gods looked at Rudra, the gods thought over Rudra, the gods praised Rudra [with the following hymn of praise] with raised hands.

2

Om!

Rudra is this exalted one and Brahmán, to him the salutation, the salutation!

,, ,, ,, Viṣṇu, ,, ,, ,,

,, ,, ,, Skanda, ,, ,, ,,

,, ,, ,, Indra, ,, ,, ,,

---

1. The text and the sense are quite uncertain here and in the following lines.

Rudra is this exalted one and Agni, to him the salutation,
the salutation

,, ,, ,, Vāyu, ,, ,, ,,
,, ,, ,, Sūrya, ,, ,, ,,
,, ,, ,, Soma, ,, ,, ,,

Rudra is this exalted one and the 8 seizors,[1] to him the salutation,
the salutation!

,, ,, ,, the 8 superseizors[1] ,, ,,
,, ,, ,, *bhūr*, ,, ,, ,,
,, ,, ,, *bhuvaḥ*, ,, ,, ,,
,, ,, ,, *svar*, ,, ,, ,,
,, ,, ,, *mahas*[2] ,, ,, ,,
,, ,, ,, the earth, ,, ,, ,,
,, ,, ,, the mid-region ,, ,,
,, ,, ,, the heaven ,, ,, ,,
,, ,, ,, the water ,, ,, ,,
,, ,, ,, the fire ,, ,, ,,
,, ,, ,, Kāla, ,, ,, ,,
,, ,, ,, Yama, ,, ,, ,,
,, ,, ,, Mṛtyu, ,, ,, ,,
,, ,, ,, the immortal ,, ,, ,,
,, ,, ,, the ether, ,, ,, ,,
,, ,, ,, the all ,, ,, ,,
,, ,, ,, the gross, ,, ,, ,,
,, ,, ,, the fine, ,, ,, ,,
,, ,, ,, the white, ,, ,, ,,
,, ,, ,, the black, ,, ,, ,,
,, ,, ,, the whole, ,, ,, ,,
,, ,, ,, the true, ,, ,, ,,
,, ,, ,, the universe, ,, ,, ,,

3

Bhūr is your beginning, *bhuvar* your middle, *svar* your head. You are omniform, Brahman. You are one, twofold, threefold.

---

1. Cf. Bṛh. Up. 3,2 and the translator's note there.
2. Taitt. 1,5.

You are growth, you are peace, you are prosperity. What is offered in sacrifice and what not offered in sacrifice, given and not given, all and non-all, whole and non-whole, done and undone, the highest of the highest (*parama-param*, that is how it is to be split[1]), the highest goal, you are it.

We have drunk Soma, have become immortal,
Have entered into the light, found out the gods!
What could the hostility harm us now,
What, O immortal, the malice of man! (Ṛgv. 8,48,3).

Before Soma and Sūrya is the subtle soul. But comprising [implicit, *hitam*] the whole world is that syllable [Om], which swallows what is Prajāpati-like, what is soma-like, the subtle soul, the seizable by its unseizable, the existence by its existence, the Soma-like by its Soma-like, the subtle by its subtle, the wind-like by its wind-like. To it as the greatest swallower, the salutation, the salutation!

In the heart all deities,
In it are the vital breaths,[2]
As the one surpassing the three moras,
You too are in the heart.

His head is to the North (Chānd. 5,10,1), his feet to the South. He who is to the North, is the sound Om, as the sound Om he is the holy call, as the holy call he is all-pervading, as all-pervading he is infinite, as infinite he is the protecting (*tāram*), as the protecting he is the pure, as the pure he is the subtle, as the subtle he is the lightning-like, as the lightning-like he is the highest Brahman, as the highest Brahman he is the one, as the one he is Rudra, as Rudra he is the ruler, as the ruler he is the exalted Maheśvara.

4

But why is he called the sound Om ?—Because, being uttered he makes the vital breaths go upwards on high, therefore he is called the sound Om.

1. But see footnote 2 under the introduction.—GBP.
2. Cf. the verse Brahma Up. 2, above.

And why is he called the holy call (*praṇava*) ?—Because being uttered, he makes the Brahman consisting of Ṛc, Yajus, Sāman, Atharvāṅgiras lean towards the Brāhmaṇas and bends it, therefore he is called the holy call.

But why is he called all-pervading ?—Because, being uttered, he pervades and permeates that quiet one (Kāṭh. 3,13), sewn lengthwise and crosswise (Bṛh. 3,6), as a lump of sesame-dough with oil, therefore he is called all-pervading.

But why is he called infinite ?—Because, when it is being uttered, no end of it is to be found athwart, upward, and downward, therefore it is called infinite.

But why is he called the protecting ? Because, being uttered, he rescues from the dire fear of conception, birth, illness, old age, death and from the transmigration of the soul and protects, therefore, it is called the protecting.

But why is he called the pure (*śu-klam*) ? Because, being uttered, he makes noise (*klandate*) and makes one tired (*klāmayati*), therefore he is called the pure.

But why is he called the subtle ? Because, being uttered, he takes possession of the body in a subtle form and tinges all the limbs, therefore he is called the subtle.

But why is he called lightning-like? Because, being uttered, he illumines it in the great unmanifest darkness, therefore he is called lightning-like.

But why is he called the highest Brahman? Because he is the highest of the highest, the highest goal, the strong and strengthens by the strong [magic power] (*bṛhatyā bṛṁhayati*), therefore he is called the highest Brahman.

But why is he called the one?—He who, the devourer of all vital powers (*prāṇāḥ*), by the act of devouring them, as being more eternal unites them and again spreads them apart, so that some hasten to their master and some others hasten to their master and yet others [as the natural powers corresponding to the Prāṇas] hasten to the South, the West, the North and the East, who is the meeting place of all here, and has become one by uniting, moves along [as the vital breath] of the creatures,—therefore he is called the one.

But why is he called Rudra?—Because his essence (*rū-pam*) is grasped instantly (*dru-tam*) only by the seers (*ṛ-ṣi*), not by other devotees, therefore he is called *Ru-dra*.

But why is he called the ruler? Because it is he,
Who rules over all the gods,
With his regal and procreative powers (cf. Śvet. 3,1),—

To you, O here, we cry out,
Like cows, which go for milking,
To the lord of what moves, to the heaven-seer,
To the lord, O Indra, of what stays (Ṛgv. 7,32,22),—
therefore he is called the ruler.

But why is he called the exalted Maheśvara?—Because he permits the devotees (*bhaktān*) in the participation of perception and is gracious towards them; because he withdraws the speech [of the Veda] in himself and again allows it to flow out (Bṛh. 2,4,10); because, giving up all forms, he raises himself and is elevated through the perception of the Ātman and the mastery of the Yoga, therefore he is called the exalted Maheśvara.

This is the knowledge of Rudra.

5

The one god in all the world-spaces,
Born of old and in mother's womb,
He was born, he will be born,
He is in men and omnipresent (Vāj. Saṁh. 32,4. Śvet. 2,16).

One Rudra there is,—[don't worship] him as second!—
Who with his regal powers rules over the world;
He dwells in the creatures and gathers them in him at the end,
When he, the guardian, devours all creatures (Śvet. 3,2).

Who, as one, presides over every womb,
Through whom the whole universe spreads out;
Who knows him as ruler, as God, liberal giver, praiseworthy

He enters into that peace for ever.
(Śvet. 4,11, cf. Śvet. 5,2. Kāṭh. 1,17).
Shunning the world, the root of the causal net,
Wisely surrendering to Rudra all acquisition,

[they] acknowledged Rudra as the unity, as the eternal, the senior in refreshment and energy,[1] the creatures, as the one who cuts their bonds of death.

Thus it happens that, by means of that [sacred sound], when he penetrates into the soul, [the Īśvara] grants peace, the release of creatures (*paśu*) from their bonds (*pāśa*) by the three-and-halfth mora [of Om].

The first mora [of Om$=a+u+m$] has Brahman as its deity and is red in colour; he who meditates on it continuously, goes to the abode of Brahmán.

The second mora has Viṣṇu as its deity and is black in colour; he who meditates on it continuously, goes to the abode of Viṣṇu.

The third mora has Īśāna as its deity and is brown in colour; he who meditates on it continuously, goes to the abode of Īśāna.

But the three-and-halfth mora has all these as its deities, is unmanifest, goes out into the wide, is pure and resembles a mountain-crystal in colour; he who meditates on it continuously, goes to the abode of the bliss.

Therefore one should revere this! The silent ones (ascetics) proclaim it worldlessly, because there is no grasping of it.

That is the prescribed way to the North, by which the gods go (Chānd. 5,10,1), and the fathers and the Ṛṣis to the highest of the highest, to the supreme goal.

Minute like hair's tip, in the midst of heart,
Omnipresent, the God, golden dear,
The wise who sees him as dwelling in himself,
He alone attains peace, and none else.
[Leaving] anger to him, greed and worldly desires,

---

1. *iṣamūrjena* : the compound *iṣam-ūrja* is formed ungrammatically from the constituents *iṣam ūrjam*. Similarly below, p. 8,5. We have come across a similar example [*tamasaḥ paryam*] above, Maitr. Up. 6,24.

shunning the world, the root of the causal net
Wisely surrendering to Rudra all acquisition,

they acknowledged Rudra as the unity; for Rudra is the controller through eternal, old refreshment-and-energy and austerities. What is called fire is ashes, and what wind, is ashes; and what water, is ashes; and what earth, is ashes; and what ether, is ashes; and the whole universe is ashes, and the mind and these eyes! Because this is the vow of the Pāśupata, viz. that he covers his limbs with ashes, therefore this is the Pāśupata form of prayer, so that the creation be freed from his bonds.

6

To Rudra, who is in fire, in water,
Who has entered plants and creepers,
Who has become all these creatures,

to this Rudra, salutation, as Agni!

To Rudra, who is in fire, in water,
Who has entered plants and creepers,
Who has become all these creatures,

to this Rudra, salutation, salutation!

Rudra who is in water, Rudra in plants, Rudra in trees, Rudra by whom the world is held on high, by whom is supported the earth in a two-fold or three-fold form as supporter, and the snakes who dwell in the atmosphere, to this Rudra, salutation, salutation!

[Rudra as Prāṇa in the human head :]

When Atharvan sewed together
His head and the heart in him,
He stimulated him over the brain,
As purifier, from the head down.

This head belongs to Atharvan,
A cask stuffed with gods,

This head is guarded by Prāṇa,
Food and Manas in union.[1]

Nine heavens there are, guarded by divine community,
Nine atmospheres, and nine of these earths;
He who is seven lengthwise and crosswise in all,
From him nothing exists apart.

Nothing is earlier than him, nothing later,
Nothing what had been or was going to be;
With a thousand feet and only one head
He pervades the world and makes it roll.

From the Eternal, time is born,
From time he is called the pervader,

for the pervader is the exalted Rudra. When Rudra lies down in the manner of a serpent's coils, then the creatures are withdrawn within. When he breathes out (Bṛh. 4,5,11), there originates darkness, from darkness the water; when he stirs in the water with a finger, what is stirred becomes cold in the cold and, when it is stirred, it becomes foam; out of the foam originates the (universe-) egg, out of the egg Brahmán, out of Brahmán the wind, out of the wind the sound Om, out of the sound Om Sāvitrī, out of Sāvitrī Gāyatrī, out of Gayātrī the worlds (cf. Ṛgv. 1,164,25. Chānd. 3.12).

They praise Tapas and truth when they pour out the sweet drink, who does not forget (liberation). Indeed, this is the highest Tapas, is water, light, essence, the Immortal, Brahman (cf. above, Amṛtabindu-Up., 10, footnote).

Bhūr, *bhuvaḥ*, *svar*! Om ! Salutation! –

7

(Cf. Mahā Up. 4)

The Brāhmaṇa who studies this Atharvaśiras, one who is not an authority on scriptures becomes an authority on scriptures, an uninitiated becomes initiated; he is purified by fire, purified

1. Atharvav. 10,2, 26-27, whose readings we have followed. The purifier who, rising to the head, stimulates man, is the Soma. cf. our explanation of the hymn, *Gesch.d.Phil.* I. 269.

by wind, purified by Soma, purified by truth; he is known by all the gods, is meditated upon by all the Vedas [which appear here as persons], becomes one who has bathed in all the holy bathing places, and all sacrifices are performed by him. Sixty thousand Gāyatrī stanzas are muttered by him, a hundred thousand [stanzas] of the Itihāsa-Purāṇas and of the Rudra-hymns are muttered by him, ten thousand Praṇavas are muttered by him. He purifies the assembly as far as his sight reaches *ācakṣuṣaḥ*) he purifies up to the seventh generation (ancestors and descendants): thus has the exalted one promised.

He who mutters the Atharvaśiras once, becomes pure, purified, fit for activity?—he who mutters it a second time, attains supremacy over the host of the supreme god; he who mutters it a third time, enters into a similar existence.

Om! The truth! Om! The truth! Om! The truth!

ATHARVAŚIKHĀ UPANIṢAD

The name of this Upaniṣad "The tip of the Atharvan" seems to be an imitation, if not an outdoing, of the title of the Atharvaśirá Upaniṣad, with which as a model the Atharvaśikhā Upaniṣad shows close relationship, in that it takes up once more some topics touched by it in order to present them more closely.

The first is the symbolical interpretation of the sound *Om*, whose moras are treated of, in connection with Atharvaśiras 5, according to the following diagram :

Moras	*Worlds*	*Vedas*	*Main Gods*	*God-hosts*	*Metres*	*Fires*	*Colours*
a	Earth	Ṛgv.	Brahmán	Vasus	Gāyatrī	Gārha-patya	Red
u	Atmos-phere	Yajurv.	Viṣṇu	Rudras	Triṣṭubh	Dakṣiṇa	Black
m	Heaven	Sāmav	Rudra	Ādityas	Jagatī	Āhava-nīya	White
Reverberation—		Athar-vav.	Ekarṣi (Puruṣa Īśāna.)	Maruts	Virāj	Fire of univer-sal des-truction	All-col-oured.

Then follows a section (extremely obscure on account of the uncertainty of transmission and the inadequacy of the commentary) on the illumination of the highest knowledge which appears suddenly with the buzzing of the reverberation. To this are joined some break-neck etymologies, of the kind of the Atharvaśirá Upaniṣad and partly practically borrowed verbatim from it (as, e.g. those of *oṁkāra* and *praṇava*). As the deity of the three-and-halfth mora here appears Īśāna, as previously Ekarṣi and Puruṣa (and therefore probably to be identified with them). But what is new is that at the end our Upaniṣad adds, on the authority of a Śloka cited, as the fifth and the highest god Śiva, to the four gods Brahman, Viṣṇu, Rudra and Īśāna, represented by the sound Om,—(Śiva) whom the Atharvaśirá Upaniṣad yet does not know or recognize (otherwise the Upaniṣad would not have probably let him slip in its derivations of names), and whom our Upaniṣad identifies with the sound Om itself,—as its (Om's) true content. The emphatic way in which Śiva, this old epithet of Rudra, is elevated here to the top of deities makes the impression of lateness and it should not be improbable that our Upaniṣad forms a transitional link from Rudra, Īśāna etc., to Śiva which later prevails as the main name.

Om !

1. Pippalāda, Aṅgiras and Sanatkumāra asked the holy Atharvan :

Which meditation enjoined as the highest is to be meditated ?

What does this meditation consist of ?

Who is the meditator ?

What is the object of the meditator ?

Thereupon Atharvan replied to them :

Om, this syllable is enjoined as the highest to be meditated. Om, this syllable contains four quarters, four gods, four Vedas. This syllable consisting of four quarters is the highest Brahman.

Its first mora, the earth, is the *a*-sound. It (*a*-sound) is, consisting of verses, the Ṛgveda, it is Brahmán, the Vasus, the Gāyatrī, the Gārhapatya fire.

Its second mora, the atmosphere, is the *u*-sound. It is, consisting of sacrificial formulae, the Yajurveda, it is Viṣṇu, the Rudras, the Triṣṭubh, the Dakṣiṇa fire.

Its third mora, the heaven, is the *m*-sound. It is, consisting of songs, the Sāmaveda, it is Viṣṇu,[1] the Ādityas, the Jagatī, the Āhavanīya fire.

The fourth, the half mora, which is at the end of the syllable, is the fragmentary *m*-sound. It is, consisting of the Atharvan-songs, the Atharvaveda, it is the fire of universal destruction, the Maruts, the Virāj, the wisest. This mora is Shining with light, in its own lustre.

The first mora is red, dedicated to Brahmán and has Brahman as its divinity.

The second mora is bright, dedicated to Rudra and has Rudra as its divinity.

---

1. Read Rudra, which occurs in Nṛsiṁhap. 2,1 and Nṛsiṁhott. 3 [and also here in the editions of the Atharvaśikhā Up. available to me.—GBP.].

The third mora is black, dedicated to Viṣṇu, and has Viṣṇu as its divinity.[1]

The fourth mora is lightning-like, multi-coloured and has Puruṣa as its divinity.

That is the Om-sound with its four quarters and its four (fires as) heads. The fourth quarter is the half mora; it is pronounced materially in three ways, short, long or extra long.

om, *om*, *om*

The fourth is the calm-self (*śāntātman*) which, in the employment of the extra long pronunciation, must come suddenly as an illumination of the self, and not in a similar way [i.e. not materially as a continuous buzzing of *m*]. It is this latter [Om-sound] which, as soon as it is uttered, [sends upwards] all the vital breaths suddenly; and just because it sends them upwards (*ūrdhvam utkrāmayati*), it is called the Om-sound (*Om-kāra*).

2. And it is called Praṇava because it makes all the Prāṇas bow down (*praṇāmayati*) to itself;[2] because it makes them bow down, therefore, it is called Praṇava.[2] Because it is fourfold, therefore it is the origin of the Vedas and the gods;[3] because they are to be grasped (*dheya*) in it, therefore it is called All-grasper (*saṁdhartar*), and because it saves (*saṁtārayati*) from all griefs and fears, it is so [called] from the saving from all these. As Viṣṇu it conquers all [perhaps because it reminds of *vijayiṣṇu*]; as Brahmán it has pulled out (*abṛhat*) all organs [from their activity]. Since he fixed them through meditation and since Viṣṇu fixed them in the Manas in the highest Ātman

---

1. The second and the third mora seem to be confused here erroneously. The commentator comforts himself by saying that Brahmán, Viṣṇu and Śiva are ultimately identical. [There is no such confusion in the editions available to me.—GBP].

2. There is obviously a tautology. Editions available to me explain instead the name *pralaya* in the first sentence thus : *prāṇān sarvān pralīyate iti pralayaḥ*.—GBP.

3. The expression *veda-deva-yoniḥ* refers to the foregoing comparison of the four moras with the Vedas and gods. The expression recurs at Brahma Up. 1 (above) where, however, this connection is missing, and so it is to be looked upon as an imitation of our text.

[appearing] at the end of the reverberation, they further meditate on the Lord (*Īśāna*) as the object of meditation, for by the Lord the whole world is set to activity. Brahmán, Viṣṇu, Rudra and Indra have been brought forth by him, similarly all organs along with creatures. His divine majesty has become the cause, the universe, the blissful [Śiva], as the ether standing unshaken in the mid-air.

Brahmán, Viṣṇu and Rudra too,
The Lord and also the Blissful (*Śiva*)
Fivefold as these five gods
The holy sound is proclaimed.

Therefore one who gives himself up to him even for a moment, obtains a higher reward than by a hundred sacrifices. But from all knowledge, Yoga-practice and meditation, all that relates to the Om-sound is to be meditated as the only blissful (*Śiva*), indeed the Om-sound is *Śiva*.

So let a man give up everything else and study this [Upaniṣad] ! Then is the twice-born released from a further stay in mother's womb,—released from a further stay in mother's womb.

NĪLARUDRA UPANIṢAD

The most important older monument from the theology of Rudra, this precursor of Śiva, is the *Śatarudriyam*, properly probably (as already derived in the Śatap. Br. 9,1,1,2) *Śāntarudriyam* "Song for the pacification of Rudra", Vāj. Saṁh. 16 (Taitt. Saṁh. 4,5). Although this text has no relation whatever with the Upaniṣadic thought, still it was so renowned, and so often mentioned in the Atharva-Upaniṣads (Jābāla 3. Kaivalya 24. Atharvaśiras 7. Mahā. 4. Nṛsiṁhap. 5,10, p. 106), that many a compiler of the Upaniṣads did not want to dispense with it (particularly in view of the role which Śiva plays in the Atharva-Upaniṣads). While the collection of 108 Upaniṣads, as it is before us in the Telugu ed., leaves this song as far as we see, it is wholly admitted in the collection of Daraschakoh as *Schat Roudri* (Anquetil II, p, 171-196). The collection which we have taken as the basis, on the other hand, contains only an extract from it (with some other ornamentation) under the name *Nīlarudra Upaniṣad* (the esoteric doctrine of the dark Rudra).

The original meaning of Rudra is disputed. But if we keep in mind the predominant features of his image, and moreover consider, that he is the most dreaded god, and that no other natural phenomenon is so immediately fearful to the man originally as the flash of lightning, then it becomes probable that *Rudra* (properly probably "the shining one") was originally nothing else than a personification of the descending and striking lightning. He holds the lightning in the hand (*vajrabāhu*), loves forests, mountain summits, and tree-tops (*parame vṛkṣe āyudhaṁ nidhāya*, Vaj. Saṁh. 16,51), is called a man-slayer, animal-slayer, and his back is red, while his belly (the foot prints which he leaves behind where he lies down) is black (Atharvav.—15, 1,7). Also the further main feature, that he brings healing medicines, is easily understood when one considers that the thunderstorm cleans the atmosphere and banishes infectious emanation.

As the translation shows, this character is maintained very distinctly in our Upaniṣad which (verses 4-17) is a cento from variously mutilated verses of the Śatarudriyam, to which are added (verses 18-20) some verses from the Vāj. Saṁh. 13. The snakes shooting down from the air could in the same way be lightnings.—Quite obscure is the third part (verses 21-26), whose first verse has got in here perhaps only accidentally, through the mention of the word *Nīlagrīva*, while the verses which follow seem to speak of a law-suit between the brown, brown-eared aborigines and the Āryas, whom Śiva helps. Atharvav. 2,27,6 is related, and since here also a herb is spoken of, so the verse 21 also can perhaps be brought in this connection, only when a more readable text, than the wholly degenerate (in both editions) one which stood at our disposal, becomes available.

1

1. I saw you, yea, coming down
From the heaven upon the earth here,—
I saw the shooting Rudra,
The dark-necked, curly-haired.

2. From heaven he descended, dreadful,
And planted his feet on the earth;
O men ! see him bright-red,
The dark-necked, see him there !

3. Rudra, who doesn't strike men,
Comes with healing medicines,
May the flatulence, which robbed you
Of sleep, vanish away.

4. Salutation to your world-kindness,
Salutation to your world-anger
Salutation to your arms,
Salutation to your arrows too.[1]

5. The arrow, which, O rejoicer-in-hills,
You hold in your hand to shoot,
Make it gracious to us, hill-guardian,
May it not strike my people.[2]

6. With words in a pleasing voice
We call you hither, O mountain-lord,
So that all that lives by us,
Be healthy and happy in mind.[3]

7. With your kindest arrow
And your gracious bow
And your gracious bow-shot
Pity us, so that we may live.[4]

1. Cf. Vāj. Saṁh. 16, 1.
2. Vāj. Saṁh. 16, 3.
3. Vāj. Saṁh. 16, 4.
4. Cf. Vāj. Saṁh. 16, 11.

8. With your gracious appearance,
Not terrible, not harmful,
With your most wholesome appearance,
O mountain-dweller, show yourself to us.[1]

9. The one who shines, dark and red,
And brownish and in blazing red,
The thousands of Rudras darting
To all sides around,
I beg their fury away from us.[2]

2

10. They saw you descending,
With a dark neck, in blazing red,
They saw you, the cowherds,
And the women fetching water,
Yea, everybody saw you,—
Salutation to you, whom they saw.[3]

11. Salutation to him, the dark-haired one,
Who, the thousand-eyed, comes as a hero,
And to all his legions too
Let me pay a tribute of salutation.[4]

12. Salutation to your weapon,
The relaxed, daring,
Salutation to your two arms,
To your bow, I have offered.[5]

13. Relax at both the ends
The string of your bow,
Throw away from us, revered one !
The arrows from your hands.[6]

---

1. Vāj. Saṁh. 16, 2 (according to which the text is to be corrected); Śvet. 3,5.
2. Vāj. Saṁh. 16,6.
3. Cf. Vāj. Saṁh. 16,7.
4. Vāj. Saṁh. 16,8.
5. Vāj. Saṁh. 16,14.
6. Vāj. Saṁh. 16,9.

14. Relax, O gracious one, now
Your bow, O thousand-eyed one;
In hundred quivers break off
Your arrows and bring us help.[1]

15. His bow is now stringless,
His quiver without an arrow,
His missiles have disappeared,
Bliss-bringer is his sheath of sword.[2]

16. May the missile shooting from your bow
Pass by us in all directions,
Indeed, loosen your quiver itself
And keep it far away from us.[3]

17. Or rather take up as weapon
Your bow, O prosperous god,
With it as defender from diseases
To protect us from all sides.[4]

18. Salutation to the snakes also,
To such as are on the earth,
Also to the snakes in atmosphere,
Salutation to those in heaven.[5]

19. Those in the radiant regions of heaven,
Those too, that are in the sun's rays,
And those that live in the watery abyss,
Salutation to these snakes too.[6]

20. Who as arrows of the imps
Shoot down from trees above,
And those who nest in earth-holes,
Salutation to these snakes too.[7]

1. Vāj. Saṁh. 16.13.
2. Vāj. Saṁh. 16.10.
3. Vāj. Saṁh. 16.12.
4. Vāj. Saṁh. 16.11.
5. Vāj. Saṁh. 13.6.
6. Vāj. Saṁh. 13.8.
7. Vāj. Saṁh. 13.7.

3

21. He who is the Blue-necked god (*Śiva*) to his people,
He who is quite Hari (*Viṣṇu*) to his own,
Him with a many-coloured tail, O healing herb,
Quick grind to pieces, Arundhatī.

22. The [goblin] is brown and brown-eared,
But with a circle of black neck is Śiva,
Through him, Śarva, the black-haired,
Through Bhava, who the father (read *pitrā*) of the winds is.

23. Through him with eyes enormous,
Strike [read : *hata*] by the brown, him who only speaks a word,
Through him wholely dark-haired
At work, a hero's work.

24. Check the demand that he makes,
So that we could share it here,
Salutation to Śiva, Salutation to Śarva,
Salutation to him, the ever-young fighter !

25. Salutation to him, the black-haired,
When he comes to the assembly
And lets his fawn-coloured mules,
And asses graze around.

26. Salutation to him, the black-haired,
When he comes to the assembly,
—When he comes to the assembly.

KĀLĀGNIRUDRA UPANIṢAD

[It will strike anyone who comes to India that the natives often wear on the forehead a mark applied in red or some other colour, consisting of a small round fleck or also of several lines drawn vertically or horizontally, which often cover the whole forehead and, to our feeling, do not exactly contribute to heighten the beauty. These marks, called *tilaka* or *puṇḍra*, are (apart from their use as an ornament of women) sectarian marks, which are applied newly every morning after the bath with a certain ritual; through them the Indian openly makes as it were a silent confession of his faith before the whole world, while in other countries even priests would like to conceal what could draw attention to their church.—*Tripuṇḍram*, with which our Upaniṣad occupies itself, is also a similar mark of a Śaiva sect, described as consisting of three horizontal streaks made with ashes on the forehead, cranium, shoulders and the breast, thus in all five times, to the accompaniment of certain formulas. It is a great proof of the accommodating capacity of the Vedānta doctrine, when it knows how to attribute an allegorical significance even to this formality in that it sees in the three streaks the three sacrificial fires, three sounds of the syllable Om, three Guṇas, three worlds, three Ātmans, three powers, three Vedas, three [Soma] pressings and the three forms of the god Śiva and grants him, who knows this as such, all sorts of religious gains.—Thus here in the case of a thoughtlessly observed custom a direction on to the higher and the spiritual is given to the mind and with that a stimulus to a further activity with it.]

1

Once it happened that Sanatkumāra asked the exalted Kālāgnirudra: "Teach me, O exalted sir, the truth in respect to the rule of the Tripuṇḍram (a sect-mark consisting of three streaks) and what material, which place, how much, of what extent and which streaks, which divinity, which formula, which powers and which reward there are."

The exalted one said to him: "The material should be the ash of fires. One should grasp it with the five Brahman-formulas *sadyojātam* etc. (Taitt. Ar. 10, 43-47), consecrate it with the formula *agnir iti bhasma* etc. (Atharvaśiras 5), take out with the formula *mā nas toke* (Ṛgv. 1, 114, 8) and, [after consecrating] with the formula *tryambakaṁ yajāmahe* (Ṛgv. 7, 59, 12) should apply it as three lines across on the head, forehead, breast and shoulders under the three *tryāyuṣa*-formulas, *tryambaka*-formulas and *triśakti*-formulas.

This is the Śambhu-vow, which is taught in all the Vedas by those versed in the Veda. Therefore one desirous of liberation should practise it, so that he is not born again. And this, O Sanatkumāra, is its [of the mark] extent: it stretches threefold from the forehead down to the eyes and goes from the centre of one eye-brow [to the other].

2

Its first line is the Gārhapatya fire, the *a*-sound, the Rajas, the terrestrial world, the external Ātman, the acting power, the Ṛgveda, the morning pressing [of the Soma], and Maheśvara is its divinity.

Its second line is the Dakṣiṇa fire, the *u*-sound the Sattvam, the atmosphere, the inner Ātman, the willing power, the Yajurveda, the midday pressing [of the Soma] and *Sadāśiva* is its divinity.

Its third line is the Āhavanīya fire, the *m*-sound, the Tamas, the heaven, the highest Ātman, the perceiving power, the Sāmaveda, the evening pressing [of the Soma], and *Śiva* is its divinity.

Therefore, he makes the Tripuṇḍram from the ashes. He who knows this, whether he be a Brahman-student, a house-holder, a forest-resident or an ascetic, he is thereby purified of all the major sins and minor sins. Thereby all the gods are meditated upon by him, he is known by all the gods, becomes one who has bathed in all the holy bathing places, one who has all the time muttered the Rudra-prayer. And after enjoying all the pleasures he enters, giving up the body, into union with Śiva and does not return—and does not return."

Thus spoke the exalted Kālāgnirudra.

One who recites it here, he also attains to a similar state. *Om Satyam.*

Thus reads the Upaniṣad.

KAIVALYA UPANIṢAD

[Depending in a manifold way on older ideas and expressions, but not without its own inner experience, our Upaniṣad portrays the Kaivalyam, 'the absoluteness', i.e. the state of man who on the way of renunciation (*tyāga*) has become free of all attachment to the worldly and who, consequently knows and feels himself only as the one divine essence that lives in all. Particularly beautiful it is when from stanza 18 onward the pupil himself begins to speak in order to give expression to his consciousness of identity with God, which may appear exaggerated to a Westerner.

There is only a difficulty about the concluding passage in prose, which all of a sudden, recommends the study of the Śatarudriyam (Vāj. Saṁh. 16) and adds to it all sorts of promises in the style of the latest Upaniṣads. Nārāyaṇa is silent on it. Śaṁkarānanda's opinion, that only such people are here meant as would not be able to grasp the Ātman in the way described, is in no way indicated by the text. If the passage has not come to be attached, through a sheer accident, to the end of an Upaniṣad which is so entirely different from it in spirit and bearing, then an inference could be advanced that our Upaniṣad originally formed an epode to the Śatarudriyam, which would then again be referred in the concluding passage.]

Om !

Once it happened that Āśvalāyana approached the Supreme one and said to him:

1. Proclaim to me, O Sir, the secret
Of the highest Brahman-lore, which the good adore,
By which the wise, quickly freed of sins,
Enter into that Person, higher than the highest.[1]

2. Then spoke to him the Grand Father of all:
"Know, since you practise, with a pious mind:
Not through works, through children, through richness—
Through renunciation they attained immortality.[2]

---

1. According to Muṇḍ. 3,2,8.
2. =Mahānār. 10, verse 21.

3.[1] On the other side of heaven, in the depth of heart,
What shines, therein go the penitents;
Those who grasp the Vedānta-doctrine's meaning
Full of renunciation, the penitents, of pure being,

4.[2] In Brahman's world at the time of final end
They are all released by the Imperishable.—
Enthroned in joy in a secluded place,
Purified, with neck, head and body still,[3]

5. Remaining in the last Āśrama, restraining
The senses, to the teacher devoutly bowing,
Meditating the pure, dustless heart-lotus
And the griefless pure one situated therein,

6. The inconceivable, unmanifest, infinite,
Calm, blissful, eternal, the Brahman's source,
The one, without beginning, middle and end,
The wonderful lord full of intelligence and bliss,

7. The supreme god and lord, Uma's companion,
With dark neck, three eyes, wholely calm,—
Meditating him, all-seeing, primordial source of all,
The wise goes to the other side of darkness.

8. He is Brahmán, Śiva, Indra,
Imperishable, the supreme sovereign,
He is Viṣṇu, he the Prāṇa,
The fire of death and the moon.

9. It is he, all that originated,
And what originates in eternity,
Who knows him conquers death,
There's no other way to salvation.

10. He who sees himself in all beings
And all beings in him,

---

1. 3ab=Mahānār. 10, verse 21.
2. 3cd 4ab=Muṇḍ. 3,2,6. Mahānār. 10, verse 22.
3. Cf. Śvet. 2,8.

He goes thereby, and in no other way,
Into the abode of the highest Brahman.

11.[1] Making himself the lower churn-wood
And the Om-sound the upper one,
The wise rubs the fire of knowledge
And diligently burns down the sin.

12. When his self is blinded by the Māyā,
He dwells in the body and strives after works,
In women, food drink and enjoyments
He finds satisfaction in the wakeful state.

13. And in the dream too, tasting joy and sorrow,
The soul fashions a world through self-deception;
And when in deep sleep all illusion vanishes,
Shrouded by darkness the soul goes into bliss.

14. And again through the works of former lives
The soul goes into dream and wakefulness;
And playing it dwells in the triad of states,
Until it falls to its share to perceive
That rich, whole, supporter, partless, bliss,
In which the triad of states comes to rest.

15.[2] From him is born the Prāṇa,
The Manas and the group of senses,
The ether, wind, light, water,
And the earth, which bears all.

16. Brahman, the supreme soul of all,
The great resting place of universe,[3]
The subtlest of the subtle,[4] eternal
You yourself are it, and it's you !

1. Cf. Śvet. 1, 14.
2. =Muṇḍ. 2,1,3.
3. Cf. Mahānār. 11,7.
4. Cf. Muṇḍ. 3,1,7.

17. In waking, dreaming, deep sleep
What you see spread out,
Know yourself to be that Brahman,—
Then all the chains fall down."—

18. "What as experience, its object,
The experiencer, are known in the three states,
Different from them, the witness,
Pure intelligence, blissful I ever am !

19. In me was born everything,
In me alone everything abides,
In me it's dissolved, I myself am
That Brahman, the one without a second.

20. I am minutest of the minute, none the less
Great I am, I'm this diverse, rich universe,
I am the ancient, am the spirit, the Lord,
Wholly golden I am, of blissful appearance.

21.[1] Without hands and feet, I have infinite power,
I see without eyes, hear without ears;
I am the knower, and apart from me
There's no other knower in eternal times.

22. Through all the Vedas I am to be perceived,
I am the Veda-perfecter, Veda-knower,
Imperishable, I am free from good and bad,
Free from birth, without body and mind.

23. For me there's no earth, and no water,
No fire, no wind and no ether."
He who has thus found the highest Ātman
In the depths of heart, partless, secondless,

24. All-seeing, free from being and non-being,
To his share falls the pure supreme Ātman.

1. Cf. Śvetaśva. 3,19.

He who studies the Śatarudriyam, is purified by fire, purified by wind, purified by the Ātman, purified of alcoholic drink, purified of Brāhmaṇa-murder, purified of the theft of gold, purified of [the fault of failing to do] what is prescribed and of [that of doing] what is prohibited. Therefore he goes into the *Avimukta* [who has no need of liberation at all]. Rising above the Āśramas, one should mutter it always, or once [daily].

Through this the knowledge is obtained,
Which destroys the ocean of Saṁsāra;
Therefore, who finds him thus,
Attains the reward of absoluteness (*kaivalyam*).

e. Viṣṇu Upaniṣads

MAHĀ UPANIṢAD

NĀRĀYAṆA UPANIṢAD

ĀTMABODHA UPANIṢAD

NṚSIṀHAPŪRVATĀPANĪYA UP.

NṚSIṀHOTTARTĀPANĪYA UP.

RĀMAPŪRVATĀPANĪYA UP.

RĀMOTTARATĀPANĪYA UP.

MAHĀ UPANIṢAD[1]

[On the monuments of the Nārāyāṇa cult mentioned above [Mahānārāyaṇa-Upaniṣad, introduction to the 11th Anuvāka] now follows this small Upaniṣad, *kat'āntiphrasin* called 'the great' which, as it seems, pursues the goal of showing Nārāyaṇa as a higher being in comparison with the principles of the Sāṁkhya system as also with the gods Śiva and Brahmàn. According to Chapter 1 Nārāyaṇa projects out of himself 'the twentyfivefold Puruṣa', i.e. the twentyfive principles of the Sāṁkhyas, substituting Tejas (which, according to Chapter 3, later on, is formed from the primordial waters and so is akin to them) in the place of Prakṛti and Ātman in that of Puruṣa. The form of narration is patterned on the Creation myths in the Brāhmaṇas and it particularly reminds of the Taitt. Br. 2,2,9. the Pañc. Br. 6,1 and the Śatap. Br. 6,1,1 (*Gesch.d.Phil.* I, p. 202, 183.199). Chapter 2 describes how *śūlapāṇiḥ puruṣaḥ* (i.e. Śiva) springs out of Nārāyaṇa, whose limbs consist of holy exclamation, songs and metres of the Veda (cf. *mantramūrti* as an epithet of Śiva). Finally, according to chapter 3, there originates from Nārāyaṇa's meditation the god Brahmān and through the latter's meditation again the Veda along with the metres and holy exclamations. In respect of form the Taitt. Ār, 1,23 (*Gesch.d.Phil.* I, p. 197) is particularly comparable here. The verses which further follow are entirely patched up from the Mahānārāyaṇa 11, and the variants are in no way happy (e.g. *śikarādibhis* for *śirābhis*). Finally there follows as chapter 4 a series of promises which agree almost verbatim with the Atharvaśiras 7 and are probably borrowed from there with necessary changes.]

1

Now, then the Mahā-Upaniṣad-text.

Nārāyaṇa, verily, was alone, they say; there was no Brahmán no Īśāna, no water, no Agni and Soma, no heaven and no earth here, no stars, no sun, but only he, the Nara (*Puruṣa*) alone. A

1. On the sequence. Finally follow such Upaniṣads as worship Viṣṇu in one form or another : *Mahā*, *Nārāyaṇa*, *Ātmabodha*, *Nṛsiṁhatāpanīya* and *Rāmatāpanīya*, according to the lists of Colebrooke and Nārāyaṇa with the sequence maintained, and the *Ātmabodha-Upaniṣad* (it is true that it is not counted by Nārāyaṇa, but is regarded as an appendix of the Nārāyaṇa Upaniṣad and commented upon) inserted. Here the order of succession which results from the lists seems to agree fully with the historical order of origination as it will be clear in the following.

sacrificial hymn of praise is uttered by him, as he remains absorbed in meditation. Therein originated fourteen Puruṣas (men) and a girl, viz: the ten Indriyas, the Manas as the eleventh, the Tejas as the twelfth, the Ahaṁkāra as the thirteenth, as fourteenth the Prāṇa, it is the Ātman, as fifteenth the Buddhi. Besides the five subtle elements and the five gross elements. This is the twentyfivefold Puruṣa. The [primordial] Puruṣa appointed him the creator. Yet his creatures are not born without the year, but they are born from the year.

2

Then Nārāyaṇa, desirous of another, once more meditated in his mind. As he stood absorbed in meditation, there was born from his forehead a three-eyed Puruṣa holding a trident, possessing about him beauty, truth, chastity, austerity, renunciation, intelligence and mastery; but the Om-sound and the three Vyāhṛtis (*bhūr*, *bhuvaḥ*, *svaḥ*) the Ṛcs, Yajus', Sāmans, Atharva-Aṅgiras' and all metres, they abided in his limbs.

3

Then Nārāyaṇa, desirous of another, once more meditated in his mind. As he stood absorbed in meditation, sweat came out of his forehead. It expanded into these primordial waters. In them was born the Tejas as a golden egg. Therein was born the god Brahmán with four faces. He meditated towards the East, and there was born the exclamation *bhūr*, the metre Gāyatrī, the Ṛgveda;—towards the West, and there was born the exclamation *bhuvar*, the metre Triṣṭubh, the Yajurveda;—towards the North, and there was born the exclamation *svar*, the metre Jagatī, the Sāmaveda;—towards the South, and there was born with the exclamation *om janad*, the metre Anuṣṭubh, the Atharvaveda.

Om!

To the god with thousand heads,
Thousand eyes, bringing every happiness,
Who, the eternal, transcends all,
The all, Nārāyaṇa, Hari.

The Puruṣa, who is all this,
Who is the enlivener of the world,

The wise lord of all, who,
Omniform, resides in the waters.

Like a lotus-calyx it hangs,
Almost like a flower-cup,
In the heart, with drops of dew[1] as if
Swollen, it hangs downwards.

In its midst a great fire,
All-fire, flaming in all directions;
In it a pointed flame,
A fine one, striving upwards,

And in the midst of the pointed flame
The Puruṣa, the highest self,
He is Brahman and Īśāna,
The eternal, supreme lord.[2]

4

(Cf. Atharvaśiras 7).

The Brāhmaṇa who studies this Mahā-Upaniṣad text, one who is not an authority on scriptures becomes an authority on scriptures, an uninitiated becomes initiated; he is purified by Agni, purified by Vāyu, purified by Sūrya, purified by Soma, purified by truth, purified by all; he is known by all the gods, is meditated upon by all the Vedas, becomes one who has bathed in all the holy bathing places, and all sacrifices are performed by him; Sixty thousand Gāyatrī stanzas are muttered by him, a hundred thousand [stanzas] of the Itihāsa-Purāṇas and of the Rudra-hymns are muttered by him, ten thousand Praṇavas are muttered by him. He purifies the assembly as far as his sight reaches, he purifies up to the seventh generation (ancestors and descendants); thus has the exalted Hiraṇyagarbha promised.

By muttering one attains immortality,—one attains immortality.

1. Read : *śīkarādibhiḥ*.
2. After this, editions available to me read huge passages, as if to make the name *Mahā*-significant !—GBP.

NĀRĀYAṆA UPANIṢAD

[Like the Mahā Upaniṣad, the Nārāyaṇa Upaniṣad also extols Nārāyaṇa as the principle of gods and beings. Only it speaks less in the style of the Brāhmaṇa myths and instead makes more use of older Upaniṣadic passages. But a new element, which had not come to be used till now, is the one which becomes prevailing in the still later Upaniṣads, viz. the cult of the formula, whose appearance here (as in a different way in our own time again) is a symptom of necrosis of the philosophical thought. The formula, whose meditation instead of that over objects enters into our Upaniṣad, reads : *Om ! namo Nārāyaṇāya* ! "Om ! Salutation to Nārāyaṇa!"—Since it first appears only in the last two chapters, after chapter three had already concluded with the promises, the inference suggests itself that the whole Upaniṣad might have been pieced together from passages belonging to different times.]

1

Once it happened that the Puruṣa Nārāyaṇa desired to beget creatures. There was born from Nārāyaṇa the Prāṇa.

The Manas and the group of senses,
The ether, wind, light, water,
And the earth, which bears all,

From Nārāyaṇa was born Brahman,
,, ,, ,, ,, Rudra,
,, ,, ,, ,, Prajāpati,
,, ,, ,, ,, Indra,
,, ,, were ,, the eight Vasus,
,, ,, ,, ,, the eleven Rudras,
,, ,, ,, ,, the twelve Ādityas,

all gods, all Ṛṣis, all metres and all beings are born from Nārāyaṇa only and merge in Nārāyaṇa,—and merge in Nārāyaṇa.

2

Nārāyaṇa is the eternal, one god,
Nārāyaṇa is Brahmán also,
,, ,, Śiva ,,
,, ,, Śakra ,,

Nārāyaṇa is the twelve Ādityas also,
„ „ the Vasus and Aśvins also,
„ „ all Ṛṣis also,
„ „ the time also
„ „ the quarters also,
„ „ below also,
„ „ above also,
„ „ corporal and uncorporal also,
„ „ the inner and the outer also,

indeed, this whole universe, "what was and what is yet to be" is Nārāyaṇa. Nārāyaṇa is thus the eternal, spotless, inexpressible, changeless, artless, pure, one god, there is no second apart from him.

Choose Rudra as your charioteer,
Use your Manas as reins,
Then go to the supreme hereafter,
To the eternal abode of Viṣṇu,
—to the eternal abode of Viṣṇu.

3

This, verily, is the Upaniṣad-text of Nārāyaṇa. Verily, he who studies the Upaniṣad-text of Nārāyaṇa is freed of all fearful, he obtains all desires and all worlds, and entering into Brahmanhood he goes into immortality,—he goes into immortality.

4

One should first utter *Om*, then *namo*, and afterwards Nārāyaṇāya. *Om* is one syllable, *namo* are two syllables, Nārāyaṇāya are five syllables. This is the octo-syllabic metrical line of Nārāyaṇa. He who studies this octo-syllabic metrical line of Nārāyaṇa reaches the full span of life without a mishap, he enjoys happiness in offspring, growth of prosperity, possession of cattle, and he further participates in immortality,—and he further participates in immortality.

5

He (Nārāyaṇa) merged into one with the inner bliss, the Brahman, the Puruṣa, the holy syllable consisting of *a*, *u* and *m*, it became the sound *Om*.

The Yogin who has seen this,
Is free from birth and Saṁsāra.

And he who worships the formula : *Om namo Nārāyaṇāya*, he goes to Vaikuṇṭha's (Viṣṇu's) heaven. That city is here, this lotus-flower (Chānd. 8,1,1), consisting wholly of intelligence, that is why it is just like a flash of the lightning (Kena. 29-30).

So pious was Devakī's son,
So pious was Madhusūdana,

as it is said, [because he perceived] him who dwells in all beings, one, Nārāyaṇa, the cause, the *a*,[1] the highest Brahman in the Om sound.

He who studies this Atharvaśiras,[2]—if he studies it in the morning, then he annihilates the sins committed at night, if he studies it in the evening, then he annihilates the sins committed in the day; if he studies it at midday, facing the sun, then he is freed of the five major sins and the five minor sins, participates in the merit which is the goal of all Vedas, and attains communion with Nārāyaṇa,—attains communion with Nārāyaṇa.

1. Other editions available to me read *akāraṇam* 'causeless' which is certainly better than *akāram* which Deussen seems to have read.—GBP.

2. Here appellative : "the main part of the Atharvaveda." One Ms. reads *atharvāṅgirasam* (Jacob, *Concordance*, s.v.)

ĀTMABODHA UPANIṢAD[1]

["This Ātmabodha Upaniṣad", says the commentator, "serves the purpose of explaining the octosyllabic [formula of the] Nārāyaṇa Upaniṣad. For it happens that one Veda-text serves to explain another, as e.g. the Brāhmaṇas which explain the Mantras". Actually, however, the present text is a sheer, word-to-word repetition of the Nār. Up. 5 and the additions are partly of no importance, partly misleading. Thus, when the *Vijñāna-ghana* (=*kāraṇarūpa*) is regarded as not the Ātman itself but a product of him, while immediately afterwards the *kāraṇarūpa* is identified with Nārāyaṇa. And the verse about Devakīputra also is, as the supplements show, understood differently from us at Nār. Up. 5 and, we believe, mis-understood. Also the citations from the Bṛh. 4, 4, 19, Ait. 3, 3-4 and Ṛgv. 9, 113, 7 patched up at the end announce the complete lack of originality of the work which we do not ignore only for the reason that it is admitted by the *Oupanek'hat* and commented upon by Nārāyaṇa].

Om ! Salutation !

[Nārāyaṇa entered] into the inner bliss, the Brahman, the sacred sound consisting of *a*, *u* and *m*, into this syllable, the Praṇava, which became the sound Om.

The Yogin, who desires this,
Is freed of birth and Saṁsāra.

Om ! Salutation to Nārāyaṇa, the holder of conch, disk, and mace ! Therefore, he who worships the formula: *Om, namo Nārāyaṇāya* ! attains Vaikuṇṭha, the heaven of the holy. And the city which is here, the Brahman-city, the lotus flower as the house, the Ātman who dwells in it, in the middle of this golden flower, from him springs out what is of the nature of cause, of the nature of consciousness, consisting wholly of knowledge; that is why it is just like a flash of lightning, its light is like a lamp.

So pious was Devakī's son,
So pious was Garuḍadhvaja,
So pious was Puṇḍarīkākṣa,
So pious was Madhusūdana.

1. The title alternates optionally with *Ātmaprabodha-Upaniṣad.*

for he had perceived him who dwells in all beings, one, Nārāyaṇa, of the nature of cause, of the *a*,[1] the supreme Brahman.

Who on Viṣṇu, free from pain and illusion,
Meditates, he is never ruined,
Fearless, he goes from duality to nonduality.

But

"From one death into another he falls,
"Who believes in seeing plurality here" (Bṛh.4,4,19).

In the midst of the heart-lotus flower is "all this guided by consciousness, established in what is guided by consciousness; the world is guided by consciousness, consciousness is its basis, consciousness is Brahman. Rising above this world by means of this conscious self, he [Vāmadeva] obtained all desires in that heaven and has become immortal,—has become immortal" (Ait. 3,3-4).

"Where light is without cessation,
"Where heaven's splendour is based,
"In that world, O purifier,
"In that eternal one, put me" (Ṛgv. 9,113,7).

Thus one goes to immortality,—thus one goes to immortality. Om, salutation !

One who meditates over the Ātmaprabodha-Upaniṣad devotedly only for an hour, for him there is no return,—for him there is no return.

1. See the note under the *Nārāyaṇa-Upaniṣad* on this.—GBP.

NṚSIṀHA-PŪRVA-TĀPANĪYA UPANIṢAD

Tapanam is the burning, pain-suffering, ascetic self-sacrifice, *Nṛsiṁha-tapanam* the ascetic self-surrender to Nṛsiṁha, therefore *Nṛsiṁha-tāpanīya-Upaniṣad* "the esoteric doctrine concerning the ascetic surrender to Nṛsiṁha." It consists of two halves, one more exoteric (*Nṛsiṁha-pūrva-tāpanīya-Upaniṣad*), which is dedicated to the earlier elementary surrender to Nṛsiṁha, and one more esoteric (*Nṛsiṁhottara-tāpanīya-Upaniṣad*), which is dedicated to the later, higher surrender; the former consists of five parts, the latter of a single main part; both are together considered as six Upaniṣads.

While the Upaniṣadic doctrine had reached to the recognition of one Brahman-Ātman, the monistic tendency, which is found in every religion, led to it so that the popular religious thought and worship also gained two chronologically or spatially different peaks in India (just as in Greece it centred around Zeús in the post-Homeric time), the one in *Śiva* (*Mahādeva-Īśvara*) who had arisen out of the Vedic Rudra and Agni, the other in the old-Vedic sun-god *Viṣṇu,* who again was worshipped in various forms, particularly as *Nṛsiṁha, Rāma, Kṛṣṇa* (which were united as different Avatāras of one Viṣṇu by a later age). Whereas both the last-named gods [*Rāma, Kṛṣṇa*] seem to have arisen through a deification of human, historical persons, Nṛsiṁha, the 'Man-lion', i.e. 'divine lion' (*nṛ* "man, hero, god"; cf. e.g. Ṛgv 4, 25, 4 : *Indrāya nare naryāya, nṛtamāya nṛṇām*), is originally probably only "the powerful divine hero" into which the solar power was personified. (That the form as half-man half-lion should have nothing to do with the Assyrian or any other imagination whatever, is probably the simple explanation of the name.) In this form as *Nṛsiṁha* (*Narasiṁha,* occasionally also *Nārasiṁha,* cf. *Nara*, and beside it *Nārāyaṇa*) Viṣṇu was worshipped by a pretty exclusive and therefore, as it appears, little spread sect, whose symbolical book is the present Upaniṣad in its both parts; they can be conveniently distinguished (with Weber) as the exoteric and the esoteric part; both swear allegiance to the Nṛsiṁha faith and both remain thereby under the influence of the Upaniṣadic doctrine; the difference can be described most briefly by saying that in the first part the Upaniṣadic doctrine is put in the service of the Nṛsiṁha faith (*philosophia ancillatur theologiae*), in the second part the Nṛsiṁha faith is put in the service of the Upaniṣadic doctrine (*theologia ancillatur philosophiae*).

The first part (*Nṛsiṁha-pūrva-tāpanīya*), with which we are concerned first, teaches the worship of Viṣṇu through a sacred formula composed in the Anuṣṭubh metre whereby, however, the worship aims more at the formula than at the god and it plays a similar role, only it is carried further wide than the role played by, say, Vyāhṛtis, the Sāvitrī (cf. e.g. Maitr. 6, 6-7) in other texts, and by the holy sound Om in so many Ātharvaṇa

Upaniṣads. As in the Om-sound, similarly in the Nṛsiṁha formula also the whole Veda is comprised; it is the *Mantrarāja,* the 'king of formulas', which was of service in the world-creation (1, 1), it deals with all worlds and all Vedas (1, 2), is identical with the four moras of the Om-sound (2, 1); like Brahman, it has the Māyā as its creative power (*śakti*), and the Ākāśa as the semen (*vījam*), i.e. as the starting point of creation ("from this Ātman the Ākāśa is born, from the Ākāśa the wind" etc. Taitt. 2, 1), and the incessant repetition and artistic writing down (worn as an amulet) of this formula assures superabundant reward. Just as a prince does not appear without the retinue, so this Mantrarāja has three (1, 3) or subsequently (4, 1-2) four *Aṅga-mantras* 'limb-formulas' or 'sub-formulas' in his retinue, to which, as a further corona, is added, corresponding to the 32 syllables of the royal formula, one more crowd of 32 formulas (4.3). As it is necessary to have the Mantrarāja always before the eyes for an understanding to both the Nṛsiṁha texts, we will introduce it along with the four Aṅgamantras here in advance, in text and translation.

The Mantrarāja.

Ugram vīram, mahā-Viṣṇum,
Jvalantaṁ, sarvatomukham
Nṛsiṁhaṁ, bhīṣaṇaṁ, bhadram,
Mṛtyu-mṛtyuṁ namamy aham.

The terrible, mighty, great, Viṣṇu,
Burning in all the directions,
As Man-lion, fearful and gracious,
As the death of deaths, I adore him.

The four Aṅgamantras.

I. The Praṇava.

Om !

II. The Sāvitrī :

Ghṛṇiḥ, sūrya, Ādityaḥ,
the glow, the sun, Āditya.

III. The Lakṣmī-yajus (also Yajurlakṣmī).
The beauty-formula.

Om ! bhūr lakṣmīr, bhuvar lakṣmīḥ,
suvaḥ kālakarṇī, tan no
mahālakṣmīḥ pracodayāt

Om ! earth luck and atmosphere luck,
And heaven luck, black-eared,—
So may the great luck promote us !

IV. The Nṛsiṁha-gāyatrī.

Om ! Nṛsiṁhāya vidmahe,
vajranakhāya dhīmahi,
tan naḥ siṁhaḥ pracodayāt.

Om ! Let us think, well aware
Of Nṛsiṁha, the lightning-nailed,
May the Lion promote our thought.

NṚSIṀHA-PŪRVA-TĀPANĪYA UPANIṢAD

The auspicious let us hear with ears, o gods,
The auspicious let us see with eyes, o holies,
With firm limbs, praising, able-bodied,
Let's reach the God-ordained span of life ! (Ṛgv. 1.89.8).
May Indra, the highly renowned, grant us well-being,
Well-being god Pūṣan, the lord of all riches,
Well-being Tārkṣya, whose felly remains undamaged,
May Bṛhaspati, too, grant well-being to us (Ṛv. 1.89,6).
Om, peace ! Om, peace ! Om, peace !

1.1

[Prajāpati created the world by means of the Nṛsiṁha formula.]

Om !

"Verily this world was water, waving. There Prajāpati was born alone on a lotus-leaf. In his mind (*manas*) a desire (*kāma*) arose : 'I will create this world !' Therefore what a man aspires after in his mind, he speaks it out with the speech, accomplishes it with his activity. On this is this verse (Ṛgv. 10,129,4):

"There arose out of it desire first,
It was the first outpouring of mind's semen.—
The being's roots in the non-being found
The searching wise in the urge of heart."

It comes to him, what he aspires after [who knows thus]! —He (Prajāpati) practised penance; after practising penance" (from the beginning upto here = Taitt. Ār. I, 23, *Gesh. d. Phil.* I, 196), he saw this *Mantrarāja* (royal formula) relative to Nṛsiṁha and composed in the Anuṣṭubh metre; with it he created the whole world, whatever exists. Therefore they say: this whole world is Anuṣṭubh, whatever exists. "From the Anuṣṭubh, indeed, are born these creatures, having been born they live by the Anuṣṭubh, and departing, they again go back into the Anuṣṭubh" (according to Taitt. 3, 1-6). On this is this (verse): "The Anuṣṭubh is the first, and the Anuṣṭubh is the last; for the

Anuṣṭubh is Speech; (the creatures) depart by the Speech, and they are born by the Speech"; and it is indeed said: "The Anuṣṭubh is the highest of all the metres" (Taitt. Saṁh. 5,4,12,1).

1.2

[The four lines of the formula deal with the four world-regions with all their contents, and the four Vedas also.]

The earth with its oceans, its mountains, its seven islands,—that one should know as the first line of that song [the Mantrarāja].

The atmosphere, as populated by the bands of Yakṣas, Gandharvas, Apsaras',—that one should know as the second line of the song.

The heaven, as populated by the Vasus, the Rudras, the Ādityas, and all gods,—that one should know as the third line of the song.

The undefiled, self-essence of the Brahman, dwelling "in the highest space" (Taitt. 2,1),—that one should know as the fourth line of the song.

He who knows this, attains immortality.

The four Vedas, Ṛg-, Yajur-, Sāma and Atharvaveda, with their Aṅgas (*Gesch. d. Phil.* I, 51) and Śākhās (*Gesch. d. Phil.* I, 65),—they are the four lines.

What is the meditation [of this song], what its divinity, what its limbs, what their divinities, what its metre, what its poet,[1] thus [one shall ask oneself incessantly.]

1.3

[Introductory over the first three of the four limb-formulas of the royal formula.]

Thus said Prajāpati: Verily, he who knows that beauty-anointed, octo-syllabic line of the Savitar formula as a limb (an *Aṅgamantra*) of that song, is anointed with beauty.

All the Vedas have the Praṇava [the holy Om-sound] as the beginning; if he knows this Praṇava also as a limb [as Aṅgamantra] of that song, he conquers the three worlds.

1. Probably Prajāpati is to be understood as the poet.

There is a sacrificial formula, the great Lakṣmī (luck) consisting of twentyfour syllables; if he knows this also as a limb of that song, he becomes rich in life, fame, honour, knowledge and mastery.

Therefore one should know this song along with its limbs [the Aṅgamantras]; and he who knows it, attains immortality.

The teachers do not permit the Savitar-formula, the holy sound and the Lakṣmī-formula to a woman, to a Śūdra. One should know well the thirtytwo-syllabic song, and he who knows it, attains immortality,—but if a woman or a Śūdra knows the Savitar-formula, the Lakṣmī-formula, the Praṇava, he goes downwards after death. Therefore one should never proclaim these to them! If one proclaims these to them, the teacher goes downwards after death.

1.4

[After a repeated identification of the formula with the highest divinities, the first two syllables of each of its four lines are inculcated.]

Thus spoke Prajāpati :

Agni, verily, the Vedas, this universe and all beings, the vital breaths and organs, animals, food, the immortal, the supreme ruler, the self-ruler, the far-and-wide-ruler,—this one should know as the first line of the song.

The sun in the form of Ṛc, Yajus, Sāman and Atharvan, 'the golden man within the sun' (Chānd. 1,6,6),—this one should know as the second line of the song.

He who rules over plants, the lord of the stars, the Soma,—this one should know as the third line of the song.

"It is Brahmán, Śiva, Hari, Indra, Agni, the eternal, the supreme lord" (Taitt. Ār. 10,11,12; also Mahānārāyaṇa-Up., 11th Anuvāka, verse 12, above),—this one should know as the fourth line of the song.

And he who knows it, attains immortality.

Om ! One should know *ugram* as the initial song of the first line, *jvalan-* as that of the second, *nṛsiṁ-* as that of the third, *mṛtyu-* as that of the fourth.

And he who knows it, attains immortality.

Therefore one should not proclaim this song everywhere; if one wants to impart it, one should impart it only to one's son, if he is desirous of learning it, or otherwise to a pupil.

1.5

[The second pair of syllables of each of the four lines, with a preceding and following glorification of the formula.]

The Man-lion who rests in the milk-ocean, 'the highest step' (Ṛv.1,22,20) meditated upon by the Yogins, one should know it as the song.

And one who knows it, attains immortality.

One should know *vīram* as the end-song of the first half of the first line,*-taṁ sa-* as that of the second, *-haṁ bhī-* as that of the third,*-mṛtyuṁ* as that of the fourth.

And one who knows this, attains immortality.

Therefore he who has learnt this song from the mouth of some teacher is liberated from the Saṁsāra thereby, helps liberate, strives for liberation; he who mutters it has a vision of God in this very body of his. Therefore this is the gate of liberation in the Kali age, none else attains liberation. Therefore one should know the song with its limbs. He who knows it strives for liberation.

1.6

[The third pair of syllables, along with glorification.]

Om !

"As law, truth, supreme Brahman,
The Man-lion-formed, black-brown Puruṣa.
"The chaste, with eyes odd" (Taitt. Ār. 10,12; Mahānār-Up., 12th Anuvāka, above).
The black-and-red Śaṁkara,

the husband of Umā, the lord of animals, the wielder of bow, of infinite brilliance [I invoke, he who is] "the master of all knowledge, the lord of all beings, Brahman as the over-lord, the over-lord of Brahman" (Taitt. Ār. 10,47), the one to be praised according to the Yajurveda,—this one should know as the song.

And one who knows it attains immortality.

One should know *mahā-* as the initial song of the final half of the first line,*-rvato-* as that of the second, *-ṣaṇaṁ* as that of the third, *namā-* as that of the fourth.

And one who knows it attains immortality.

Therefore this song is the supreme Brahman, which consists of being, intelligence and bliss;[1] he who knows it as such becomes immortal here itself. Therefore one should know the song along with its limbs.

And one who knows it attains immortality.

1.7

[The fourth pair of syllables of each of the four lines, along with glorification. Preliminary to the interweaving of the Om-sound.]

"With this, verily [i.e. with the thousand-year sacrifice in the original passage] the all-creators created the world; since they created all, so they are called all-creators. Everything originates after them, and they [those who perform a hundred-year sacrifice or those who teach it] (Taitt. Br. 3,12,9,8) attained a common life and a common world with Brahman,—therefore one should know this song along with its limbs.

And one who knows it attains immortality.

One should know *-Viṣṇum* as the final song of the first line, *-mukham* as that of the second, *bhadram* as that of the third, *-myaham* as that of the fourth.

And one who knows it attains immortality.

He himself [Prajāpati] has manifested all this. Relative to the Ātman, to the Brahman, one should know the worship with that Anuṣṭubh.

And one who knows it attains immortality.

And if one, whether a woman [only the Aṅgamantras were forbidden to women at 1,3 above, not the Mantrarāja] or a man, desires to stay here on the earth, the [Mantrarāja] grants to him mastery over everything, and wherever he may die, there

1. *Sat-cid-ānanda*; this could (apart from Taitt. 2, 1) possibly be the first occurrence of the celebrated formula.

the God (of the Mantrarāja) imparts to him at the end of his life the highest, delivering Brahman, by which, (already) immortal, he then attains to immortality. Therefore one mutters this [Brahman in the form of the *Om* sound] at intervals in the song; therefore this limb of the song is Prajāpati, and therefore one who knows it as such becomes this limb of the song, becomes Prajāpati.

Thus reads the great Upaniṣad. And one who knows this great Upaniṣad, he becomes, when he has performed the preparatory worship, the great Viṣṇu,—the great Viṣṇu.

Second Upaniṣad

[After a myth about the delivering power of the Nṛsiṁha formula (patterned upon Pañcav. Br. 22, 12; cf. above, Chānd-Up., fourth Khaṇḍa) there follows the identification of its four lines with the four moras of the Om-sound, in which the corresponding passage of the Atharvaśikhā Upaniṣad (above) is borrowed verbatim and adapted to serve the purpose of our Upaniṣad.]

Om !

Once upon a time the gods were afraid of death, sins and the Saṁsāra. They took their refuge in Prajāpati. He administered to them this royal formula addressed to Narasiṁha and composed in the Anuṣṭubh metre. With that they conquered death, surmounted sins, surmounted the Saṁsāra. Therefore one who is afraid of death, sins and the Saṁsāra should grasp this royal formula addressed to Narasiṁha and composed in the Anuṣṭubh metre. He then conquers death, surmounts sins, and surmounts the Saṁsāra.

Of this Praṇava [Om-sound], verily,[1] "the first mora, the earth, is the *a-* sound. It is, consisting of verses, the Ṛgveda, it is Brahman, the Vasus, the Gāyatrī, the Gārhapatya fire",—this is the first line [of the royal formula].

"Its second mora, the atmosphere, is the *u-* sound. It is, consisting of sacrificial formulas, the Yajurveda, it is Viṣṇu, the Rudras, the Triṣṭubh, the Dakṣiṇa fire",—this is the second line.

---

1. All the passages enclosed in the quotation marks are taken verbatim from the Atharvaśikhā above.

"Its third mora, the heaven, is the *m-* sound. It is, consisting of songs, the Sāmaveda, it is Rudra, the Ādityas, the Jagatī, the Āhavanīya fire",—This is the third line.

"The fourth, the half-mora, which is at the end of the syllable, is the Soma world, the Om-sound [for this the Atharvaśikhā reads : is the broken down *m-* sound]. It is, consisting of the Atharvan songs, the Atharvaveda, it is the fire of universal destruction, the Maruts, the Virāj, the highest wise, the resplendent",—this is the fourth line of the song.

2.2

[The Nṛsiṁha formula as the king of formulas (*mantrarāja*) has five attributes, viz. heart, head, hair-tuft, armour and missile, to which the four lines of the formula with the Praṇava as the fifth correspond. They are interwoven in the following, and so also the worlds which they symbolise.]

The first line is octo-syllabic, and the three [remaining] lines [also] are octo-syllabic; thus thirtytwo syllables result; the Anuṣṭubh, verily, is thirty-two-syllabic; by the Anuṣṭubh the whole world has been created and by the Anuṣṭubh it is reabsorbed again.

That same [Mantrarāja] has five attributes [*aṅgāni* : heart, head, hair-tuft, armour and missile]; the four lines correspond to the four attributes and the whole [of the formula] furnished with the Praṇava corresponds to the fifth. Of the five [formulas formed from the attributes]: *om* to the heart *namaḥ*, *om* to the head *svāhā*, *om* to the hair-tuft *vaṣaṭ*, *om* to the armour *hum*, *om* to the missile *phaṭ*, the first is combined with the first line [*ugraṁ vīraṁ mahāviṣṇum, oṁ hṛdayāya namaḥ*], the second with the second [*jvalantaṁ sarvatomukham, oṁ śirase svāhā*], the third with the third [*nṛsiṁhaṁ bhīṣaṇaṁ bhadram, oṁ śikhāyai vaṣaṭ*], the fourth with the fourth [*mṛtyumṛtyuṁ namāmy aham, oṁ kavacāya hum*] and the fifth with the fifth [*om ! ugraṁ vīram mahāviṣṇuṁ jvalantaṁ sarvatomukhaṁ nṛsiṁhaṁ bhīṣaṇaṁ bhadraṁ mṛtyumṛtyuṁ namāmy aham, om astrāya phaṭ*]; because these worlds are interwoven into one another, therefore the constituents [of the lines and formulas] also are interwoven into one another.—"Om! This syllable is the whole world" (Māṇḍ.1); therefore the sound Om has a place before and after each syllable [of the above five combinations. Thus : *om u om, om gram om, om vi om, om ram om* and so on]; the syllables are to be thus designed (drawn), as the Brahman-knowers teach.

2.3

[Enumeration of the eleven words of the formula, along with glorification.]

In this [Mantrarāja], one should know, at the first place stands *ugram*—and one who knows this attains immortality,—at the second place *vīram*, at the third *mahāviṣṇum*, at the fourth *jvalantam*, at the fifth *sarvatomukham*, at the sixth *nṛsiṁham*, at the seventh *bhīṣaṇam*, at the eighth *bhadram*, at the ninth *mṛtyumṛtyum*, at the tenth *namāmi*, at the eleventh *aham*.

One who knows this attains immortality.

The Anuṣṭubh has eleven words, by the Anuṣṭubh this whole world has been created, and by the Anuṣṭubh everything is reabsorbed again. Therefore one should understand this whole world as of the nature of Anuṣṭubh; and one who knows this attains immortality.

2.4

[The eleven words of the formula are explained etymologically and these explanations are embellished with Vedic citations, which often have very little connection with the matter in hand. Atharvaśiras 4 (above) seems to have been in the mind as the model.]

It came to pass that the gods said to Prajāpati: Now why is it said *ugram*?—And Prajāpati said: Because by his majesty he lifts up (*udgṛhṇāti*) all worlds, all gods, all selves, all beings, creates continually, expands and causes to live, while he is caused to be elevated and is elevated,—

> Praise the celebrated young car-warrior,
> Who like a fierce lion terribly attacks;
> Be gracious to the singer, highly-praised lion !
> Let your troops fell someone other than us !
>
> (Ṛgv. 2,33,11, free)—

therefore it is said *ugram*.

Now why is it said *vīram*?—Because by his majesty he puts to rest all worlds, all gods, all selves, all beings (stand away from them, *viramati*), creates continually, expands and causes to live,—

Through which a hero, energetic, virtuous,
Presser, the friend of gods is born (Ṛgv. 3,4,9),

therefore it is said *vīram*.

Now why is it said *mahāviṣṇum*?—[Because it is he,] who permeates all worlds and causes them to permeate him, like oil with regard to the lump of ground sesamum interwoven lengthwise and crosswise by it, mutually is permeated by them,—

He, than whom no higher one exists,
Who has entered into all the beings,
Yea, beyond whom nothing else exists,
Prajāpati, endowed with offspring,
Pervades the three world-lights of sixteen parts,—
(Vāj. Saṁh. 8,36, free, cf. *Gesch. d. Phil.* I, 191).

therefore it is said *mahāviṣṇum*.

Now why is it said jvalantam?—Because by his majesty he inflames all words, all gods, all selves, all beings, causes to flame, is inflamed, causes himself to inflame,—

1

"Mover,[1] stimulator, bright, shining, illuminator, flaming, inflammer, burning, kindling, scorching, glittering, sparkling, pretty, embellishing, beautiful (Taitt. Br. 3,10,1,2),—therefore it is said *jvalantam*.

Now why is it said *sarvatomukham*?— Because even without sense organs he sees everywhere, hears everywhere, goes everywhere, takes everywhere, and going everywhere, stays everywhere,—

"The one, who formerly became the world,
From whom was born the protector of the universe,

1. The passage contains only an enumeration of the fifteen hours of the days of the second half of the month, as Weber, *Ind. Stud.* IX, 94 observes.

In whom the world merges in final destruction,
Him I adore, active everywhere",—

therefore it is said *sarvatomukham.*

Now why is it said *nṛsiṁham*?—Because of all creatures man (*nṛ*) is the bravest and the loftiest, and the lion (*siṁha*) is the bravest and the loftiest, therefore the highest god became the man-lion. For the imperishable one takes this form for the well-being of the world,—

"Viṣṇu is glorified for this great deed,
Like a roaming, wild animal, that dwells in mountains,
He, under whose three mighty steps,
The creatures all have a secure home (Ṛgv. 1,154,2)—

therefore it is said *nṛsiṁham.*

Now why is it said *bhīṣaṇam*?—Because he, at whose sight all worlds, all gods, all beings run away from fear, is not afraid of anything whatsoever,—

"Out of his fear the wind purifies,
Out of his fear the sun rises,
Out of his fear hastens Agni
And Indra and the Death, the fifth" (Taitt. 2,8)—

therefore it is said *bhiṣaṇam.*

Now why is it said *bhadram*?—[Because] he, being himself auspicious, always grants good luck, "glittering, sparkling, pretty, embellishing, beautiful" (Taitt. Br. 3,10,1),—

"The auspicious let us hear with ears, O gods,
The auspicious let us see with eyes, O holies,
With firm limbs, praising, able-bodied,
Let's reach the God-ordained span of life"!
(Ṛgv. 1,89,8)—

therefore it is said *bhadram.*

Now why is it said *mṛtyumṛtyum*?—Because, the moment he

is thought of, he slays the death and the sudden (or accidental) death,[1]—

"He who gives breath, gives strength,
Whose command everybody hears, the very gods too,
Whose reflection the Immortal, who's the death of Death,
Which the god, whom we may worship through sacrifice?"
(Ṛgv. 10,121,2, free)—

therefore it is said *mṛtyumṛtyum*.

Now why is it said *namāmi*?—Because [it is he] to whom all gods bow down, also the seekers of liberation and the Brahman-students,—

"Now Brahmaṇaspati is speaking forth
A formula full of praise,
In which Indra and gods rejoice,
Varuṇa, Mitra, Aryaman" (Ṛgv. 1,40,5)—

therefore it is said *namāmi*.

Now why is it said *aham* ?—
"I am the first-born of the cosmic order,
Before the gods, at the fountain of Eternal,
Who serves out to me, delights me thereby,
For I am the food, I eat the food-eater,
I am above this whole world.

He who knows this shines like gold!—Thus reads the great Upaniṣad (Taitt. 3,10, above).

THIRD UPANIṢAD

[In a sacred formula, three parts are usually distinguished : (1) *vījam* "the germ", i.e. the first syllable, (2) *kīla* or *kīlaka* "the stem", the middle syllables from the second up to the penultimate, (3) *śakti* "the power" (the crown, as it were, or the fruit of it), i.e. the last syllable. In the following, the Vījam (*u*) and Śakti (*-ham*) of the Nṛsiṁha formula are interpreted allegorically. *Śakti*, the creative power of Nṛsiṁha, is the *māyā* and Vījam, the seed, out of which the whole world has developed, is the *Ākāśa* (space, ether) (in accordance with the oft-quoted passage, Taitt. 2,1: "Out of this Ātman the Ākāśa is born, out of the Ākāśa the wind" etc.)]

1. The original 'Abertod', which seems to be Deussen's own coinage, is not quite clear to me.—GBP.

Once upon a time the gods said to Prajāpati: "Teach us, O respected sir, the *Śakti* (power) and the *Vījam* (seed) of the Mantrarāja, composed in Anuṣṭubh and relating to Nṛsiṁha. And Prajāpati said:

It is this Māyā of Narasiṁha which creates the universe, protects the universe, and reabsorbs the universe. Therefore one should know this Māyā as the *Śakti* (creative power); one who knows this Māyā as the Śakti, he surmounts the sin, surmounts death, he also attains immortality and obtains great luck.—The Brahman-knowers inquire: is it [the Śakti, the final syllable of the formula] to be uttered short or long or extra-long (*ham*, *hām*, *hā-ām*)?—When it is [uttered] short, one thereby burns all sin and attains immortality; if long, one obtains great luck and attains immortality; if extra-long, one becomes wise and attains immortality. Therefore the following is said by the Ṛṣi by way of indication;

So drink it now, aspiring and victorious (Ṛgv. 6,17,2)!
Luck, beauty, press-stone, little mother and earth-cow,
And Indra's weapon, which is counted as the sixth,
I know them as sprung from Brahman, all alike,
And implore them for the protection of my life.

The Ākāśa, verily, is the highest goal of all beings. For all beings are born from the Ākāśa; from the Ākāśa, after they are born, they live; and departing from here, they are again merged in the Ākāśa [patterned on Taitt. 3, 1ff]. Therefore one should know the Ākāśa as the *vījam* (world-seed). Therefore the following is said by the Ṛṣi by way of indication (Kāṭh. 5,2. Mahānār. 10.6, following. Ṛgv. 4,40,5):

In ether he is sun-swan, Vasu in air,
Hotar on the altar, guest at the doorstep,
He dwells in man and wideness, in rule, in space,

Springs from waters, kine, law, mountains as the great law—he, who knows this.—Thus reads the great Upaniṣad.

Fourth Upaniṣad

[Just as a king does not appear without retinue. similarly the formula-king (*mantra-rāja*), i.e. the Nṛsiṁha formula is accompanied by four sub-formulas which are here (after the mention of the first three in anticipation at 1, 3) presented according to their text. What is remarkable here is the openness with which the Māṇḍūkya-Upaniṣad is plundered for the sake of explaining the Om-sound. Upon the four sub-formulas follows at 3 yet another swarm of small formulas which are wholly devised on the pattern of Atharvaśiras 2.]

4.1

Om!

And the gods said to Prajāpati: Teach us, O respected sir, the Aṅgamantras (accompanying formulas) of the Mantrarāja, composed in Anuṣṭubh and relating to Nṛsiṁha.—And Prajāpati said:

The *Praṇava*, the *Sāvitrī*, the *Yajurlakṣmī* and the *Nṛsiṁha-gāyatrī*,—these one should know as the Aṅgas. And one who knows this, attains immortality.

[First Aṅga : the *Praṇava*]

"Om! This syllable is the whole world. Its explanation is as follows:

"The past, the present and the future, all this is the sound Om. And besides, what still lies beyond the three times, that also is the sound Om.

"All this, verily, is Brahman, but Brahman is this Ātman (the soul), and this Ātman is fourfold.

"The *Vaiśvānara*, present in the wakeful state, perceiving outwards, seven-limbed, having nineteen mouths, the enjoyer of the gross, is its first quarter.

"The *Taijasa*, present in the state of dream, perceiving inwards, seven-limbed, having nineteen mouths, the enjoyer of the selected, is its second quarter.

"The state where he, asleep, no more experiences any desire and sees no vision is deep sleep. The *Prājña*, present in the state of deep sleep, become one, consisting wholly of knowledge through and through, consisting of bliss, the enjoyer of the bliss, having conscience for his mouth, is its third quarter.— He is the lord of all, he is the omniscient, he is the inner guide, he is the cradle of the universe, verily he is creation and disappearance of creatures.

"That which is neither inward-perceiving nor outward-perceiving, nor both-way perceiving, neither conscious nor unconscious, that which does not consist of knowledge through and through, neither invisible, unhandlable, ungraspable, uncharacterizable, inconceivable, unnamable, established in the certitude of one's own self, that which extinguishes the expanse of the universe, calm, auspicious, without the second,—that is the fourth quarter, that one should know as the Ātman." (This whole observation on the Praṇava is borrowed, almost wholly unchanged, from the Māṇḍūkya-Up. 1-7).

4.2

[Second Aṅga : the *Sāvitrī.*]

Further the Sāvitrī, i.e. the Gāyatrī, consisting of the sacrificial formula [*ghṛṇiḥ sūrya' ādityaḥ* Taitt. Ār. 10,15] by which the whole world is pervaded; *ghṛṇiḥ* are two syllables, *sūria* are three, and *āditya* are three; this is an octo-syllabic line, anointed with beauty, of the Savitar-formula; and who knows it thus, he is therefore anointed with beauty. This is said by ṛc (Ṛgv. 1, 164,39):

The sound of hymn in the highest heaven,
Propped on which gods all are enthroned,
If one doesn't know it, of what use the hymn?—
We, who know it, are assembled here.

Verily, he who knows Sāvitrī, requires no Ṛc, no Yajus, no Sāman any longer.

[Third Aṅga : the *Lakṣmī-yajus* or the *Yajur-lakṣmī.*]

Om! bhūr lakṣmīr, bhuvar lakṣmīḥ,
suvaḥ kālakarṇī, tan no
mahālakṣmīḥ pracodayāt!
(Om! earth luck, and atmosphere luck,
And heaven luck, black-eared,[1]—
So may the great luck promote us!)

1. As a rule black ears otherwise denote bad luck. So we have here, as a counterpart to euphemism, a 'Dysphemismus', which is not so easy to understand psychologically as the other. (The use of terms of abuse as fondling expressions is analogous.)

This is the sacrificial formula *Mahālakṣmī*, a twentyfour-syllabic Gāyatrī. Verily Gāyatrī is all this, whatever exists. Therefore, he who knows this Mahālakṣmī contained in a sacrificial formula obtains great bliss.

[Fourth Aṅga : the Nṛsiṁhagāyatrī.]

Om! Let us think, well aware,
Of Nṛsiṁha, the lightning-nailed,
May the Lion promote our thought.
(after Taitt. Ār. 1, verse 31).

Verily, this Nṛsiṁha-Gāyatrī is the basic reality of gods and the Vedas. He who knows this is of the nature of basic reality.

4.3

And the gods said to Prajāpati : By which formula must the God be praised so that he is pleased and shows himself ? Tell it to us, O exalted sir !

Then prājāpati said:[1]

Om! He who is the exalted god Nṛsiṁha and is also		Brahmán,	to him the salutation, the salutation!		
,,	,,	Viṣṇu	,,	,,	,,
,,	,,	Maheśvara	,,	,,	,,
,,	,,	Puruṣa,	,,	,,	,,
,,	,,	Īśvara,	,,	,	,,
,,	,,	Sarasvatī,	,,	,,	,,
,,	,,	Śrī,	,,	,,	,,
,,	,,	Gaurī,	,,	,,	,,
,,	,,	Prakṛti,	,,	,,	,,
,,	,,	the Ignorance,[2]	,,	,,	,,
,,	,,	the sound Om,	,,	,,	,,

1. The whole following formula is patterned on Atharvaśiras 2 (above).

2. To the first five the following five are allotted as wives, as remarked pertinently by Weber, with whom we adopt the analysis *avidyā*; the scholiast of course reads *vidyā*.

Om! He who is the exalted god Nṛsiṁha and is also	the Vedas with Aṅgas and Śākhās	to him the salutation, the salutation!
" "	the five fires	" " "
" "	the 7 Vyāhṛtis,	" " "
" "	the 8 world-guardians,	" "
" "	the 8 Vasus,	" " "
" "	the Rudras,	" " "
" "	the Ādityas,	" " "
" "	(the 8 seizors) ((Bṛh. 3,2))	" " "
" "	the 5 elements,	" " "
" "	the three-worlds,	" " "
" "	the time,	" " "
" "	Manu,	" " "
" "	the death,	" " "
" "	the Yama,	" " "
" "	the god of death	" " "
" "	the Prāṇa,	" " "
" "	Sūrya,	" " "
" "	Soma,	" " "
" "	the Jīva (soul),	" " "
" "	the Virāj,	" " "
" "	the universe,	" " "

And Prajāpati said to them [further]: Always praise the God with these formulas so that being pleased he will show himself to you.

Therefore he who always praises the God with these formulas gets a view of the God and attains immortality,—and he who knows this also attains immortality. Thus reads the great Upaniṣad.

FIFTH UPANIṢAD

[If the substitution of formula in the place of thought is a sign of decadence, then the last step in this direction is taken when, as taught here, the formula is put down artistically and worn as an amulet of magical potency, on neck, arm or hair-lock;—and the sadness over seeing the most spiritual and the most sublime of all religions going to the grave in this way is not mitigated by the consideration that we see similar phenomena making their appearance in other walks of religious and philosophical development. In glaring contrast to these symptoms of marasmus stand the extravagant promises, in which the second half abounds.]

5.1

Om!

Once the gods said to Prajāpati: Explain to us, O exalted sir, the circle, (the diagram), which is called the great circle, the one which the Yogins call the all-wish-fulfilling gate of liberation. —And Prajāpati said:

This great circle *Sudarśanam* (the discus of Viṣṇu; originally the solar discus "beautiful to look at") has six spokes; therefore it has also six spokes and six wings. Verily there are six seasons; it corresponds to the seasons. In the middle is the navel; for the spokes are established in the navel. And all this is surrounded by the Māyā; but the Māyā does not touch its self (Ātman); therefore from the outside it is surrounded by the Māyā.

Further there is a circle with eight spokes and eight wings; for the Gāyatrī has eight syllables; it corresponds to the Gāyatrī. From outside it is surrounded by the Māyā. Verily this Māyā appears in every field (as its surrounding).

Further there is a circle with twelve spokes and twelve wings; for the Jagatī has twelve syllables; it corresponds to the Jagatī. From outside it is surrounded by the Māyā.

Further there is a circle with sixteen spokes and sixteen wings; for "the Puruṣa consists of sixteen parts" (Chānd. 6,7,1, but in a different sense), but the Puruṣa is this whole world; and it corresponds to the Puruṣa. From outside it is surrounded by the Māyā.

Further there is a circle with thirtytwo spokes and thirtytwo wings; for the Anuṣṭubh has thirtytwo syllables; it corresponds to the Anuṣṭubh. From outside it is surrounded by the Māyā.

This Sudarśana circle is formed by the Spokes; the Vedas, verily are the spokes; it revolves around in wings; the songs [Chandas], verily are the wings.

5.2

The great circle Sudarśanam is this circle. At its centre, at the nave, is the delivering sign (*tārakam*); the syllable, which denotes Narasiṁha (viz. *Om*), it is this one syllable.

On the six wings stands the six-syllabic Sudarśanam ["a six-syllabic *Sudarśana-mantra*" Schol.; which one, not said; perhaps: *Om namaś cakrāya*].

On the eight wings stands the octo-syllabic Nārāyaṇam [probably: *Om namo Nārāyaṇāya*].

On the twelve wings stands the twelve-syllabic Vāsudevam [perhaps: *Om namo bhagavate Vāsudevāya*].

On the sixteen wings stand the firsts of the letters of alphabet [according to the scholiast: "the initial signs of a letter-formula" *mātṛkāmantrasya*, i.e. probably of a formula whose lines or words begin with the fourteen vowels *a ā i ī u ū ṛ ṝ ḷ ḹ e ai o au*] along with points [Anusvāra and Visarga] as the sixteen parts.

On the thirtytwo wings stands the thirtytwo-syllabic king of the formulas, relating to Narasiṁha and composed in Anuṣṭubh.

This is the great circle, which is the gate of liberation, fulfilling all desires and consists of the Ṛcs, the Yajus', the Sāmans, the Brahman, the immortality.

To its east are situated the Vasus, to the south the Rudras, to the west the Ādityas, to the north the Viśve devāḥ, at the nave Brahmán, Viṣṇu and Maheśvara, on its side the sun and the moon.[1] On this is the verse (Ṛgv. 1,164,39):

The sound of hymn in the highest heaven,
Propped on which gods all are enthroned,
If one doesn't know it, of what us the hymn?–
We, who know it, are assembled here.

If one knows this great circle, whether he is a child or a youth, he is great, he is a teacher, he is the instructor of all the Mantras (Vedic songs and formulas). One sacrifices through Anuṣṭubh [in that one knows and recites it], one offers a song of praise through Anuṣṭubh.

This[diagram], which slays evil spirits and protects from death, after receiving it from one's preceptor, one should tie it on the neck, arm, or the hair-tuft.

1. Accordingly the whole Mahācakra-diagram would look something like this : see p. 830a.

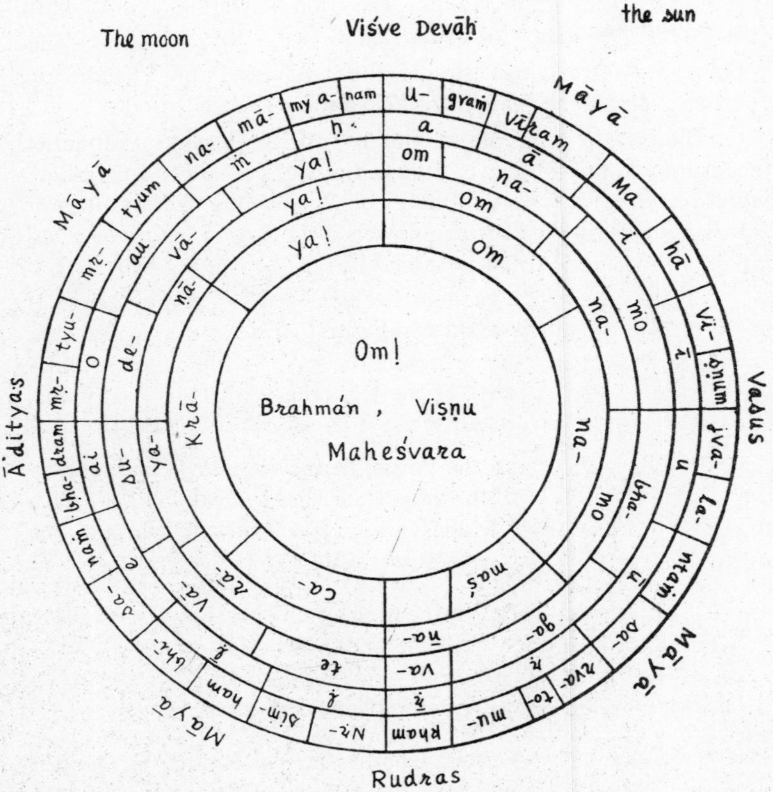

It is worth naticing that the old Vedic gods lie outside the circle, in the realm of the Māyā.

This formula is of so much use, that one had as it were given away the whole earth with the seven islands as the Dakṣiṇā) (sacrificial reward).—Therefore, trusting in it when one gives away whatever it may be, that serves as [sufficient] Dakṣiṇā.

5.3

The gods once said to Prajāpati: Propound to us, O exalted sir, the reward of this formula-king, composed in Anuṣṭubh and relating to Nṛsiṁha.—And Prajāpati said:

One who always studies this formula-king, relating to Nṛsiṁha and composed in Anuṣṭubh, he is purified by Agni,[1] purified by Vāyu, purified by Āditya, purified by Soma, purified by truth, purified by worlds, purified by Brahmán, purified by Viṣṇu, purified by Rudra, purified by the Vedas, purified by everything, —purified by everything.

5.4

One who always studies this formula-king relating to Nṛsiṁha surmounts death, surmounts embryo-killing, Brāhmaṇa-killing, man-killing, all killing, surmounts Saṁsāra, surmounts everything—surmounts everything.

5.5

One who always studies this formula-king relating to Nṛsiṁha composed in Anuṣṭubh, he makes Agni spell-bound, makes Vāyu spell-bound, makes Āditya spell-bound, makes Soma spell-bound, makes the water spell-bound, makes all gods spell-bound, makes all evil spirits spell-bound, makes the poison spell-bound, —makes the poison spell-bound.

5.6

One who always studies this formula-king relating to Nṛsiṁha, composed in Anuṣṭubh, he wins the world *bhūr*, wins the world *bhuvar*, wins the world *svar*, wins the world *mahar*, wins the world *jana*, wins the world *tapas*, wins the world *satyam*, wins the whole world, —wins the whole world.

---

1. This same or a similar formula is usually found in later Upaniṣads: Cf. Rāmottaratāp. Appendix p. 381. Kaivalya, end, p. 464. Atharvaśiras 7. Mahā. 4, p. 96 (Jacob). Mudgala 4 Telugu ed. p. 529, 14).

5,7.

One who always studies this formula-king relating to Nṛsiṁha, composed in Anuṣṭubh, he charms men towards him, charms gods towards him, charms the Yakṣas towards him, charms all towards him,—charms all towards him.

5.8

One who always studies this formula-king relating to Nṛsiṁha, composed in Anuṣṭubh, he thereby offers the Agniṣṭoma[1], offers the Ukthya, offers the Ṣoḍaśin, offers the Vājapeya, offers the Atirātra, offers the Aptoryāma, thereby he offers all sacrifices,—offers all sacrifices.

5.9

One who always studies this formula-king relating to Nṛsiṁha, composed in Anuṣṭubh, he thereby studies[2] the Ṛcs, the Yajus', the Sāmans, the Atharvan, the Aṅgiras, the Śākhās, the Purāṇas, the Kalpas (ritualistic Sūtras), the song-verses, the verses of man-praise and the Praṇava, but one who studies Praṇava, he thereby studies everything,—he thereby studies everything.

5.10

A hundred uninitiated are equal to one initiated [i.e. a *Brahmacārin*]; a hundred initiated are equal to one householder (*Gṛhastha*); a hundred householders are equal to one forest-resident (*Vānaprastha*); a hundred forest-residents are equal to one ascetic (*Yati*, i.e. *Saṁnyāsin*); a full hundred ascetics are equal to one who mutters the Rudrajapa [probably the Śatarudriyam or the Nīlarudropaniṣad borrowed from it]; a hundred who mutter the Rudrajapa are equal to one who studies the Atharvaśiras and the Atharvaśikhā; and a hundred who mutter the Atharvaśiras and the Atharvaśikhā are equal to one who studies the Mantrarāja.

---

1. On these forms of one-day Soma-sacrifices, cf. e.g. Ait. Br. 3, 39ff. (Introduction to the Aitareya-Upaniṣad, above).
2. For the following enumeration, cf. Taitt. Ār. 2, 10 (pp. 240 ff).

This, verily, is the highest abode of one who studies the Mantrarāja, where no sun heats, no wind blows, no moon shines, no stars shine, no fire burns, no death breaks in, no pain approaches, the truly blissful,[1] supremely blissful, eternal, calm, ever auspicious, worshipped by everybody right from Brahmán, to be meditated upon by the Yogins, having gone where the Yogins do not return again.

On this is the verse :

And the highest step of Viṣṇu
The patrons see for ever
Like an eye, stationed in heaven.

And wondering over this highest step
Of Viṣṇu, the priests, wide awake,
Enkindle the sacrificial fire.[2]

And this falls to the share of one who is desireless,—this falls to the share of one who is desireless, who knows it thus. Thus reads the great Upaniṣad.

1. Deussen seems to have analysed *sadānandam* (usually dissolved into *sadā+ānandam*) into *sad+ānandam*.—GBP.

2. For these two verses forming a favourite conclusion of many an Upaniṣad, see note at the end of the Āruṇeya Upaniṣad above. —GBP.

NṚSIṀHA-UTTARA-TĀPANĪYA UPANIṢAD

As we saw, in all the five Upaniṣads it consists of, the *Nṛsiṁhapūrvatāpanīya* pursues as its goal the cult of the Nṛsiṁha-formula; the formula is the idol whose worship is demanded there and everything that comes in of the philosophical elements enters into the service of this goal. In this form the work might have satisfied the religious needs of the masses in whose hands everything finally becomes an idol; in any event, through the interspersed philosophical suggestions a vague suspicion of a deeper content might have been awakened and kept alive in common people also to whom it would remain incomprehensible.

To unfold this deeper content for those few, who were receptive to it, and to whom the Pūrvatāpanīya served only as a preliminary stage, is the aim of the *Nṛsiṁha-uttara-tāpanīya-Upaniṣad*. Although the Nṛsiṁha-formula continues to be held in high honour with the identification of Nṛsiṁha with the supreme Ātman, still it plays there a subordinate role; the whole stress falls on a complicated philosophical unfoldment which, to be sure, is essentially based on older passages, particularly of the Māṇḍūkya Upaniṣad, but is not wanting in new and, at times, particularly towards the end, remarkably deep-going views.

The fundamental view is the one of a four-fold identity which we can put down in the equation :

$$\textit{Ātman} = \textit{Om} = \textit{Brahman} = \textit{Nṛsiṁha},$$

wherein *Ātman* as the psychic principle is equated, by means of the *Om*-sound with the *Brahman* as cosmic principle and all the three, in their turn, are seen symbolically in Nṛsiṁha. To this fundamental view is added, as a continuous fundamental doctrine, that the Ātman (identical with *Om*, *Brahman*, *Nṛsiṁha*) persists in full purity only in his supreme, sixteenth aspect as a completely passive subject of perception (*avikalpa*), while with his fifteen subordinate forms he projects into the world and conditions its reality, but that this whole reality of the world and his fifteen subordinate forms are nothing when looked at from the highest point of view. The inner unity of the Ātman in all beings is thereby brought to view by the artistically executed interweaving of all forms with each other.

First, in union with the Māṇḍūkya Upaniṣad, the four states of the Ātman are distinguished :

I. The waking and the (gross) world of waking.

II. The dream and the (subtle) dream-world.

III. The deep sleep and the seed-world, cause-world (cf. Gauḍap. 1,13 : *vījanidrāyutaḥ prājñaḥ*, above).

IV. The Turīya (sc. *ātmā*, or the Turīyam, sc. *sthānam*), the fourth state, the spectatorship, in which the union of the subject and the object takes place under the persistence of consciousness, whereas in the third it is accompanied by a dissolution of it (cf. Gauḍap. 1,12: *turyaṁ tat sarvadṛk sadā*, above).

Each of the first three states is mixed with all the four states, is therefore 1. gross (waking), 2. subtle (dream), 3. seed (deep sleep), 4. Turīya (spectator).

As against this, there is a different fourfold division in the Turīya (and in the other three states in so far as they have a share in it). The Turīya is :

1. *ota* "inwoven" (*Bṛh.* 3,8) as the intellectual element running through the whole world;

2. *anujñātṛ* "Affirmer" (alternating with *anumantṛ*[1] "Consenter" not in the sense of Schopenhauerian" affirmation of the will to the life", (will's acceptance of life) but as the spiritual which alone gives a positive substance to the objects ("the thinking makes this wholly unsubstantial world substantial" Nṛsiṁhott. 8b, below).

3. *anujñā* "Affirmation", the very same after stripping off personality (related to *anujñātṛ* in the same way as the impersonal *Brahman* to the personal *Īśvara*).

4. *avikalpa* "Indifference", the complete effacement of all differences, so that only the pure, objectless subject of perception remains. (Main passages explaining these four basic concepts are below).

Inasmuch as waking, dream and deep sleep have a share in the Turīya, they also contain *ota, anujñātṛ, anujñā* and *avikalpa* and by this very means they "flow into" the Turīya (*turīya-avasita*). But all the three states (waking, dream, deep sleep) and the first three determinations of the Turīya also (*ota, anujñātṛ, anujñā*) are wholly "only deep sleep, dream and sheer delusion". Only *avikalpa* is completely real "for the Ātman has thinking as the only taste."

This highest state, attained after severing all worldly tastes, is "the fourth of the fourth" (*turīya-turīya*), is the Ātman himself in his purest form, and the description in the last chapter how he is to be felt and found by becoming conscious (*anubhava*) of him as the self in us, and not through intellectual activity is among the most beautiful and most precious that the ancient Indian plunge into the secrets of the inner self has brought to light.

---

1. The expression perhaps goes back to the Bhag. G. 13,22 : *upadraṣṭā-'numantā ca.*

NṚSIṀHA-UTTARA-TĀPANĪYA UPANIṢAD

Om !

The auspicious let us hear with ears, O gods,
The auspicious let us see with eyes, O holies,
With firm limbs, praising, able-bodied,
Let's reach the God-ordained span of life ! (Ṛgv. 1,89,8).

May Indra, the highly renowned, grant us well-being,
Well-being god Pūṣan, the lord of all riches,
Well-being Tārkṣya, whose felly remains undamaged,
May Bṛhaspati, too, grant well-being to us (Ṛgv. 1,89,6).
Om, peace! Om, peace! Om, peace !

FIRST KHAṆḌA

[At first, in conjunction with a passage from the Māṇḍūkya, the Om-sound is set forth as a unity in which *Brahman* (objective) and *Ātman* (subjective) fuse together. Both, Brahman and Ātman, are (as is unfolded again in the continuation of the Māṇḍūkya Upaniṣad theory of the four states of the Ātman) : (1) gross (world of waking,—waking), (2) subtle (dreamworld,—dreaming), (3) uniform (seed-world,-deep sleep), (4) *Turīya*, spectator, the pure subject of perception. Each of the first three states is *caturātman* "four-substanced", i.e. mixed with the three other states so that each of them contains (a) the gross, (b) the subtle, (c) the seed, (d) the spectator. Another fourfold division occurs in the Turīya, wherein the same is (a) *ota*, (b) *anujñātṛ*, (c) *anujñā*, (d) *avikalpa*; also the first three states have a share in these four determinations, through which they flow into the Turīya. Only the last of these determinations *(avikalpa)* is wholly free from the illusion of mundane life.]

Om !

Once the gods said to Prajāpati: Proclaim to us the Om-sound which, being that Ātman, is minuter than the minute.— Let it be so, said he.[1]

"Om ! this syllable is the whole world. Its explanation is as follows. The past, the present and the future, all this

1. Prajāpati begins his discussion with the Māṇḍūkya Upaniṣad, from which the whole portion enclosed in the quotation marks is taken.

> is the sound Om. And besides, what still lies beyond the three times, that also is the sound Om. All this, verily, is Brahman, but Brahman is this Ātman."

While one makes this Ātman one with Brahman by means of the word Om, and makes the Brahman one with the Ātman by means of the word Om, one should experience that one, ageless, immortal, fearless in the word Om, should merge in it this whole three-body world,—for one should know that the world consists of it,—and should compress it in the word Om. Thereby one should combine the three-body Ātman and the three-body supreme Brahman into each other, so far the latter is gross and the former experiences the gross, the latter is subtle and the former experiences the subtle, the latter is uniform and the former experiences bliss.

> "This Ātman is fourfold. The one present in the "wakeful state", perceiving the gross, seven-limbed, having nineteen mouths, experiencing the gross four-substanced *Viśva*, "Vaiśvānara is his first quarter. —The one present in the state of dream" perceiving the subtle, "seven-limbed, having nineteen mouths", experiencing the subtle, four-substanced "*Taijasa*", Hiraṇyagarbha "is his second quarter.—The state, where he, asleep, no more experiences, any desire and sees no vision is deep sleep. The one present in the state of deep sleep, become one consisting wholly of knowledge through and through, consisting of bliss, experiencing the bliss, having consciousness for his "mouth", four-substanced, "*Prājña*", *Īśvara* is his third quarter. He is the lord of all, he is the omniscient, he is the inner guide, he is the cradle of the universe, verily he is creation and disappearance of creatures."

All these three are in reality only deep sleep, dream and sheer delusion; for the Ātman has thinking as the only taste. But as far as the Fourth is further concerned, he is also four-substanced, so far as in the *Turīya* (Fourth) fuses each of the other three by virtue of the *Inwoven*, *Affirmer*, Affirmation and Indifference [properties inherent in all of them]. And even of these the [first] three are only deep sleep, dream and sheer delusion : for [the Ātman] has thinking as the only taste. On him there is this instruction :

> Not perceiving the gross and not perceiving the subtle, not both-way perceiving, neither conscious nor unconscious, also not consisting of knowledge through and through, invisible, uncharacterizable, established in the certitude of his own self, extinguishing the expanse of the universe, auspicious, calm, without the second,—that is [the fourth quarter], that "precisely" is the Ātman, that precisely "one should perceive",—

and the *Īśvara* (the personal God) also is devoured by the *Turīya* (the Fourth),—by the *Turīya*.[1]

SECOND KHAṆḌA

[As it was previously a connecting link between the Ātman and the Brahman, the Om-sound is a connecting link between the Ātman and the material world, on the one side through its three moras (*a*, *u*, *m*), on the other as the whole (*om*). Each of the three states of the Ātman (waking, dream, deep sleep) is the gross, the subtle, unity and spectator; similarly each of the three moras (*a*, *u*, *m*) contains the gross, the subtle, unity and spectator, so that *a* corresponds to the waking, *u* to the dream, *m* to the deep sleep. Similarly the Om-sound as a whole corresponds to the Turīya, so far as he bears on himself the four determinations of these (*ota*, *anujñātṛ*, *anujñā*, *avikalpa*). Through these four determinations the world becomes a reality (*nāma-rūpa-ātmaka*); through them the Turīya projects, by means of the Om-sound, into the objects.—To the end the Nṛsiṁha-formula is described as a means to elevate oneself to the Turīya, thus preparing for the next section.]

Of this Ātman one should know that in waking he is dreamless and without deep sleep, in dream he is waking and without

1. The Turīya is the abyss, which swallows even the personification of the divine as Īśvara. What a grand doctrine for instead of the occidental. "If the ruler of the world had not been too great even to the theory."—Weber understands the words *Īśvaragrāsas turīyaḥ* in the opposite way, meaning that the Turīya is supposed to be swallowed by the Īśvara (*Ind. Stud*. IX, 128. 131).—At this stage of understanding the judgment (passed ibid. p. 137; and repeated complacently by the young) ; "The mystical profound sense becomes rampant non-sense",—would probably seem to be premature.

deep sleep, in deep sleep waking and dreamless, in the Turīya waking, dreamless and without deep sleep, that he is unchangeable eternal bliss, having the only taste (of thinking), that is how one should know him.

He is the one who sees the eye, who sees the ear, who sees the speech, who sees the *Manas,* who sees the Buddhi, who sees the Prāṇa, who sees the darkness, who sees everything. Therefore he is another from the universe, an essentially different one.

He is the spectator (*sākṣin*) of the eye, spectator of the ear, spectator of the speech, spectator of the Manas, spectator of the Buddhi, spectator of the Prāṇa, spectator of the darkness, spectator of everything. Therefore he is the unchangeable great spirit, the dearest of all the world, verily one must know him as consisting of bliss through and through. Shining gloriously before this whole world,[1] having the only taste [of thinking], not aging and not decaying, immortal and fearless, he [the Ātman] is the Brahman.

And one should also make him, consisting of four quarters, one with the unborn [*Prakṛti, Māyā, Avidyā*] by means of the moras and further by means of the [whole] Om-sound.

> "The one present in state of waking"[2] four-substance *Viśva*, "*Vaiśvānara* is the" four-form "*a*-sound; verily the *a*-sound is four-form by reason of the forms of the *a*-sound: the gross, the subtle, the seed and the spectator, "from the reaching or from the first existence", and from being gross, being subtle, being the seed and being the spectator; "He who knows this, verily attains" this whole world "and becomes the first".
>
> "The one present in the state of dream" four-substanced "*Taijasa*", *Hiraṇyagarbha* "is the" four-form "*u*-sound"; verily the *u*-sound is four-form by reason of the forms of the *u*-sound: the gross, the subtle, the seed and the spectator, "from the high-holding or from the being-on-

1. Cf. Taitt. Br. 2,8,8,8: *brahma jajñānam prathamam purastāt* (*Gesch. d. Phil.* I, 251).

2. The following whole portion enclosed in the quotation marks is taken from the Māṇḍūkya Upaniṣad.

"both-the-sides" and from being gross, being subtle, being the seed and being the spectator; "he who knows this, "verily, holds high the tradition of knowledge and is "equally respected by both the sides".

"The one present in the state of deep sleep" four-substanced "*Prājña*", *Īśvara* "is the" four-form "*m*-sound" verily the *m*-sound "is four-form by reason of the forms of the "*m*-sound": the gross, the subtle, the seed and the spectator, "from constructing "or also from annihilating" and from being gross, being subtle, being the seed and being the spectator; "he who knows this verily constructs this whole world and is also its annihilation".

Thus one should re-find all the Mātrās in each individual Mātrā.[1]

Further the Turīya who, as self-ruler, self-Īśvara, self-luminious, devours even the Īśvara (the personal God), is four-substanced as *ota*, *anujñātṛ*, *anujñā* and *avikalpa*.

The Ātman is similar to the *ota* ["woven into" the world] as the whole world to the rays of the time-fire and of the sun (read *kālāgni-sūrya-usraiḥ*) at the time of the end.

And the Ātman is the *anujñātṛ* (affirmer) of this world because he gives it his own self and [thereby] makes this world visible—that is, makes it his own self [which is luminous]—as the sun the darkness.

And the Ātman has *anujñā* (affirmation) as his own taste because, by his very nature, he is pure thought, comparable to the fire after it has consumed the fuel.

And the Ātman is the *avikalpa* (indifference), so far as he is not accessible to words and thoughts.

The Om-sound has also thought for its form, and it is four-form; and this four-form Om-sound is, by means of the Inwoven the Affirmer, the Affirmation and the Indifference, the Ātman himself. And this world has names and forms for its substance

1. The variant reading : *amātramātrāyām pratimātrāḥ kuryād*, "one should re-find every individual mora in the moraless mora", not supported by the comm., which Weber follows is, as he rightly observes, also linguistically doubtful, but it would point to what now follows admirably well.

by reason of the Turīyaness alone or the thought form character [included in the Om-sound] as also by means of being inwoven, being the affirmer, being affirmation and being indifference—for the whole universe also is [on account of its very substance] of the form of indifference, and there is no difference [between Ātman, Om-sound, universe]. And on this is this instruction:

> "The fourth is moraless, unhandlable, extinguishing the expanse of the universe, auspicious, without a second,—the syllable Om, the Ātman himself. One who knows this has his [individual] self merged in the [highest] self". (Māṇḍ. 12).

Such a man will know the Turīya through the Anuṣṭubh relating to Nṛsiṁha, the formula-king. For this [formula-king] discloses the Ātman, is capable of collecting all [duality], not tolerating arrogance, the master, all-pervading, always blazing, free from the nescience and its effects, abolishing the bond of one's own self, always without a second, having the form of bliss, the foundation of all, pure being, he is the I himself wholly freed from nescience, darkness and delusion.

Therefore one should, in this way, make one this Ātman and the highest Ātman; one who accomplishes it, is a man, is Nṛsiṁha himself !

Third Khaṇḍa

[The four lines of the Nṛsiṁha-formula correspond to the four moras of the Om-sound (*a*, *u*, *m*, half mora), and, therefore, they also contain, like the latter, the Turīya in themselves and they thereby become a means to rise above the world to the Turīya, to absorb the whole world in the Turīya.]

Verily, what is the first mora of the Om-sound, that is the first line [of the Nṛsiṁha-formula]; the second corresponds to the second, the third to the third; the fourth mora is, according to its substance, In-woven, Assenter, Assent, Indifference; finding with it and with the fourth line the Turīya of four substances, one should, meditating by means of it, absorb [the world] in the Turīya.

> Verily, of this Om-sound,[1] "the first mora, the earth, "is the *a*-sound. It is, consisting of verses, the Ṛgveda, is Brahman, the Vasus, the Gāyatrī, the Gārhapatya fire." This is the first line [of the formula-king].

It is, however, four-substanced in all the four lines by reason of the gross, the subtle, the seed and the spectator.

> "The second mora, the atmosphere, is the *u*-sound. It is, consisting of sacrificial formulas, the Yajurveda, is Viṣṇu, the Rudras, the Triṣṭubh, the Dakṣiṇa fire."

This is the second line [of the formula-king]. It is, however, four-substanced in all the four lines by reason of the gross, the subtle, the seed and the spectator.

> "The third mora, the heaven, is the *m*- sound. It is, consisting of the songs, the Sāmaveda, is Rudra, the Ādityas, the Jagatī, the Āhavanīya fire."

This is the third line [of the formula-king]. It is, however, four-substanced in all the four lines by reason of the gross, the subtle, the seed and the spectator.

> "The fourth, the half-mora, which is at the end of the syllable, is the Soma world, the Om-sound. It is, consisting of the Atharvan songs, the Atharvaveda, is the fire of universal destruction, the Maruts, the Virāj, the highest wise" called "the shining."

This is the fourth line [of the formula-king]. It is, however, four-substanced in all the four lines by reason of the gross, the subtle, the seed and the spectator.

Refinding all the Mātrās in each individual Mātrā, one should, meditating on him who has the forms of the Inwoven, Affirmer, Affirmation and indifference, absorb [the world in him];—thus one becomes wise, immortal, sacrificing the consciousness, pure, reposing, and free from obstructions. Perceiving the [Ātman]

---

1. What follows is taken from the Nṛsiṁhapūrvat. 2, 1 (above) which, in its turn, from the Atharvaśikhā 1. (above).

through restraining the breath, renouncing the whole world here below itself, and freeing oneself completely from the expanse of plurality one becomes the whole, the fundamental four-substanced one, who consists of Amṛtam, the fundamental four substanced one, who consists of the universe.

Then, on this great throne [of one's own heart] one should install, as the fiery Om-sound on the basic fire (Bṛh. 5,9), this four-into-seven-formed, four-substanced Ātman along with his retinue, i.e.

the sevenfold [as earth, *a*-sound, Ṛgveda, *Brahmán*, Vasus, Gāyatrī, Gārhapatya], four-substanced *a*-sound as *Brahmán* in the navel,

the sevenfold [as atmosphere, *u*-sound, Yajurveda, Viṣṇu, Rudra(s), Triṣṭubh, Dakṣiṇa], four-substanced *u*-sound as *Viṣṇu* in the heart,

the sevenfold [as heaven, *m*-sound, Sāmaveda, Rudra Ādityas, Jagatī, Āhavanīya], four-substanced, *m*-sound as *Rudra* between the brows,

the sevenfold [as Soma-world, *Om*-sound, Atharvaveda, fire of universal destruction, Maruts, Virāj, the highest wise], four-substanced, four-into-sevenfold [as the content of all the preceding ones], four-substanced *Om*-sound as *Sarveśvara* at the end of these twelve [sounds, *a*, *u*, *m* each of which is four-substanced], and,

the sevenfold [as before], four-substanced, four-into-sevenfold [as before], four-substanced, *Praṇava* [the Om-sound along with its constituent parts] consisting of bliss and Amṛtam at the end of these sixteen [the sounds *a*, *u*, *m*, *om* each of which is four-substanced].

Thereupon, with the [*Praṇava*] consisting of bliss and Amṛtam one should worship those—*Brahmán*, *Viṣṇu*, *Rudra*, *Maheśvara*] in a four-fold way, as also specially *Brahmán*, *Viṣṇu* and *Rudra*, all three as separate and again all three as not separate, after one has worshipped them in the form of their attribute in a fourfold way by means of offerings, should compress as attributeless [*caturdhā' liṅgān*, Telugu ed.], should then pervade the threefold [gross, subtle, of the form of seed] body with the heat [of the basic fire mentioned above], should inflame the Ātman located in them, and, supporting himself on that heat which issues out of the spirituality of the Ātman for strength, one should establish, by means of the qualities [gross, subtle, causal] the unity [first] in the [cosmic] great-gross, then he should compress the great-gross in the great-subtle and the great-subtle in the great-causal and, meditating on that which has the forms of the In-woven, Assent, Assenter and Indifference by means of the moras, should merge the world in it.

Fourth Khaṇḍa

[The Ātman, "who, as Turīya, shines on the tip of the Om-sound" (*turīya-oṁkāra-agra-vidyota*), is identical with Nṛsiṁha, as is shown by an inspection of the words in the Nṛsiṁha-formula.]

This Ātman, the highest Brahman, the Om-sound, who shines as Turīya at the tip of the Om-sound, one should, with Anuṣṭubh, worship, win his favour, should compress him in the word Om and think over him as [one's own] I.

This Ātman, the highest Brahman, the Om-sound, who shines as Turīya at the tip of the Om-sound, one should then worship as eleven-substanced (through the eleven words of the Mantrarāja) Ātman Nṛsiṁha, should compress him in the word Om and think over.

This Ātman, the highest Brahman, the Om-sound, who shines as Turīya at the tip of the Om-sound, one should then think over through the Praṇava, should picture him to oneself, through Anuṣṭubh, as the nine-fold in the selves [of the first nine words of the Mantrarāja] filled with being, thinking and bliss, the Ātman filled with being, thinking and bliss, as the highest Ātman, the highest Brahman, should then grasp it as the self itself through the word I and should make him one with the Brahman, in mind or also through the Anuṣṭubh.[1]

He, verily is *nṛ* (man, hero), for this nṛsiṁha is everywhere and at all times all-animating; and *siṁha* (lion) is this highest god, for it is he who is everywhere and at all times all-animating,

1. The first of these three sections seems to refer to the meditation of I, the second to that of Nṛsiṁha, the third to that of the unity of the two in the Brahman.

who devours everything. So he is wholly *nṛ-siṁha*; and this one is the Turīya.

He is *ugra*, he is *vīra*, he is *mahān*, he is *Viṣṇu*, he is *jvalan*, he is *sarvatomukha*, he is *nṛsiṁha*, he is *bhīṣaṇa*, he is *bhadra*, he is *mṛtyumṛtyu*, he is *namāmi*, he is *aham*.

Thus applying oneself to the Yoga, one should meditate upon the Anuṣṭubh with reference to the Brahman and with reference to the Om-sound.

On this are these verses:
Install on the throne the lion; your children,[1]
Offshoots of the world of sense, seize and hit with horns
Of the Om-sound, bull; the unreal,[2] quivering,
Throw before the lion to eat, then you are a hero !

Fifth Khaṇḍa

[The word *Om* signifies, in its three sounds, Nṛsiṁha : This latter is *a* as *āptatama* (reaching most), *u* as *utkṛṣṭatama* (most exalted), *m* as *mahāvibhūti* (the all-powerful), which is then further carried on in the case of the words of the Nṛsiṁha-formula. The first two of the three predicates mentioned are formed according to the Māṇḍūkya Up. 9-10 (above).]

Now, as for the *a*-sound, it means the one reaching most; for it refers to the Ātman, Nṛsiṁha, the Brahman; this is the one reaching the most; for he is the witness, is the lord; therefore he is omni-present; for he (read *sa hi idaṁ sarvam*) is this universe, is the one reaching most. For this universe is only the Ātman, a sheer delusion.—He is *ugra* as the one reaching most, is *vīra* as the one reaching most, is *mahān* as the one reaching most, is *viṣṇu* as the one reaching most, is *jvalan* as the one reaching most, is *sarvatomukha* as the one reaching most, is *nṛsiṁha* as the one reaching most, is *bhīṣaṇa* as the one reaching most, is *bhadra* as the one reaching most, is *mṛtyumṛtyu* as the one reaching most, is *namāmi* as the one reaching most, is *aham* as the one reaching most.—Indeed, the God Nṛsiṁha is the Ātman, is the Brahman. One who knows this, is "without desires, free from desires, of satisfied desires, his own desire;

1. The material objects.
2. The Māyā.

his animal spirits do not go out but, assembled, they stay there itself, for he is the Brahman and he is merged in the Brahman" (Bṛh. 4,4,6 and 3,2,11, above).

As for the *u*-sound, it means the most exalted; for it refers to the Ātman, Nṛsiṁha, the Brahman; therefore it is the reality as having the being; for apart from it there exists no other thing [which would be] imperceptible, which does not receive its light from the Ātman. For he alone is self-luminous, not attached, and the Ātman does not see anything other [than himself]. Therefore it [exaltedness] is not to be found otherwise, but that exaltedness is peculiar to the Ātman alone.—He is *ugra* as the exalted, is *vīra* as the exalted, is *mahān* as the exalted, is *viṣṇu* as the exalted, is *jvalan* as the exalted, is *sarvatomukha* as the exalted, is *nṛsiṁha* as the exalted, is *bhīṣaṇa* as the exalted, is *bhadra* as the exalted, is *mṛtyumṛtyu* as the exalted, is *namāmi* as the exalted, is *aham* as the exalted. —Therefore, one should know the Ātman as such; indeed the god Nṛsiṁha is the Ātman. One who knows this is "without desires, free from desires, of satisfied desires, his own desire; his animal spirits do not go out, but, assembled, they stay there itself, for he is the Brahman and he is merged in the Brahman" (Bṛh. 4,4,6 and 3,2,11).

As for the *m*-sound, it means the omni-potent; for it refers to the Ātman, Nṛsiṁha, the Brahman; therefore it is the unbounded (*analpa*, Chānd. 7,24,1), indivisible, self-luminous; indeed, Brahman is the one reaching most, most exalted, and this Brahman is also the omni-scient, exercising great magic art, omni-potent. It is *ugram* as the omni-potent, is *vīram* as the omni-potent, is *mahad* as the omni-potent, is *viṣṇu* as the omni-potent, is *jvalan*[1] as the omni-potent, is *sarvato-mukham* as the omni-potent, is *nṛsiṁham* as the omni-potent, is *bhiṣaṇam* as the omni-potent, is *bhadram* as the omni-potent, is *mṛtyumṛtyu* as the omni-potent, is *namāmi* as the omni-potent, is *aham* as the omni-potent.

Therefore one should search, with the *a*-sound and the *u*-sound, this Ātman as one searching most, most exalted, purely

1. Read *jvalad*.—GBP.

spiritual, all-seeing, being all-witness, all-devouring, being the object of all love, consisting of being, thinking and bliss, having only one taste, shining gloriously before this whole world (*Second Khaṇḍa*, above), and should know him, with the *m*-sound, as the highest Brahman, reaching most, most exalted, purely spiritual, omni-potent, consisting of being, thinking and bliss, having only one taste.—Indeed, the god Nṛsiṁha is the Ātman, is the highest Brahman. One who knows this is "without desires, free from desires, of satisfied desires, his own desire; his animal spirits do not go out, but, assembled, they stay there itself, for he is the Brahman and he is merged in the Brahman" (Bṛh. 4,4,6 and 3,2,11).—Thus spoke Prajāpati.

Sixth Khaṇḍa

[There are two stages, a lower one, in which the duality—the evil—is not yet fully overcome, but continues to remain within the Ātman, and a higher one, in which the Ātman, after extinction of all duality, purely negative, remains as a void (*śūnyam*). The latter stage is busy practically in the detachment from the world and all its interests.—The whole section interrupts the instruction of the gods by Prajāpati and ideologically also takes an isolated position.]

The gods desired to know this Ātman. Then the demonic evil wanted to devour them. Then they thought : Well ! Let us devour that demonic evil !—Then it happened that they knew, through the Nṛsiṁha-Anuṣṭubh, that Ātman shining at the tip of the Om-sound, who is [really only] the Fourth of the Fourth[1], as *ugra* and non-*ugra*, *vīra* and non-*vīra*, *mahān* and non-*mahān*, *viṣṇu* and non-*viṣṇu*, *jvalan* and non-*jvalan*, *sarvatomukha* and non-*sarvatomukha*, *nṛsiṁha* and non-*nṛsiṁha*, *bhīṣaṇa* and non-*bhīṣaṇa*, *bhadra* and non-*bhadra*, *mṛtyumṛtyu* and non-*mṛtyumṛtyu*, *namāmi* and non-*namāmi*, *aham* and non-*aham*. Then for them that demonic evil transformed itself into the light that consists of being, thinking and bliss. Therefore, one[2]

1. Of the four attributes of the *Turīyam*, Inwoven, Assenter, Assent, Indifference, only the last belongs to the Ātman in the strictest sense; the first three are only "deep sleep, dream and pure delusion" (above) :

2. My conjecture, that the Nominative is to be read instead of *apakvakaṣāyam* (*Bibl. Ind.*, Weber), was subsequently confirmed by the Telugu ed.

whose sin is not eradicated should know in this way through the Nṛsiṁha-Anuṣṭubh the Ātman shining at the tip of the Om-sound, who is the Fourth of the Fourth. For him the demonic evil transforms itself into the light which consists of being, thinking and bliss.

The gods, striving to be beyond that light and having misgivings of duality,[1] and having searched further through the Nṛsiṁha-Anuṣṭubh at the tip of the Om-sound, the one who is the Fourth of the Fourth, reached in him as the goal through Praṇava. Then that light shining gloriously before this whole world became, for them, the lightless, secondless, unthinkable, attributeless, self-luminous void (*śūnyam*) consisting wholly of bliss.—One who knows this becomes the self-luminous, highest Brahman.

The gods "stood away from the desire for sons, from the desire for possessions, from the desire for world" (Bṛh. 3,5,1. 4,4,22) and from the useful means thereto, and moving about without self-esteem, without residence, without family, without hair-tuft, without sacrificial thread, like blind, deaf, fool, impotent, dumb, insane, they became "calm, tamed, renouncing, patient and collected" (Bṛh. 4,4,23), "delighting in the Ātman, playing with the Ātman, pairing with and taking delight in the Ātman" (Chānd. 7,15,2), and perceiving the Praṇava to be the highest Brahman, as the void shining through itself, passed away in it.

Therefore, one who follows the way of life of the gods, he passes away in the Om-sound, the highest Brahman. He sees in his self the (highest) self, the highest Brahman. On this is this verse:

> In three horns (*a*, *u*, *m*) the hornless (*turīya*),
> In three horns seize the lion!—
> Joining the horn (*m*) to the two horns (*a*, *u*)
> Leisurely sit the three gods (*Brahmán*, *Viṣṇu*, *Rudra*).

Seventh Khaṇḍa

[Three sections, which are supposed to establish the identity of the Ātman and Brahman in a playful way through the word Om and Nṛsiṁha.

1. *bhayaṁ paśyantas*, cf. Chānd. 8,9,1 *bhāyaṁ dadarśa*. Our myth is patterned on the one narrated there.

(1) *a* is Ātman, *m* is again the Ātman, *u* is the lion who connects the two. (2) *a* is Ātman, *m* is Brahman, which two are bound together by the sound *u*. (3) *a* is Brahman, *m* the Ātman, both joined through *u*. In between different ideas are inserted which, very important in themselves still make a heterogeneous impression in this context and are perhaps taken over from somewhere else.]

(1) *a-u-m=Ātman-lion-Ātman*

Once it happened that the gods said to Prajāpati: Instruct us further, O exalted sir.—Be it so, said he.

One should search, by means of the *a*-sound, the Ātman, for it is unborn, unageing, unfading, immortal, fearless, without grief, without delusion, hungerless, thirstless and secondless [and all these ten predicates begin with *a* in Sanskrit],—then with the *u*-sound he should search for the highest lion, for he is exalted, begetting, has come in from above, raising up high, looking up high, working up high, going up high, shining up high, roving up high and above transformation [and all these ten predicates begin with *u* in Sanskrit],—hereupon, catching the prior half of the *u*-sound, one should turn into the lion the Ātman as the *a*-sound, —further, catching that lion by the posterior half [of the *u*-sound], one should, by means of the *m*-sound, make him one with that Ātman, for he is great, powerful, observing bounds, liberated, the grand god, the grand master, the grand being, the grand spiritual, the great bliss and the high authority [and all these ten predicates begin with *m* in Sanskrit].

One who knows this, he, bodyless, organless, breathless, without darkness, consisting only of being, thinking and bliss, becomes the self-ruler.

(2) *a-u-m*=Ātman—exclamation of assent—Brahman.

Some one asks somebody : Who are you ? He answers : *aham* (I). Similarly, all that exists. Therefore *aham* (I) is a name for all (Bṛh. 1,4,1,). Its initial letter and the *a*-sound [in Om] is the same, for the Ātman [signified by the *a*-sound of Om] is all, for he is within all, for all this cannot exist without having an Ātman (a self, substance), all this is therefore Ātman. Therefore, one should investigate the Ātman, the self of all, by means of the *a*-sound which expresses the self of all.

Further, all this (this whole world) is Brahman which consists of being, thinking and bliss. For all this consists of being, thinking and bliss. That is, firstly, all this is being; for *one* says [of all that exists] : That is a being. Further, all this is thinking (spirit, *cit*) also, for it shines and appears [is imagination]. If you ask : What is 'being" the reply is : it is becoming conscious, that this is and this is not. But what is becoming conscious ? It is this and is not this, thus can one reply, not with words but only through becoming conscious.[1] Similarly one can explain the thinking and the bliss not through words but one can understand only by becoming conscious of them. Similarly, everything else in the world must be conscious of [the thinking and the bliss, of which it consists]. This is the highest bliss. —That Brahman therefore [whose essence one must thus experience innerly] is called [in the nominative] *brahma*. Its final syllable and [in Om] the *m*-sound [the *ma*-sound as it is called in Sanskrit] is the same. Therefore one should investigate the highest Brahman by means of the *m*-sound [*ma*-sound]. If it is asked: Is this so [is the Brahman the Ātman]? Then the reply, without hesitation, is: *u* [which is here supposed to mean 'yes'].[2] Therefore one should search for the Ātman with the *a*-sound and should, without hesitation, bind him with the *m*-sound as the Brahman through the *u*-sound.

One who knows this, he, bodyless, organless, breathless, without darkness, consisting only of being, thinking and bliss, becomes the self-ruler!

a-u-m=Brahman—exclamation of assent—Ātman.

This whole world is Brahman, because it is eternal, [and this] because it is *ugra*, *vīra*, *mahat*, *viṣṇu*, *jvalat*, *sarvatomukha*, *nṛsiṁha*, *bhīṣaṇa*, *bhadra*, *mṛtyumṛtyu*, *namāmi* and *aham*; and the Brahman is this eternal one, because it [likewise] is *ugra*, *vīra*, *mahat*, *viṣṇu*, *jvalat*, *sarvatomukha*, *nṛsiṁha*, *bhīṣaṇa*, *bhadra*, *mṛtyumṛtyu*, *namāmi* and *aham*. Therefore, searching for the

1. Cf. Bṛh. 3,4,2, above. Like *Uṣasta* there, Weber (*Ind. Stud.* IX, 157) thinks: "Now, to say the least, this is settling things cheaply".—Yājñavalkya may answer him also.

2. *U-kārasya avadhāraṇa-arthatvaṁ lokaprasiddham*, Schol.

highest Brahman with the *a*-sound, one should search with the *m*-sound the [Ātman as] promoter of the Manas and the organs and [as] spectator of the Manas and the organs.—[An incidental remark on the Ātman:] When he, (asleep) does not supervise the universe, then the universe is merged in him; and when he wakes up again, the universe emerges out of him. After protecting the universe and again withdrawing it within, crushing, burning and devouring it, he [once more] gives away his self [as the self] of the objects and all the same[1] continues to be super-*ugra*, super-*vīra*, super-*mahān*, super-*viṣṇu*, super-*jvalan*, super-*sarvatomukha*, super-*nṛsiṁha*, super-*bhīṣaṇa*, super-*bhadra*, super-*mṛtyumṛtyu*, super-*aham* "in his own majesty" (Chānd. 7. 24,1). —Therefore one should, without hesitation, bind this [Ātman as the *m*-sound] with the highest Brahman as the content of the *a*-sound through the *u*-sound.

One who knows this, he, bodyless, organless, without darkness, consisting only of being, thinking and bliss, becomes the self-ruler!

On this is the verse :

Dragging the half-horn (*u*) to the horn (*a*),
One should bind it (*u*) with the horn (*a*);
And similarly through this (*u*), that horn (*a*)
One should bind in the last horn (*m*).

EIGHTH KHAṆḌA

[The identity of the Nṛsiṁha-Ātman and the Om-sound is demonstrated in this way, that both are *ota, anujñātṛ, anujñā, avikalpa*. In the strictest sense, of course, the Ātman is *avikalpa* alone, and even if he is also described as non-*avikalpa* side by side, there is no contradiction, because (as the following last section will work out in details) that, which makes him non-*avikalpa*, possesses no reality.]

Now through the Turīya [and its four specifications, *ota, anujñātṛ, anujñā, avikalpa*, the identity of Ātman and Om is shown].

a. Woven lengthwise and crosswise [in the world] is that Ātman, the lion. For this whole world is in him; for he is the

1. For this idea, cf. Bṛh. 5,1 above.

self of all, he is all. And yet [in reality] he is not inwoven for this Ātman is without a second, one and undifferentiated. For the object is not existent but he, as if inwoven, is wholly being, wholly thinking, wholly bliss, having only one taste, incomprehensible, without a second whatsoever.

Woven lengthwise and crosswise is the Om-sound also; for when one is asked : Is it so ? Is it not so ? One answers with "Om" (yes). The Om-sound is indeed the speech; and speech is this whole world; for here is nothing that does not have a name. The Om-sound also consists of thinking; and the whole world consists of thinking.

Therefore, both these [Ātman and Om] are one in the highest God. That is the immortal, fearless one, the Brahman. For Brahman is the fearless one; one who knows this becomes the fearless Brahman. This is the secret instruction.

b. Assenter is this Ātman; for he assents his self as [the self of] the whole world. Verily this world is not 'self-possessed' in itself. And yet [in reality] he is not inwoven and not assenter; for nothing sticks him, and he is unchangeable, for there is no being apart from him.

Assenter is the Om-sound also, for one assents with the word "Om" (yes). The Om-sound is indeed the speech; and the speech assents the whole world. The Om-sound also consists of thinking; and the thinking (spirit, *cit*) makes this whole unsustained world substantial.

Therefore both these [Ātman and Om] are one in the highest God. That is the immortal, fearless one, the Brahman. For Brahman is the fearless one; one who knows this becomes the fearless Brahman. This is the secret instruction.

c. This Ātman has assenting as the only taste. For it consists of knowledge alone. It shines gloriously before all this world: therefore it consists of thinking (spirit) alone. And yet [in reality] it is not inwoven and not assenter [therefore not assent also]; for only so far as the Ātman is the assent, this world is an existent one.

The Om-sound also has assent as the only taste, for one assents with the word "Om" (yes). The Om-sound is indeed the speech, for it is speech that assents. The Om-sound also consists of thinking, for it is thinking that assents.

Therefore both these [Ātman and Om] are one in the highest God. That is the immortal, fearless one, the Brahman. For Brahman is the fearless one; one who knows this becomes the fearless Brahman. This is the secret instruction.

d. This Ātman is indifference, because it is without a second. The Om-sound is also indifference, because it is without a second; for the Om-sound consists wholly of thinking.

Therefore both these [Ātman and Om] are one in the highest God.

It is without differentiation and yet not without differentiation; and therein is no split (no contradiction); for there is no split in the Ātman. One who accepts a split, as it were, in it, is split hundredfold and thousandfold, "is entangled in death after death" (Bṛh. 4,4.19).

Therefore this one without a second, the self-shining supreme bliss is the Ātman. It is the immortal, fearless one, the Brahman. For Brahman is the fearless one. One who knows this becomes the fearless Brahman. This is the secret instruction.

Ninth Khaṇḍa

[The Ātman alone is real, all else, even the *Jiva* (the individual soul) and the Īśvara (the personal God) rest only on the Māyā. The nature of the Māyā, however, cannot be questioned, because it has no reality. The Ātman, on the other hand, cannot, of course, be grasped by way of perception, which sets itself face to face against the object as something other but can be possibly grasped through an inner consciousness (*anubhava*), in so far as it is our self. This inner vision finds its expression in the syllable Om, which is the Ātman itself.]

Once it happened that the gods said to Prajāpati: Instruct us, O exalted sir, on this Ātman as the Om-sound. —Be it so, said he.

Spectator and consenter is this Ātman, the lion. Consisting of thinking and unchangeable, he is the perceiver everywhere. For there is no possible proof for the existence of a duality, and only the secondless Ātman can be proved. There is something other as it were only through the Māyā; verily the Ātman alone is the highest one and he is all that exists; for this results out of the state of deep sleep (*prājñaiḥ*). The whole world is ignorance, is this Māyā. But the Ātman is the highest self and is self-luminous. He perceives and perceives not; for his perception is without an object. it is becoming conscious (*anubhūti*).

But even the Māyā, which is of the nature of darkness, is perceived through becoming conscious [of the Ātman as the only real] as motionless, illusory, endless void. This is its nature. But although it manifests now this, now that and constantly disappears, it is looked at as the Ātman by the fools. The Māyā lets the Ātman appear only as being and again as not being [disappearing], while it shows him and shows him not, and, to be sure, in the state of freedom [as God] and non-freedom [as soul]. That is, just as a seed of the fig tree, same in itself, possesses the potentiality of many fig trees, similarly the Māyā also, although one [possesses the potentiality of plurality in it]. For, just as the fig-tree, same in itself, although it is one, brings forth many fig trees stretching out beyond itself,[1] all of which have it as their seed, and which is full and whole in each of them, similarly the Māyā also manifests many locations [of the soul], stretching out beyond itself,[1] existing full and whole and similarly manifests the Jīva and Īśvara (the individual and the divine soul), and in doing so, it still remains only a deception and ignorance. It is manifold but firmly fitted together and rich in sprouts; and just as it is not itself different from its Guṇas [*Sattvam, Rajas, Tamas*], similarly in its sprouts also it is not different from its Guṇas, but is everywhere illuminated by the spirit as Brahman, Viṣṇu and Śiva. Its threefoldness and its character as the source everywhere stem from this Ātman alone. Further he is threefold as the I-conscious *Jīva*, as the ruling *Īśvara*, and as the all 'I'-conscious *Hiraṇyagarbha*. For this last one who, like Īśvara, has perceptible spirituality and is omnipresent, is the Īśvara as the animater of doings and perceptions, is all and consists of all. All the Jīvas also consist of all, only that they are restricted in all their states.

This Ātman, having created elements, organs, the Virāj, natural divinities and the sheaths (Taitt. 2) and having entered

1. The reading at both the places, in editions available to me, is *svāvyatirikta*—"not different (or apart) from itself".—GBP.

in these, remains undeluded and in rest and appears to be deluded as it were and in activity only through the Māyā.

Therefore this secondless Ātman is consisting of being alone eternal, pure, wise, real, liberated, undefied, all-pervading, supreme, known by these proofs as the inner one through and through : the whole world consists of existence alone, what exists is the Brahman which has been there from time immemorial; for nothing else is known here by becoming conscious (*anubhava*); and no ignorance is possible in the Ātman, known by becoming conscious, self-luminous, who is all-perceiving, unchangeable, secondless. See here itself the pure being, and that everything else is non-being, for that is the truth ! Thus it is proved [by becoming conscious], the ancient, beginningless one, which abides in itself, consists wholly of bliss and thinking, still it is not provable (by reflection).

It is Viṣṇu, Īśāna, Brahmán, is also everything else and omnipresent. Therefore everything is the Ātman who is pure, not formed externally, wise and of the nature of joy. And this world is not devoid of Ātman and yet it is not the Ātman; for he existed already there before it. But this universe has been never there at all, but only the Ātman, abiding in his own majesty, absolute, one, who is a spectator, self-luminous.

But does this persistent world-expanse spring from the Ātman ?

Undoubtedly ! For it is he, who brings forth all this as it is, the seer in the seer, the spectator, changeless, perfect, devoid of ignorance, very evident to—not the external but—the internal observation, above the darkness. So say, do you see him now well ?

—We see him, although he is incomprehensibly small.

He is not small, but he is the spectator [the subject of perception], without difference, without a second; without joy and sorrow and without duality is the highest Ātman, all-knowing, unending, indivisible, secondless, everywhere consciousness[1] [of the objects] by reason of Māyā, but again not

1. "alterwärts Bewusstsein". So Deussen seems to have split original *sarvadāsaṁvittir* into *sarvadā+saṁvittir*. But, as in other editions, a better split is : *sarvadā+asaṁvittir*, which accords well with the following denial: *nāsaṁvittiḥ* "but not [really] unconsciousness."—GBP.

unconsciousness, because self-luminous.— You yourselves are it ! Can he now be possibly seen by [himself as] the secondless? Certainly not ! For he would be a second, if he were not yourself !

—Explain it to us, O exalted sir, said the gods.

You yourself are he, I say. If he were seen by you, then you would not perceive (know) the Ātman [as he is the self, none other]. Verily the Ātman is without any attachment to the world. Therefore you yourself are he, and the light, with which you shine, is your own. Indeed, this world is only you yourselves, for you consist wholly of being and consciousness.

—Certainly not! said they; for then we would be without any world-attachment, so they said.

How could he be seen otherwise? said he.

—We do not know it, said they.

Therefore you yourself are he, and the light, with which you shine, is your own. As such you are not even consisting of being and consciousness. For these two are only [the Brahman], as it shone gloriously before, [but in truth] it is incomprehensible, secondless.—Then say now: Do you know him [the Ātman]?

—We know that he is higher than the known and the unknown, said they.

And he said: Verily, this secondless, called Brahman from the greatness (*bṛhat*), is eternal, pure, enlightened, liberated, true, subtle, perfect, secondless, consisting only of being, bliss and thinking, is the Ātman himself and incomprehensible for everybody.

Therefore, though not seeing him, you should see him with the word Om. This is the truth, is the Ātman, is the Brahman, for the Brahman is the Ātman. Indeed this is not to be doubted: *Om* is the reality; that is what the wise see. Indeed, this soundless, touchless, formless, tasteless, odourless, what cannot be spoken, taken, gone to, emptied, procreated, without Manas, without Buddhi, without Ahaṁkāra, without Cittam (see Sarva-Upanisad-sāra footnote above), without Prāṇa, Apāna, Vyāna, Udāna and Samāna, without sense-organs, objects, instruments, without mark, without attachment, without properties, without change, without designation, without Sattvam, Rajas and Tamas, the unborn, Māyāless, that is what the Upaniṣads teach as shining gloriously, shining suddenly, shining gloriously before this whole world, secondless,—see, I am he, and he is I!

And he further said: Do you see him now, or do you not see him?

—We see, they said, that he is higher than the known and the unknown.—But where does this [Māyā] stay and how? they asked further.

—Why this question?

—O, just for nothing, said they. [We now know that Māyā is nothing.]

You are a wonder [because you know Ātman, Kāṭh. 2,7], and again you are not [for everybody, like you, is the Ātman], so said he. So give your assent to him with *Om* and express him.

—We know him and yet we know him not, so they said. But it is not so also [the Ātman is above these contrasts of knownness and unknownness], they added.

Then just express him, for he is self-known [even without perceiving him], said he.

—We see him, O exalted sir, and yet we see him not. We cannot express how he is. Salutation to you! Be kind to us, so they said.

Don't be afraid, said he, ask what you will.

—What is this assenting [through the sound Om]?

It is the Ātman himself, said he.

—There, they said, we all bring you salutation, as we are.

Thus it happened that Prajāpati instructed the gods, instructed [the gods].

On this is the verse:

Knowing the Inwoven through Inwoven,
Know further the Assenter then,
The Assent and then the secondless
Grasping, enter into the Spectator!

RĀMA-PŪRVA-TĀPANĪYA UPANIṢAD

The Rāmatāpanīya Upaniṣad, as the title, form and the execution show, was later revised after the model of the Nṛsiṁha-tāpanīya Upaniṣad, if not originally composed according to it, particularly in so far as two parts, an earlier, elementary (*pūrvā*) and a later, higher (*uttarā*) were designed for this Upaniṣad also. But while the *Nṛsiṁha-uttarā* is in its way an original and supremely important work, the *Rāma-uttarā* consists mostly of borrowings, which show, for the most part, no close relation to the *Rāma-pūrvā* and which were probably tagged on to them to shape the whole after the model of the *Nṛsiṁha Upaniṣad.*

The *Rāma-pūrvā,* on the other hand, is a complete whole in itself in a much higher degree than the *Nṛsiṁha-pūrvā,* in which the more concrete incarnation of Viṣṇu as Rāma appears in the place of Nṛsiṁha; for the rest, the whole thing amounts, here also as there, to the correct construction of a diagram (*yantram*; probably to be worn as an amulet) which, in accordance with the later age, is far more artificial than the one depicted at the Nṛsiṁhap. 5, so that, particularly on account of the uncertainty of many a statement, a definite reconstruction of it would be scarcely possible. Everything else, what the Upaniṣad contains in the prior half (verses 1-57) and the latter half (verses 58-94), and particularly the graphic portraits of Rāma and his surroundings (verses 23-28 and 48-57) have only one aim, viz. to prepare for the diagram and to underline its importance, partly also to motivate its construction.—Accordingly, we distinguish three main parts on the whole :

I. Preliminary (verses 1-57).

II. The construction of the diagram (verses 58-84).

III. Epilogue (85-94).

I. *Preliminary* (verses 1-57)

Verses 1-6. Etymologies of the word Rāma.

Verses 7-10. Rāma is an incarnation of the Brahman.

Verses 11-13. A preliminary announcement of the formula-king *Rāṁ Rāmāya namaḥ* and of the diagram whose most important part it is supposed to be.

Verses 14-23. The formula-king *Rāṁ Rāmāya namaḥ*. Its germ (*Rāṁ*) implies the whole world, because it contains the *Prakṛti* (*Sītā*) and the *Puruṣa* (*Rāma*). The remaining words (*Rāmāya namaḥ*) signify the highest doctrine of the Vedānta, the identity of the individual and the highest soul (verse 19). Value of the formula-king and wearing of it on the chest (verses 20-23). This wearing of the formula-king on the chest is naturally to be distinguished from the wearing of the same in 32 spokes of the diagram (verse 69) described later. For the rest, however, it is to be held fast that in the following (verses 23-58) it is not yet so much a graphic representation of one kind or the other, as only a dignified preparation for it; for this purpose the poet first imagines how Rāma sits with Sītā and Lakṣmaṇa, how the gods worship Rāma, how the Ṛṣis praise his deeds, and finally how he, after accomplishing heroic deeds, sits on the throne, surrounded by his loyal followers. It is, therefore, incorrect and misleading for the whole comprehension, when Weber finds, in verse 23 (page 293) "statements on the form and the surroundings, in which Rāma is to be represented for the purpose of the diagram". Hereby it is not the question of representations but only of imaginary ideas of Rāma's form, surroundings and heroic deeds for the purpose of his worship, which Weber's scholiast (page 293; compare, on the other hand, the observation under verse 52 below) seems to confirm: "In order to describe (*nirūpayitum*) the diagram used for worship, the poet launches forth [before-hand] in 34½ verses (23-57) into the form, surroundings, glory and history of Rāma to be worshipped". Accordingly the concluding words (verse 58) are not to be translated as : "Thus (the diagram) has been stated in brief. Now (follows) its detailed description", but rather as : "This is said for the purpose of instruction (*uddeśataḥ*). Now follows the directions (*nirdeśas*) to that (the diagram already announced in verse 13)". On a closer observation, this preliminary section is divided into the following three parts :

Verses 23-28. The poet imagines Rāma with Sītā on his lap and Lakṣmaṇa standing nearby (as represented in so many sculptures). As these figures form a triangle, so "the end (*namaḥ*), name (*Rāṁ*) and the dative (*Rāmāya*)" of the formula king also are fancied as a triangle.

Verses 29-47. Further the poet describes how the gods approach Rāma to glorify him (verses 29-34), and the sages to sing his heroic deeds, while the main events of the Rāmāyaṇa are briefly recapitulated (verses 35-47).

Verses 48-57. In this connection the poet imagines, how Rāma sits on the throne, in a hexagon (as the model of the hexagon of the diagram which follows later) surrounded by the principal six heroes, around whom the gods and the sages throng. If this whole group, floating before the poet's eyes, is neither to be brought into harmony with the previously described triangle (Rāma, Sītā, Lakṣmaṇa) nor (as Weber also remarks under verse 60) with the dispositions of the diagram described later (58ff), then the explanation is just this, that in the whole section up to the verse 57 there is no question of any graphic representation, but only of alternating pictures floating before the poet's fantasy which, as also the historical digressions, only serve to enhance the worship of Rāma and thereby to bring into light the importance of the diagram which now follows.

II. *The Construction of the Diagram* (Verses 58-84)

The form of this diagram, compared with that of the Nṛsiṁhapūrvā (above) is considerably complicated, still it is simpler than it would appear at first sight. Only it must be grasped firm that entire figures are to be drawn concentrically and that of the three circles mentioned in verse 62 the first is described within the hexagon, the second circumscribes the hexagon, the octagon circumscribes this second circle and [finally] the third circle circumscribing this octagon is described (*ṣaṭkoṇasya upari ekaṁ vṛttam, madhye ca ekam, patra-agre ca ekam,* Nārāyaṇa in the Calc. ed. p. 331, 6). Accordingly the figure would be constructed like this: In the middle, the hexagon with an inscribed circle; the hexagon is circumscribed by another circle, this latter by an octagon, this latter by a circle, this latter once more by an octagon, this latter by a circle, this latter by a dodecagon, this latter by a circle, this latter by a sixteen-angle figure, this latter by a circle, this latter by a thirtytwo-angle figure, this latter by a circle, this latter finally by a square. If now one replaces, outside the hexagon, the entire straight lines, which run from the periphery of the inner circles to that of the outer ones, by wavy lines like a circumflex, then we get two eight-petal lotus flowers, one twelve-petal one, one sixteen-petal one and probably also one thirtytwo-petal lotus flower, like a big wheel, all placed one around the other; the tips of the petals lie on the circumscribing circle, the filaments are to be regarded as being towards the side of the inscribed circle. On the filaments and cusps, occasionally between the latter, letters, syllables and names are written down, as the text prescribes them. On the outermost thirtytwo-petal lotus-flower is put down the Mantrarāja, whose germ (*Rāṁ*) already formed the kernel of the whole. Consequently, the Nṛsiṁha-formula, or even the Mālāmantra, is probably hardly to be understood below the Mantrarāja, but rather the formula-king *Rāṁ Rāmāya namaḥ* which, with the preceding and the following *om*, put down four times, would fill up the 32 wings. (The Mantrarāja formed the outermost circle in the Nṛsiṁha Mahācakra Diagram also, above).

As a supplement, the Mālāmantra, to be put down on the inner, eight-petal lotus flower, is taught (verses 74-80) by means of a secret alphabet which substitutes words in the place of syllables.

III. *Epilogue* (verses 85-94)

Verses 85-91. The poet calls upon to worship Rāma after a proper preparation and to invoke him by imagining him how he sits on his throne carried and surrounded by different kinds of beings, in the course of which all sorts of elements of earlier and later mythology, of myths about deities and heroic legends, the Vedāntic forms of the Ātman and the Guṇas and the Bhāvas of the Sāṁkhya doctrine run side by side.

Verses 92-94. In the end the poet offers his homage to Rāma and promises liberation to those who worship him duly and study the present Upaniṣad.

RĀMA-PŪRVA-TĀPANĪYA UPANIṢAD

I. *Preliminary part, verses* 1-57.

Verses 1-6 : Etymologies of the name Rāma

1. The great Viṣṇu, all spiritual,
   Grew up in Daśaratha's house,
   In Raghu's race, the all-giver (*rā-ti*),
   Who rules (*rā-jate*) over the kingdom of earth (*ma-hī*).

2. That's why he was called *Rā-ma*
   By the wise ones in this world,—
   Or because the profusion of his power
   Brought the demons (*Rā-kṣasas*) to the death (*ma-raṇam*).

3. Or also because of loveliness (*abhi-rāma*)
   Rāma's name is world-renowned;—
   Or because, like *Rā-hu* the moon (*ma-nasija*),
   Himself mortal (*ma-rtya*), he the demons (*Rā-kṣasa*)

4. Deprived of their lustre, also because showing
   To the kings (*ma*) worthy of rulership (*rā*)
   Through his model the path of duty
   And of knowledge, to him who names him,

5. Of renunciation, who contemplates on him,
   Of godliness, to him who adores him,—
   For this reason too, on the earth
   Staying, Rāma was justly named.

6. And because the Yogins delight (*ra-mante*) in him,
   Who's eternal bliss and spirituality,
   So it is that through the word *Rāma*
   The Brahman itself is named as he.

Verses 7-10 *:* Rāma is an incarnation of the Brahman

7. The Brahman, all spiritual, secondless,
   Without parts, without body,

Is still looked upon as multiform
To serve the purpose of worship.

8. To the deities endowed with forms
Are assigned sex, limbs and weapons,
Two, four, six, eight, ten, twelve,
Sixteen, eighteen, even a thousand hands,

9. Which with a variety of insignia,
Conches and others, are furnished,
One attributes to them also colour.
Weapons, powers and military forces;—

10. One similarly assigns to Rāma's body,
Accepted as the Brahman itself,
An army, as also the four other[1]
Attributes of a sovereign.

Verses 11-13 : Preliminary Announcement of the Formula-king

11. Encompassing the Brahman and everything,
Named significantly after Rāma,
The formula ought to be muttered,
If the deity is to be gracious to you.

12. Our formula deals with everything,
for which one sacrifices and works;
Since it rescues (*trā*) him, who muses (*man*) over it,
Therefore it is called *Man-tra* (the formula).

13. The diagram, which now follows,
Is the embodiment of the two gods (Brahman and Rāma).
Do not worship without a diagram,
If the deity is to be gracious to you.

Verses 14-23 : The formula "*Rāṁ Rāmāya namaḥ*"

14. Self-existing, all luminous, having
Endless forms, he shines by himself,

1. Ministers, territory, fortresses, treasure and the army were usually reckoned as the five basic elements (*prakṛti*) which, along with the prince, form the kingship.

Through whose Jīva-ness this universe,—
Whom he the creation, sustenance, end,—

15. Through whose causeness, spiritual force
And the qualities Rajas, Sattvam and Tamas.
As the fig seed[1] already contains
The large grown up tree,

16. So the germ of the word *Rāma*
Contains the whole animate world in it.
On R are founded the three forms,[2]
On it the three forces too.[3]

17. Worship Sītā and Rāma as arising out of it;
From them proceeds the creation, sustenance and end
Of the twice seven worlds, and in the worlds
Rāma lets himself be born a man through the Māyā.

18. Salutation to him, the Ātman, the world-breath!
Praise his oneness with the primordial Guṇas!

19. The word *namas* here[4] means Jīva,
The word *Rāma* means the Ātman;
But the dative in- *āya*
Aims at the consubstantiality of the two.

20. The formula is the glorifier,
And Rāma the glorified;
The two thus united surely bring
Reward to all who use it.

21. Just as a person bearing a name, turns
Towards the one who calls by that name,

---

1. The metaphor taken from the Nṛsiṁhottarat. 9 (above).
2. According to Nārāyaṇa in the Poona ed. and Weber's scholiast, in *Rāṁ* (=*R*+*a*+*a*+*m*) Brahmán (*a*), Viṣṇu (*a*) and Śiva (*m*) rest on *R*. On the other hand, according to the commentary printed under Nārāyaṇa's name in the Calcutta ed., which, less correctly, is thinking of the whole word *Rāmaḥ*, *R* is Kṛṣṇa (Viṣṇu), *ā* Brahmán, *maḥ* Maheśvara.
3. Creation, sustenance, dissolution (*Nārāyaṇa*).
4. In the formula-king : *Rāṁ Rāmāya namaḥ*.

So also the formula, budding from the germ,
Turns towards him who employs it.

22. The Germ and the Force one should wear
On the right and the left breast;
Not without them the *Stem*[1] between,
That fulfills all the desires,—

23. As here so with all
The formulas the procedure is same.—

[Verses 23-29: Portrayal of Rāma seated with Sītā and Lakṣmaṇa]

Being eternal, here on earth too
Rāma is like fire in lustre;[2]—

24. Yet, becoming cool-rayed,
Like *Viśva* to the Agni-Somite world,
He glows along with Sītā,
Like the moon with the moon-light;

25. Subdued through her as Prakṛti,
Wearing matted hair and a yellow garment;
Two-armed, with ear-rings and pearl-strings,
He sits there, wielding a bow.

26. Adorned with eight boldnesses,
Of cheerful countenance, confident of victory,
On his thigh the world-mother,
The divine Prakṛti.

27. Kausalyā's son is made happy,
Embraced with both arms by her,
Gold-hued, decked, attentive,
And wearing a garland of lotuses.

1. The Germ (*vīja*) of the formula is *Rāṁ*, the Stem (*kīla*) is *Rāmāya na-*, and the Force (*śakti*) is *-maḥ*.

2. As Weber observes, the verse could also mean according to the mystic alphabet taught later in verses 74-80 : "*Rāmaḥ* is *ananta* (=*ā*) with *tejas* (=*R*), *vahni* (=*R*) and *-maḥ*".

28. To his right stands Lakṣmaṇa,
Wielding a bow in hand,
His younger brother, gold-hued,
The three forming a triangle.

29. Similar is the case with the formula :
The end, the name and the dative[1]
Give it, too, a triangular form.

[Verses 29-34: Portrayal of Rāma, as the gods worship him]

The gods approached him,

30. Who sat under the wish-fulfilling tree,
To praise him as the lord of the world:
"Salutation to Rāma, taking form at will!
To him possessed of magical powers!

31. Salutation to him as the Om-sound,
Who is the ur-form of the Veda,
To him as the bearer of loveliness,
As the embodiment of the Ātman!

32. Adorned with Sītā's figure,
Rakṣas-killer, of beautiful limbs,
To the gracious hero of the Raghus,
Who killed the ten-headed one.

33. "O Raghu-hero, bringer of prosperity,
With a large bow, highest prince!
Utter destroyer of the ten-headed man,
Grant us both, protection and prosperity.

34. Grant us divine rulership,
Strike them all, including *Khara!*"—

---

1. The name Rāma (*svam*) along with the dative form in which it stands (*ṅe-tayā*) [Read: *ṅentayā*, GBP] and with the *aṇu*, which here probably denotes the lightly reverberating *namas* forms a triad corresponding to that triangle (Rāma, Sītā and Lakṣmaṇa). The commentary in Weber explains quite differently; the commentators certainly tried to help here and in many following passages as well as they could, and nothing more remains for us also.

The gods, praising him thus,
Remained with him, full of joy.

[Verses 35-47: Portrayal of Rāma, as the Ṛṣis praise him]

35. Then the sages thus praised him :
"The demonical Rāvaṇa
Who, Rāma's (*Rā-*) wife, dwelling in forest (*-vana*),
Abducted for his own ruin.

36. Who, therefore, was called *Rā-vaṇa*
Or from the force of his roaring (*rāva*).
Then for this reason, Rāma,
Seeking Sītā, along with Lakṣmaṇa

37. Wandered all over the earth,
Looking around in search of the queen;
Killed the demon Kabandha,
Went, as instructed by him (Rām. 3,73,26[1]), to Śabarī,

38. Honoured by her and by Wind's son (Hanumān),
The two called the king of apes (Sugrīva),
And told him the whole story
From the beginning to the end.

39. He, doubtful of Rāma's strength,
Showed him the huge body of Dundubhi
As a test to prove his strength;
Rāma hurled it far away,

40. Piercing seven Sāla trees at once
Delighted stood Raghu's scion !
Then the prince of apes, rejoicing,
Went to Bālin's city with Rāma.

41. The younger brother (Sugrīva) called out Bālin,
Whereupon with rapidity
The latter rushed out of the house;
A battle ensued; Rāghava

1. Cf. Baroda Crit. ed. 3.69. 19-20.—GBP.

42. Slew Bālin and installed
Sugrīva on his throne.
Then summoning the apes
Sugrīva said : You knowers of regions,

43. Go ye this very day and
Bring back Maithilī, quick, at work !
Then came, jumping over the sea,
Hanumān to the city of Laṅkā,

44. Saw Sītā, killed the demons,
And, having burnt their city,
He came and narrated everything
To Rāma as it had happened.

45. Then Rāma, burning with anger,
Called the hordes of apes
And with them and their weapons
Marched to the city of Laṅkā.

46. After seeing Sītā[1] there,
He fought with the lord of Laṅkā,
Killed him and Kumbhakarṇa, in battle
And also the conqueror of Indra,

47. And having installed Vibhīṣaṇa
As king on the throne of Laṅkā,
And taking Janaka's daughter on lap,
He returned homeward with them all.

[Verses 48-57 : Portrayal of Rāma, as he sits on the throne after accomplishing heroic deeds.]

48. On the lion-seat here sits
Raghu's scion with two arms,
Wielding a bow, glad at heart,
Adorned with every ornament,

---

1. "Nachdem er dort erblickt Sītā" (orig.). Deussen is nodding. The Skt. original runs : *tāṁ dṛṣṭvā tadadhīśena sārdhaṁ yuddham akārayat*. Here it is clear that the pronouns *tām* and *tad-* refer to one and the same thing, viz. Laṅkāpurī which occurs in the previous stanza. Besides, it is well known that Rāma did not see Sītā until after the end of the war.—GBP.

49. With the instructive posture of the right hand,
Announcing power with the left hand,
Distributing instruction with pleasure,
Wholly spiritual, the highest God;

50. To his left and right
He has Śatrughna and Bharata,
Attentive Hanumān in front,
The three forming a triangle;

51. After Bharata comes Sugrīva,
After Śatrughna Vibhīṣaṇa;
Chowrie and parasol in hand,
Lakṣmaṇa in the background,

52. Who, with the two palmleaf-holders (Sugrīva and Vibhīṣaṇa)
Forms another triangle :
Thus originates a hexagon.[1]—Rāma
Firstly, with his own long limbs;[2]—

53. Secondly, with Vāsudeva and others
Furnished, to the south-west, and so on;—
Thirdly, with Vāyu's son,
With Sugrīva and Bharata,

54. With Vibhīṣaṇa, Lakṣmaṇa,
Aṅgada, Arimardana

---

1. 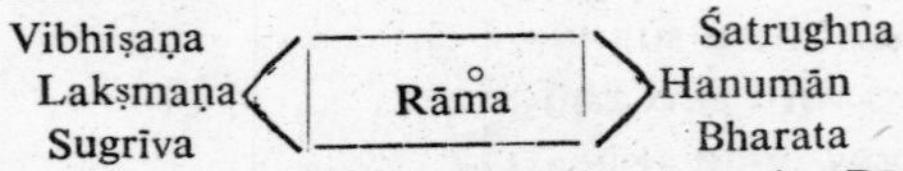

2. The first covering (*āvaraṇam*) protecting Rāma consists of his own powerful limbs (*sva-dīrgha-aṅgaiḥ*); cf. Rāmāy. 1,1,10: *ā-jānu-bāhuḥ* etc. The commentators speak of vowel lengths with which Rāma is supposed to be surrounded, and so they seem already to be thinking of a drawing (*vinyaset*, to verse 53),—but hardly correctly, for up to the verse 58, it is probably only a question of changing, imaginary pictures of Rāma and his surroundings represented for the purpose of worship.

And Jāmbavān he is furnished;—
With Dhṛṣṭi and Jayantaka,

55. With Vijaya and Surāṣṭra,
Akopa, Rāṣṭravardhana,
Dharmapāla and Sumantra
Is he fourthly surrounded;—

56. Fifthly by Indra and Agni,
Dharma, Rakṣas and Varuṇa,
Wind, Moon, Lord, Creator, Ananta,
By these ten is he enriched.

57. From outside deck him the weapons
Of gods, Nīla and his people,
And the sages like Vāmadeva
And Vasiṣṭha sit around him

58. This should suffice as instruction.—

II. *The construction of the Diagram*, verses 58-84.

[Verses 58-74 : Its figure along with the entries]

Now the description of the diagram:
Draw two triangles as pockets* within the hexagon,
In the midst write twice *Om*.

59. Between the two write the germ *Rāṁ*,
Write below it in Accusative
What you desire; he who desires
Should stand above it in Genitive.

60. On the sides write twice '*Give*!'
Within the germ the *Ramā;*
All this with two *Om*-sounds,
Surround, pure of heart and mind.

61. Write in the six angles
The long-syllabic germ with the heart-formulas;[1]

*The original 'tascht' is not quite clear to me.—GBP.

1. With the formulas on the heart, head, hair-tuft, armour, eyes and weapons.

Write *Ramā* and *Māyā* on the sides,
Anaṅga on the vertex of angles.

62. Write "Anger" between vertices,
On its sides skilfully the "sound".
Three circles with eight petals
Of the lotus-flower write down.

63. Write the vowels [on] the filaments,
The eight consonants [on] the petals,
On them write the Garland-formula's (verses 74-80) syllables,
Having the number six of the Waves.[1]

64. At the end only five syllables.
Then again an eight-petal lotus
With eight Nārāyaṇa syllables
And the *Ramā* on the filaments.

65. A twelve-petal lotus flower
Circumscribes this, on which
Write the twelve-syllabic formula:
Om namo bhagavate Vāsudevāya.

66. In a circular form on the filaments
Write letters from *a* to *kṣa*.
Then follows a sixteen-petal lotus,
On whose filaments write "shy".

67. On the petals write twelve-syllabic
Formula with *huṁ*, *phaṭ* and *namas*.[2]
In between write the formulas
Of Vāyu's son and others.

68. *Hṛṁ*, *Sṛṁ*, *Bhṛṁ*, *Vṛṁ*, *Lṛṁ*, *Śṛṁ* and *Jṛṁ*,[3]
write these exactly;—and around these

1. The six waves are : hunger, thirst, grief, infatuation, old age and death. —GBP.

2. Nārāyaṇa gives *na* and *maḥ* separately, which is better as it matches with the 16 petals well. —GBP.

3. The seven initial letters enumerated here (with a vocalised *ṛ*, along with an Anusvāra) of names Hanumān (*Hṛṁ*), Sugrīva, Surāṣṭra, Sumantra

Draw, with thirtytwo spokes,
A great wheel,—with resonance and point (i.e. probably: with *Oṁ*).

69. Write carefully on its wings
the letters of the formula-king (verses 14-23).
The eight Vasus and eleven Rudras
You should meditate thereby.

70. Along with the twelve Inas (Ādityas) and Dhātar;
Also the *Vaṣaṭ* exclamation; around it
With thunderbolts, tridents
A square near three lines,

71. With doors, with zodiac's
Pictures and serpents adorned.
Thus concluding the magical circle,
In its poles and between them

72. Write down the two formulas
Of Nṛsiṁha and Varāha.
As the former is meant *Kṣrauṁ*
With point, resonance and power,

73. A formula known as Nṛsiṁha
Used for annihilation of the Grahas.
The germ of the Sūkara-formula
With *h*, *u*, point and resonance

74. Is the *huṁ*-syllable.—

[Verses 74-81 : Information on the Mālāmantra (verse 63) by means of a mystical alphabet.]

The garland-formula
of Rama is now taught:[1]

(*Sṛṁ*), Bharata (*Bhṛṁ*), Vibhīṣaṇa, Vijaya (*Vṛṁ*), Lakṣmaṇa (*Lṛṁ*), Śatrumardana (*Śṛṁ*), Jāmbavān, Jayanta (*Jṛṁ*) are to be brought up to the required sixteen (Cf. verses 53-55) through Aṅgada, Akopa (*Aṁ*), Dhṛṣṭi, Dharmapāla (*Dhṛṁ*) and Rāṣṭravardhana (*Ṛṁ*), allegedly included in 'and'.

1. The letters (enclosed in brackets) which are here presented through mystical names, yield the 47-syllable Mālāmantra : *om* ! *namo bhagavate*

tāro (*oṁ*) and natiḥ (*namo*) nidrāyāḥ (*bha-*)
smṛtir (*-ga-*) and medas (*-va-*), kāmikā (*-t-*)

75. Joined with rudra (*-e*), vahnir (*Ra-*),
medhā (*-gh-*) adorned with *amara* (*-u-*),
dīrghā (*-na-*) with krūra (*-ṁ*), hlādinī (*-da-*),
Then comes dīrghā (*-n*) with mānada (*-ā-*)

76. kṣudhā (*-ya*), krodhinī (*ra-*), amoghā (*-kṣ-*),
viśvam (*-o-*) further, with medhā (*-gh-*) then
Combined, dīrghā (*-na-*) jvālinī (*-v-*)
With sūkṣmā (*-i-*), mṛtyurūpiṇī (*-śa-*),

77. Then hlādinī (*-d-*) with pratiṣṭhā (*-ā-*),
tvaj (*-ya*), kṣvelaḥ (*ma-*), prīti (*-dh-*), amarā (*-u-*),
jyotis (*-ra-*), tīkṣṇā (*-p-*), then agniḥ (*-ra-*),
śvetā (*-sa-*) with anusvāra (*-ṁ-*) then,

78. kāmikā's fifth (*-na-*), then lāntaḥ (*-va-*),
Then tāntānta (*-da-*), dhānta (*-n-*) follows,
Then ananta (*-ā-*), and then vāyu (*-y-*),
dīrgha (*-ā-*), viṣa (*-m-*) with sūkṣma (*-i-*) follows;

79. kāmikā (*-ta-*), kāmikā (*-t-*), rudra (*-e-*),
Then follow sthirā (*-ja-*) sa (*-s-*) e (*-e*),
tāpinī (*va-*), bhūr (*-l-*) then with dīrgha (*-ā-*),
anilo (*-ya-*), 'nalo (*R-*) 'nanta (*-ā-*) then,

80. kāla (*-m-*) with nārāyaṇa (*-ā-*),
prāṇa (*-ya*), ambhaḥ (*v-*), with vidyā (*-i-*) then,
pītā (*-ṣ-*) with rati (*-ṇa-*) and lānta (*-v-*),
Then yoni (*-e*), at the end natiḥ (*namaḥ*).

81. This, of Guṇa consisting, Guṇa-ending
Is the fortyseven-syllabic formula.—

Raghunandanāya, rakṣoghnaviśadāya, madhura-prasanna-vadanāya, amitatejase, valāya, Rāmāya, Viṣṇave namaḥ ! "*Om* ! Salutation to the holy scion of Raghu, celebrated as the killer of the Rakṣas', having a lovely, gracious face, with immeasurable strength, to Vala, to Rāma, to Viṣṇu salutation!"

[Verses 81-84 : Glorification of the diagram described]

In the sequence depicted
Write, for the crowned Rāma,

82. This all-encompassing diagram
Glorified by the Ṛṣis!
Which to the worshipper brings
Liberation, strengthens health and life,

83. Bestows sons to the sonless,—
In one word, through this
The Dharma and the other three
Are fully accomplished in an instant.

84. As a riddle of deep significance
Even for God is difficult to understand
The diagram described thus.
Don't give it to a common man!

III. *Epilogue*, verses 85-94.

[Verses 85-91 : Exhortation for worship of Rāma]

85. Whatever of the elements on you, purify, worship the doors,
In the Padmāsana or any other posture, cheerful,
Worship duly the throne-seat, below, above,
The sides and the central lotus-flower;

86. On a soft, smooth carpet, offering
Worship to the teacher on his pearl-seat
Meditate on the seat borne by the Śakti,
Tortoise, snake, earth lotus-flower.

87. Worship Vighna, Durgā, Kṣetrapāla, Vāṇī
Along with their germ-sounds,[1] then at the foot.

1. Thus, *Oṁ viṁ vighnāya namaḥ, oṁ duṁ durgāyai namaḥ* etc.—GBP.

Of the throne the Dharma in the south-east,
And, thus progressing, their negations on the poles.[1]

88. In the middle of the seat think of the sun, moon and fire
One upon another, which worship through *a u m*,
Also Rajas, Sattvam, Tamas, as three circles
Following one another, worship them along with the germ-syllables,

89. In the world-poles and the sub-poles
Worship Ātman, Antarātman, Paramātman,
In the inner one the Jñānātman, on the sides
Māyā, Vidyā, Kalā and Paratattvam.

90. The spotless one and the other power,
Then worship and invoke thereby God Rāma.
Worship him through limbs, forms, Hanumān's troop;
Through Dhṛṣṭi's troop, world-guardians and the weapons,

91. Vasiṣṭha's band of seers, through Nīla's troops
With sandle-wood win over Rāma as the first one;
Worship him with best, manifold gifts
And offer him the soft muttering with all propriety.

[Verses 92-94 : Promises to those who worship Rāma properly]

92. Thus I glorify Rāma as the world-sustainer,
As the holder of mace, lotus, conch and discus
As Being, Intelligence, Bliss, overcomer of worldly being.—
He, who meditates him thus, attains liberation.

93. The all-pervading, Raghu's son, who formerly
Disappeared with conch, discus, mace, lotus,
With Ramā, with the brothers and followers
And his city, all-world-container,

1. In the south-east, south-west, north-west and north-east *Dharma, Jñāna, Vairāgya* and *Aiśvarya* should be worshipped, in the east, south, west and north *Adharma, Ajñāna, Avairāgya* and *Anaiśvarya*. The juxtaposition of these eight is not so seldom as Weber p. 324 thinks; they are found e.g. in the Sāṁkhyakārikā 44-45 also.

94. He who worships him, enjoys fulfilment of desires
And, like He, rises to the highest place.
One, who this holy song, joyfully and piously
Recites, spotless he attains liberation,
—Recites, spotless he attains liberation.

RĀMA-UTTARA-TĀPANĪYA UPANIṢAD

This work owes its origination probably only to a desire to set up a corresponding Rāma-uttarā to match the Nṛsiṁha-uttarā. To this purpose all sorts of Upaniṣadic passages were snatched up and a form appropriate to the Rāma-cult was given to them, either by explaining away or by modifying the original intention, which reminds somewhat of those Roman empresses and ladies which caused the head of the Greek statues to be struck off in order to replace it by their own likeness.

The first two chapters of the Jābāla-Upaniṣad form the basic texture as sections 1 and 4, between which are inserted as sections 2 and 3, two passages borrowed from the Tāraka- and the Māṇḍūkya-Upaniṣad, and a doxology modelled on Nṛsiṁhapūrvatāp. 4, 3, (as this latter, in its turn, on Atharvaśiras 2) is appended as section 5.

1. At first the Jābālop. 1 is reproduced, which teaches that he who dies in *Avimuktam* (a locality in Banaras) immediately attains liberation through Rudra, but that the Saṁnyāsin, wherever he may be wandering, has *Avimuktam* by his side. The solution of the riddle follows in the next chapter, Jābālop. 2. Our Upaniṣad appropriates this also, however only as section 4, as two other passages are inserted before it.

2. The first of these insertions is the Tāraka-Upaniṣad (Anquetil II, 378-379), preserved only in the Oupanek'hat[1] which extols the Om-sound as *tāraka* 'deliverer', distinguishes six elements in it (*a*, *u*, *m*, half-mora, *bindu*, *nāda*), and in the end assures that one who knows *Om*, would attain to *Avimuktam* (*so'vimuktam āśrito bhavati*; in Anquetil : *scit, quod in locis benedictis, quod sedes liberation is est, sit,* i.e. he knows, that he is in Avimuktam).—This mention of Avimuktam, along with the similarity of wording, may have been the main reason for requisitioning the Tāraka-Upaniṣad; and add to this the ease with which the Rāma formula : "*Om! Rāṁ Rāmāya namaś, candrāya namo, bhadrāya namaḥ*" lent itself substitute the elements of the Om-sound (the passage in Anquetil is not quite clear) mentioned in the Tāraka-Upaniṣad. Apart from this substitution of the formula the rest of the Upaniṣad seems to be bodily incorporated; but

---

1. On the other hand the Tārasāra-Upaniṣad, incorporated as No. 91 of the Muktikā collection, is a compilation, partly abridging partly amplifying, from the Rāmottaratāpanīyā which it apparently presupposes (and, indeed, including sections 6 and 7 which are not found in most of the manuscripts and in Nārāyaṇa, perhaps with the exception of the longer Purāṇa passage). In the place of the formula-king relating to Rāma it has the formula : *Om namo Nārāyaṇāya* and it glorifies it as the deliverer (*tārakam*) from the Saṁsāra.

since it glorifies, not Rāma, but the Om-sound and its constituents, so a reinterpretation of it as referring to the Rāma myth was required.

3. This takes place in the following section, which first identifies in four Ślokas the *a*-sound (*viśva*) with Lakṣmaṇa, the *u*-sound (*taijasa*) with Śatrughna, the *m*-sound (*prājña*) with Bharata, the half-mora with Rāma and the entire Praṇava with Sītā as the *Mūlaprakṛti.* Since this whole construction is based essentially on the Māṇḍūkya-Upaniṣad (above), so the Māṇḍūkya-Up. 1-7 is cited verbatim, as if a commentary on it. A reference to the identity of the individual soul with the supreme soul, personated as Rāma, forms the end.

4. Only now our compilator goes back to the Jābāla-Upaniṣad, copying word to word its second chapter, in which *Avimuktam* is explained as referring to the spot between the eye-brows and the nose, as a result of which the earlier statement, that the wise has the *Avimuktam* always by his side becomes intelligible only now.—Meanwhile this thought is either no more understood by our author or it is clouded by him, inasmuch as he narrates in the verses which follow how Rāma has given a boon to Śiva, promising that all those who die in *Avimuktam* will attain liberation,—whereby *Avimuktam* is again restricted to a locality in Banaras.

5. As Rāma is placed above Śiva in the preceding section, he is placed above Brahmán in this section, in that the personal Brahmán extols Rāma as the essence of all gods, words and beings in 47 formulas. In form and contents the whole is an imitation of the Atharvaśiras 2 and the Nṛsiṁha-pūrvat. 4, 3.

The sections 6-7 added by Weber are missing in most manuscripts but all the same, they, along with the whole of the rest of the Upaniṣad were presupposed and utilised by the Tārasāra-Upaniṣad of the Muktikā-collection (cf. the preceding footnote).

RĀMA-UTTARA-TĀPANĪYA UPANIṢAD

1

Cf. Jābāla-Up. 1 (above).

Bṛhaspati said to Yājñavalkya : "[Tell me that] which is next to Kurukṣetram itself as a sacrificial place of the gods and as the Brahman-seat of all beings."—He said : "Verily, *Avimuktam* is the [true] Kurukṣetram, the sacrificial place of the gods and the Brahman-seat of all beings.

Therefore, wherever he may be wandering, he should think : here, verily, is the [true] Kurukṣetram, the sacrificial place of the gods and the Brahman-seat of all beings. For here, when the vital breaths depart out of a person, Rudra imparts the saving formula, by which one participates in immortality, participates in liberation. Therefore, one should revere *Avimuktam*, one should not leave *Avimuktam* [which is not left] !" "It is so, O Yājñavalkya."

2

[Borrowed, with necessary modifications, from the Tāraka-Upaniṣad *Oupnek'hat* II, 378 ff).]

Then Bharadvāja asked Yājñavalkya, What is the saving one and wherefrom does it save ?—Yājñavalkya said : the saving one is, followed by the point (*ṁ*), dīrgha (*ā*) after anala (*r*), once more,[1] *māya namaḥ, candrāya namaḥ, bhadrāya namaḥ* [therefore together : *Rāṁ Rāmāya namaś, candrāya namo, bhadrāya namaḥ,* " Salutation to Rāṁ Rāma, the moon, the gracious."

The syllable Om is to be worshipped as [the sounds, *varṇāḥ*] consisting of Brahman, called being, thinking and bliss.

The sound *a* is its first constituent, *u* the second, *m* the third, the half-mora the fourth, the Anusvāra the fifth, the reverberation the sixth. Because it saves, therefore the Om-sound is

1. What is repeated is *dīrghānalam* only, i.e. *Rā.*—GBP.

called the saving one, this you should know as the saving Brahman, you should worship, mark this well. Because it saves from conception, birth, old age, death, Saṁsāra and from the great fear, therefore it is called the saving one.

The Brāhmaṇa who always studies this saving one, it saves him from all sin, it saves him from death, from the killing of a Brāhmaṇa, from the killing of embryo, from the killing of a hero, from all killing, from Saṁsāra, from everything. He attains *Avimuktam*, he becomes great and enters immortality.

3

[Explanation of Om-sound as referring to the Rāma-myth, followed by a reproduction of the Māṇḍūkya-Up. 1-7 (above) and the Nṛsiṁhott. 2 (above).]

Sprung from the *a*-sound,
Lakṣmaṇa is like the *Viśva*;
Sprung from the *u*-sound,
Śatrughna is the *Taijasa*.

Sprung from the *m*-sound,
Bharata is like the Prājña;
To the half-mora corresponds Rāma,
The Brāhmic bliss embodied.

Nestling close against Rāma,
As the bestower of bliss on the world,
Creating, sustaining, dissolving all
The beings, one should know her,

That exalted Sītā,
She who's called the *Mūla-Prakṛti*;
Because she Praṇava (Om-sound) is,
So the Brahman-knowers call her Prakṛti.

"Om ! This syllable is the whole world. Its explanation is as follows. The past, the present and the future, all this is the sound Om. And besides, what still lies beyond the three times, that also is the sound Om. All this, verily, is Brahman, but Brahman is Ātman, and this Ātman is fourfold.

"The *Vaiśvānara*, present in the wakeful state, perceiving outwards, seven-limbed, having nineteen mouths, the enjoyer of the gross, is his first quarter.

"The *Taijasa*, present in the state of dream, perceiving inwards, seven-limbed, having nineteen mouths, the enjoyer of the selected, is his second quarter.

"The state, where he, asleep, no more experiences any desire and sees no vision, is deep sleep. The *Prājña*, present in the state of deep sleep, become one, consisting wholly of knowledge through and through, consisting of bliss, the enjoyer of the bliss, having conscience for his mouth, is his third quarter. He is the lord of all, he is the omni-scient, he is the inner guide, he is the cradle of the universe, verily, he is the creation and the disappearance of all creatures.

"That which is neither inward-perceiving nor outward perceiving nor both-way perceiving, that which does not consist of knowledge through and through, neither conscious nor unconscious,—invisible, unhandlable, ungraspable, uncharacterizable[1] unnamable, established in the certitude of his own self, that which extinguishes the expanse of the universe, calm, auspicious, without the second,—that is the fourth quarter, that is the Ātman which should be known" (above).

Ever shining, free from nescience and its effects, is this Ātman, who exempts from the bonds, always foreign to the duality, having the form of bliss, the basis of all, pure existence, throwing off nescience, darkness and infatuation. "I am he", so should one think; the word "I" denotes Om, That, the Being, that is the supreme Brahman, that is Rāmacandra. I am That which consists of Intelligence, am Om, That, Rāmabhadra, the supreme light. One should grasp the Ātman in the word "I" and should unite him in spirit with Brahman.

He, who always, with sincerity
Acknowledges, "I am Rāma",
He no longer belongs to the Saṁsāra,
He is Rāma himself.

1. Only here there are some minor variations from the text of the Māṇḍūkya-Upaniṣad, and these too not in all manuscripts.

Thus runs the Upaniṣad; he who knows this, becomes a liberated one.—Thus spoke Yājñavalkya.

4

[Cf. Jābāla-Up. 2 (above)]

Then Atri said to him; Yājñavalkya ! That infinite, unmanifest Ātman, how can I perceive him? —And Yājñavalkya said : That indestructible, infinite, unmanifest, having perfect bliss as the only taste, spiritual Ātman,—this infinite, unmanifest Ātman, he is to be found in the Avimuktam. —But where is the Avimukta-place to be searched for? It is to be searched between the Varaṇā and the Nāsī.—But what is the Varaṇā and what the Nāsī ? — Varaṇā is so called because it wards off (*vārayati*) [from the Ātman] all the faults committed by the body-organs; Nāsī is so called because it destroys (*nāsayati*) all the sins committed by the body-organs. — But where is the place of this Avimuktam? — It is the meeting place between the eye-brows and the nose. For this is the meeting place between the heavenly world and the highest world [of the Ātman]. Therefore the knowers of the Brahman worship this connecting place as the union-time (twilight). For in Avimuktam, so they know, one should revere him [the Ātman]. He who knows thus, proclaims his knowledge as *avimuktam* (unforgettable).

And Yājñavalkya further said to him voluntarily (unasked) :

In Kāśī Rāma's formula
Was muttered by the bull-bannered (Śiva),
Through thousands of Manu-ages
With worship, offerings and prayers.

Then spoke, pleased thereby, Rāma,
The holy one, to Śaṁkara (Śiva) :
You may, what you wish for, choose,
I grant it to you, O highest God !

Then the God requested Rāma, consisting of being, intelligence bliss:

Whoever dies in the Maṇikarnī pond,
In my temple, or on Gaṅgā's bank,

Grant him liberation !
Nothing further remains for me to wish.

Then the exalted Rāma said :

Whoever, O chief of gods,
Dies anywhere in your domain,
Be it even a worm, a beetle,
He will be liberated instantly.

In the idols of stone
I myself shall ever abide
To bring about liberation of all
In Avimuktam, your domain.

Who, devout, with this formula
Worships me here, him I shall declare
Free of all sins, worry not,
Even if he were a Brāhmaṇa's murderer.

He, to whom by you or by Brahmán
Is disclosed my six-syllabled formula,
Shall be liberated in his life-time,
And, liberated, he shall merge in me.

If you will whisper my formula
In the right ear of even a dying man,
Whoever he may be,
He shall be liberated, O Śiva !

He, who also sees the Avimuktam spoken of by Śrī-Rāmacandra, destroys thereby the sins sticking to him from previous births.

5

[Cf. Atharvaśiras 2 and Nṛsiṁhpūrvat. 4, 3 (above)]

Then Bharadvāja said to Yājñavalkya : With which formulas must the illustrious Rāma be glorified so that he is pleased and shows himself ? Tell us that, O exalted sir !

Then Yājñavalkya said: The God Brahmán, instructed by the illustrious Rāma, glorifies him in return by this formula:

The great Viṣṇu, all-sustainer,
The free-from grief Nārāyaṇa,
Knowing complete bliss alone,
Consisting of highest light as his essence
Was praised by the devout Brahmán
As the highest God.

Om ! The illustrious Rāma is this exalted one and	the secondless Ātman consisting of the supreme bliss, who is the supreme Brahman;	*bhūr*, *bhuvaḥ*, *svaḥ*. salutation to him, salutation !
,, ,,	the complete indivisible Ātman;	,, ,,
,, ,,	the Amṛtam of the Brahman-bliss;	,, ,,
,, ,,	the saving Brahman;	,, ,,
,, ,,	Brahmán, Viṣṇu, Īśvara who is the soul of the Vedas;	,, ,,
,, ,,	who is all the Vedas along with Aṅgas, Śākhās and Purāṇas;	,, ,,
,, ,,	the individual soul;	,, ,,
,, ,,	the inner soul of all beings;	,, ,,
,, ,,	the beings, like gods, Asuras and men;	,, ,,
,, ,,	the Avatāras, such as Fish, Tortoise etc;	,, ,,
,, ,,	the Prāṇa;	,, ,,
,, ,,	the essence of the four-fold inner organ;	,, ,,
,, ,,	Yama;	,, ,,
,, ,,	the end-maker;	,, ,,
,, ,,	the Death;	,, ,,
,, ,,	the Immortal;	,, ,,
,, ,,	the five elements;	,, ,,

,,	,,	the movable and the immovable;	,,	,,
,,	,,	the five fires;	,,	,,
,,	,,	the seven Vyāhṛtis;	,,	,,
,,	,,	the knowledge;	,,	,,
,,	,,	Sarasvatī	,,	,,
,,	,,	Lakṣmī:	,,	,,
,,	,,	Gaurī;	,,	,,
,,	,,	Jānakī;	,,	,,
,,	,,	the three worlds;	,,	,,
,,	,,	the sun;	,,	,,
,,	,,	the moon;	,,	,,
,,	,,	the stars;	,,	,,
,,	,,	the nine planets;	,,	,,
,,	,,	the eight Vasus;	,,	,,
,,	,,	the eight world Guardians	,,	,,
,,	,,	the eleven Rudras;	,,	,,
,,	,,	the twelve Ādityas;	,,	,,
,,	,,	past, present, future;	,,	,,
,,	,,	the one, who, as Virāj,	,,	,,
,,	,,	fills the Brahman-egg through and through;	,,	,,
,,	,,	Hiraṇyagarbha;	,,	,,
,,	,,	Prakṛti;	,,	,,
,,	,,	the Om sound	,,	,,
,,	,,	the three and half moras;	,,	,,
,,	,,	the supreme Puruṣa;	,,	,,
,,	,,	Maheśvara;	,,	,,
,,	,,	Mahādeva;	,,	,,
,,	,,	*Om! Namo Bhagavate*	,,	,,
		Vāsudevāya; the great Viṣṇu;	,,	,,
,,	,,	the highest Ātman;	,,	,,
,,	,,	Jñāna-Ātman;	,,	,,
,,	,,	the Ātman, having being, intelligence, bliss and second-lessness as the only taste;	,,	,,

The God is pleased if the Brahman-knower glorifies the God with these forty-seven formulas at all times. Therefore, one who glorifies the God with these formulas at all times gets a sight of the God and attains immortality, — and attains immortality.

F

SUPPLEMENT

Containing the still remaining
Upaniṣads of the *Oupnek'hat*

I. BARK'HE SOUKT (PURUṢASŪKTAM)
II. TADIW (TAD EVA)
III. SCHIW SANKLAP (ŚIVASAṀKALPA)
IV. BASCHKL (BĀṢKALA)
V. TSCHHAKLI (CHĀGALEYA)
VI. PANKL (PAIṄGALA)
VII. MRAT LANKOUL (MṚTYULĀṄGALA)
VIII. ARK'HI (ĀRṢEYA)
IX. PRANOU (PRAṆAVA)
X. SCHAVANK (ŚAUNAKA)

PREFATORY NOTE

The Persian-Latin trantlation of the *Oupnek'hat* (above; Upaniṣads of the Atharvaveda, Introduction, section 3) is the form in which the Upaniṣads became known to Europe for the first time and made a deep influence on the Western thought, particularly through the agency of Schopenhauer's philosophy. The reader will, therefore, desire to find again all the fifty Upaniṣads of the Oupnek'hat in our collection. We have already met with forty of them so far, since even 11. *Sarbsar* and 19. *Schat roudri* may be taken as sufficiently represented in an abridged form through the Aitareya Upaniṣad and the Nīlarudra Upaniṣad respectively. With that ten texts remain, of which 40. *Bark'he soukt*, 8. *Tadiw*, 22. *Schiw sanklap* stem from the Vājasaneyi-Saṁhitā, 44. *Baschkl* is claimed to have been taken from the Ṛgveda, and 45. *Tschhakli* from the Yajurveda, while 32. *Pankl*, 42. *Mrat lankoul*, 47. *Ark'hi*, 41. *Pranou* and 49. *Schavank* are ascribed to the Atharvaveda. Four of these texts, viz. *Baschkl*, *Tschhakli*, *Ark'hi* and *Schavank* are, as far as we know, not yet discovered in the Sanskrit original[1] and so they must be translated from Anquetil Duperron's Oupnek'hat. To these one more, *Pranou*, was added in the first edition, which could now be translated from the Sanskrit original also (see below, *Pranou*, Introduction). In the case of the remaining five Upaniṣads the translation does not conform to the Oupnek'hat with its numerous, additions, variant readings and misunderstandings but to the most original form every time in which the passage exists.

---

1. All these four Upaniṣads are now available in the Sanskrit original. They are included in the *Unpublished Upaniṣads*, edited by the Pandits of Adyar Library under the supervision of Dr. C. Kunhan Raja, Adyar 1933. The pages concerned are : 15. *Bāṣkalamantropaniṣad* (this is the title of the Upaniṣad in this collection) pp. 37-39, followed by an anonymous commentary on it, pp. 39-47; 8. Chāgaleya-Upaniṣad, pp. 23-25; 4. Ārṣeya-Upaniṣad, pp. 7-9; 19. Śaunaka-Upaniṣad, pp. 51-54. Although there are certain additions and omissions, and also different readings as compared with the Persian-Latin version, even a cursory examination will suffice one to come to the conclusion that the text is essentially the same in both the versions. A detailed comparison of the two versions, although it will be very instructive in itself, is not attempted here, in view of the limited scope of the present work. I have, however, occasionally made some references to the Adyar edition where I thought it was necessary. For the rest I have confined myself to translating Deussen's original.—GBP.

I. BARK'HE SOUKT (PURUṢA-SŪKTAM)

[This text contains the Puruṣa-song (Ṛv. 10, 90=Vāj. Saṁh. 31, 1-16) along with its continuation as Uttaranārāyaṇam (Vāj. Saṁh. 31, 17-22). Since for explanation we refer to our work on this text (*Allg. Gesch. d. Phil.* I, 150-158. 288-291), we restrict ourselves here to reproducing the translation given there.]

ṚGVEDA 10, 90

1. The Puruṣa with a thousand heads,
With thousand eyes, thousand feet
Covered on all sides the earth everywhere
And yet overflew ten fingers high above it.

2. Puruṣa alone is this whole world,
And what was, and what lasts in future,
He is the lord of immortality,—
That, which lives on food.

3. So great is this, his majesty,
Yet more elevated than it is the Puruṣa himself,
All creatures are only a quarter of him,
His three quarters are immortal above.

4. Three quarters of him soared up high,
One quarter grew up here in this world,
To spread out as everything,
What is preserved with food, and what without.

5. From him, the Puruṣa, was born
Virāj, from Virāj, the Puruṣa;
Born, he extended himself beyond the earth
Forward, backward and in all places.

6. When with the Puruṣa as the offering
The gods performed a sacrifice,
The spring became the clarified butter,
The summer the fuel and autumn the offering.

7. The Puruṣa, who was born before,
was consecrated on grass as sacrificial beast,
Him they offered in sacrifice, the gods,
The deceased and the seers assembled.

8. From him, the victim burnt as all,
Flew down sacrificial mucilage with butter mixed,
From it were created animals in the air
And those that live in forest and at home.

9. From him, the victim burnt as all,
The hymns and the psalms originated,
From him the 'state'-songs[1] altogether
And what exists of the sacrificial formulas.

10. From him originated the horse, and those
That have incisors on both the sides,
From him originated the species of cow,
The specialities of the goat and the sheep.

11. In how many parts was he transformed,
When they cut the Puruṣa in pieces ?
What did his mouth become ? what his arms,
What his thighs, what his feet ?

12. His mouth then became the Brāhmaṇa,
From the arms the Rājanya was made,
The Vaiśya from the thighs,
From the feet the Śūdra came forth.

13. From his Manas originated the moon,
The eye is now seen as the sun,
Indra and Agni were born from his mouth,
Vāyu, the wind, from his blowing breath.

14. From his navel originated the atmosphere,
From his head the heaven was created,
The earth from his feet, from the ear
Were made the directions and the world.

1. 'Prunklieder'. The word carries with it the idea of something ostentatious, gorgeous and ceremonial.—GBP.

15. Seven sticks served them as enclosure,
Three times seven served as fire-wood,
When the gods, preparing for that sacrifice,
Bound the Puruṣa as the sacrificial victim.

16. The gods, sacrificing, worshipped the sacrifice,
And that was the first of sacrificial acts;
Of mighty being, they pressed to heaven,
Where the old, departed gods abide.

VĀJASANEYI-SAṀHITĀ 31,17-21

17. Created from waters and the sap of earth,
In the beginning he went forth as Viśvakarman;
Tvaṣṭṛ comes to develop the form for him;
So the first origin of man is Godhead.

18. I know that Puruṣa, the great,
Who, like the sun, shines beyond the darkness;
Only who knows him, escapes from the realm of Death,
There is no other way to go.

19. The Prajāpati works in the womb,
The unborn is born in many ways;
How he springs up, only the wise see,
All beings are established in him.

20. Salutation to him who, warming,
Illumines the gods, is their priest,
Who was born before them,
To him resplendent, Brahmanlike.[1]

21. Creating him, resplendent, Brahmanlike
The gods then said :
"To the priest, who knows you,
May the gods be subject !"

---

1. The absence of any mark of punctuation (by oversight ?) after verse 20 makes it one continuous sentence with 21 which is confusing and makes Deussen's construction obscure. Moreover it does not agree with the Sanskrit original which clearly makes 20 and 21 two independent sentences.—GBP.

22. Beauty and prosperity are your wives, Day and Night your sides, the stars your body, the Aśvins your jaws. May the prompter promote, promote that [world] for me, promote the universe for me.

II. TADIW

(TAD EVA, Vāj. Saṁh. 32, 1-16)

[Cf. for explanation of this song *Allg. Gesch. d. Phil.* I, 291-294, and with regard to the inserted verses ibid. pp. 132-133, 191.]

1. It, forsooth, is Agni, Āditya,
It is Vāyu and Candramas,
It is the pure one, the Brahman,
The waters and Prajāpati.

2. All divisions of time sprung
From the lightning (Kena 29), from the Puruṣa;
Not in height, nor in breadth,
Nor in the middle is he encompassable.

3. There is no image of him,
Who is called the great majesty.

In the beginning he went forth as a golden embryo;
As soon as born, he became the lord of world;
He steadied the earth and the heaven,—
Who is the god, whom we shall serve with offerings ?
(Ṛv. 10,121,1).

Who, when it breaths, and when it closes eyes,
Governs the living world as the only king,
Ruling over the biped here and the quadruped,—
Who is the god, whom we shall serve with offerings ?
(Ṛv. 10,121,3).

Through whose power are snowy mountains,
The ocean, the world-stream, of whom they talk idly,
Whose arms are the poles of heaven,—
Who is the god, whom we shall serve with offerings ?
(Ṛv. 10,121,4)

He who gives breath, gives strength, whom all,
When he commands, obey, even the very gods,

Whose reflection is immortality, whose the death,—
Who is the god, whom we shall serve with offerings ?
(Ṛv. 10,121,2)

May he not harm us, he, the creator of earth,
Who created the heaven too, true to law,
Who created the waters, mighty, resplendent,—
Who is the god, whom we shall serve with offerings ?
(Ṛv. 10,121,9)

He, above whom nothing higher exists,
Who has entered into each and every creature,
Prajāpati, confering gifts of progeny,
Penetrates, of sixteen parts, the three world-lights.
(Vāj. Saṁh. 8,36)

Indra, the prince, and Varuṇa, the king,
Who made for you this [Soma] drink in the beginning;
They both drink, and I drink after them,
May the Goddess Speech enjoy the Soma. (Vāj. Saṁh.8.37)

4. He is the god in all world-spaces,
Born of old and in mother's womb;
He was born, and born he will be,
He is in men, and present everywhere.

5. He who was born before all others,
Who transforms himself into all the beings,
Prajāpati, confering gifts of progeny,
Penetrates, of sixteen parts, the three world-lights.

6. By whom was the heaven, the fastness of the earth,
The splendour of the sun and firmament made firm,
Who in the mid-region measures out atmosphere,—
Who is the god, whom we shall serve with offerings ?
(Ṛv. 10,121,5)

7. Whom the warriors in both armies look up to,
Relying on help, anxious in heart,
From whom the sun rises and shines far off,—
Who is the god, whom we shall serve with offerings ?
(Ṛv. 10,121,6)

When, of old, the great waters came,
Pregnant with cosmic embryo, begetting the fire,
He went forth thereof as the vital breath of gods,—
Who is the god, whom we shall serve with offerings?
(Ṛv. 10,121,7)

Who, the mighty one, himself surveyed the waters
That were pregnant with power and begot the sacrifice,
He, who was the only god among the gods,—
Who is the god, whom we shall serve with offerings?
(Ṛv. 10,121,8)

8. Vena[1] sees it, the highest, concealed,
In which the whole world has its only nest,
The point of union and departure of the world,
The omnipresent one, woven lengthwise and crosswise in beings.

9. May the Gandharva, acquainted with the eternal,
Announce his secret, this wide-spread world,
Three quarters of it remain concealed from us,
One, who knows this, would be the father's father.

10. He, our relative, father, care-taker,
Knows the dwelling places and beings all;
There where the gods, attaining eternality,
Soared high to the third world above.

11. Going around all beings, all worlds,
Going around all regions and directions,
He penetrated to the order of the First-born,
And entered the self with his own self.

12. At once he went around the earth and haven,
Went around the worlds, directions and light-region;
He unravelled the web of the cosmic order:
He saw it and became it, for he was it.

1. The original version may be Atharvav. 2, 1, 1 (*Allg. Gesch. d. Phil.* I, 253), the above modification probably being under the influence of the Bṛh. 3,6.8 (above).

13. The wonderful lord of the dwelling,
The beloved friend of Indra,
I have invoked for gift and wisdom. Svāhā! (ṚV.1,18,6)

14. The wisdom, which the hosts of gods,
And which the Pitṛs prize,
With that wisdom may you today,
O Agni, make me wise ; Svāhā !

15. Wisdom may Varuṇa grant me,
Wisdom Agni, Prajāpati,
Wisdom Indra and Vāyu,
Wisdom the creator may grant to me. Svāhā !

16. The Brāhmaṇa-class and the warrior-class
May bless this good fortune of mine,
May the gods grant me highest fortune !
To you, O fortune, Svāhā !

III. SCHIW SANKLAP
(ŚIVA-SAṀKALPA, Vāj. Saṁh. 34, 1-6)

[The *Manas*, whose friendly disposition is solicited here is the Ātman as shown by the Bṛh. 4,3 (above), the text which is most closely related to it. The beautiful song stands on the same level as the verses Bṛh. 4, 4, 8ff as also Kena, Kāṭhaka and Īśa, many reminiscences from which are found here.]

1. The divine one, that wanders far off
From the wakeful, wanders in the sleep too,
Wandering far and wide, the only light of lights
(Bṛh. 4,4,16),
May that Mind be friendly disposed to me !

2. By which the efficient wise do their works
In sacrifices and in festive gatherings,
What lives in man as the wonder from antiquity
(Kena 3,15),
May that Mind be friendly disposed to me !

3. That as consciousness, intelligence and determination,
As the undying light dwells in man,
Without whose assistance no hand can move (Kena 3,19),
May that Mind be friendly disposed to me !

4. Who this whole world, past and future,
The immortal one, all things in it contains,
By whom flares up the sacrifice with seven priests,
May that Mind be friendly disposed to me !

5. In whom the Ṛcs, the Sāmans and the Yajus,
Are firmly established like spokes in a nave,
Into whom is woven everything that men think,
May that Mind be friendly disposed to me !

6. That which like a good driver the horses (Kāṭh. 3,3)
Leads men securely as by the reins,
Firm in heart and yet the quickest of the quick (Īśā 4),
May that Mind be friendly disposed to me !

IV. BASCHKL
(Bāṣkala-Upaniṣad)

[The name of this Upaniṣad, preserved only in the Oupnek'hat as *Baschkl* or *Baschkel*, is explained by Weber, probably correctly, as *Bāṣkala*-Upaniṣad[1] and is referred to the half-lost Bāṣkalas, a school of the Ṛgveda (to which our Upaniṣad is claimed to belong), although the Upaniṣad before us shows no relationship whatever with what is known about the Bāṣkalas, and, according to its contents, cannot possibly go back to a time in which the Upaniṣads, as appendices to the Brāhmaṇas or the Āraṇyakas, formed the dogmatic textbooks of particular Veda schools.[2]

A legend occurring at Ṣaḍv. Br. 1, 1 (perhaps based on the misunderstood Ṛgv. verse 8,2,40, cf. *Ind. Stud.* IX, 40) reports that Indra *Medhātithiṁ ha Kāṇvāyanaṁ meṣo bhūtvā jahāra*, "in the form of a ram, is said to have kidnapped Medhātithi, son of Kaṇva." Our Upaniṣad is joined to this legend (quite similarly as the Kāṭhaka-Upaniṣad to the Naciketas legend) with a view to expressing the essential fundamental doctrines of the Upaniṣadic teaching, through Indra who discloses himself and (as in the Kauṣ. 3) appears as the representative of the Ātman. To all appearances, the form was, perhaps even including the initial passages,[3] metrical. For the age of composition, what is even more characteristic than the reminiscences of the Ṛgv., Bṛh., Chānd., Kāṭh., and Śvet. is that the doctrine of the five fires (Chānd. 5, 10) is presupposed as well-known, that the Ātman is repeatedly described as 'witness' (*sākṣin*, first Śvet. 6, 11), and that even the fire (*aurva*) burning in the ocean is mentioned, which does not occur in any other Upaniṣad known to us. This could possibly be, like many others, an addition of the commentary repeatedly interwoven, particularly at the beginning by the Persian translators;[4] the colossal freedom with which they have handled the text here as elsewhere is in marked contrast with the colossal faithfulness of Anquetilean translation and which, as long as the Sanskrit text is not found, does not make it possible to look at the present Upaniṣad in any other way but through the mist, as it were, throughout.]

Once it so happened that the wise Indra, in the form of a ram, approached Medhātithi, the son of Kanva, and lifted him up

1. Bāṣkalamantropaniṣad in the Adyar ed.—GBP.
2. The Sanskrit original in the Adyar ed., however, certainly gives the impression of an archaic language.—GBP.
3. Deussen's conjecture is now confirmed by the Adyar ed. in which this entire Upaniṣad is in a metrical form.—GBP.
4. But all these features are found in the Adyar ed. of this Upaniṣad. —GBP.

against his wish and carried him to heaven. Then Medhātithi, indignant at his forceful abduction, said to Indra the excited words: "You know, who you are; I know only that you are strong and move away quickly. One who sees you thus will not believe that you are one of the rams as they move about on the earth while you move along without touching the earth. Nobody burdened with a body can fly to the higher worlds, as you do it. You are all-knower, so tell me who you are; if not, then I, a Brāhmaṇa, will strike you with my anger.

The mighty Indra, all-seeing,
Who grants desires, conquers the hordes
Of enemies, snatches off everything,
For whom I practised the Tapas, [1]

Who sees me, wherever he be,
Who wields lightning in his hand
To strike one who, deviating
From law, goes a crooked way. [2]

Now that much against my will
I have fallen into your hands,
Whither will you, wonderful sir, take me,
And where is your kingdom? [3]

Where could my father possibly be ?
Sleeps he, that he has no news
of you, who are robbing me,
And of me, of whom you robbed him ? [4]

And the gods in the luminous heaven,
In west and south, in east and north,
And those that live in the higher regions,
Do they know, that you are robbing me ? [5]

If I have duly performed their worship,
Why don't they set me free;
Wherein could I have made a mistake,
That they approach me not for help?" [6]

Then Indra smiled and he said, in order to banish the doubt from his heart: "Who do you think holds you now in protection and custody? You feel yourself oppressed by me and yet you do not know who I am and that I cannot release you without bringing you to my abode.

I am the one, who rewards the sacrifice,
I am the Mantra, that consecrates oblations,
I the fire that consumes the offerings,
I am the witness of all the things. [1]

I nourish the gods too; all the worlds,
The Brahman-egg, I fashioned as my abode.
I am separated from all in the world,
And yet bound up with all in the world.[1] [2]

I am the great speech which, divided,
Disseminates itself as manifold speeches.[2]
It is I, who killed the demon Vṛtra,[3]
When he lived in the mountains as a serpent.[4] [3]

With my thunderbolt I terrify all.
I make nourishment grow, I am the wing
of what flies; the victories, which Indra
Won with his hosts,—I was their winner! [4]

Who would know me,—who would define?
I slew all enemies, me slew none.
I give food; who, possibly, would be able
In all the worlds my power to see? [5]

I am the one, am the light, I appear,
Assuming various forms through magical powers.[5]

---

1. As the Ātman, the subject of the cognition, he is mixed up with everything that is objective and yet stands apart from it as something different.
2. Cf. Ṛgv. 10,125,3.
3. "Occidens *tòn* Bratr nomine schaittani."
4. Ṛgv. 1,32,2 : *áhiṁ párvate śiśriyāṇám.*
5. Cf. Ṛgv. 6,47,18 : *Indro māyā́bhiḥ pururū́pa īyate.*

I fear nothing; am within all
As the inner guide,[1] as the witness of all.[2] [6]

None can ever surpass me in greatness,
Earth and heaven,—I spread them out.
For the kings I make food from sacrifice;
To those who sacrifice gladly, I distribute rewards. [7]

I know the centre of the earth, am the first parent,
The father and the mother of this world.
I make, that it rains down from the sky,
I create the dew that falls from atmosphere. [8]

I know the Vedas, sacrifices, metres
And treasures, am the fire in the ocean (*Aurva*),
That burns incessantly; am the Nāciketa-fire,
The pure, which they on the altar pile. [9]

I am the priests, who in the course of sacrifice
Early at dawn, before the birds fly out,
Pour the sacrificial offerings in the fire
And send forth the fire's praise in loud tones. [10]

One-wheeled is the car with twelve spokes,[3]
Which in the course of a year ascends to heaven;
It's the sun, who in twelve months
Encircles the world,—I am his charioteer. [11]

And he, who day by day multiplies his light,
Swells his body and lets rain down again,
The waters, which are the origin of life,[4]
I am this being too, am the moon. [12]

And he, who in the world of living beings
Moves about between them, above them,
Who, purifying, sweeps through the entire universe,
I am this being too, am the wind. [13]

---

1. As *antaryāmin*, Bṛh. 3,7.
2. As the *sākṣin*, Śvet. 6.11.
3. Cf. Ṛgv. 1,164,2.11 (*Allg. Gesch. d. Phil.* I, 108.111).
4. Cf. Chānd. 5, 3-10 (above).

And she, who deep down in her bowels
Holds the world of plants well concealed,
And sends it up to the sacrificer's gratification,
I am this being too, am the earth. [14]

It is I who, becoming the vital breath,
Enters into all forms, great and small
And circulates in all beings high and low.
He who knows me in the heart's space, becomes me. [15]

Fivefold and tenfold[1] I am, one and thousand,
Spread out infinitefold in this world.
He, who knows this, spreads out like me,
He, who doesn't know this, knows not himself. [16]

I am not to be obtained by works,[2]
Not by scriptures' knowledge, not by numerous fasts,
Not by charity either, practised manifold,—
Still all come to me by all the ways. [17]

Who is it, that kills and takes prisoner?
Who is the ram, that carried you from there?
It is I, who appears in this form,
It is I, who appears in all the forms. [18]

When someone is frightened of something or the other,
I am it, the one who is frightened, and the one who frightens,
Yet in the greatness there's a difference:
I devour everybody, me devours none. [19]

You have, O Medhātithi, for my sake,
Put up with much penance and self-torture;
To lead you to truth, to the pure existence,
I descended down in the form of ram. [20]

Along that way, which leads to truth,
Along that way you shall shortly reach the truth:

---

1. Chānd. 7,26,2 (above).
2. Cf. Kāṭh. 2,23 (above).

Luminous I am, eternal, bondless,
What was and is and shall be,—I am all. [21]

What I am and what you are, I and you
And you and I, know that I am that all!
Doubt no more! You were previously ignorant,
Experienced you are now; doubt not further. [22]

It is I, who nourishes, who brings about
The returns of all acts, it is I, who
Holds the universe sheltered in his protection;
I am shaped into this entire world. [23]

As Rudra I am the destroyer of this world,
Shaking everything; I am the Death, too,
I am the ordainer of misery and plague;
I am the lord of the world, am its soul (*haṁsa*). [24]

I am free from grief and free from old age,
I am the ancient one, free from all;
Verily, I am the universe, am the universe.
I am also the one, who brings the offering. [25]

On all sides I am the face (Ṛgv. 10.81,3)
All-embracing, lord, witness, I am.
All-pervading, kind to all,
The one I am; what exists, I am it." [26]

V. TSCHHAKLI
(CHĀGALEYA-UPANIṢAD ?)[1]

[The wise *Tschhakli*, after whom this Upaniṣad is named, is explained as *Chāgaleya* by Stenzler and Weber, and we could not think of any better substitute for this inference[1], since *cākrāyaṇa* (Chānd. 1, 10) is far removed phonologically, and also because at Bṛh. 3,4 it is reproduced as Tschekraïn. We also agree with Weber in the explanation of *Nimkehar* as the Naimiṣa-forest (*Naimiṣāraṇyam*) and *K'herk'hit* as the *Kurukṣetram*.[2]

The theme of the Upaniṣad is not strictly fixed; in the beginning the question is whether the birth decides a Brāhmaṇa; further on, whether the essence of man is to be seen in his body or in his soul. Anyway, by reconciling the two one can set up the basic thought, that the birth does not decide a Brāhmaṇa because while the body alone is born, the essence of man is however to be seen in his soul.

It is difficult to arrive at the age of the Upaniṣad on the basis of its contents, for the question wherein lies the essence of a Brāhmaṇa was possible at any time from the Chāndogya 4,4 down to the Vajrasūcikā and the comparison of body and soul with car and its driver could be equally regarded as independent of the Kāṭh. 3,3 or dependent on it. The 'living like children' seems certainly to presuppose the Bṛh. 3,5, unless one thinks of something like the dwarfish Vālakhilyas.

To judge by the form the text certainly makes the impression of belonging to a very late date, but we do not know how much of it is to be put to the account of the explanations added by the Persian translators.[3]]

Once the Ṛṣis performed a sacrifice on the bank of Sarasvatī. There sat among them a Brāhmaṇa[4] of whom the Ṛṣis said:

---

1. The name *Chāgaleya* is now confirmed by the Adyar ed. and so the question-mark in the title can now be removed.—GBP.

2. *Naimiṣa* and *Kurukṣetra* are exactly the words found in the Adyar ed.—GBP.

3. The language of the Sanskrit original preserved in the Adyar ed. on the other hand makes the impression of being considerably old and typically Upaniṣadic. Besides there are certain details, e.g. the long list of sacrificial rites, which, now found in the Adyar ed., is missing in the Persian-Latin version. The Persian translator has also dropped some proper names (which appear in the Adyar ed.), we do not know why. Lastly, the lacuna towards the end in the Adyar ed. can be fortunately filled with the assistance of the Persian-Latin version.—GBP.

4. In the Adyar ed., the name of this person is specifically mentioned as *Kavaṣa Ailūṣa*. This seems to be borne out by the Ait. Br. 2.19 which mentions this initial part of the story and where Kavaṣa Ailūṣa is called *dāsyāḥ putra*. He is however positively called *abrāhmaṇa*.—GBP.

"We must exclude him, for his mother is a maidservant and it is against the rule that such a one should be present at a sacrifice." — Thereupon the Brāhmaṇa said: "O venerable sacrificers and Veda-knowers, what is this greatness of yours which is not supposed to be there in me ?"—And they said : "This is our greatness that we are born Brāhmaṇas."—And he said : "What is that Brahman in you which is not supposed to be there in me ?"—The Ṛṣis said : "He who is born in a Brāhmaṇa family and performs the work of a Brāhmaṇa, the works which are laid down in the Veda, he is a Brāhmaṇa."

Then he showed to them a corpse[1] which was lying on the bank of the river; and he said to them : "Even this one, who lies here dead, is a Brāhmaṇa and has performed all the works [of a Brāhmaṇa] laid down in the Veda; why is not this corpse called a Brāhmaṇa ? If you regard the body as a Brāhmaṇa, then you must regard this one also a Brāhmaṇa; for, the works have not departed from the body."—The Ṛṣis said : "We do not know what has departed from it, after the departure of which we no longer call him a Brāhmaṇa."—He said: "There was a holy place in the Naimiṣa-forest (*Nimkehar*), where the Brāhmaṇas performed a sacrifice. This dead one was at that time of the sacrifice one of those Brāhmaṇas, knew all the knowledge[2] and performed the works. What has become of this knowledge of his ?" — At this the Ṛṣis were perplexed, they approached him as pupils and said to him: "We do not know it ! Let us be your pupils, teach us !"—But he said smilingly : "That is surely against the grain that a lower one should have so great and noble persons as pupils !"—The Ṛṣis said : "If it is so, then do not accept us as pupils, but advise us whither we should go !" He said : "Those who live like children, have assembled in Kurukṣetram (*K'herk'hit*); so get up and go to them; they will impart to you the truth about this."

At this the Ṛṣis got up and went towards Kurukṣetram to them who lived like children. As they reached there, the latter

1. The Adyar ed. mentions the name Ātreya at this stage itself, which is quite logical.—GBP.

2. The Adyar ed. here contains a long list (repeated further on) of sacrificial rites which is absent in the Persian version.—GBP.

inquired after what they wanted and said: "We live like children; why have you come to us, you who are great and old and wise and versed in the Veda? Here also are similar ones, who are old and wise and great and versed in the Veda and possessed of great richness; why do you not go to them instead of to us?" —When the Ṛṣis heard these words, they were perplexed, they looked at one another and said: "He who advised us to approach you as pupils to their teachers, has sent us, and trusting in him we have come to you."—"Then say what you want from us" they said.—And the Ṛṣis said: "When the Brāhmaṇas in the Naimiṣa-forest performed a sacrifice, there was among them one Brāhmaṇa descended from Atri, who knew all the knowledge[1] and performed all works. Now, after he has died and his body fallen down, what has become of his knowledge?"—They said: "A custom has been handed down to us by our ancestors that we do not admit as a pupil anyone who has not already waited upon us for a year. If you are willing to stay here for a year and wait upon us, then we will talk to you."

And they remained there for a year and waited on them. Then they living as children said to the Ṛṣis: "Now that you have waited upon us for an year, we will talk to you".—And they took them by the hand and led them by a way along which the car-drivers passed with their cars; and they said: "O lovers of truth, do you see this?"—"What?" said they.—"The car" they said.—The Ṛṣis said: "We indeed see the car, but why do you want us to see it?"—They said: "As the car-horses, like sea waves, spring and run, similarly the car too springs and runs; whichever way the horses go, thither goes the car and brings the passenger to the destination. This is how it happens." The Ṛṣis said: "So it is, and all travel by the car, till they reach their destination in the evening."

At this the driver pulled up the car, got down and unharnessed the horses. Then they said to the Ṛṣis: "Look, how now the car, like a sheer piece of wood, stands there, without going, running about or moving." "What is it", they asked,

1. The long list of sacrificial rites is repeated here also in the Adyar ed.—GBP.

"that has left the car, so that, instead of running, it stands motionless ?"—The Ṛṣis said : "The car-driver has left it".—At this they said : "Just as you are seeing the car standing motionless, after the car-driver has left it, similarly, O lovers of truth, this body also is motionless after the soul (*jīvātman*) has left it. It is the soul which moves the body; the senses are the horses of the car, the sinews are the ropes which hold its parts together, the bones are the wooden parts, the blood is the oil which one drips in so that it would move; the work is the stick with which one drives the horses; the speech is the rattling of the car, the skin is its covering.—And just as the car-driver leaves the car, as a result of which it stands motionless, similarly the soul also leaving the state of wakefulness goes into the state of dream, and leaving the state of dream into the state of deep sleep (*suṣupti*), which is of the nature of perception (*prajñā*). And when the soul leaves this state also and liberates itself and does not return here any more and sets free the body, then this car of body stands motionless and no longer creaks, and gives out a foul smell, and they do not touch it, and dogs and crows and vultures and jackals lacerate it."—

There the Ṛṣis understood what the truth is, and that it is the soul with whose departure the body becomes a corpse, and that the body is low and the soul is high and that the body can never be called high and the soul low.

When the Ṛṣis had grasped this truth well, they touched their feet and said : "Verily, we have nothing good which we could offer and give you as a gift equivalent to what you have taught us. Here we stand with respectfully joined hands."—

The Ṛṣi Chāgaleya told this story and said these Mantras of the Veda :

> Just as a car without a driver
> Does not run, rattle and move,
> So also the body when
> It's left by the departing soul.
> And as the implements of a car
> Are idle without a driver,

So also the organs of the body[1]
Are idle without the soul.

And even though for the dead
All his own people may mourn,
Still they accomplish thereby
Nothing of use to the dead body.

1. The manuscript on which the Adyar ed. is based breaks off here in the midst of the third quarter. This shows how sometimes, may be rarely, even the Persian translation may be valuable for restoring the original text where the Indian sources fail.—GBP.

VI. PANKL

(PAIṄGALA-UPANIṢAD)

[The text of this Upaniṣad which, so far as known to us, was sought in vain uptill now, we have discovered it as a part of Paiṅgala Upaniṣad, admitted as No. 59 in the Muktikā-collection. The first Adhyāya of this work, rich in contents, deals with cosmology, in a combined view of Vedānta and Sāṁkhya, often reminding one of the Vedāntasāra, the second similarly the physiology, the third the 'great words', viz. *tat tvam asi,* and the reward of its meditation, the fourth finally the freedom of the liberated. From the initial portion of this fourth Adhyāya originates the text of the *Pankl* of the Oupnek'hat which evidently shrinks remarkably in the Sanskrit original. A comparison of it (as we reproduce it here word to word as much as possible and without taking into consideration the Oupnek'hat) with Anquetil's translation provides us with a good example of the great liberty with which the Persian translators handled the text.]

Then Paiṅgala asked Yājñavalkya: "What does a man of knowledge do and how is his behaviour (*sthiti*)?"

Then Yājñavalkya said: "The seeker of liberation endowed with freedom from self-conceit rescues twentyone ancestors (*kulam*); the knower of the Brahman thereby alone hundred and one ancestors.

Know the Ātman to be a car-traveller,
The body is the car,
The Buddhi is the driver,
Know the Manas to be the reins.[1]

The senses are called the horses,
The sense-objects their roads;
As swiftly flying divine cars
The wise regard the hearts.

What's furnished with Ātman, senses, body
The Ṛṣis call him 'experiencer' (Kāṭh. 3,4).
Through him, immediately comprehensible,
Dwells in heart Nārāyaṇa.

---

1. Kāṭh. 3,3 The following verses are Kāṭh. 3,4. in an expanded form.

After the termination of acts begun
His doings are like a serpent's slough,
The souls change their house like the moon,[1]
When liberated, they have no house.

Whether he casts off his body at a holy place or in the hut of an eater-of-dogs'-flesh,—he goes to absoluteness.

Whether one offers him to space
Or covers him with the earth,
Such a man never wanders
To another birth again.

No fire-customs, no impurity (Manu, 11, 184),
No meal-ball, no water-offerings,
No offerings-to-the-deceased are needed
By the Bhikṣu who has become Brahman.

Why cook, what is already cooked ?
Why burn, what is already burnt ?
When the fire of knowledge burns it,
The body requires no customs.

Until one outgrows the world-illusion,
One shall obey the teacher,
Shall respect as the teacher
The teacher's wife and the children too.

One who has a pure heart and has become pure spirit should say : 'I am he' with patience,—'I am he' with patience".

1. *Candravac carate dehī, sa muktas' ca aniketanaḥ*. As the moon lives in another lunar mansion every night, so also the soul in a different body in every life. In Oupnek'hat the stanza is put at a wrong place and is completely misunderstood : *se ipsum potest—similem lunae lumini effectum —ex obscuritate monscientiae* [?] *liberatum facere* ["Itself it can—an effect similar to the moon's light—free from the darkness of ignorance make"].

VII. MRAT LANKOUL
(Mṛtyu-Lāṅgala[1] Upaniṣad)

[This Upaniṣad occupies itself with one of those Mantras (occurring often since Ṛgv. 7,59,12 onwards), which are believed to be of service in 'the warding off of [premature] death' (*mṛtyuvijaya*). For this purpose the formula Taitt. Ār. 10, 12 is enjoined here. This is preceded by a formula, which forms the end of the Taitt. Ār. 10, 11 in the Atharva-recension, according to which the corrupt text had to be corrected. Every word of the formula, if forgotten, brings nearer the hour of death by a month.—The expression *mṛtyulāṅgalam*,[1] 'the plough of death', which is handed down in the majority of manuscripts as the title, is probably to be explained in this way that the Death, as a hunter, sets his snares (*pāśa*) which he hides on the field under stubble and the bushes; by our formula, as by a plough, these snares are ploughed up and thereby rendered harmless.—Our translation follows Col. Jacob's edition (*Indian Antiquary* 16, 287), utilising the variants from Burnell's edition mentioned by him.]

Om! We will explain the Plough of Death. Of this formula of the Plough of Death, the metre is Anuṣṭubh, the divinity Kālāgnirudra, the poet Vasiṣṭha: its application is at the approach of death which has Yama as its divinity (read : *Yaṃa-devata-mṛtyūpasthāne*).

"Now the Yoga : my tongue is speaking sweet; I am not in the time, but the time itself.[2]

Ṛtaṁ satyaṁ paraṁ Brahma
Puruṣaṁ kṛṣṇapiṅgalam
Ūrdhvaliṅgaṁ virūpākṣam;—
Viśvarūpāya namo namaḥ !
Oṁ, krāṁ krīṁ, svāhā.'

(As law, truth, highest Brahman,
The dark-and-yellow Puruṣa,
With Liṅgam above, odd eyes [I invoke];—
Salutation to him assuming all forms !)"

1. °*lāṅgūla*° is found in some editions, which seems to be presupposed by the Persian translator.—GBP.

2. The words which follow next in the text are probably only an explanatory gloss; *sphena*—(read : *śyāma*)—*kapila-rūpāya* is an explanation of *kṛṣṇapiṅgalam*.

One who recites this Mṛtyu-lāṅgala [-Mantra] in the morning, at noon and in the evening is exonerated from a Brāhmaṇa's murder, from a gold-thief he becomes a non-thief, from a polluter of teacher's bed a non-polluter, he is immediately freed from all major sins and minor sins.

This formula, once recited, brings the same reward as eight thousand Gāyatrīs; one who teaches it to eight Brāhmaṇas goes to the world of Brahmán and Rudra; one who does not impart it becomes spotted, scabby or has diseased nails. One who does not retain it when it is imparted to him, becomes blind, deaf or dumb.

When death approaches, this formula is forgotten within six months before it; [if not, then] Yama, the venerable lord of justice, can be pacified by the aforesaid recitation of this great Mantra called Mṛtyulāṅgala.

From whom the word *ṛtam* disappears,
He dies after six months;
After five, if *satyam* also disappeared,
After four, from whom *paraṁ Brahma* too;

After three, if *puruṣam* also disappeared
After two, from whom *kṛṣṇapiṅgalam* also,
From whom *ūrdhvaliṅgam*, after a month,
After a fortnight, when *virūpākṣam*,
After three days, when *viśvarūpam*,
Namo namaḥ, immediately afterwards,
—*namo namaḥ*, immediately afterwards.

VIII. ARK'HI
(ĀRṢEYA UPANIṢAD[1])

[The explanation of the name *Ārk'hi* as *Ārṣeyā* (from *ṛṣi*) given by Weber (*Ind. Stud.* IX, 48) is to be certainly preferred to that as *Ārṣikā* (from *ṛṣika*) also given by Weber, *Literaturgesch.* 2. ed. p. 180, for the contents consist in a conversation of the five old-Vedic Ṛṣis, *Viśvāmitra, Jamadagni, Bharadvāja, Gautama* and *Vasiṣṭha* on the nature of the Brahman. For the time of composition, the following remark[2] at the end that *posteri tou K'hak rek'heschir, propter tò invenire hunc ātma, maschghouli igni Beischavantr fecerunt* is conclusive in the first instance. By the Ṛṣi *K'hak* is not to be understood Kapila (as Anquetil the author of the variant *Kapl* and Weber accept as possible), but *Aśvapati Kaikeya*; for he develops at Śatap. Br. 10,6,1. Chānd. 5, 11-24 (above) before six Brāhmaṇas the doctrine of *Agni Vaiśvānara* as *Ātman Vaiśvānara.* Following the model of this passage the five Ṛṣis of our text define the Brahman successively as the atmosphere, the Ākāśa, the solar light, the light of the lightning and that, *de quo non possunt dicere : hoc et illud est*, where probably there was Yājñyavalkya's formula *neti, neti* in the text (Cf. Bṛh. Up. Brāhmaṇas 3 and 9, Introductions, above). Further, back references, as the proofs show, down to the Praśna and possibly to the Māṇḍūkya, seem to occur. For the rest, the bearing of the text is pretty ancient; we may recognise in it a beautiful echo of the thoughts of the ancient Upaniṣads.]

Once the Ṛṣis assembled to investigate the truth; not to refute one another, but to learn the truth from one another.

There *Viśvāmitra* spoke first to show off his knowledge : "What is on the earth and in the heaven, immovable, not contained in anything else, containing everything in itself, like the Ākāśa which, immovable, contains everything and is not contained in anything and in which the rumbling clouds, flashing with lightning, appear thundering terribly,—this I know as the Brahman. For even if one burnt it with fire and moistened it with water and bound it and fastened together with leather straps and beat it with iron hammers and pierced it with needles and embedded it on spikes and bored through it with iron nails and smeared it with mud and hewed it with the axe and stabbed

1. *Unpublished Upaniṣads*, Adyar, pp. 7-6.—GBP.
2. Not found in the Adyar ed.—GBP.

in the heart, still all this would leave behind no trace on it, none can restrain it, none can go beyond it."

But the Ṛṣi *Jamadagni* did not approve of these words, for he thought that what is on the earth and in the heaven is transitory and is limited, because it is between the earth and the heaven, and he said : "What you are talking about, that is the atmospheric world (*antarikṣaloka*); this I look upon as an unfolded power (*mahiman*) of the Brahman, not as the Brahman for this atmospheric world is contained in it. One who worships this atmospheric world, which is its unfolded power and is contained in it, he is, like this atmospheric world, contained in the world and transitory. And one who worships this atmospheric world as the Brahman, he continually undergoes decay because he worships the unfolded power which is in the Brahman and does not know the Brahman."

And the other said : "What do you then know, which always persists and does not disappear ?"

Then Jamadagni said : "that wherein the earth and the heaven are, which has established in itself the earth and the heaven, and is not established in something else, which one cannot reach, not even so much as see, and which is not surrounded by anything else,—this I know as the Brahman. For in it the world-lights revolve diversely and they do not disappear and do not fall down, also they do not go astray and are not tired; and if one were to run for his whole lifetime, one would not be able to reach it, not even so much as to see it.

Some say:[1] it is the water (*āpas*); others : the darkness (*tamas*, Ṛgv. 10,129,2); yet others : the light; still some others : the Prāṇa; many : the Ākāśa; yet some others : the Ātman."

But the Ṛṣi *Bharadvāja* did not approve of these words and said : "One who knows thus, does not thereby know the highest reality: for even this, which you know, is transitory; for what is within the world is limited and therefore imperfect, and it makes [limited and therefore] imperfect what is outside the world. Even this I look upon as an unfolded power of the

1. This paragraph falls out of the tone of the whole text and thereby reveals its identity, pretty clearly, as an interpolation already present in the Sanskrit original. [It is found in the Adyar ed. also. —GBP.]

Brahman and not as the Brahman; it is the Bhūtākāśa (the space as element), which surrounds this world and is yet within [the Brahman]. One who worships this Bhūtākāśa, which is its unfolded power and is contained in it, he is, like this Bhūtākāśa, contained in the Brahman and transitory. And the one who worships this Bhūtākāśa as the Brahman, does thereby evil and continually undergoes decay. But one who knows this Bhūtākāśa as only contained in the Brahman and worships, he reaches the full old age and subdues[1] everything."

And the other said : "What do you then know, which always persists and does not disappear ?"

Then Bharadvāja said : "That light, which is there in the sun's disk and revolves continually and shines and glows and is very bright and directs everything towards itself,—this I know as the Brahman. For it is always like itself and appears the same from afar and near, and is turned towards all sides (Chānd. 2,9,1 and the note); and even if one were to run and jump, in order to reach it, still he cannot reach it, he cannot even approach it. For in the vicinity it looks distant and from distance near, and nobody can conquer its greatness."

But the Ṛṣi *Gautama* did not approve of these words and said : "Even this is transitory; because its light lasts, only so long as it is connected with the sun's orb. Also its light is perceived by a mere look by the wise and the ignorant, the unthinking, the laymen, whether they live on islands or in mountains, and even by those to whom the revelation of the scriptures has not reached;[2] but the light of the Brahman is not of this kind, for none, to whom it is not taught, can see it. I look upon the sun's light as an unfolded power of the Brahman. Who thus knows the sun's light as an unfolded power of the Brahman and worships [it] and the golden Man (*puruṣa*), who is seen within the sun with golden hair, all golden down to the tips of nails,[3]—who worships the sun's

1. The reading before the Persian translator seems to have been *vaśīyān*, in the Adyar text it is *vasīyān* :—GBP.

2. The Adyar ed. reads names of certain uncivilized peoples here : *Puṇḍrāḥ Suhmāḥ Kulumbhā Daradā Barbarāiti*.—GBP.

3. The agreement with the Chānd. 1,6,6 is so far-going that we may well look upon this as a citation from this passage and translate accordingly.

light thus, he is great among all the beings, he is the foundation and the support of all, he reaches the full old age, and everything lives in his shade. The sun, when he rises, cannot surpass the greatness of the Brahman, but is inferior to it and rises in obedience to its command (Cf. Kāṭh. 4,9). Who now looks upon the sun as rising by himself, and worships, does thereby evil and continually undergoes decay. But one who knows the sun's light as an unfolded power of the Brahman and worships and knows that he rises at its command, he enters the Light and reaches the full old age, and everything lives in his shade who, knowing thus, worships."

And the other said : "What do you then know, which always persists and does not disappear ?"

Then Gautama said : "That shining and quivering lightning, which appears near from a distance and distant from near, which is not equalled by anything hurled in swiftness,—this I know as the Brahman."

But the Ṛṣi Vasiṣṭha did not approve of these words and said : The lightning is recognized by the rumbling of the clouds and the flash and then it disappears. It is perceived by a mere look by the wise and by the ignorant, while they show it to one another; but the light of the Brahman is not of this kind, for none, to whom it is not taught, can see it; and one to whom it is taught, sees the light of the Brahman in his own heart. I look upon the light of the lightning as an unfolded power of the Brahman, not as the Brahman. One who knows the lightning as an unfolded power of the Brahman and worships, he reaches the unfolded power, reaches the full old age, and everything lives in his shade."

And the other said : "What do you then know, which always persists and does not disappear ?"

And Vasiṣṭha pondered over and said : "That, of which you say : 'It is not so, it is not so' (*neti, neti*), that is the Brahman. This Brahman is the Ātman, infinite, unaging, boundless; not external and not internal, all-knowing, of the form of light, without hunger and without thirst; he leads from ignorance over to the other bank (cf. *avidyāyāḥ paraṁ pāraṁ tārayasi*, Praśna 6,8); he is the light in the heart; he is the lord of the universe, the commander of the universe, the sovereign of the universe (Bṛh. 4,4,22), the dwelling of the universe; him nobody conquers; he is the creation and the dissolution of the creatures (cf. Māṇḍ. 1,5); he is the praise-worthy guardian of the universe.

The descendants of [*Aśvapati*] *Kaikeya* worshipped[1] the fire Vaiśvānara as this Ātman (Śatap. Br. 10,6,1. Chānd. 5, 11-24). As such they worshipped at the sacrifices Indra, because he grants help to the hosts and brings about sacrifices and is very great and accepts the offerings; he is the guardian of creatures, and everything approaches him and praises him with the formulas of the Veda. His treasure-house is this entire earth, he kills the demon Ahi. He is in the ocean, he grants everybody efficiency through his power; one who knows him, invokes him before every activity."[2]

When the Ṛṣis heard these words of Vasiṣṭha, they agreed to it, that one must, therefore, know the Brahman, [they] paid him respect there and then and became his pupils.

Salutation to Agni !
Salutation to Indra !
Salutation to Prajāpati !
Salutation to the Brahman !

1. This reference is not found in the Adyar ed.—GBP.

2. This paragraph is seen with considerable additions and omissions in the Adyar ed.; moreover, it consists of verses there.—GBP.

IX. PRANOU
(PRAṆAVA UPANIṢAD[1])

[A *Praṇava-Upaniṣad* (that is how the title is to be explained without doubt) is found in a manuscript form in Fort St. George (Taylor, *Catalogue* II, 472), in Tanjore (Burnell 33b), in Jammu (Stein's *Catalogue* p. 31) and in Madras (*Catalogue of the Government Oriental Manuscripts Library*, p. 52); the third cannot be our Upaniṣad, for in that case it would be fractional, since it consists of fourteen lines; whether the others, remains to be seen. Meanwhile we are attempting to sift out from the diffused and probably here also strongly interpolated Persian-Latin translation a conjectural text of the original work. But we remark that this attempt is a completely hypothetical one, particularly considering the abstruse contents of the work. It is divided in three Brāhmaṇas : the first considers the Praṇava, i.e. the syllable *Om* according to its letters and sounds and its indispensability at the beginning of every Vedic study and the sacrifice;—the second Brāhmaṇam confirms this indispensability through a myth;—the third makes the Prajāpati answer thirtysix questions concerning the Om-sound. Here also the more coherent presentation of the answers seems to be the original and the prefixing of the thirtysix questions a later subscription of the contents (cf. Praśna 4, above). We have tried as far as possible to correlate questions and answers through common numbering; but already Anquetil (II, 748) no more knows now to help; several passages are partly misunderstood, and partly not understood at all even by him or quite probably by his Persian predecessors. We can scarcely hope that we have always hit the mark in our attempt to bring about clarity everywhere. But the picture of the Upaniṣad as given by our translation will essentially be a correct one. [After Bloomfield's discovery, as said in the Foreword, of the Sanskrit text of the Praṇava-Upaniṣad in the Gopatha-Brāhmaṇam I, 1, 16-30, we have added in this second edition a translation of the occasionally difficult and considerably corrupt Sanskrit original running throughout side by side with our original translation from Anquetil Duperron, because a comparison of the two versions is not without interest.]

FIRST BRĀHMAṆAM

The Bráhman created Bráhman in a lotus-flower. The latter deliberated : "Which is the one word by which all desires are obtained and all worlds, gods, Vedas, sacrifices, rewards of the sacrifices, everything movable and the immovable is known?"

---

1. Adyar ed., pp. 32-77.—GBP.

—And he practised Tapas. After he had practised the Tapas, he saw that syllable, which consists of two letters and four moras, which is all-encompassing, all-ruling, ever new, the Brahman. Then he obtained all desires, all worlds, gods, Vedas, sacrifices, all the movable and the Immovable.

Through the first letter he perceived the water (*āpas*) and the acquisition (*āpti*); through the second the fire and the light.

The first mora, the *a*-sound, is the earth and the fire, the plants, the Ṛgveda, *bhūr*, the Gāyatrī, the ninefold Sāman, the East, the spring and with reference to the self, the language, the tongue and the speech.

The second mora, the *u*-sound, is the atmosphere and the wind, [the Yajurveda], *bhuvar*, the *Triṣṭubh*. the fifteenfold Sāman, the West, the summer, and with reference to the self the breath, the nose and the smell.

Praṇava Upaniṣad

(From the Gopatha-Brāhmaṇam I, 1,16-30.)

First Brāhmaṇam = (Gop.B.I, 1,16-22.)

16. The Bráhman created Bráhman in a lotus-flower. This Brahmán, when he was created, hit upon the idea : "Which is the only syllable, through which I can obtain all desires, all worlds, all gods, all Vedas, all sacrifices, all speech, and all rewards and all beings, movable and immovable ?"—And he practised the Brahman-conduct. Then he saw the syllable "Om", which consists of two letters and four moras, which is all-encompassing, all-ruling, ever new, the Brahman, the exclamation signifying the Brahman, having Brahman as its divinity. By that he obtained all desires, all worlds, all gods, all Vedas, all sacrifices, all speech, all rewards and all beings, movable and immovable.

Through its first letter he obtained the water and the moisture [read : *apas snehañca*]; through its second letter he obtained the fire and the lights.

17. Through its first phonetic mora he obtained the earth, the fire, the plants and trees, the Ṛgveda, the exclamation

The third mora, the *m*-sound, is the heaven and the sun, the Sāmaveda, *svar*, the Jagatī, the seventeenfold Sāman, the North, the rainy season, and with reference to the self the light, the eye and the sight.

The fourth mora, the Anusvāra, is the water and the moon, the Atharvaveda, *janas*, the Anuṣṭubh, the twentysevenfold Sāman, the South, the autumn, and with reference to the self the heart, the knowledge and the known.

The reverberation is the Vedāṅgas, creation and dissolution, the Veda-discourses, the great formulas, the Upaniṣads, the Vedic injunctions, the seven Vyāhṛtis, the seven tones, and art, dance, speech and music; and the songs of Citraratha and the other [Gandharvas]; the lightning, the Bṛhatī, the thirtythreefold Sāman, the direction above, the four months of the remaining seasons, and with reference to the self the ear, the voice and the hearing.

This Praṇava, the one syllable, originated before the Tapas, is the Brahman, the seed of the Veda; all Mantras have sprung from this Praṇava.

[read: *vyāhṛtim*] *bhūr*, the Gāyatrī metre, the Stoma Trivṛt, the eastern direction, the season of spring, and with reference to the self the speech, the tongue and the taste, these organs.

18. Through its second phonetic mora he obtained the atmosphere, the wind, the Yajurveda, the exclamation *bhuvar*, the Triṣṭubh metre, the fifteenfold Stoma, the western direction, the season of summer, and with reference to the self the breath, the nose and the smelling of the odour, these organs.

19. Through its third phonetic mora he obtained the heaven, the sun, the Sāmaveda, the exclamation svar, the Jagatī metre, the seventeenfold Stoma, the northern direction, the season of rain, and with reference to the self the light, the eye and the sight, these organs.

20. Through its phonetic mora *va*-(?) he obtained the water, the moon, the Atharvaveda, the stars, as the sound *Om* their own self, as the sound *janar* that of the Aṅgiras', the Anuṣṭubh metre, the twentyonefold Stoma, the southern direction, the

And this is the work of the Praṇava : When one studies the Vedas without Tapas, attendance on the teacher, or at a forbidden time, then their power declines and they do not remain; but through the Praṇava, which is the essence of the Atharvaveda, they get back their power and remain again. And just as a child at birth, if its position is disastrous, kills the mother, and if it is favourable, frees her, similarly in the case of study the Mantras go well by the Praṇava and remain and in the case of the sacrifice, through the Praṇava the sacrifices become faultless.

Therefore it is said : "The Praṇava is the one syllable which they utter at the beginning of every sacrificial act and at its end."

> The syllable of the hymn in the highest heaven,
> Supporting on which the gods all are enthroned,
> If one doesn't know it, what's the use of the hymn?—
> We, who know it, are assembled here.[1]

This syllable is the Praṇava.

He who has a desire, may observe abstinence for three nights, sleep on straw, sit silently facing the East and every night he

---

season of autumn, and with reference to the self the Manas, the knowledge and the known, these organs.

21. Through the hearing of the *ma*-sound he obtained the epic and the mythological poems, the Veda-discourses, the Nārāśaṁsa songs, the Upaniṣads, [the contents] of the Vedic injunctions, the [seven] exclamations *vṛdhat*, *karat*, *guhat*, *mahat*, *tat*, *śam* and *om*, the various kinds of string music, salutary owing to its tunes, the [seven] tunes, dance, song and music, he further obtained the divine song of Citraratha, the light of lightning, the Bṛhatī metre, the three-times-ninefold and thirty-threefold Stoma, the firm direction above, the seasons of winter [*hemanta*] and post-winter [*śiśira*], and with reference to the self the ear, the sounds and the hearing, these organs.

1. Ṛgv. 1, 164,39; the last line is misunderstood by the Persian translators, unless they had a different reading before them.

should go over the Praṇava mentally a thousand times; then he will receive his desired object and will obtain the fruit of his sacrificial acts.

SECOND BRĀHMAṆAM

When Sudhā,[1] the city of Indra, was stormed on all sides by the Asuras, the gods were afraid and said : "Who will conquer the Asuras?" They said to the Om-sound, the first-born of the Brahman: "You are the strongest amongst us; let us conquer the Asuras through you !"—"What will be my reward?" said he.—They said : "What do you demand?"—The Praṇava said: "That they shall not study the Veda without first uttering me; and that if they do not utter me first, the study of the Veda shall not bring any fruit !"—"Let it be so", said they. Then the gods attacked from the place where the sacrifice was, from the

---

22. This Ṛg-verse consisting of only one syllable originated as the Bráhman before Brahmán and Tapas as the Atharva-seed of the Veda; from it the Mantras originated. This [Praṇava] however, verily, when one makes the Mantras defective or injures them or makes them unusable by studying them without Tapas, unobediently at a forbidden time, then it restores them to their power through the energy of the Atharvan; the Mantras could turn towards me [inimically], just as the embryos could wish to kill [read: *abhijighāṁseyus*] the mother, [so he thinks] and he first employs the Om-sound and restores it to its powers through this Ṛc; it is also employed before the sacrifice and after so the sacrifice spreads through it on all sides.

This very thing is said in a verse:
"She, who is employed first,
On the syllable of this Vedic Ṛc in the highest heaven"...
(Atharvav. 9,10,18=1,164,39).[2]

---

1. *Sudhāyām=svarge* (Sāyaṇa to Ait. Br. 3, 47, 8). Weber thinks of *Sobha* (cf. *Ind. Stud.* II, 38n.)
2. Actually only the second line is found at the Vedic place mentioned. —GBP.

north (above, Chānd. Up. 4,17,9, note), said "Om!" and defeated the Asuras by the help of the Praṇava.

Therefore one says the word *Om* in all sacred activities, and one who does not know it, he is not capable of accomplishing the activity; but one who knows it, he has the Veda in his power. That is why when one utters it at the beginning of the Ṛgveda, it is the Ṛgveda, of the Yajurveda; the Yajurveda; of the Sāmaveda, the Sāmaveda. And in every work, because one utters Praṇava at the beginning that is its form,—the form of it.

Third Brāhmaṇam

They asked [Prajāpati] with regard to the Om-sound :

1. Which is its root (*Prakṛti*)?
2. What its pronunciation ?
3. How does it get into the Sandhi ?
4. Should one treat it as masculine, feminine or as neuter ?
5. Is it singular, dual or plural ?

When a Brāhmaṇa has a desire, he should repeat to himself this syllable a thousand times, after he has observed abstinence for three nights and sat silently on the straw, facing the East; then all his desires come true and so also all his sacrificial acts. —Thus reads the Brāhmaṇam.

Second Brāhmaṇam = Gop. B. I, 1,23.

23. There is a city of Indra by name Vasordhārā (Goods' flood); the Asuras stormed it on all sides; then the gods were afraid and said: "Who will ward off these Asuras?"—They saw the Om-sound, the first-born son of Brahman. To him they said : "Let us conquer these Asuras with yourself as the mouth !"—He said : "What will be my reward ?"—"Choose a gift", said they.—"I will choose it", said he. And he chose a gift : "The Brāhmaṇas shall not recite the Veda-word without uttering me first, and if they do not utter me first, it shall be ineffective (*abrahman*)!"—"Let it be so" said they. Then the gods came into a close combat with the Asuras from the northern side of the sacrificial place and the gods defeated the

6-13. Can it be put into the case-relations: 6. "it", 7. "from it", 8. "with it", 9. "in it", 10. "by it". 11. "out of it", 12. "to it"? 13. and through which suffixes are these relations with it shown ?

14. Is it to be uttered in a low, medium or loud tone ?

15. Is its meaning changed if a sound is prefixed to it [e.g. in *śom*, Taitt. Up. 1,8], and can its sounds be modified [e.g. in prolating, Atharvaśikhā 2, or the substitution of the Anusvāra *ṁ* in the place of *m* with Virāma] ? [The sense is uncertain, for the answer which follows is incomplete.]

16. What is its interpretation? What is after it and after what is it formed ?

17-21. How many Mātrās has it ? How is it composed ? How many signs has it ? How many sounds ? What is it followed by ?

22. With which organ is it uttered ?

23[a]. How is it uttered ? 23[b]. How is its pronunciation taught ?

24. Which is its metre ?

25. What is its colour ?

Asuras from the place of the Āgnīdhrīya fire by means of the Om-sound.

Because they defeated them, therefore the Om-sound is uttered first, and one who does not know the Om-sound, he is powerless; but one who knows it, he has the Veda-word in his power. That is why the Om-sound is the Ṛc in the Ṛc, the Yajus in the Yajus, the Sāman in the Sāman, the Sūtram in the Sūtram, the Brāhmaṇam in the Brāhmaṇam, the Śloka in the Śloka, the Praṇava in the Praṇava.—Thus reads the Brāhmaṇam.

Third Brāhmaṇam=Gop. B. I, 1,24-30.

24. We are asking questions about the Om-sound :

1. Which is its root ?
2. Which is its stem ?
3. What is its connection with noun and verb (*nāmākhyātam*)?
4. What is its gender ?

26. What is its main effect ?
27. How frequently is it uttered?
28. Which narration serves as its explanation?
29. In which sound [of *Om*] is the Ṛgveda, in which the Yajurveda, in which the Sāmaveda?
30. Why do the reciters of the Veda first utter the Praṇava?
31. Which is its divinity?
32. Which is the right time to say it?
33. What is the explanation of its sounds?
34. Which is its abode (*loka*)?
35. And which is the place, where it sprang up?
36. With what is it connected in the body?

Prajāpati said: Splitting these thirtysix questions I will explain the Praṇava.

---

5. What its pronunciation ?[1]
6. Which its case ?
7. What its suffix ?
8. What its accent ?
9. What its preposition ?
10. What its particle ?
11. What its analysis ?
12. What its modification ?
13. What its element that undergoes modification ?
14. How many moras has it ?
15. How many letters ?
16. How many syllables ?
17. How many words ?
18. What is its consonantal euphony ?
19. What effects augmentation of its reverberation [read: *nāda*] ?[2]
20. Its phoneticians?

1. 'Aussprache'. *vacanam* should rather mean number.—GBP.

2. Deussen's proposed emendation and interpretation are questionable. *Sthāna, anupradāna* and *karaṇa* respectively mean (1) point of articulation, (2) mode (or effort) and (3) the organ (i.e. the mobile organ of articulation). But see 27. below.—GBP.

1. Its root is *ap*, according to others *av*; according to the former it surrounds (*āpnoti*), according to the latter it supports. But the surrounding is more than supporting; and *ap* (the water) is so called because, like Brahman, it surrounds.

2. Its pronunciation is joint or separate; whether the letters are pronounced jointly or separately, it gives the same meaning.

3. The sounds, with which it enters into the Sandhi (*a*, *ā*), give up their pronunciation, but maintain their meaning (Pāṇ. 6.1.95).

4. It undergoes no difference in pronunciation as masculine or feminine, (is uttered with a loud voice[1]) and can be constructed with a masculine, feminine or neuter [adjective] equally well.

5. (The answer is inserted in 23).

6-13. It can be put into the case-relations 6. "it", 7. "from it", 8. "with it", 9. "in it" 10. "by it", 11. "out of it", 12. "to it". 13. In all these cases it remains the same (without suffix).

14. (The answer is inserted in 23.)

15. (The answer is inserted in 23.)

---

21. As what do they pronounce it?
22. Which is its metre?
23. What is its colour?

Thus read the prior questions. Now follow the latter:

24. Its formula?
25. Its ritual?
26. Its Brāhmaṇam?
27. Its Ṛc?
28. Its Yajus?
29. Its Sāman?
30. Why do the Brahman-teachers place the Om-sound at the beginning?
31. What has it as its divinity?
32. What its luminary-principle?
33. What its etymology?
34. What its place?

1. Answer to 14; out of place here.

16. The *a* (in *ap* 'water') becomes *o*, and the *p m* and out of these two signs, the sound *o-m* is formed.

17-21. Its Mātras are three *a*, *u*, *m*. It is uttered (above, Atharvaśikhā 1) with three reverberations (*mad*=*nāda*?). The reverberation is its fourth element. Thus it consists of three and a half Mātras.

22. It is uttered with the lips.

23[a]. For *o*, the throat is widened, for *m* the lips are closed;—(Answer to 19:) It has two marks not one;—(Answer to 15:) The addition of the Virāma does not change its meaning;—(Answer to 14:) It can be uttered in a low, medium or lord tone;—(Answer to 5:) It can be used as singular, dual or plural.

23[b]. The ancestors have thus uttered and handed it down, so that the students need not ask such questions; for they know that its pronunciation can be learnt by merely hearing.

Now among the juniors in Kanyakubja there was the learned *Anheh,* who discussed with the wise similar questions. And he asked the Ṛṣis: "Which is the way to pronounce the Praṇava

---

35. Which its origin?

36. What its connection with the self?

These are the thirtysix questions. The earlier and later form three groups, each consisting of twelve; according to these we will explain the Om-sound.

25. Indra asked Prajāpati: O holy one, consecrating myself [by taking the fuel-sticks], I ask you.—Ask, my dear, so said he. —What is this Om-sound ? Whose son is he? What is its metre ? What is its colour? And as what does the priest reach that Brahman? For it is for that reason that he immolated first [as it were] that Om-sound which brings welfare. In the Ṛgveda the Om-sound is with the Svarita tone and monosyllabic; in the Yajurveda the Om-sound is with the three accents as its tone and monosyllabic; in the Sāmaveda the Om-sound is with the long-drawn tone and monosyllabic; in the Atharvaveda the Om-sound is with a short tone and monosyllabic; with Udātta as the tone it is dissyllabic, viz. as *a* and *u*; there are three and a half moras, for which there is an indication in the *m*-sound, as

badly, so that one knows that it is badly pronounced; and which is the way, of which they say, it is correctly pronounced?" [And they answered]: "There are six characteristics of its pronunciation: place of its articulation, mode, correctness, quantity, duration and the acts in which it is to be uttered. For that they praise the speaker. But one who does not know these six, cannot pronounce the Praṇava correctly."

24. Its metre is the Gāyatrī; for the gods pronounce it in one word.

25. Its colour is white (see above Atharvaśiras 5 and Atharvaśikhā 1).

---

they say (?). As regards the first mora, it has Brahmán as the divinity, is red in colour, and one who meditates over it constantly, goes to the abode of Brahmán. As regards the second mora, it has Viṣṇu as the divinity, is black in colour, and one who meditates over it constantly, goes to the abode of Viṣṇu. As regards the third mora, it has Īśāna (Śiva) as the divinity, is brown in colour, and one who meditates over it constantly, goes to the abode of Īśāna. As regards the three-and-the-halfth mora, it is dedicated to all the divinities, goes into the ether when it manifests itself and resembles a pure crystal in colour; one who meditates over it constantly, he goes to the nameless abode and it is the origin of the Om-sound. If a Brāhmaṇa does not know this, then a repeated initiation by the teacher is [necessary]; therefore the word of our Brāhmaṇam is to be taken care of like a firebrand which is not to be touched (*alātavyo*).[1] Its family? He is a son of Brahman; its metre is Gāyatrī, its colour white. He is preferably masculine [*puṁso vatso*?][2]. Rudra is its divinity. Such is the Om-sound of the Vedas.

26. Which is its root? the root is *āp*; some think it is *av*. But the semantic accord is closer than the formal accord; so it

1. H.C. Patyal (unpublished dissertation on the Gopatha-Brāhmaṇa) translates: "He is of the lineage of Lātavya" (i.e. a descendant of Latu). The text still remains obscure.—GBP.

2. 'male-calf' (Patyal).—GBP.

26. The way of its effect is that it is uttered at the beginning.

27. Twofold, is the answer [is the *Om*-sound to be uttered, viz. firstly (if we have understood the passage correctly) in the form of the four *Vyāhṛtis*, secondly as the Praṇava].

I. There are the Mantras, the Vidhis and the Brahman as parts of the Vedas, viz. of the Ṛgveda, Yajurveda, Sāmaveda; and the Atharvaveda, whose glory (*mahiman*) is the Praṇava. What is uttered at the beginning of the four Vedas is particularly the glory of the four Vedas. These are four words: *Om* at the beginning of the Atharvaveda, *bhūr* of the Ṛgveda, *bhuvar* of the Yajurveda, *svar* of the Sāmaveda. II. But the glory of all is *Om*, in so far as it is uttered at the beginning of all the four Vedas; if not, their power decreases, and they do not yield any fruit.

---

comes from *āp* and means that the Om-sound surrounds [*āpnoti*] everything. That it is a radical compound, corresponds to the fact. A nominal stem is not noticeable. The name suffix [for *m*] is pertinent, and the grammarians mention it expressly under the exceptions. It is an adverbial compound (*avyayībhūtam*); this name is significant and means that as such it never changes. For it is said:

> What remains the same in the three genders,
> In all cases and numbers
> Remains unmodified, is called indeclinable (*avyayam*).
> (Mahābhāṣyam I,1,38, p. 96, 16.)

Which is dropped as a changeable element? A vocalisation takes place. Of the root *āp*, the letters *ā* and *p* must be modified. In its initial the Om-sound is modified; the second element is the sound *m*. Thus the monosyllabic *Om*-sound consisting of two letters results as *Om*.

27. How many moras? The initial contains three moras, for it becomes pluta at the beginning;[1] the *m*-sound is the fourth mora. What is its place? The two lips are its place, and as effecting the augmentation they are a twofold place. The dipthong [*au*] and the low-sounding *a* come out of the throat with the

---

1. Of vedic recitation.—GBP.

28. After the passing of the *Satyam* and the *Tretā*, at the beginning of the age *Dvāparam* the Ṛṣis discussed: "Now they will perform sacrifice without sufficient knowledge of the Ṛg-, Yajur- and Sāmaveda and their work will be defective and without fruit; how may such a harm affect the works ?" They were seized with fear for the ancestors had not left any instructions as to what is to be done, should the Vedas become fruitless. And they said: "Come on. Let us go all together to Atharvan, worthy of veneration, and request him to grant us freedom from fear, and instruct us in this matter." And they thought: "How will he talk to us, if we do not approach him submissively ?" And they went thither and approached him in submissiveness. But having admitted them as pupils Atharvan said to them: "My pupils utter at the beginning of the study of all the Vedas that great word which stands at the head of the Veda which is named after me; thereby the Mantras of the Vedas bring fruit. If you do not say the beginning of the Atharvaveda in the works of your Vedas, then your works will be defective and fruitless and will harm him who offers and also him who makes offer. Therefore

---

[consonantal] supplementation mentioned earlier. The first stands there to bring about an open sound, the second [*m*] stands there to bring about a consonant. A consonantal euphony does not take place. As far as the verbal form, preposition, grave, circumflex, gender, case and the pronunciation[1] are further concerned, it is given by the old teachers studying its constitution, who say: "One learns it only by hearing, one does not ask about a cause". But the wise Pañcālacaṇḍa of the opposite party asked them and said: "You should some time point out to me by turn and individually (*anu u pṛthag*?[2]) the mistakes which one is likely to commit in the matter of the Udgītha" Therefore one should be attentive to the division according to letters, syllables, words and signs; one thus holds in honour the speech which is prized by the wise. Therefore we discuss the cause,

1. See our note under 5.—GBP.
2. The Bibliotheca Indica ed. reads *babhūvāṁ vu pṛthag*, the Adyar ed. *babhūvāṁbuḥ* p°. The text continues to be obscure.—GBP.

teach your descendants, to do so; thus the Ṛg-, Yajur- and the Sāmaveda will bring fruit". Then the Ṛṣis said: "Be it so, O venerable one; we are free from fear and grief and are full of joy."

29. (The answer is missing; it is to be gathered from the Brahmavidyā, Atharvaśikhā 1 and the First Brāhmaṇam of this Praṇava-Upaniṣad.)

30. Therefore it happens that the students of the Veda utter the great word *Om* before the Mantras, works and the sections of the Veda, viz. of the Ṛg-, Yajur- and Sāmaveda.

31-34. When they utter the Praṇava at the beginning of the Ṛgveda, its divinity is Fire, its light the Praṇava, its metre the Gāyatrī, its place the earth; and they begin with the first verse of the Ṛgveda, because it praises the fire (Ṛgv. 1,1,1: *agnim īḷe* etc.)

And when they utter the Praṇava at the beginning of the Yajurveda, its divinity is Wind, its light the Praṇava, its metre the Triṣṭubh, its place the atmosphere, because it praises the rain (Vāj. Saṁh. 1,1,1: *iṣe* [=*vṛṣṭyai*] *tvā* etc.)

And when they utter the Praṇava at the beginning of the Sāmaveda, its divinity is the Sun, its light the Praṇava, its metre

---

because we believe that this contributes to the health of letters and we, who know the six Vedāṅgas, study it in this way.

What is its metre ? Its metre is the Gāyatrī, for the Gāyatrī of the gods is declared as mono-syllabic and white in colour. So much about the two groups of twelve each. This therefore is its analysis, the explanation of the meaning of its root, its phonetical treatment and explanation of its metre. Now as far as the last two groups of twelve each are concerned, the esoteric teaching of the Veda [regarding the Om-sound] has been explained. Formula, ritual and sacred speech are found in the Ṛg-, Yajur-, Sāma- and Atharvaveda, but this is a sacred exclamation as it is used in turn in the four Vedas, viz. the exclamations: *Om bhūr*, *bhuvar* and *svar*.

28. As a means to put to the test the non-circumspect, the following is handed down. At the beginning of the *Dvāparam*

the Jagatī, its place the heaven, and they begin with the first verse of the Sāmaveda, because it praises the fire (Sāmav. 1,1,1: *agna' āyāhi* etc.)

And when they utter Praṇava at the beginning of the Atharvaveda, its divinity is the Moon, its light the Praṇava, its metre all metres, its place the water, and they begin with the first verse of the Atharvaveda because it praises the water (Atharvav. 1,6,1[1]: *Śaṁ no devīr* etc.)

35. This is the water from which everything movable and immovable has sprung up. Therefore everything is water, one should know, and everything Atharvaveda. Therefore the water and the Praṇava is the same; for the water is called *ap* and *ap* is, as *o*, the initial sound of the Praṇava. Therefore the Ṛṣi Vyāsa has said, those who follow the injunctions of the Atharvaveda, do not study any Veda on the last day of the month of Śrāvaṇa, because it will not bring any profit. Therefore one who desires to claim the Vedas should study the Atharvaveda; without this, it is profitless. The Sāmaveda is

---

age a particular Ṛṣi, author of a fault just here, hit upon an idea of drinking Soma by means of the three Vedas and thought that that should suffice. The consequence of this was that the Ṛg-, Yajur- and the Sāma- songs lost their lustre. Then the great Ṛṣis lamented and said: "We have come to great grief and fear, and that [which is to be done] is not transmitted by the ancestors. Come on. Let us go all together to [Atharvan] worthy of veneration". [The latter said to them:] "I shall be the shelter of all of you".—"Be it so" said they and stood silently. "Not, if you do not approach submissively", said he. "We will approach you submissively" they said and prostrated themselves before him. But after admitting them as pupils he said: "You should employ every time as the beginning the exclamation proper to me; that is how they recite, those who are my pupils.

The Soma is not to be drunk except by those who knows the Bhṛgu-and the Aṅgiras-formulas (the Atharvaveda); otherwise

1. This is the reference to the current Śaunaka recension. The stanza is 1,1,1 (and hence the symbol of the Atharvav.) in the now discovered Paippalāda recension,—GBP.

the greatest, because it brings the fruit if one reads it with Tapas; but the Atharvaveda brings this fruit even without Tapas. Therefore, one who studies the Atharvaveda knows the three other Vedas also, for they are contained in it.—Thus reads the instruction of the Veda.

36. But the main result of the Atharvaveda is that one suffering from the ignorance of the Ātman is cured by the Praṇava which is the beginning of the Atharvaveda. And it is the fruit of the meditation of the Praṇava that one becomes the pure Ātman. By meditating over the Praṇava one should unite in the heart the individual and the highest soul; then one leaves all scriptures and remains as consisting of the highest Ātman: "I am Om! this is the state of the submerging; in this state one lets go all duality and obtains indistinguishable submerging (*nirvikalpa samādhi*), in which one remains without "I" and without "this" as the pure Ātman.

---

the sacrificial priests perish, the scrificer is covered with impurity and the holy scripture also remains dusty. So you should teach it in an ever continuing tradition to each coming generation, then the lustre will not be lost". – "Be it so, be it so, O sir", with these words they assented him, prospered and were free from grief and fear. Therefore the teachers of Brahman employ the Om-sound at the beginning.

29. What divinity has it? For the Ṛcs the divinity is Agni, the same the light-principle, the Gāyatrī the metre, the earth the place. *Agním īḷe puróhitam yajñásya devám ṛtvíjam, hótāram ratnádhatamam* Ṛgv. 1,1,1), beginning with these words they study the Ṛgveda.

For the Yajus' the divinity is Vāyu, the same the light, the Triṣṭubh the metre, the atmosphere the place. *Iṣe tvā ūrje tva, vāyava stha devo vaḥ savitā prārpayatu śreṣṭhatamāya karmaṇe* (Vāj Saṁh. 1,1,1), beginning with these words they study the Yajurveda.

For the Sāmans the divinity is Āditya, the same the light, the Jagatī the metre, the heaven the place, *Agna' āyāhi vitaye gṛṇāno havyadātaye, ni hotā satsi barhiṣi* (Sāmav. 1,1,1), beginning with these words they study the Sāmaveda.

One who has understood these questions well becomes omniscient, he knows the answer to all questions.

For the Atharva-songs the divinity is the moon, the same the light, all metres the metre, the water the place. *Śam no devīr abhiṣṭaye* (Atharvav. 1,6,1),[1] beginning with these words they study the Atharvaveda. The whole host of beings, movable and immovable, springs from waters, therefore everything has come from water, everything comes from the Bhṛgu- and Aṅgiras-songs. The other three Vedas have gone into Bhṛgu- and Aṅgiras-songs. Therefore, the water is called *ap*, and the origin of waters is from the Om-sound. Therefore Vyāsa[2] said formerly : "One who is initiated by a knower of the Bhṛgu- and Aṅgiras-songs, should study the other Vedas, but even without being initiated by another, one may study the Bhṛgu- and Aṅgiras-songs."[3] Also in the Sāmaveda a supplementary text says : "Therefore also one who learns as the Brahman-student the Bhṛgu- and the Atharvan-songs, he has thereby learnt everything".—Thus reads the Brāhmaṇam.

30. With reference to the self :

The Om-sound is the healing of the Ātman and the liberation of the Ātman. Shutting his Ātman in himself one should meditate on the thought, based only on the union with it, [thought] of its [of the Om-sound] real sense;[4] then one elevates oneself above the Vedas and obtains the full reward of the

---

1. This is the reference to the current Śaunaka recension. The stanza is 1,1,1 (and hence the symbol of the Atharvav.) in the now discovered Paippalāda recension.—GBP.

2. In the Adyar ed. the Upaniṣad ends abruptly with *caitasmād Vyāsaḥ*, the editor there however does not seem to be aware of the abrupt termination.—GBP.

3. Deussen's translation of this last clause is not quite correct. (Had he a different reading before him ?) Patyal (ibid) translates better : "and he who is consecrated elsewhere, should not study the Veda of the Bhṛgus and Aṅgiras."—GBP.

4. I have translated Deussen literally. The sentence remains obscure. Unconvincing is Patyal's translation also : "Having stopped the anxiety about creatures, (which is) the only union (with Om), he should think about the (supreme) spirit."—GBP.

highest inner self; that is the meaning [of the Om-sound]. One who meditates on it [Om-sound], subjected to reflection, having the nature of knowledge, through corresponding questions and answers, appropriate to the word, he is an expert, powerful and wanted at every Vedic conference. — Thus reads the Brāhmaṇam.

X. SCHAVANK

(ŚAUNAKA UPANIṢAD)[1]

[The wise "Schavank", to whom the teaching of this Upaniṣad is attributed, is without doubt *Śaunaka* (cf. Oupnek'hat I, 375 with the Muṇḍ. 1,1,3, above), although a Śaunaka Upaniṣad, as far as we know, is nowhere else mentioned. The legend imitated from the old myth of war between the Devas and the Asuras forms the contents in order to glorify the Om-sound (*praṇava*). The demons attack thrice, at 1. Prātaḥsavanam, 2. Mādhyandinasavanam and 3. Tṛtīyasavanam the sacrificial priests and receive from them as settlement. 1. drops of sacrificial clarified butter, 2. sacrificial water, 3. tips of sacrificial grass with which they thrice defeat the gods headed by 1. Vasus, 2. Rudras, 3. the Jagatī, and since these do not feel sufficiently strong, Indra prefixes them every time with the Om-sound, as a result of which the demons are defeated. But twice the demons recover from their defeat while the Praṇava, ashamed of showing himself to the gods, withdraws himself from the Mātrās into the reverberation (cf. also the Chānd, 1,4), and only the third time, when he appears in his full glory, he defeats the demons for ever.

The Praṇava- and Śaunaka-Upaniṣad are closely connected in purpose, contents and bearing; in the glorification of the Om-sound they go farther than all other Upaniṣads received by us and as such are not without interest. Unfortunately, even now the latter had to be understood only through the muddy medium of the translation of a translation,[2] both of which, the one through excessive freedom and the other through excessive faithfulness, have equally contributed much to disfigure the contents. We may hope to have reconstructed correctly the original text on the whole; but in many individual case. we were left to our own guess and we cannot everywhere assume responsibility for having handled it correctly.]

The gods and demons were preparing for war; Indra however had not yet joined the gods.

1. In the morning pressing the gods placed the Ṛṣis and the Vasus in front to conquer the demons and prepared for the war. But during the course of the sacrifice the demons appeared and said to the Ṛṣis : "Let us sacrifice with you so that today we shall win a victory over the gods ! "The Ṛṣis were frightened and gave them that much clarified butter which one is to pour

1. The Adyar ed. pp. 51-54.—GBP.
2. Now, of course, we have the Sanskrit original in the Adyar ed. —GBP.

in the fire at a sacrifice and said : "With this you will conquer the gods." The demons took it and with it they conquered the gods. Then Indra said to Gāyatrī : "Lead the gods to victory !" She said : "I see the gods retreating, what can I do with them?" Then Indra made Praṇava the constant beginning of the Gāyatrī and said : "This one will protect you." Then Gāyatrī said : "If this one leads me, then he will take a share in my fame." Indra said : "Do not be afraid that he will share with you. His greatness is superior to all and does not share in the greatness of others. The whole world rests on his greatness. You have nothing to do with the Praṇava but have to go to the Vasus for help."— "Om" (be it so), said the Gāyatrī. The Praṇava said : "It is my condition that they begin every work with me. If not, then I shall not help them."—"Om" (be it so), said the gods. That is to say, when one says "Om", all names and forms are contained in it; for the Praṇava is everything and contains everything; therefore one calls it "the one syllable" (*eka-akṣaram*, allegedly from *aś* surround, pervade *vyāptau*). Therefore one says : "Om, I will do this", and when they allow him this, they say "Om", and when they wish to speak, all say "Om". This sound grants victory and is constant and contains in it all beings; it is only a syllable and yet infinite; being infinite, it is one and contains all forms, sounds, smells, tastes and touches. Therefore they call the Praṇava Indra. Verily, all syllables and all beings are linked with this one syllable, all the Vedas and all the sacrifices are under its power. And just as everything is under Indra's power, because he is the king above all, so everything is under the power of Praṇava; he is the king of all syllables.

Therefore they utter the Praṇava softly and lightly in the mornings; for when the demons were near, the gods uttered it softly; there the Praṇava became light to them and said : "Lightly I shall crush your enemies".

Therefore, the Mantras also, which are preceded by the Praṇava, are said softly in the morning; and because the Gāyatrī was linked with it, therefore all the Mantras, which they recite in the morning, are linked with Gāyatrī, and the gods of the morning offerings are the Vasus.

Then the Praṇava said : ''While I am everything and the beginning of the Gāyatrī, what will be my reward for the help I give to the gods ?"

Indra said : "This, that they first utter you in the Sāmans, and when they sing the Sāman, they will sing you as all the syllables." Therefore it happens that when they sing the Sāman, they sing the Praṇava as all syllables.

The Praṇava pondered: "If I am as all syllables, then the gods will see all my forms, and that is not good." Then he withdrew all his forms within himself and concealed himself in the reverberation; he was hornless (without the moras). Therefore they ran after the hornless one, in order to search for him. And they said : "The power, the seed, the light, the indestructible, the flawless, all that is the reverberation." Therefore one obtains the light, the indestructible, the flawless through the reverberation.

And it happened that the demons were defeated and the gods won.

This Praṇava is Indra, is everything that exists. The Gāyatrī, the Sāman, the Vasus, the morning pressing, all that is the Praṇava. Indra is the movable and the immovable. so they say but Indra is the Praṇava.

2. But the defeated demons gathered again and as the midday-pressing Sāman was being chanted, they made their appearance at the sacrifice. The Ṛṣis were frightened and gave them of the water which is used at the sacrifice and said : "With this you will conquer the gods." The demons were desirous of conquering the gods with the water. And Indra sent the Rudras with the gods in the battle, but the gods were defeated by the demons. Then Indra said to Triṣṭubh: "Go to them for aid !" "She said: "The gods are defeated, what can I do with them ?" Then Indra again said to the Praṇava : "Place yourself at the head of the Triṣṭubh". The Praṇava said : "What will be my reward ?" Indra said : "What I am, that you are; they will pronounce you as my form."

The Praṇava pondered : "The gods will see full truth about me, and that is not good". Then he withdrew all his forms within himself and concealed himself in the reverberation.

Therefore they do not pronounce its third horn (*m*), but an Anusvāra (*ṁ*) in its place.

And it happened that the demons were defeated and the gods won.

Therefore the gods at the midday-pressing are the Rudras, and their metre is the Triṣṭubh.

3. But the demons prepared once more and as the evening-pressing Sāman was being chanted they appeared at the sacrifice. The Ṛṣis were frightened, they tore off the tips of the blades of the sacrificial grass, gave them to the demons and said : "With these you will conquer the gods." Then Indra said to Jagatī : "Go to the gods for aid !" Then Jagatī said : "The gods are defeated, what can I do ?" Then Indra placed the Praṇava at the head of the Jagatī. The Praṇava said : "What will be my reward, that I help the gods?" Indra said : "They will pronounce you with the Udgītha, so that your glory will be visible." And he made the Āditya[1] the leader of the gods. Therefore, the divinity of the evening-pressing is the Āditya and their metre the Jagatī. The Praṇava perceived : "The Udgītha is the manifestation of the Āditya, the manifestation of the Brahman, and I am the manifestation of the Brahman and not different from him." And he walked with his full form, which he had previously concealed in the reverberation, in front of the Āditya, and the Āditya made him his weapon. Then he defeated the demons, and they were scattered as dust, so that they could not again come together. That the Praṇava appeared in his full form, thereby he earned great fame, for the Praṇava is the pinnacle of greatness. All beings are contained in him, and his abode is in the reverberation, for in it he had concealed himself.

Therefore, what one desires, one should request him for it, and the worship one performs belongs to him.

Therefore it is said :
The Praṇava[1] has four horns, three feet,
Two heads, seven hands, threefold is he

1. The German original has singular but the plural (as supported by the Adyar ed.) is evidently intended.—GBP.

Bound, great, loudly roaring, shining brightly,
Having entered into all the living beings. (cf. Ṛgv. 4,58,3)

His four horns are the 3½ moras; his three feet are *a*, *u* and *m*; his two heads *o* and *m*; his seven hands are the seven notes (*svara*), because he is sung in all the seven. Threefold bound are its three letters (*a*, *u*, *m*) with the three fires, the three worlds and the three Vedas; like these he is also talked of.

The Praṇava is Indra and therefore great.
Therefore it is said :
The lord over all gods, great is Indra,
Granting greatness, mitigating grief, full of light,
Helping all, ruler, mighty, granting strength,
Sustaining the universe, well-disposed to all.

Because Indra supports himself in this way, therefore it was said that the Praṇava rings loudly; and it rings loudly because all, who worship him, earn great fame. That he has entered into all living beings (*prāṇin*) means that he dwells in all beings (*bhūta*). Therefore one should worship Indra by the syllable *Om*.

Thus spake the revered Śaunaka.

---

1. Apparently the Persian-Latin version read here *Praṇavo* for *vṛṣabho* of the ṚV (which latter is found in the Adyar ed. also).—GBP.

INDEX

The figures refer to the pages. The abbreviations Mu, Da, Co and Nā signify the Upaniṣadic collections of the Muktikā-Upaniṣad, Darashakoh (Oupnek'hat), Colebrooke and Nārāyaṇa respectively. [N (after a page-reference)=foot Note.]

etc., which is then further analysed into *akṣara*-s 881. The meanings often pass over into one another
Akṣi-Upaniṣad (only Mu) 557
Ālambāyanīputra N. of a teacher, 543
Ālambīputra, N. of a teacher, 543.
alātacakram, the firebrand circle, 363
Alātaśānti "Extinction of the firebrand" (title of Gauḍ. Kār. IV) 608, 626 ff
All-atonement sacrifice (*sarvaprāyaścittīyam*) 648, 649
Allopaniṣad (an Islamic Upaniṣad) 556
All-property sacrifice (*sarvavedasa Kratu*) 268 N, 270, 275
alms-giving (liberality, *dānam*), as cardinal virtue, 508 praised 262, 264; is duty of a *Gṛhastha* 98 and for him means of Knowledge 499. Its essence is asceticism 253; it comes in the place of Dakṣiṇā 115. The Saṁnyāsin should live on alms alone 455, 576, 738, 748, 750, 754, 761, 766, but should not give any alms 750 (? cf. the note)
ama and *sā* "he and she" (in word-play on *sāman*) 76 ff. (Cf. 137), 407
āmaṁsi āmaṁhi te mahi 532
Ambā-s and *Ambāyavī*-s, groups of Apsaras' in the Brahman-world, 27
Ambarīṣa, N. of a king, 332
ambayāḥ, rivers in the Brahman-world 27
ambhaḥ, the heavenly ocean, 13
Ambhiṇī, as a female teacher, 544
Amitaujas, sofa in the Brahman-world, 27
Amṛtabindu-Upaniṣad 692-698; (Mu, Da, Co, Nā) 556, 560, 561, 563, called *Amṛtanāda-Up.* by those who give the name *Amṛtabindu-Up.* to the Brahmabindu-Up. (Mu, Da and Śaṁkarānanda).
amṛtaṁ satyena channam 424
amṛtam, nectar, ambrosia, 103ff, 648, 886
Amṛtanāda-Upaniṣad, Name of the *Amṛtabindu-Up.* acc. to some (q.v.)
amulet, possibly already 278; 664, 828, 830, 859. cf. applying and diagram
ana (=*prāṇa*) breath, vital breath, 136, 406, 407, 420, 524
Ānabhimlāta, N. of a teacher, 442
anaḍvān, bull, the sun 320. Brahman 677, 680
ānanda 1) bliss (q. v.); 2) carnal pleasure 30, 42, 48-50, 245 N. 436 (504), 479
ānandamaya (*puruṣa*, *ātman*, *kośa*), 234, 237, 240, 246, 611 (825, 838, 883), 657, 659
ānandasya mīmāṁsā, consideration of bliss, 239 ff, 491 ff
Ānandavallī, N. for Taitti. Up., 2 (232-240)
Anaṅga ("bodyless"), epithet of the god of love, 872
Ananta, king of the snakes (=Śeṣa), 871
Anantaka, chief of the snakes (prob. =Ananta), 664
Anaraṇya, N. of a king, 332
ancestors (forbears) 164, 209, 331, 499, 527, 549, 550, 934, 937
ancestors (manes) and the world of ancestors 239, 297, 421, 448, 528.
ancestor-worship, 41 (Introd.) 148, 264, 290, 415, 464, 653-654
ancient (original), the, is Brahman 283, 285, 314, 775 (Rudra), 794, 908; the ancient Brahman 249, 498
Āndhra-recension (of the Mahānār. Up.) 247
Aṅgada, son of the monkey-king Bālin and comrade-in-arms of Rāma, 870
aṅgam limb; 1) subsidiary rite 21; 2) subsidiary formula, see *Aṅgamantra*-s; 3) Ancillary treatises of the Veda, see *Vedāṅga*-s
Aṅgamantra-s, the four subsidiary formulas of the Nṛsiṁha formula (*Praṇava*, *Sāvitrī*, *Lakṣmī* and *Gāyatrī*) 810, 814, 825 ff
anger of a Brāhmaṇa dangerous even for gods 904; cf. 277
Aṅgir as ancestral teacher of Angiras, probably derived from it, only 570, 571
Aṅgiras 1) plur., mythical beings, mediators between gods and men, whence in the Ṛgv-Agni said to be their first; so (along with *Vasu*-s, *Rudra*-s *Āditya*-s, *Sādhya*-s) 381. The songs of the Atharvaveda are ascribed to them, along with *Atharvan*, therefore they are called *Atharva-Aṅgirasaḥ* (q.v.), also *Aṅgirasaḥ*, *Bhṛgu-Aṅgirasaḥ* 939, 940, 941 or (sing.) Aṅgiras (832). 2) Sing., ancestor of the

Āraṇyaka-s (forest texts), a class of Vedic texts, 3, 12; remcommended only to the Saṁnyāsin 742
Arimardana (=*Śatrughna*) 870
arka (ray, fire, song of praise) 350, 401
Ārṣeya-Brāhmaṇam of the Sāma-veda 61, 62
Ārṣeya-Upaniṣad 919-923; (only Da) 560
Ārtabhāga Jāratkārava, N. of a man (participating in a discussion), 450-452
Ārtabhāgīputra, N. of a teacher, 543
arteries wrap the heart 258.—101 arteries extend from out of the heart 196, 299; they are filled with five-coloured sap 57, 195, 489, 497 (six-coloured 368, 673), corresponding to the five-coloured solar rays 196, 497. According to another view 72,000 arteries spread in the pericardium, 429, (understood differently 670, 674). These 101 or 72,000 arteries are the seat of the soul in the deep sleep, 196, 429, cf. 727. A combination of the two views enumerates 727210201 arteries, 595, or declares the 101 arteries as the most prominent, 673. In the body 700 arteries are enumerated, 644; three main arteries 649, their names *Iḍā*, *Piṅgalā* and *Suṣumnā* 674
arthavāda, a constituent part of the Brāhmaṇas, 1
Aruṇa, (father and) teacher of Uddālaka, 544
āruṇa (*—ketuka*) *agni*, a particular kind of piling up the altar, 219, 269
Arundhatī, a healing plant, 787
Āruṇeya- (*Āruṇi*- *Āruṇīya*- *Āruṇika*-) *Upaniṣad* 741-743 (Mu, Da, Co, Nā) 556, 559, 561, 563
Āruṇī, son of *Aruṇa* (see *Uddālaka Āruṇī*) 25 ff, and (incorrectly) grandson of the same (see *Auddāki Āruṇi*) 277. —Questions Prajājāpati 741 (cf. however *Ā. Suparṇeya*). An ascetic of past 761
Āruṇi Suparṇea questions Prajāpati 263 ff. cf. 741
Arunmukha-s (*Arurmagha*-s) vanquished by Indra 45
Ārya, belonging to the three upper castes, 3
Aryaman N. of an Āditya, 221, 231, 823
Āryā—metre, used only at 690
āśāmbara 754 (=*digambara*); see naked
āśīḥsamṛddhi, fulfilment of desire, 72
Āśrama-s, the four stages of life as *Brahmacārin*, *Gṛhastha*, *Vānaprastha* and *Saṁnyāsin* in which the life of an Ārya is supposed to proceed, 3; on its origin 97-98, 341, 619, 764 ff; one gone beyond them 734; cf. the *atyāśramin* 301, 326
Āśrama-Upaniṣad 764-766; Mu (partly as Bhikṣuka) 557, Co 561, Nā(?) 564
Āśramin 341 (=*snātaka*) 735
Aśvala, N. of a Hotṛ priest, 446
Āśvalāyana asks 791; *Ā. Kausalya* 589-595; *Ā.* the pupil of Śaunaka, 7, 11
aśvamedha, horse-sacrifice, 12, 219, 269, 328, 391, 452ff; re-interpreted 399ff
Aśvapati 332; *Ā. Kaikeya* king 149, 919 (K'hak)
aśvattha, tree (*ficus religiosa*) 296 (256, 313, 348, 256)
Aśvin-s, Vedic pair of gods, 440ff, 540, 896; as teachers 443, 506; are Nārāyaṇa 804; *Āśvinaṁ śastram* 8
asambhava, *asambhūti* "dissolution" (=*vināśa*; contradictory opposition instead of the contrary), 550.
asaṅga "not sticking" to the world, to the objective, is the *puruṣa* (the subject of cognition) 463, 473, (481, 499, 505), 488, 634, 635, 637, 847, 857
āsanya prāṇa=*mukhya-prāṇa* (q.v.) 405
ashes, the body becomes ashes 519, (551). Everything is ashes 776 (790). Sacrifice (vainly) in ashes 155. Drink ashes 750. Besmear oneself with ashes 776 (790). Touching with ashes 664
aṣṭācatvāriṁśa, a *Stoma* consisting of 48 verses, 62
Aṣṭādhyāyī, the 11th book of Śatap. Br., 390
aṣṭarātra, a nine-day Soma-ceremony, 63
Asita Vārṣagaṇa, N. of a teacher, 544.
asceticism (penance, mortification, *tapas*), of the world-creator 238, 349. (weakening him) 401, 418, 590, 813; abstractly as creative principle 291, 573. As product

of creation 266, 603. Is specially the duty of the Vānaprastha 98, 499, 578, 579, 591, 600. (all these passages have the Āśrama-s in view). A° is every virtue 253, 264, but the renunciation (*nyāsa*) stands higher 263, 267. By itself alone it does not bring peace 126, it brings only a transitory reward 464, leads only to Pitṛyāna 528, also 145 (differently 576); Brahmacarya stands higher 195; A° is to be combined with the study of the Veda 228. Is of worth in so far as it frees from evil 343 and as the foundation 213, and as the preparatory means of knowledge 26, 243 ff, 308 (731, 732), 326, 331, 342, 584, 590, 592, 904, still it must be genuine 585. Note 3; it helps to steady the heart 738, and is to be practised moderately by the Saṁnyāsin 748. It takes the place of the cult of sacrifice 115, 267, but is itself replaced by the sufferings of life and death 513, by the sound *Om* 284, by pure knowledge 573 (734). Rudra practises asceticism 776, is himself asceticism 777

asparśayoga, nontouch Yoga, 608, 624, 626

Asura-s, demons, a class of beings beside gods and men, 400, 508, 886; are pupils of Prajāpati 508, but are misinstructed by him, by Brahman, by Bṛhaspati in the form of Śukra 383. They are defeated by Rāma 869, are perishable 333, they are sought to be exorcized 382. In battle with gods, Indra etc., or with the sense organs, they are at first victorious 58, 69, 404, oppress the city of Indra 929, their weapons are made of sacrificial ingredients 943ff, and by similar one they are defeated by gods 265

Āsurāyaṇa, N. of a teacher, 443, 506; differently 543

Āsuri, N. of a teacher, 443, 506; differently 543

Atharva=Atharvan

Atharvan, mythical priest of antiquity; participates in the creation 734, 776; instructed by Brahmán 571, instructs *Aṅgir* 571, *Pippalāda*, *Aṅgiras* and *Sanatkumāra* 780, the Ṛṣis of antiquity 937. (Plur.) authors of the Atharvaveda 680, 681, therefore *Atharvānaḥ* 814 and (sing.) 832 the songs of the Atharvaveda

Atharvan Daiva, N. of a teacher, 443, 506

Atharvāṅgirasaḥ, the songs of the Atharvaveda, 103, 237, 372, 436, (370), 476, 503, 593, 770, 773, 800, 941

Atharvaśikhā-Upaniṣad 780-782, mentioned 832; (Mu, Da, Co, Nā) 557, 559, 561, 563

Atharvaśiras, "main part of the Atharvan" 805, 778(?)

Atharvaśira'-Upaniṣad 770-778, mentioned 832; (Mu, Da, Co, Nā) 556, 559, 561, 563

Atharva-Upaniṣads, classified, 567; editions 558, 559, 639N. 640N.

Atharvaveda, the fourth Veda, 1; this name first occurs 572 (previously *Atharvāṅgirasaḥ*, *Ātharvaṇa* scil *Veda* etc.)

Atidhanvan Śaunaka, N. of a teacher, 80

Atigraha, "super-seizor", eight 449 ff, 771; cf. *graha*

Āṭikī, N. of a woman, 81

Atirātra, Soma-sacrifice with 29 Śastras 8, 63, 378, 832

ātithyam, Ceremony in Soma-sacrifice, 8

ativāda, the talking down [i.e. surpassing somebody in speaking] from which

ativādin, talking down [i.e. surpassing somebody in speech], 185. 343 N 1, 583

Ātmabodha- (*Ātmaprabodha-*) *Upaniṣad* 807-808, 808. (only Mu, Da) 557, 559 (on Nā, cf. 565, 807).

Ātman (masc.), breath, vital breath, 121 (in a citation). 1) The self 18, 34, 37, 96, 210, 236ff, 285, 360 (*nirātman*), 413, 416, 434 ff. 469, 501ff. The individual person, 77, 421, 548, person 129. Reflexive pronoun 73, 89 etc. The body 57-58, 85, 96 (embodiment). 225, 227 (world-body). 235 (trunk). 292, 298, 400, 424, 427; *śārīra ātman* 236, 481, 492. The true essence of anything 53ff, 58, 422, 435. The essence, spirit 401. 2) The (individual) soul 51, 111, 163 (*jīva ātman*), 168, 169 (of plants), 204, 287, 290, 292, 293, 306, 307, 314, 337, 413, 440, 469 (manas). 493, 498, etc., as essence or unity of vital

B

that *Ātman* appears as the more recent and more distinctive expression, *Brahman* the older and more recognized, 52 (425), 454 etc.; therefore *bráhman* for 5) "principle" in general, e.g. 305 Note 1. 476 ff. Where the two expressions are differentiated, there *brahman* is the cosmic principle, to be determined, *ātman* the psychic, determining, principle 110 ff, 495, 838, 851 ff.—The Brahman has, according to 107 (Ṛgv. 10, 90, 3) four feet, which are determined variously 116, 124 ff, 386, 516 ff. The gods are dependent on its will, 211 ff; the world is the Brahman-egg 117, 741, 887, 905; the popular gods and deified heroes are its manifestations, 343, 863; the (neutr.) Bráhman created the (masc.) Bráhman 926. The *Bráhman* as teacher 444, 506, 544.—Cf. lower and higher knowledge

Brahmán (masc.) 1) the god Brahmán, the personified Bráhman, 27, 106, 205, 343, 344, 346, 570, 571. (Born out of Nārāyaṇa 800, 803; worships Rāma 885 ff) *Brahmán Svayambhū* as teacher 21; *Brahmán, Viṣṇu, Śiva* (*Rudra, Īśvara*) 647, 856, 886; *Brahmán, Viṣṇu, Rudra, Turīyam* 728, 844, 849. 2) The fourth and the highest of the priests (Ṛtvij) 1, 9, 131, 267, who supervises over the sacrifice 133, 447

brāhmaṇa, Brahmin (significant), 120, 455; what determines him 910. As a sub-class of the Brahmacārin 764. — *brāhmaṇa, rājan, vaiśya* 36; *brāhmaṇa, rājanya, vaiśya, śūdra* 414, 894

brāhmaṇācchaṁsin, a sacrificial priest, assistant of Brahmán, reinterpreted 650

brahmaṇaḥ parimaraḥ, a ceremony, 9, 38, 245

brāhmaṇam, a class of Vedic texts, 1, 2, 217, 389

Brahmaṇaspati, a Vedic god (cf. *Bṛhaspati*) 407, 647, 823

Brahman-city (body) 191, 581, 599. (Brahman-dwelling) 585, 726, 805, 807

Brāhmaṇic dignity (*brahmavarcasam*) 109, 151, 153, 154, 244 ff

brahmarandhram, opening in the scull through which the soul departs; the thing already from 196 226. onwards, the name first, 719

brahmatatamam 18, Note

Brahma-Upaniṣad 726-732. Mu (as *Brahma-* and *Parabrahma-Up.*) 556-557. Co, Nā 561, 563

brahmavidyā, lore of prayer 176, 177, 180; lore of Brahman 413 (perhaps double-meaning). 571 ff etc. (misused, perverted) 663

Brahmavidyā-Upaniṣad 668-670. (Mu, Da, Co, Nā) 557, 559, 561, 563.

brahmodyam, rivalry in [discussion of] sacred objects, 445, 462, 464.

brain-shell (*śaṅkha*), perhaps more correctly (cf. 379, 710) heart-shell 669

Bṛhadāraṇyaka-Upaniṣad 399-544, (Mu, Da) 556, 559

Bṛhaddiva Sumnayu, N. of a teacher 22

Bṛhadratha, N. of a king, 331 ff

Bṛhajjābāla-Upaniṣad (only Mu) 557

Bṛhannārāyaṇa-Upaniṣad, see *Mahānārāyaṇa-Up*.

Bṛhant, a subclass of brahmacārin, 764

Bṛhaspati, Vedic god (=*Brahmaṇaspati*) 71, 96, 221, 231, 239-240, 813, 837; (differentiated from *Brahmaṇaspati*) 407; instructed by Yājñavalkya 758 (881). As teacher of demons 383 (probably therefore later the founder of the Cārvāka doctrine)

Bṛhaspatisava, one-day Soma-rite, 62

bṛhat, N. of a Sāman, 9, 28, 68, 93, 265, 380, 679

Bṛhatī (metre of 8+8+12+8 syllables) 10, 407, 927

Bṛhatsena, instructs Indra, 663

bricks (in Agnicayanam), 278, 371

bridge (damn, *setu*), the Ātman as b° 194. (381), of immortality 326, 581. The Nāciketa fire as b° 287

bubbles and ocean 681

buddhi, as specification of the individual soul, 321; perception in general, consciousness, understanding, thinking, insight 288, 312 (315), 370, 659, 794, intention 720. As special faculty beside *manas* 287, 288, 298 (368). 335, 353, 599, 619, 641, 650, 800, 840, (stamping the ideas of the *manas* into resolutions, whereupon they are executed by the *manas* through the organs of action)

buddhi-indriyāṇi "sense organs", five, first 434, 337, 644, 651, (fivefold *buddhi*) 642
Buddhistic and Buddhism 2, 329, 332 Note 3, 341, 382, 449, 451. Note, 513, 569, 607 (*atyantaśūnyavāda*)
Buḍila Āśvatarāśvi 149, 152, 518
bull, as teacher, 123
buzzing in the ears, whence, 109, 362, 512

C

Caikitāyana Dālbhya, N. of a participant in a discussion, 79
cakṣus, eye, q.v. and man in eye
Cākṣuṣī, a spirit in the Brahman-world 27
calmness (*śama*) 228, 262, 264, 366, 636. The calm (*śānta*) 110, 500; 326, 335 (366), 380, 576, 586, 694, 792, etc. The calm self (*śāntātman*) 289, 345, 781
Caṇḍāla 146, 155, *Cāṇḍāla*, a despised caste, 490, 728
Candra, *Candramas*, moon (-god), corresponding to the Manas 406, 894, 906 etc. (see moon)
Cannapurī (Madras) 4
car (and car-rider) 287, 310, 335, 337, 911 ff, 915
carakādhvaryu-s, followers of the Black Yajurveda, 390
case-relations, different, 931, 933
caterpillar (and blade) 495, 727
catuḥṣṭoma, a one-day Soma-rite 8, 62
caturhotāraḥ, a four-priest litany 327
cāturhotracayanam, a particular form of piling up altar, 219, 269.
cāturmāsyāni, four-month sacrifices 12, 21, 268, 269, 327, 390, 574
caturviṁśa, day of beginning of *Gavām ayanam*, 8-9
cause, of the nature of (*kāraṇa-rūpa*) : Nārāyaṇa 805, 808; on the other hand it springs out of him 807
Chāgaleya (?) Ṛṣi 912
Chāgaleya-Upaniṣad (? *Tschhakli*) 909-913. (only Da) 560
Chandoga-s, the singers of the Sāmaveda, 61
Chāndogyabrāhmaṇam of the Sāmaveda 61. Contents 63
Chāndogya-Upaniṣad 68-205. (Mu, Da) 556, 559
chandoma, N. of a Stoma, 62
childlikeness, as condition of the man of knowledge, 455, 910, 911
children, unnecessary for the man of knowledge, obstructive 366
chronology of the Upaniṣads 271-272, 301, 328-329, 579, Notes 1-2. 687 Introd. 713, 781 N3
citations. *Ṛgveda* : (1, 18, 6) 252; (1, 22, 20-21) 743; 833; (1, 40, 5) 823; (1, 50, 10) 116; (1, 89, 8.6) 813; 837; (1,89,8) 822; (1, 90, 9) 222; (1, 91, 16, 18) 35; (1, 114, 8) 319; 789; (1, 116, 12) 440; (1, 117, 22) 441; (1, 154, 2) 822; (1, 164, 12) 591; (1, 164, 20) 316; (1, 164, 39) 316; 826; 830; 929; (1, 164, 49) 542; (1, 189, 1) 519, 551, (2, 21, 6) 38; (2, 33, 11) 820; (3, 4, 9) 821; (3, 29, 2) 291; (3, 36, 10) 38; (4, 26, 1) 413; (4, 27, 1) 19; (4, 40, 5) 255, 293-294; (5, 78, 7-8) 540; (5, 82, 1) 138; (6, 17, 2) 824; (6, 47, 18) 442; (7, 32, 22) 774; (7, 59, 12) 789; (8, 6, 30) 116; (8, 48, 3) 772; (9, 96, 6) 254-255; (9, 113, 7) 808; (10, 81, 3) 251, 311; (10, 85, 22) 539; (10, 90) 893; cf. 257; (10, 90, 1-2) 313-314; (10, 90, 3) 107; (10, 97, 15) 646; (10, 121, 1-8) 250; (10, 121, 2) 823; (10, 121.3) 317; (10, 129, 4) 813; (10, 184) 540. —*Atharvaveda* : (3, 20, 1) 760; (4, 1, 1) 734; (6, 96, 1) 646; (7, 81, 5) 36 (7, 81, 5.6) 35; (10, 2, 26-27) 777; (10, 8, 9) 430; (10, 8, 16) 292; (10, 8, 27) 315; (10, 8, 29) 508; (11, 4, 13) 578; (11, 8) 736-737; 750; (18, 1-4) 735.—*Vājasaneyi-Saṁhitā* : (8, 36) 821; (11, 1-5) 309; (13, 6.8.7) 786; (16, 1.3.4) 784; (16, 2-3) 312; (16, 11.2.6.7.8.14) 784-785; (16, 9, 13, 10, 12.11) 785-786; (31, 18) 312; (31, 17-22) 250. 895; (32) 897; (32, 1) 250-315; (32, 2.3.4) 250-251; (32, 2.3) 318-319; (32.4) 311, 774; (32, 8-12) 251; (34, 1-6) 901.— *Taittirīya Saṁhitā* : (7, 5, 24) 375. —*Taittirīya-Brāhmaṇam* : (3, 10, 1, 2) 821; (3, 12, 9, 8) 817. *Taittirīya Āraṇyakam* : (1, 23) 813; (3, 10, 1, 1) 822; (10, 11-12) 917; (10, 12.47) 816; (10, 43) 789. —*Mahābhāṣyam* (1, 1, 38) 936. Cf. also the reminiscences of : *Āśvalāyana-Gṛhyasūtram* : (1, 13, 7) 35. *Mānavadharmaśāstram* : (3, 76) 378. —*Sāṁkhyakārikā* : (24) 339; (41) 360; (53) Cf. 340; (63) 339; (65) 338

E

kaivalyam (*kevalatvam* 361) state of absoluteness (liberation) 300, 791ff, 795, 916
kaivalya-Upaniṣad 791-795, (Mu, Da, Co, Nā) 556, 559, 561, 564
Kāla, the time, personified 677, 680, 719, 771. Brahman as time 355.
Kalā, part, personified 876
Kālāgni, the world-destruction fire, 792, 841
Kālāgnirudra, Rudra as world-destroyer, 917; teaches 789 ff
Kālāgnirudra-Upaniṣad 789-790, (Mu, Co, Nā) 557, 561, 564
Kālakañja-s, (cloud-) demons vanquished by Indra, 45
Kali (m.), the fourth and the worst of the four Yugas (*Kṛtam* or *Satyam, Tretā, Dvāpara, Kali*), began on the 18th Febr. 3102 B.C. and lasts 432000 years, only 816
Kālika, N. of a chief of snakes, 664
Kalisaṁtaraṇa-Upaniṣad (only Mu) 557
Kam, joy 400; as designation of Brahman 127 (like *Katama* 261, 265, *sukham* 187 and usually *ānanda* 232. etc)
Kambalāśvatara, N. of a chief of snakes, 664
kāmyāḥ paśavaḥ and *iṣṭayaḥ*, animal sacrifices and other sacrifices, undertaken for the accomplishment of specific objects 269
Kaṇṭhaśruti-Upaniṣad 747-51, (Mu as *Saṁnyāsa-Up.* and *Kaṭha-Up.*) 557. (Co, Nā) 561, 563
Kaṇva 1) old-Vedic Ṛṣi; 2) a prince, father of Medhātithi 903
Kāṇva, off-shoot of the Vājasaneyins, 390. — *Kāṇva-* and Mādhyandina-recension 488 N. 530N
Kāṇvīputra, N. of a teacher, 543
Kanyakubja, a city on the upper Gaṅgā (now Kanauj), 934
kapila 319 "red-brown" (gold-coloured), not *Kapila*
Kāpīputra, N. of a teacher, 543
Kapyāsa-lotus 77
Karkoṭaka, chief of snakes, 664
karmadevāḥ, gods, so become by meritorious deeds, 239, 492. Examples 495
karman (work), what doesn't die of man, 449, 452; cf. 495
Kārśakeyīputra, N. of a teacher, 543
Kārttika, N. of a month (Oct.-Nov.) 765
Kāśi-s, N. of a people, 52, 462, with the later capital *Kāśī* (Benares) 884
Kaśyapa, old-Vedic Ṛṣi, 430.—*Kaśyapa Naidhruvi*, N. of a teacher, 544
Kāṣāyaṇa, N. of a teacher, 505-506.
Katama, superlative of *Ka* or *Kam* (q. v.), 261, 265
Kaṭha-s, a school of the Black Yajurveda, 269
Kāṭhakam, Brāhmaṇa-work, contents, 269
Kāṭhaka-Upaniṣad, 275-300, (Mu, Da, Co, Nā) 556, 559, 561, 563
Kaṭha (*rudra*)-*Upaniṣad* (Mu) 557.= (Co, Nā) *Kaṇṭhaśruti-Up.* 3-5
Kātyāyanī, wife of Yājñavalkya, 434, 501
Kātyāyanīputra, N. of a teacher, 542
Kauṇḍinya, N. of a teacher, 442, 505
Kauravyāyaṇīputra, N. of a teacher, 508 (not in the lists.)
Kauśika, N. of a teacher, 442, 505.
Kauśikāyani, N. of a teacher, 443, 506
Kauśikīputra, N. of a teacher, 543
Kauṣītaki, N. of a teacher, 29, 34, 75; cf. *Kahola*
Kauṣītakin-s (—*Śāṁkhāyana*-s), a school of the Ṛgveda, 21
Kauṣītaki-Upaniṣad 25-58. (Only Mu, Da) 557, 559
Kausalya Āśvalāyana, N. of a participant in a discussion, 589, 595
Kausalyā, mother of Rāma, 866
Kautsa, N. of a teacher, 544
Kena-(*Talavakāra*-) *Upaniṣad* 209-213, (Mu, Da, Co, Nā) 556, 559, 561, 563
Khara, Brother of Rāvaṇa, slain by Rāma, 867
Khilakāṇḍam of the Bṛh. Up., 391 Contents 396, 507
Kim, prob. the god *Ka* (q. v.), conceived impersonally, 261
kings (or warriors), wiser than Brāhmaṇas and teaching them 25(?) 52 ff, 56, 79, 143, 173, 428, 526 ff,
kleśa, plague, misery, vexation 306; five (of Yoga) 306N18
knots of the heart 189, 299N 4, 581, 586, 660. K° of ignorance 579. For the origin of this concept, cf. 448 Introd.
kośa, the five sheaths (Taitt. 2) 233ff; so named first 365, 366, 621, 659, 855.
krama, southern progress of the sun, 356, (*dakṣiṇam ayanam*) 590

kramamukti, gradual liberation (the Devayāna as a merely preliminary stage of liberation) 297, 302, 308, 582
kramapāṭha, a way of Vedic recitation, 10
kratu, sacrificial rite, particularly Soma-ceremony (*Ind. Stud. II* 97 Note) 62, 265, 317, 377, 578, 778, 782, 832
Kratu Prajāpati, one of the seven or ten (enumerated Manu, 1, 35) prajāpatis, i.e. world-creating Ṛṣis, 333, 334-335
Krauñcikīputra, N. of a teacher, 543
Kṛṣṇa Devakīputra, as pupil of Ghora Āṅgirasa, 115; also as a man 805, 807
Kṛṣṇa-Upaniṣad (Mu, Nā) 557, 564
kṣatram, *kṣatriya*-s, the warrior-caste, 143, 204, 286, 414, 593. etc., explained as life 515
kṣetrajña, the conscious principle (*jña*) in contrast with *Pradhānam* 325, with *Liṅgam* (subtle body) 335, 345 or with the whole body 681, 728. Bhag. G. XIII
kṣetrapāla, a divinity guarding the fields, 875
Kṣurikā-Upaniṣad 672-675. (Mu, Da, Co, Nā) 557, 559, 561, 563
Kubera, god of richness, living in Himālaya cf. 112
Kulika, N. of a chief snake, 664
Kumārahārita, teacher, 443, 506, 535
Kumbhakarṇa, a brother of Rāvaṇa, slain by Rāma 869
Kuṇḍika-Upaniṣad (only Mu) 557, (Co, Nā 561, 563. *Saṁnyāsa-Up.*)
Kuru-s 81, 133 (?), *Kuru*-s and *Pañcāla*-s 52, 446, 471, two tribes (in the region of Delhi)
Kurukṣetram, land of the Kurus, 758, 881, (K'herk'hit) 910
Kuśri, N. of a teacher, 544
kūṭastha, defined 660
Kuṭīcara, a class of ascetics, 742; a sub-class of the Parivrājakas 765; cf. 741
Kutsāyana, N. of a poet, only 344
Kuvalayāśva, N. of a prince 332

L

Lakṣmaṇa, younger brother of Rāma 867 ff, 882
Lakṣmī, luck, beauty, Goddess of luck and beauty 824, 887. *Lakṣmī-yajus* of the *Nṛsiṁha*-formula 810, 815, 826
Laṅkā, residence of Rāvaṇa in Ceylon and Ceylon itself 869 ff.
laying of formulas etc. on the parts of body 719, 743, 789 ff, 866
lelāyati iva 314 N2, 486
leprosy; scab 120, cf. 918
liberation (*mokṣa*, *mukti* etc.) "from all bonds" 308, 310, 318, 322, 324, 775; bondage and liberation 325, 374 etc.; portrayed 496; defined 658. The soul is liberated from eternity 367, 629, 637; liberation is freeing from the Manas (as the organ of desire) 374, 688; liberation texts thrown away 374, 688, 707
life-span, hundred years (autumns) 38, 280, 547; hundred and sixteen, 114
lightning, as symbol of the timelessness of Brahman, 208, 212, 250, 432, 511, 807. criticised adversely 922. —the *Om*-sound shines like a flash of lightning 385
liṅgam, mark, 690 (Phallus 917); attribute 690; essence, nature 308. The inner man 495, the "subtle body" (the psychic organism) 298 Note 1, 323 Note 4, 353, 367. *liṅgam nirāśrayam* 360, Note 1, (*liṅgaśárīram*) 660
liquor, spirituous (*surā*) 146, 795; (*madyam*) 150
literary circle of the Upaniṣads : 176 ff (180), 436 (476, 503, cf. the observation 503), 572 (first mention of the six Vedāṅgas), 575 Note 2, 655 (*purāṇam*, *nyāya*, *mīmāṁsā*, *dharmaśāstram*), 832 (*śākhā*-s etc.) 886 (*aṅga*-s) *śākhā*-s, *purāṇa*-s)
Lokāyatika-s, materialists, 618 cf. 199 ff, 282, 382, 383
lotus-flower 129, 339, 347, 702; cf. heart as lotus-flower
love-spell 32
lower and higher knowledge (*aparā* and *parā vidyā*) mean 571 only Karmakāṇḍam and Jñānakāṇḍam; corresponding is 600 (348), 615, 619, 728 lower and higher Brahman. But when both these (*om*) are explained as *word-brahman*, and are distinguished from the wordless, highest Brahman 361, 689, herein lies the transition to the doctrine of *aparam* and *param* (*saguṇam* and *nirguṇam*) *brahma* (and correspondingly *vidyā*) in

sense 15, 406, 439, 447, 451. The tendency to identify the Manas with the Brahman 243, 479, 738, 901, and to conceive it as creating the world 401, 420, is probably based on the as yet incomplete separation of the subject of perception and the Manas. The Yoga is based on the bringing of the activity of the Manas to standstill, 373, 608, 624 ff, 686, 687, 688, 694, 720, 721
Mānasi, the genius of mind in the Brahman-world, 27
Maṇḍalabrāhmaṇa-Upaniṣad (only Mu) 557
maṇḍalam, circle, ambiguous 692
Māṇḍavya, N. of a teacher, 544
Māṇḍūkāyani, N. of a teacher 544
Māṇḍūkāyanīputra, N. of a teacher, 543
Māṇḍūkīputra, N. of a teacher, 543
Māṇḍūkya-Upaniṣad 611-615 (Mu, Da, Co, Nā) 556, 559, 561, 564
Maṇikarṇī, a holy Tīrtham in Benares, 884
Māṇṭi, N. of a teacher, 443, 506
mantra-s, songs and formulas of the Vedas (as opposed to those of the Brāhmaṇas 2, 62, 217) 177, 178, 184, 188, 573, 905, 928, 938, 944 etc. (as opposed to *vidhi* and *brahman* [=Upaniṣad ?] 936 — Formulas devised for the worship of Nṛsiṁha, Rāma etc. also so called, 864 etc.
mantrarāja, formula-king, 1) of Nṛsiṁha 810, 813 ff, 832, 833; its five attributes (heart, head, hair-tuft, armour, missile) 819; its *vījam*, *kīlaka*, *śakti* 823 ff; its limb-formulas 814, 824 ff; its diagram 830a; 2) of Rāma 859, 864; *vījam kīlaka*, *śakti* 866; diagram 871 ff. 3) of Haṁsa 717; six attributes (heart, head, hair-tuft, armour, three eyes, weapon) 719; *vījam*, *kīlaka*, *śakti* 719; diagram 719 ff
Mantrikā-Upaniṣad (Mu) 557 Note 3. (Da, Co, Nā *Cūlikā*-Up.)
Manu (man), the ancestor of the human race, standing between Prajāpati and the creatures 106, 205, 261, 413, 828. — Manu-period (*manvantaram*) 884 (consisting of 71 × 12000 × 360 years, Manusmṛti, 1, 79)
mānuṣam, the human in Nature, 438
Marut-s, wind-gods, 105, 380, 414, 780
Marut=*Bṛhadratha* 334, 368
Marut-stoma, a particular Ekāha, 62
Marutta, N. of a prince, 333
Marutvatīyam, a Śastram in the Soma-sacrifice, 8, 10
Mātariśvan (563 *-śva*) the Wind-god 211, 548, (the *Prāṇa*) 593
mātrā, mora, prosodial unit, duration of a short vowel, see *om*
mātrāsaṁsargas tu asya bhavati 504 Note
mātṛkam, state of a mother, 386
mātṛkāmantra 830
Matsya, a people, to the west of the upper Yamunā 52
maunam, silence (as religious observance), recommended 749; yet not the highest 195, 455. Cf. *muni*
māyā magic art 442, illusion, deception 308, 342 (*indrajālam*). 592, 793; delusion of empirical reality 316, 317, 618, 622, defined 661, 840. (Main text) 855 ff; more concrete as the mother of becoming, creator's power 679, 824, 865, occupying outer side in diagrams 829, cf. 876
Medhātithi son of Kaṇva, abducted by Indra 903 ff
memory (*smṛti smara*) 166 ff, 184. Request for a good memory 253, 256
mental, the, (*mānasam*) 263, 265; *puruṣo mānasaḥ* 528 Note 2
Metronyms, of teachers, how to be explained, 393
milk and butter 165, 308, 318, 690, 701, 715, 731, 732
milk-honey-butter, administered to the new-born baby, 541
milk-ocean 816
mīmāṁsā, consideration, inspection 149, 239, 422; as N. of a system 655
miner, looking for minerals in the mine (*avaṭa*) 366
mirage, *gandharvanagaram* 619; *indrajālam* 342, 382
mirror 54, 199, 297, 310, 470
Mitra, N. of an Āditya, 221, 231, 261, 542. *Mitra-Varuṇa* 381
mixed-drink ceremony, 133, 137, 521, 529 ff
moon (*Candramas*, *Candra*, *Soma*) 35, 109, 121 etc., described 906; originated out of Manas 15, 406, 894; passes through 27 'moon-stations' (Nakṣatras) 76, 95, 356, as the soul through the bodies,

916. (Sacrifice to the 'moon-stations' 218.) masculine 'moon-station' 529, Fast regulated by the lunar course 766. The moon as a station on the (Devayāna and the) Pitṛyāna, 25, 129, 145, 528 etc. Grows by the souls which reach her 25, 35, 53 Note 2 (opposite 36). —Moon in the lake 689

mother of pearl and silver 48N

mouth-rinsing (not towards the fire 92), as dressing of the Prāṇa in the Prāṇāgnihotram 137, 352, 524, 648, 760

Mṛtyu, death, god of death, 15, 16, 96, 239, 261; =Yama 275 ff, different from him 414, also 292

Mṛtyu Prādhvaṁsana as teacher, 443, 506

mṛtyujaya, formula for warding off death, 917

Mṛtyulāngala-Upaniṣad 917-918 (only Da) 560

Mudgala-Upaniṣad (only Mu) 557, 343 Note 2

Mukhyaprāṇa, vital breath in the mouth 71, 75 (=*āsanya-prāṇa* 405). Later the chief vital breath 423, 430

Muktikā-Upaniṣad (only Mu) 2, 4, 556, 557

mūlaprakṛti, ur-matter of the Sāṁkhyas, 882

muṇḍa, having the head shaved, for *Muṇḍaka-Upaniṣad* 569

Muṇḍaka-Upaniṣad 571-587 (Mu, Da, Co, Nā) 556, 559, 561, 564

Muni, as a rule the perfected "wise", 293, 499, 616, 620, 792; the hermit 262, 264, 706, 871, 876; his silence 775, cf. *maunam*. As a preparatory stage only 455

muscles, five hundred in body, 644

mystical words and formulas, intelligible only to the initiated 110N3, 137, 508, 648 Note 1; a mystical alphabet 873

N

Nāciketa agni and *Naciketas* 271 Note, 279 Note 2

Nāciketam (*cayanam*), N. of a particular form of altar-piling, 219, 269. Therefore *Nāciketa*-fire 278 ff, 906

Naciketas, son of Vājaśravasa; Gautama, Auddālaki Āruṇi, 275, 277 (Cf. 544 the names Vājaśravasa, Aruṇa, Uddālaka; see also Śvetaketu); 269 ff, 275 ff, 383

nāda, reverberation of *om* (q.v.) and of other sounds 700, 715, 719, 720 (tenfold), 781, 873, 881, 932, 934 (? *mad*) 947

Nādabindu-Upaniṣad 684-686. (Mu, Co, Nā) 557, 561, 563

Naghāriṣā, N. of a plant, 647

Nahuṣa, a king of antiquity, 332

Naimiṣa, *Naimiṣāraṇyam*, a holy forest on the Gomatī, in which Sauti narrates the Mahābhāratam to the Ṛṣis, 71, 910 (*nimkehar*)

naiṣṭhika, a life-long Brahman-student, 98, 764

Nāka Maudgalya, a Veda-teacher, 228, 535

nākasya pṛṣṭham, "the back of heaven", 452 Introd. 576

naked saṁnyāsins 754, 761

name, mere n° 162, 176. Is the immortal in man 449, 451. Names and forms (the empirical reality) 163, 204, 412, 424, 573, 586, 603, Cf. 27

names, tradition of, in Upaniṣads 155 ff

naming of the child 542

Nara=Nārāyaṇa 799

Nārada, an ancient Ṛṣi 663; is instructed 176, 753

Nāradaparivrājaka-Upaniṣad (only Mu) 557

Naraśaṁsa-songs 928

Nārāyaṇa, 1) the Puruṣa (Ṛgv. 10, 90) as the first-born 257 Introd., 257-259, 893-895. (still beside Viṣṇu) 350 (381). (=Viṣṇu) 643, 799 ff, 803 ff (=Rāma) 886. 2) A commentator on the Upaniṣads; his collection of the Upaniṣads 562 ff

Nārāyaṇa-formula, eight-syllabic 805, 830, 872

Nārāyaṇa-Upaniṣad 803-805; (Mu, Da, Co, Nā) 556, 559, 561, 564

Nāsī for *Asī*, a small river near Benares, 759, 884

nāstikyam, nihilism, 328 (340)

Naudhasam, N. of a Sāman, 28

navarātra, nine-day Soma-ritual 63, 74

nave, spokes, rim, 51, 185, 306, 421, 440, 581, 593, 603, 901

negative nature of the Ātman (cf. *neti, neti*) 283 ff, 463, 572, 613, 688, 706, 728, 749, 839, 857 etc.

net of the Ātman 311, 320. Bird and net 339 (367). spider and net

Q

R

Rudrahṛdaya-Upaniṣad (only Mu) 557
Rudrākṣajābāla-Upaniṣad (only Mu) 557
Rudrāṇī, beside Rudra 719
Rudra, songs and prayers of 778, 790, 801, 832

Ś

Śabarī, a female ascetic searched for by Rāma, 868
śabda, sound, noise 310 etc; perhaps *Nachrede* 'afterword' (=echo ?) 55 (still cf. 427)
śabdabrahman and its counterpart 362 ff, 689
Śaiva-s (followers of Śiva) 618
Śaivya Satyakāma, N. of a participant in a discussion 589, 600, (348)
Śākāyanya, N. of a sage, 331
Śākhā ("branch"), Vedic school 2, 219, 814, 828, 886
Śakra (Indra) is Nārāyaṇa, 803
Śakti, personification of the creative power, 875. cf. *vījam*
Śākvaram, N. of a Sāman, 28, 68, 381; *śakvarī* verses, the verses which underlie it, 94
Śālīnavṛtti-s, subclass of the Gṛhasthas, 764
Śambhu=*Śaṁkara* (Śiva) 350, 381. Śambhu vow, 789-790
Śaṁkara ("bringer of blessing"=*Śiva*) 685, 816, 884
Śaṁkara (=*ācārya*), author of the commentary on the Brahmasūtras and on many Upaniṣads, cf. however 498 Note. 601 Note
Śaṁkara (-*ānanda*), author of the commentary on the Kauṣītaki- and on many Atharva-Upaniṣads 22, 34 Note, 641 Note. 691, 694 N2 etc.
Śamyos, "happiness and welfare", formula, reinterpreted 650
Śāṇḍilīputra, N. of a teacher, 543
Śāṇḍilya, N. of several teachers, 111, 442, 443, 505, 506, 544. cf. 392 ff
Śāṇḍilya-Upaniṣad (only Mu) 557
Śāṇḍilya-vidyā, Śāṇḍilya's doctrine, 111 ff, 399
Śani, the planet Saturn 381
Śaṅkhapulika, N. of a chief of snakes, 664
Śāṅkhāyana, N. of a teacher, see *Guṇākhya*
Śāṅkhāyana-s, see *Kauṣītakin*-s
śānta ātman, the calm self, 289, 345, 781
Śarabha-Upaniṣad (only Mu) 557
Śārīraka-Upaniṣad (only Mu) 557, 657
śarīram, the body, described 332, 640 etc.
Śārkarākṣya, see *Jana*
Śarva, N. of a god (beside *Bhava*, *Rudra*), 678, 680, 787
Śaryātī, N. of a chief, 332
Śaśabindu, N. of a sovereign, 332
śastram 1) (fr. *śaṁs*) Recitation by the Hotar in Soma-sacrifice 8, 12, 67, 115, 227; 2) (fr. *śas*) weapon; confused by the commentators, 34
śasyā, verse or song of praise, 447 448
Śatapatha-Brāhmaṇam, Br. of the Vājasaneyi school of the White Yajurveda, contents 390-391
śatarudriyam, N. of the 16th book of the Vāj. Saṁh., 783; (as Upaniṣad only Da) 559; (abridged as Nīlarudra-Up., Co, Nā) 561, 563; is recommended 759, 795, 832
Śatrughna, brother of Rāma, 870, 882. (=*Śatrumardana*, *Arimardana*) 870, 873
Śāṭyāyana-Upaniṣad (only Mu) 557
Śaunaka, instructed by Aṅgiras, 570, 572, by Pippalāda 726, Teaches 943 ff —*Ś°* *Kāpeya* 121, *Ś°*, teacher of Āśvalāyana, 7, 11
Śaunaka-Upaniṣad 943-947 (only Da) 560
Śaunakīya-s, Śākhā of the Atharvaveda, 555
Śauṅgīputra, N. of a teacher, 543
śikhā (tip), of arrow 363; pointed flame in heart 259 , 709, 801, in head (if the comm. is right) 669-670; tuft of hair 267, 819, 830, removed by the Saṁnyāsin (as mark of family) 729 ff, 741 ff, 747 ff, 753, 761, 766
śikṣā, instruction, particularly in phonetics, 221 ff, 572
Śikṣāvallī, N. of Taitt. Up. 1 (221-231)
Śilaka Śālāvatya, N. of a participant in discussion, 79
Śilpa Kaśyapa, N. of a teacher, 544
śiras (head), N. of a formula, 376 N. 647 N4. 693 N1, 776
śirovratam, head-vow, 376N1, 569, 587

Ṣ

S

Saṁciti, the 9th book of the Śatap. Br., 390
Saṁdaṁśa, section of the Ṣaḍviṁśa-Br., 63
saṁdhi, euphony (of speech sounds) 222, 930, 933; meeting place 759; becoming one (with the Ātman) 742 *saṁdhyā*, union-time, twilight, twilight prayers, 63, 732, 754, 759 (word-play between various meanings)
Saṁhitā-s, the "collections" of Vedic songs and formulas, 1ff, (euphony 223)
saṁhitāpāṭha, a way of Vedic recitation, 10
Saṁhitopaniṣad 61, 62; cf. 222
Sāṁjīviputra, N. of a teacher, 543
Sāṁkhya-doctrine: on its prehistory 273, 302-304, 329, 571; based on it 353, 618, 619, 643; *Sāṁkhya-Yoga* 643, 646, 677, 680 ff
sāṁkhyam 'examination', not *Sāṁkhyam*, 324
Sāṁkṛtīputra, N. of a teacher, 543
saṁnyāsa, renunciation 736, 747, 749, 759, 761
Saṁnyāsa-Upaniṣad 734-739; Mu (*Kuṇḍikā-Up.*) Co, Nā. 557, 561, 563. (*Saṁnyāsa-Up*. of Mu is = the *Kaṇṭhaśruti* 1-2 [557])
Saṁnyāsa-Upaniṣads of the Atharvaveda 568, 725N1
Saṁnyāsin (*parivrājaka*, *bhikṣu*), the propertyless, wandering, religious mendicant. Origin (cf. 4, 11, 97): it seems the Gṛhastha (*pitṛyāna*, *Brāhmaṇam*) and the Vānaprastha (*devayāna*, *Āraṇyakam*) originally stood side by side as equally entitled ways of life (beside them also the life-long Brahmacārin) 97, (one after another, already 434, 501). A higher claim makes its appearance 98 and, advocated by Yājñavalkya 455, cf. 499 (correspondingly its eschatology, 521, Introd.). Out of this is evolved the Saṁnyāsin, who is often not yet differentiated from the Vānaprastha 499 (also 434, 501), 730, 735-736, 749, differentiated 97, 455, 499, 742, 759, 766. His consecration (*saṁskāra*) 734, initiation (*dīkṣā*) 736, 750. Parting from the family 743, 747, 749, 753 (accompanied by the wife 736). Final sacrificial ceremonies 734, 735, 742, 747, 749. Removal of the sacred thread (and the hair-tuft) 729, 741, 742, 747, 748, 749, 750, 753, 761. Departure and way of life 737, 742, 750, 751, 753, 754, 755, 760, 766. No Vedic study any more 741, 751, 753, 760, (exception 742). Ablutions 742, 751, avoiding of gold 754-755, *Ahiṁsā* 742, 750. The great journey 750, 760; ascendence 738-739
saṁprasāda, *saṁprasāra* 727
saṁsāra, "course (*sar*) returning (*sam*) to its starting point", the wanderings of the soul, first (cf. however 129 *āvarta* "whirlpool", better perhaps "a return" and 529 *evam eva anuparivartante*) 288 and 325, (307, 322 Brahman-wheel, cf. 26), 333, 366, 373, 629, 632, 646, 674, 711, (portrayed) 714, 795, 805, 807, 816, 818, 831, 882, 883
Saṁvargavidyā 118 ff
Saṁvartaka, A Saṁnyāsin of antiquity, 761
Sanaga, *Sanāru*, *Sanātana*, as teachers 443-444, 506
Sanatkumāra, the war-god Skanda, 173; 176, 189 as teacher; 780, 789 as student
Sanatsujāta, Ṛṣi, as teacher 718
saptadaśa, N. of a Stoma, 380
saptarātra, N. of an Ahīna, 63
Sarasvatī, 1) N. of a river between the Indus and the Gangetic regions 909. 2) Goddess of speech 542, as wife of Brahmán 827, 887
Sarasvatīrahasya-Upaniṣad (only Mu) 557
sarbsar, of Oupnek'hat (is Ait. Ār. 2) 559, 891
Sarvamedha, ten-day Soma-sacrifice, 391
Sarveśvara (lord of all) beside Brahmán, Viṣṇu, Rudra, 844
sarvopaniṣadvidyā, the Upaniṣads already as a whole 328 (334)
Sarvopaniṣatsāra (also *Sarvasāra-Up.*) 657-661; (Mu, Da, Co, Nā) 557, 559, 561, 564
Sattram, long Soma-ritual, lasting more than 12 days, 63, 268, 269; lasting for thousand years 63, 378
sattvam, being, goodness, = *buddhi* 298, 313, 342; in the cosmic sense 379; as a Sāṁkhya term 345, 678, 684, 857, 865, 876

perhaps already *salila* (491) 324 (731). (defined) 660, 794, 840 (explained) 856, 903, 906, 908
spell 32, 33, 519, 535 ff, 831 (snakes) 667, (death) 917
spider (and thread) 324, 361, 429, 572, 673, 726, 731
sṛṅkā, chain (?), 278, 281
sruva-ladle (used in sacrifice) 32, 534, re-interpreted 650
states, the four, of the Ātman : waking, dream, deep sleep and *Turīya* (q.v.)
stobha, musical sounds, as enumerated 84
stoma, the (seven) basic forms (variations) in the singing of the *stotram*, 73 (ninefold, fifteenf°, seventeenf°, twentyonef°, twentysevenf°, thirtythreef°) 380 ff. Cf. under *Sāman*
stone images, gods present in them, 885
stotram, the Sāman combined with the Ṛcs for being sung by the Udgātar and his assistants (example 67), corresponding to the *Śastram* of the Hotar, 9, 73, 82, 96, 115, 408
stuff, trash, learned (contempt of book-learning), 374, 498, 688, 689, 692, 707, 907, 940
Subālā-Upaniṣad (only Mu) 557
subduing (*dama*) 213, 228, 262, 264; as cardinal virtue 508. The subdued (*dānta*) 500 etc.
subject of perception 50, 436-437, 454, 461, 464, 490-491, 493, 503. (*paridraṣṭar*) 603, 905 N1, cf. spectator
Subrahmaṇya, a priest, assistant of the Udgātar, 9
Sudarśanam, the discus of Viṣṇu (sun-disk), 829, 830
sudhā (nectar) = *Vasor dhārā*, city of Indra, 929
Sudhanvan Āṅgirasa, N. of a Gandharva, 453
Sudyumna, N. of a prince, 332
Sugrīva, a monkey-king, 868 ff
Sūkara, (Viṣṇu as) boar, 873
Sukeśan Bhāradvāja, a participant in a discussion, 589, 602
Sumantra, a minister of Daśaratha, 871
super-creation (*atisṛṣṭi*) 412
super-godhead over the gods, 343
super-intellectual becoming one 210, 238-239, 240, 350, 360, 436-437, 493, 584, 586, 603, 625-637, cf. *yoga*
sura "god", only 328, 333, (360), 714
Surāṣṭra, a minister of Daśaratha, 871
Sūrya, sun, the sun god, 349 etc.
Sūrya-Upaniṣad (only Mu) 557
suṣumnā, the cerebral artery, *Carotis* (according to the matter already 196, 299) only 361, 673, 674, 710 (cf. 225, 595, 670)
sūtram, 1) thread 166, 348 (?); 2) sacred thread 729 ff, 741; 3) world-thread (Vāyu, Ātman) 459 (cf. 701, 730). 742. (Word-play between 2 and 3); 4) a kind of writings, aphorisms 436 (370, 503, 476), manual 2
sutya (scil. *ahan*), day of Soma-pressing
svadhā, offering to the manes 96, 593, also a mere call to them 512, 749
svāhā (hail !), an exclamation at the *havis*-offerings which one offers (*juhoti*) sitting 512, 749
svarasāman-s, certain days of *Gavām ayanam*, 9
svarita, 934
svayambhū ("being by oneself") 1) as epithet of Bráhman (neut.) 444, 507, 544; 261; 2) personified 265, 290, 549, 672
sympathy (*dayā*) as a cardinal virtue 509

T

Tadeva as Upaniṣad 897-900 (only Da) 559
tadvanam "the-longing-for-it" 212
Taijasa (dream-sleep, cf. 605) 611, (825, 882), 612-615, 838, 840, 882
Taittirīyaka's, school of Black Yajurveda 217 ff, *Taittirīya-Saṁhitā*, contents 218; T°-*Brāhmaṇam* 218; T°-*Āraṇyakam* 219
Taittirīya-Upaniṣad 221-246; (Mu, Nā) 556, 564; Taitt. 2 and 3 (Da, Co) 560, 561
tajjalān, secret name of Brahman, 110
Takṣaka, a chief snake, 664
Talavakāra-s (= *Jaiminīya*-s) a school of Sāmaveda, 61, 62. *T°-Brāhmaṇam* 61, 207N
tamas (darkness), the third Guṇa of the Sāṁkhyas; its effects 340, 345
Tāṇḍin-s, a school of the Sāmaveda, 61

434; (clairvoyant) 453, 458; (the imminent Brahman) 454, 454; (*Gārgi*) 456, 462; (five-fire doctrine) 142, 525 ff
tyam, tyad, 238, 431 ff, 469

U

ucchiṣṭa, remaining, Brahman as *u*°, 677, 680
Udaṅka Śaulbāyana, a Veda teacher, 477
Udaraśāṇḍilya, as pupil, 80
udātta 934
udbhid and *valabhid*, particular sacrifices in *Gavām Ayanam*, 62
Uddālaka Āruṇi, son of Aruṇa and father of Śvetaketu (cf. *Naciketas* as son of *Auddālaki Āruṇi* 275, and Yājñavalkya as pupil of *Uddālaka Āruṇi* 533, 544) 22, 24ff 106, 149, 152, 166, 458, 533, 535, 544, Inconsistency of tradition about him
Uddālakāyana, N. of a teacher, 505
Udgātar, "singer", chief priest of the Sāmaveda 1, 34, 67, 78, 82-83, (sing. and plur.) 131 etc.
udgītha, middle limb and main part of the fivefold as of the sevenfold Sāman 67ff, often interpreted allegorically 28, 64, 67, 68, 70, 86ff, 347, 378, 404 ff, 407, 937, 946
Udumbara-s, as a sub-class of the Vānaprasthas, 765
Ukhāsaṁbharaṇam, N. of the sixth book of Śatap. Br., 390
Ukṣasena, N. of a prince, 333
uktham, older name for *Śastram*, particularly the *Niṣkevalya-śastram* 10, 34; in a wider sense for hymn 12, words of praise 78, Ṛgveda 424. *u*° as life 515
ukthya, form of the Soma-sacrifice, 8, 378, 832
Umā Haimavatī, wife of Rudra—Śiva, 212, 792, 816
unreality of the world 156, 162, 292, 498
upādhi, determinant, only 660, 706, cf. 286
upadrava, a limb of the Sāman having seven parts, 68, 89
upahava, invitation, 63
upahavya, a sacrifice for a definite purpose, 62
upahoma, a supplementary sacrifice, 218
Upakosala Kāmalāyana, pupil of Satyakāma, 127
upāṁśu-offering 8; -container 336; *-savana*=stone 336
Upaniṣad, originally "confidential (*upa*) sitting" (as opposed to *pariṣad*); hence everything that rests on secret communication and is to be held as secret (cf. as synonyms *guhyā ādeśāh* 101, 103; *guhyam* 290, *paramam guhyam* 326) : secret watchword 31; secret name 429 (370), 511; secret (allegorical) meaning 10, 70, 85, 223; secret word or formula 743, 790, 818; esoteric doctrine 213, 480 (plur.), 884 (also false, 200, 201); so particularly at the end of expositions (*iti Upaniṣat* and so forth) 231, 240, 246 (823). 261, 263, 267, 818, 823, 828, 884; of literary works (oral or written) to be held as secret 436 (370, 476, 530); 308 (732) 320, (*guhya-upaniṣatsu*), 742, 808, 858, 928; *upaniṣadam* (Upaniṣad-work) 804, *aupaniṣada puruṣa* (Puruṣa of the esoteric doctrine) 473.—The characteristic of being secret is connected with all the meanings; for elucidation cf. the passages cited under 'warning' and. 'refusal'
Upaniṣadbrāhmaṇam (of the Talavakāras) 207N
Upaniṣad-collections, of Muktikā-Up., 556ff; of Darashakoh (Oupnek'hat) 559ff; Colebrooke's 561; Nārāyaṇa's 562
upasad, Soma pre-ritual, with abstinence, 8, 115, 268, *upasadvratam* 529
Upaveśi, N. of a teacher, 544
Uśīnara, a tribe in the Madhyadeśa, 52
Uṣasta Cākrāyaṇa, participant in a discussion, 454
Uṣaati Cākrāyaṇa, a Vedic teacher, 81
utkrama, sun's northern course 356, cf. 590 and *krama*
uvula 226, 361

V

vāc, speech, 419 ff; as teacher, 544
Vadhryaśva, N. of a warrior, 332
Vaidṛbhatīputra, N. of a teacher, 543
Vaijavāpāyana, N. of a teacher, 443
Vaikhānasa, a sub-class of the Vānaprasthas, 765
Vaikuṇṭha, N. of Indra, 53, 54, 426, of Viṣṇu 805 and of his heaven 807

Vātsīputra, N. of a teacher, 543
Vātsya, 443, 506 pupil of Śāṇḍilya, 544 his teacher
Vātsyāyana, author of *Kāmaśāstram* (manual on love) 618
Vāyu, wind, wind-god 25, 211, corresponding on the cosmic level to the Prāṇa 15, 406, 894, and like him often a symbol of Brahman 39, 118 ff, 221, 231, 423, 431 ff, 459, 938
Veda-s, orig. three (cf. *trayī*); the four 1 ff; five 176-180 cf. 370. *vedānāṁ vedaḥ* (grammar) 176, 177, 180. One, two, three or all (four) Vedas were studied 538, all (three or four) in 12 years 162 (cf. 389), in 48 years 764, "pardoned by the Veda", 326
Vedadevayoniḥ 727N1. 781N3
Vedāṅga-s, enumerated 572; 770, 814, 828, 886, 927, 938
Vedānta (the Upaniṣads, cf. 1 ff), 326, 586 (256, 792), 617, 619, 672. —Pure Vedānta Upaniṣads of the Atharvaveda, 567, 639 N. —Vedānta and Sāṁkhyam 273, 303 N, 304, 338, 340
vedi, the altar, re-interpreted 153, 267, 650
Vena, the seer, the (heavenly, later earthly) bearer of revelation, 251, 899
Vibhīṣaṇa, brother of Rāvaṇa, allied with Rāma 869 ff
Vibhu, hall in the Brahman-world, 27, 28
Vicakṣaṇā, throne in the Brahman-world, 27, 28
Vidagdha Śākalya, a Veda teacher, 466ff, 479
Vidarbhīkauṇḍinya, a Vedic teacher, 443, 506
Videha-s, a people (capital : Mithilā), to the North-East of Patna, 52, 462, 481
vidhi, (injunction) a constituent part of the Brāhmaṇas, 1 ff, cf. 31, 927, 936
vidṛti, coronal suture 13, 18 (cf. 225)
Vidyā, knowledge, is 876 the ritualistic knowledge (cf. 'lower and higher knowledge') or (with Weber) Avidyā to be read
Vidyā and *Avidyā* 281 ff; defined 658. Both rejected 549
Vidyādhara-s, areal beings in Śiva's retinue 685
Vighana, N. of an Ekāha, 62
Vighna, "remover, eliminator" (of obstructions), Gaṇeśa, 875
vigraha, "body" 350, 357, 864, 868, 882
vījam, *kīlaka*, *śakti* of the Nṛsiṁha-formula, 823-824, of the Rāma-formula 866, of the Haṁsa-formula 719
Vijarā, a river in the Brahman-world, 27
Vijaya, a minister of Daśaratha, 871
Vindhya-mountains, as southern boundary 40
Vipracitti, N. of a teacher, 443, 506
vi-ram, renounce, 514
Virāṭ (*Virāj*), mythological representative of matter, 893, 85, 122. 227N1, 481 (wife of Indra-puruṣa), 678, 680, 828, 855, 887, N. of a metre 122, 780, of an Ekāha 62
Virocana, an Asura, 198 ff
viś, the third caste, see *Vaiśya*
viśeṣa, as a Sāṁkhya term 353, (Cf. 659)
viśva, see *Vaiśvānara*.
Viśvajit, a day of Gavām ayanam, 9
Viśvakarman, all-fashioner, 318, 895
Viśvamanāḥ, N. of a teacher, 22
Viśvāmitra, old-Vedic Ṛṣi, 10, 430, 919; as teacher, 21
Viśvarūpa Tvāṣṭra, as teacher, 443, 506
Viśvarūpāḥ, as a section of the Ṣaḍv. Br., 63
Viśvasṛj, all-creator 350 (381), (plur.) 817
Viśvāvasu, a Gandharva, 539
viśve devāḥ, orig. "all gods"; then (like Vasu, Sādhya) restricted to a particular class of gods 85, 99, 380, 414, 451, 830
Viṣṇu (for his history, cf. 809) old-Vedic sun-god 222, 231, 358, 821, (blessing the foetus) 540, (as chariot-driver) 692, who traverses the heaven in three steps; his highest step (*Viṣṇoḥ paramaṁ padam*) is the dwelling place of the deceased 288, 364, 379, 706, 743, 804, 816, 833. Often in accounts, mostly together with Brahmán and Rudra-Īśāna-Śiva 343, 344, 647, 669, 701, 775, 780, 830, 831, 856, or in other combinations 685, 728, 770, 792, 886. As the Ātman 350 (381), as *Om* 362, as the Sattvam of the Sāṁkhyas 346, as Yogin 700 (714); the last sacrifice of the Saṁnyāsin

is dedicated to him, 749. Viṣṇu as Nārāyaṇa 808, as Nṛsiṁha 810ff, as Rāma 863ff
Viṣṇu-Upaniṣads of the Atharvaveda, 568, 797, 799N
viṣuvant, middle day of Gāvām ayanam, 9
vratam, vow, maxim, 91ff, 244ff, *vratamīmāṁsā* 422, *vrataṁ Pāśupatam* 776; *Śāmbhavam* 790
vrātya as Brahman 677, 680
vrātyayajña, a particular sacrifice 62
vṛṣala, for *śūdra*, 538
Vṛtra (*Ahi*), a demon slain by Indra, 905
Vyāhṛti-s, the three sacred exclamations *bhūr*, *bhuvaḥ*, *svaḥ* (q.v.) 347, 693, 800, 926-927; four 936, 938; seven 828, 927
vyāna, intermediate breath, explained 72ff; differently 336, 596
Vyaśva, N. of a teacher, 22
Vyaṣṭi (unfoldment), as teacher, 443, 506
vyaṣṭi and *samaṣṭi* 443
Vyāsa, the Ṛṣi, only 939

W

waking, dream, deep sleep, defined 658. Main texts 201ff, 486ff, 598ff, 611ff, 616, 617, 623, 630, 633ff, 727 ff, 794
warning against instructing an unworthy one 11, 106, 326, 366, 534, 816, 875
waves of Saṁsāra (cf. ocean, boat, bank), six 754, five 306
wealth, its worthlessness 434, and dangers, 282, 754-755
wind-cords 333
wing, painted 342
wishes, granted 43, 277, 332, 526; stain 374, 687; are achieved 585, fade 585
women (children, relatives) as obstacle 366; to be given up 706, 753; w° excluded 815, permitted 817
works, good and bad, annihilation of 27, 45N, 194, 240, 337, 373, 499, 581, 583; cf. 'evil'
world-egg (Brahman-egg) 117, 350, 378, 452, 741, 754, 887,— its membrane 116
worlds, mostly three 469; four 15; seven 574 (metaphorical 579), enumerated 574N, 684; nine 455-456; fourteen 741. —boundaries of w° 452. —world-stream 897
world-dissolution (through Brahman etc.) 311, 315, 317, 323, 777, 780, 820, 852
world-guardians (eight) 10, 13, 16, 828, 876, 887
worthlessness of earthly goods 280-281, 332, 434, 501

Y

Yajamāna, institutor of sacrifice, 99, 131, 227, 327, 371, 375ff, 408, 446, 650
Yājñavacas Rājastambhāyana, as teacher, 544
Yajñavalkya Vājasaneya, a celebrated Veda teacher (cf. 389, 392ff, 444ff.), 411, 434 ff, 446-505, 758-761, 881-888, 915-916. He is (in ritual texts) 533, 544 pupil of Uddālaka; cf. on the other hand 457. Considering the great role he plays in the passages mentioned, the complete silence over him in others is striking
Yājñavalkyakāṇḍam=Bṛh. 3-4; cf. 391, 392. Contents 395, 396, 444
Yājñavalkya-Upaniṣad (only Mu) 557 (=Jābāla-Up. 5-6 among others)
yajñāyajñīyam, N. of a Sāman, 28, 68
Yājñikī Upaniṣad, see Mahānār. Up.; cf. 247
Yajurveda, the 2nd Veda acc. to Indian reckoning (exceptions 260, 578, 894), cf. 1ff (Black and White) 217, 390. Mentioned as source 816
yajus, sacrificial formula (of the Yajurveda), 28, 815 etc.; as life 515
yājyā, accompanying stanza or song, 447, 448
yājyānuvākyāḥ, a section of the Maitr. Saṁh, 328
Yakṣa-s, demigods (in the retinue of Kubera) 333, 381, 382, 685, 814, 832
yakṣam, "wonderful thing", 208, 211, 509, 901
Yama, god of death, 53, 55, 112, 274ff, 341, 377, 471, 519, 551, 918; beside *Mṛtyu* 414, 771, 828, 886
Yāska, N. of a teacher, 443, 506
yati 1) Assistant in the world creation 320 and Note (cf. *Kratu*); 2) "aspirant" 45; 3) penitent,

ADDITIONS AND CORRECTIONS

Page 7, line 8 etc. : *For* Mahīdāsa, *read* Mahidāsa.
Page 8, line 10 : *For Agniṣṭoma-, read Agnīṣoma-,*
Page 8, line 21 : *For* Ṛtuyāga, *read* Ṛtuyāja.
Page 10, line 3 : Add after *First Āraṇyaka* :

1. Which hymns are to be recited by the Hotar as the *Ājya-* and *Pra-uga-śastram* at the morning-offering of the Mahāvratam (the previous day of the Gavām ayanam).
2. The *Marutvatīyam* and *Niṣkevalyam* at the mid-day offering of the Mahāvratam.
3. The Niṣkevalya-śastram continued.
4. The Niṣkevalyam as bird, whose limbs consist of hymns.
5. Continuation.—The *Vaiśvadevatam* and *Āgnimārutam* at evening-offering of the Mahāvrata-day.

Second Āraṇyaka

Page 16, line 13 : *Add after* happened that:
Agni entered into his nose as speech,
Page 16, line 18 : Delete (out-breath).
Page 16, line 32 : *For* (abhiṣṛṣṭam sat) *read abhiṣṛṣṭaṁ sat*).
Page 18, line 3-4 : *Remove the bracket after* suture *and read it after* crack',.
Page 22, line 2 : *Read Sākamaśvaḥ.* Line 12 : *Read Kauṣītakiḥ.*
Page 26, foot-note 3 : *For* jayamānaḥ *read* jāyamānaḥ.
Page 27, line 1 : *After* the lake, *add Āra.*
Page 27, line 16 : *For Ambas read Ambā*-s.
Page 27, line 17 : *After* rivers, *add Ambayāḥ.*
Page 28, line 3 : *For* aspeedy, *read* a speedy.
Page 28, line 22 : *Read* Sāmans Śyaitam.
Page 28, line 24 : *Read* Śākvaram.
Page 31, lines 13-17 : *Wrong fount ! This is a translation of Deussen's Introduction, not of the Upaniṣad.*
Page 34, last line (foot note): *Instead of the full point*, read a (!)

Page 43, last but one line : *Read* (*abhivisṛjyante*).
Page 44, line 9 : *Read* (*bhūtamātrāḥ*).
Page 45, line 12 : *For* daughter, *read* slaughter.
Page 54, line 2 : *Read a semi-colon after* me.
Page 61, line 21 : *For* Chāndogyas, *read* Chandogas.
Page 62, line 5 from bottom: *Read Sunāśīrya.*
last line : *Read Indra-stoma.*
Page 63, line 13 : *After* (of Soma); *add Viśvarūpāḥ*;
Page 63, line 15 : *Read Hotrādyupahavāḥ.*
Page 67, line 27 : *After* gift, *read* a colon *instead of* the full point. *After this, add*:

22. *abhi tvā sūra, nonumo adugdhā iva dhenavaḥ īśānam asya jagataḥ svardṛśam, īśānam, Indra, tasthuṣaḥ.*
23. *na tvāvān anyo divyo na pārthivo na jāto, na janiṣyate aśvāyanto, maghavan Indra, vājino gavyantas tvā havāmahe.*

Page 67 : *Between line* 29 *and* 30, insert a *section number* I.
Page 68, line 11 : *Read Yajñāyajñīyam.*
Page 73, line 5 from bottom : *For* of the *stotra*, *read* of the *stoma*.
Page 79, line 7 : *Delete the comma after* Caikitāyana.
Page 91, line 11 : *For* The ten parts of the Sāman, *read* Ten of these Sāmans.
Page 92, line 22 : *Read Vāmadevyam.*
Page 99, line 27 : *Read* Gārhapatya.
Page 109, line 6 : *For* mouth, *read* moon.
Page 111, line 1 : *After* intelligence, add (*kratu*).
Page 114, para 7, line 1 : *Read* Mahidāsa.
Page 115, line 21 : For Upaniṣad-, read Upasad-.
Page 117, line 21 : Read *'brahma jajñānam.*
Page 121, line 11 : *After* wind; *insert* 2.— Pages 121-122 : *Replace the paragraph numbers* 2, 3, 4, 5, 6, 7 *by* 3, 4, 5, 6, 7, 8 *respectively.*
Page 121, line 22 : *Read Kākṣaseni.*
Page 128, line 1 : *After* (are my forms) *add*: But the man, whom one sees in the sun, I am that and I am he".
Page 133, line 7 : *For* such knowledge, *read* no such knowledge
Page 137, line 8 : *Read* Satyakāma.— Line 9 : *Read* Vyāghrapād.

Page 142, line 22 : *Read* Pravāhaṇa.

Page 143, line 5 from bottom: *After* arises, *insert* the king.

Page 155, last two lines: *For* one possessed not only fixed traditions from ancient times but on the contrary, only famous names

read

one did not possess fix traditions so much as rather only famous names.

Page 168, line 5 : *After* (the breath) *read*: , the Prāṇa into the fire (heat), and the fire (heat) into the highest divinity.

Page 176, line 23 : *For* leaant, *read* learnt.

Page 203, line 5 from bottom: *Read* C before (The Supplement...).

Page 222, foot-note: line 1 : *For* every, *read* that.— Lines 2-3: *For* which the connection or junction shows, *read* which shows the connection or junction.— Lines 5-6 : *For* and therefore the Sāman which forms the balancing of both, *read* and therefore forms the Sāman, the balancing of both.

Page 227, line 23 : *For* Āgnīdhra, *read* Agnīdh.

Page 248 : *Between line* 4 *and* 5, *insert at the centre*: *Draviḍa-Āndhra*

Page 252, lines 19-28 : *Wrong fount ! This is a translation of Deussen's Notes, not of the Upaniṣad.*

Page 253, last but one line : *read miśrāmi.*

Page 256 : *Read full points after stanzas* 20, 21, 22 *and* 23.

Page 261, line 4 : *Delete the comma after* Satya.

Page 265, line 3 : *Read* Gārhapatya.

Page 265, line 5 : *Read a comma after* space.

Page 267, line 35 : *Read* Agnīdh.

Page 268, line 5 : *For Upasada-*, *read Upasad-*.

Page 279, Foot-note 2, line 7 : *Read Nāciketasa.*

Page 290, line 5 : *After* Brāhmaṇas, add: Or at the *śrāddha* meal.

Page 294, line 2 : *After* law, *complete the quotation with the inverted commas and add*: (RV 4.40.3).

Page 295 : *Delete the foot-note.*

Page 315, foot-note 2 : Delete Cf.

Page 317, *After the stanza* 10, *insert* :

Verses 11-22 glorify Rudra as the personified Brahman. Like the related section 3, 1-6, this part also mostly consists of citations.

11. Who as the only one presides over every womb (5, 2),
In whom the world dissolves and unfolds itself (Mahān. 1, 2),
Him as the lord, the God, bounteous praise-worthy
Who perceives, attains that peace for ever (Kāṭh. 1,17).

—*Substitute the stanza numbers* 12, 13, 14, 15, 16, 17, 18, 19, 20, 21 *and* 22 *in place of* 11, 12, 13, 14, 15, 16, 17, 18, 19, 20 *and* 21 *respectively.*

—St. 13, line 4 : *For* o e, *read* one.

Page 335, line 24 : *For* every, *read* individual.

„ Lines 26-27 : *For* thinking, *read* thinking of, *for* (the *Buddhi*) *read* (of the *Buddhi*) *and for* (the Ahaṁkāra) *read* (of the Ahaṁkāra).

Page 344, lines 11 and 29 : *For* Kautsāyana, *read* Kutsāyana *at both the places.*

Page 345, line 24 : *Read Viśvā.*

Page 352, line 1 : *Read paridadhāti,*

„ 8 : After (*paridadhāti*), *add* once more.

Page 357, line 19 : *Read* Prajāpati.

Page 375, line 11 : *For* 'the true law', read 'of truthful law'.

Page 376, line 19 : *For* duality)? *read* duality?).

„ line 24: *Read* lump.

Page 378, line 1 : *Read Atirātra.*

Page 382, line 5 from bottom: *Read* exorcize *for* exercise.

Page 385, line 2 : *Read paśyan.*

Page 390, line 32 : *Read Ukhāsaṁbharaṇam.*

Page 401, line 4 from bottom: *For* became, *read* becomes.—After universe, *read a comma in the place of the semi-colon.*

Page 408 : *Insert at the beginning of the page* :

24. Therefore Brahmadatta, the descendant of Cikitāna too said, as he tasted the king [Soma] : "This king shall blow up my head if Ayāsya Āṅgirasa

has sung here the Udgītha with something different from me. For even he "said he, "has sung the Udgītha through speech and Prāṇa only".

—Substitute paragraph numbers 25, 26, 27 *and* 28 *in place* of 24, 25, 26 *and* 27 *respectively.*

Page 414, line 24 : *Read* devāḥ.

Page 418, line 1 : *For* Kauṣ. 2.12.14). Because, *read* Kauṣ. 2,12-13), because.

Page 421, line 23 : *For* name, *read* nave.

Page 422, line 17 : *Read* Śaṅk.

Page 425, line 12 : *For* texts, *read* text.

„ Line 14 and footnote line 2 : *Read* Balākā *at both the places.*

Page 429, line 6 : *For* twentyseven, *read* seventytwo.

Page 443, lines 3 and 4 : *Read Vaijavāpāyana at both places.*

„ „ 8 and 9 : *Read Jātūkarṇya at both places.*

„ Lines 21 and 22 : *Read Kumārahārita* at both places.

„ Lines 2 and 3 from bottom : *Read Sanāru* at both places.

Page 444, line 26 : *Read* Maitreyī.

Page 447, lines 16-17 : *Read anārambhaṇa*

Page 453, lines 9 and 10 : *Read* Parikṣit.—Line 20 : *Read Pārikṣitas.*

Page 456.—*After line* ?2, *insert* :

—"In the worlds of the Gandharvas, O Gārgi!"

"But wherein are the worlds of the Gandharvas interwoven lengthwise and breadthwise?"

—"In the worlds of the sun, O Gārgi!"

"But wherein are the worlds of the sun interwoven lengthwise and breadthwise?"

—"In the worlds of the moon, O Gārgi!"

"But wherein are the worlds of the moon interwoven lengthwise and breadthwise?"

Page 458, line 7 : *For* has, *read* was.

„ line 30 : *For* Will, read Well.

„ Foot-note : *Read the first sentence as* : In addressing, the patronymic is used more commonly than the [personal] name.

Page 468, line 7 : *For Vaiśvo*, read *Vaiśva-*.

,, line 9 : *Read* "Three and three hundred and three and three thousand" (3306)

Page 469, line 24 ; *For* or, *read* of.

,, line 27 : *Complete the quotation after* (amṛtam).

Page 473, line 3 : *Complete the quotation after* pieces.

,, lines 11-12 : *For* it is not so such as cannot be described *read* : it is not such, not such (i.e. it cannot be described).

,, Foot-note : *change the footnote number from* 2 *to* 1.

Page 476, lines 17 and 19: *Read* Śilina *at both places.*

Page 478, line 20: *Read* Gardabhīvipīta.

Page 482, lines 16-17: *For*

I, however, prefer (differently *System des Vedānta*, p. 203) another reading of the perceptive remark (of Yājñavalkya).

read

I now prefer (differently *system des Vedānta* p. 203) this interpretation to the other one.

Page 487, line 24: *For* non, *read* not.

Page 491, para 32, lines 2-3: *For* it is...... the Brahman of this world, *read* : it ......whose world the Brahman is.

Page 495, line 12 : *For* thus, *read* this.

,, line 23: *Read a semi-colon after* (Kāma).

Page 496, Foot-note 2, line 1: *Read tṛtīyārthe*.

Page 500, line 6: *For* Brahman, *read* Brāhmaṇa.

,, line 7: *For* he is the world of Brahman, *read* he, whose world the Brahman is.

Page 503, line 13: *For* the (hymns of) the Atharvan, *read* (the hymns of) the Atharvans.

Page 506, lines 6-7: *Read Jātūkarṇya* at both the places.

,, lines 7-8: Read *Āsurāyaṇa* at both the places.

,, lines 19-20: *Read Kumārahārita* at both the places.

Page 508, line 13: *After* known, *add* (AV. 10,8.29).

Page 525, line 8: *Read* Pravāhaṇa.

,, line 9: *Read* (*paricārayamāṇam*).

Page 526, lines 2,18 and 26: *Read* Pravāhaṇa *at all places*.

Page 535, line 18, *Read* Kumārahārita.

Page 542, line 31 : *Read Pautimāṣī.*
Page 543 : *Read*, line 9, *Kāṇvī*, lines 24, 25 *Jāyantī*, lines 26, 27 Māṇḍūkī, line 32 *Vaidṛbhatī*, line 3 from bottom *Prāśnī.*
Page 544 : *Read*, line 2 *Yājñavalkya*, line 14 *Ambhiṇī*, lines 22, 23 *Māhitthi*, lines 27, 28 *Yajñavacas*. lines 12, 13 : *Delete* that of *in both places*.
Page 547, line 1 and elsewhere : *For* ĪŚA, read ĪŚĀ.
Page 548, line 1 : *Insert at the beginning* : Verses 4-5.
— *For coincidia*, read *coincidentia.*
Page 550, line 1 : *Insert at the beginning* : Verses 12-14.
Page 551 : Put stanza number 18 before the last stanza ("O Agni...").
Page 551, end: *Add* (RV 1, 189, 1).
Page 557, line 10 : *Read Turīyātītāvadhūta.*[7]
line 18 : *Read Gāruḍa.*
Page 560, foot-note : *Add at the end* : The four Upaniṣads are already available in a printed form in the Adyar edition : *Unpublished Upaniṣads*, edited by the Pandits of Adyar Library under the supervision of Dr. C. Kunhan Raja, Adyar, 1933.
Page 571, line 36 : *For* imported, *read* imparted.
Page 578, lines 24-25 : *For* (Atharvaveda), (11.4.13) *read* (Atharvaveda 11, 4, 13).
Page 579, line 15 : *For* of, read (of.
Page 581, line 30 : *For* son, *read* sun.
Page 584, line 21 : *Delete the comma after* eye.
Page 593, line 9 : Read *Prajāpati.*
Page 595, line 4 from bottom : *For* fer, *read* far.
Page 598, line 29 : *For* Sauryāṇin, read *Sauryāyaṇin.*
Page 613, line 19 : *For* other, read others.
Page 614, line 30 : *For* muchsimilar, *read* much similar.
Page 615, line 21 : *For* knowthe, *read* know the.
Page 623, stanza 28, line 3 : *For* women, *read* woman.
Page 624, stanza 33, line 3 : *For* over, *read* ever.
Page 632, stanza 63, line 4 : Read a comma in place of the full point.
Page 640, foot-note, line 2 : *After* Cod., *add* क.

Page 647, line 15 : *Read* Brahmán.
Page 647, Foot-note 6 : *Add at the end* (GBP).
Page 648. *After line* 14, *insert section number* 2.
Page 650, section 4, line 4 : *After* Pratiprasthātar, *insert* :—the Vyāna the Prastotar ;
Page 656, foot-note, line 1 : *For* source, *read* some.—*Add* (GBP) at the end of the note.
Page 660, line 12 : *For* Brahmān, *read* Brahmán.
Page 674, stanza 19, line 4 : Read a comma in place of the full point.
Page 680, stanza 13, line 2 : *Read* Prajāpati.
Page 701, stanza 7, line 4 : Read a comma in place of the full point.
Page 713, foot-note 3 : *Replace the semi-colon by a colon.*
Page 719, line 8 : *Replace the unquote-marks after* expression *by quote-marks.*
Page 735, foot-note, line 1 : *Read phalaiḥ.*—Line 2 : *Read vihitān.*
Page 736, foot-note 1, line 3 : *Read saṁnyasta.*
Page 738, line 4 : *Read* mortifies.
Page 748, line 25 : *For* over, *read* ever.
Page 749, Line 10 : For—greating, read – greeting, — Line 4 from bottom : *Delete the comma after* earthen.
Page 751, foot-note, line 5 : *For* cf., *read* of.
Page 765, *After line* 5, *insert section number* 3.
Page 766, line 7 : *For* threat, *read* thereat.
Page 769, line 2 : *Here and in the following pages, for* Atharvaśira, *read* Atharvaśira'.
Page 777, line 5 : *For* seven, *read* sewn. — Line 21 : *Read* Gāyatrī.
Page 778, line 12 : *Replace the question mark by a semi-colon.*
Page 780, line 8 : *For* meditator, *read* meditation.—Lines 26-27: *Read, as a verse-line* :
Shining with light, in its own lustre.
Page 839, foot-note, Line 2 : *Delete* instead of. *Replace the full* point by a comma.—Line 7 : *Replace the semi-colon by a colon.*
Page 842, line 21 : *For* Ātman, *read* Brahman.

Page 851, line 27 : *Before a-u-m, insert the figure* (3).
Page 856, line 4 : *For* undefied, *read* undefiled.
Page 874, stanza 76, line 3 : *After* (*-na*), *insert a comma.*
Page 876, stanza 89, line 4 : *Read Pāratattvam.*
Page 881, line 25 : After gracious", *complete the rectangular bracket.*
Page 887, line 21 : *Delete the ditto-marks.*—
Line 26 : *For* three and, *read* four.— Line 31 : *Delete ditto-marks.*
Page 926, lower section, line 4 : *For* Bráhman in; read Brahmán in.
Page 946, last line : *For* belong, *read* belongs.